Bankers and Empire

Bankers and Empire

How Wall Street Colonized the Caribbean

PETER JAMES HUDSON

The University of Chicago Press
Chicago and London

Publication of this book has been aided by a grant from the Bevington Fund.

The University of Chicago Press, Chicago 60637
The University of Chicago Press, Ltd., London
© 2017 by The University of Chicago
Published 2017
Printed in the United States of America

26 25 24 23 22 21 20 19 18   3 4 5

ISBN-13: 978-0-226-45911-0 (cloth)
ISBN-13: 978-0-226-45925-7 (e-book)
DOI: 10.7208/chicago/9780226459257.001.0001

Library of Congress Cataloging-in-Publication Data

Names: Hudson, Peter James, author.
Title: Bankers and empire : how Wall Street colonized the Caribbean / Peter
    James Hudson.
Description: Chicago ; London : The University of Chicago Press, 2017. |
    Includes bibliographical references and index.
Identifiers: LCCN 2016047600 | ISBN 9780226459110 (cloth : alk. paper) |
    ISBN 9780226459257 (e-book)
Subjects: LCSH: Banks and banking—United States—History—20th century. |
    Banks and banking—Caribbean Area—History—20th century. | Branch
    banks—Caribbean Area—History. | Capitalism—United States. | Racism—
    Economic aspects—United States. | Imperialism—Economic aspects—
    United States. | United States—Foreign economic relations—Caribbean
    Area. | Caribbean Area—Foreign economic relations—United States. |
    United States—Economic conditions—20th century. | Caribbean Area—
    Economic conditions—20th century.
Classification: LCC HG2481.H83 2017 | DDC 332.10972909041—dc23 LC
    record available at https://lccn.loc.gov/2016047600

♾ This paper meets the requirements of ANSI/NISO Z39.48-1992
(Permanence of Paper).

For D.S.G.
In memory of Reverend Delanot Pierre

CONTENTS

Dark Finance

When James Stillman, president of the National City Bank of New York, began searching for a space to replace the bank's cramped and old-fashioned headquarters at 52 Wall Street, he sought a building that could evoke the City Bank's transformation from an early nineteenth-century merchant bank into one of the most powerful financial institutions in the United States. Stillman wanted a building that signified the City Bank's new identity while recalling the old, a building that could project strength, stability, and permanence while embodying his almost metaphysical ambitions for the bank's expansion and growth.[1] Instead of constructing a new edifice from the ground up, Stillman decided to purchase and renovate the old US Customs House at 55 Wall Street. 55 Wall Street was built in 1842 as the Merchant's Exchange, replacing an older exchange building destroyed during the Great Fire of 1835. The new building was an imposing Greek Revival structure of Quincy granite that covered the city block enclosed by Exchange Place and Wall, Hanover, and William streets. Its Wall Street face was an extended colonnade of twelve thirty-foot Ionic columns, and it was crowned with a dome that was among the most recognizable features on the Manhattan skyline.[2] The US federal government purchased 55 Wall Street in 1862. Stillman and the City Bank took it over in 1899. They would transform it into one of the most opulent banking houses in the United States.[3]

Stillman wanted 55 Wall Street remodeled as a temple of finance whose design replicated the Pantheon. He sent a bank officer to Rome for study and hired McKim, Mead, and White, the architectural darlings of the corporate world, to oversee the renovations.[4] The building's interior was dynamited and its rotunda was recast as an expansive banking room appointed in brass, marble, and mahogany and illuminated by electric candelabras. Granite salvaged from the renovations was used to construct a second tier of columns in the façade on top of the first, enclosing the dome, doubling the height of the exterior, and creating an imposing stockade fronting Wall Street. The latest office technologies were installed inside: a vacuum-powered system of pneumatic tubes for internal messaging; a telephone switchboard serving ninety-three external stations and the bank's employees at their fifty-five desks; an internal dictagraph network connecting the bank's officers and department heads; direct telegraph wires leased from Western Union and the Postal Telegraph Company, linking the bank to its agents and correspondents across the United States. At the center of the room under the dome's celestial canopy, instead of an altar to the gods of Rome stood a chapel for the daemonic idols of capitalism: the City Bank's vault, a strongbox built of 300 tons of armor-plated steel enclosed in a reinforced steel cage and protected by an elaborate system of rubber tubes, iron bolts, mechanical alarms, and jets that discharged bursts of scalding steam at the mere threat of a thief or burglar, if not a defalcator or a corrupt banker.[5]

On December 19, 1908, a caravan of clerks, tellers, and runners shouldered leather satchels containing $10,000 each and marched the City Bank's half-billion dollar cash reserve from the old premises at 52 Wall Street across the street to number 55 (fig. I.1).[6] Days later, the new building was opened to hundreds of City Bank employees, who, visiting with their families, marveled at the new building and gasped in astonishment and wonder at the towers of gold bars and paper currency stacked within the vault. Critics and commentators fawned over the renovations and commended Stillman for preserving the original façade and bucking current trends in corporate architecture by refusing to erect another Bessemer steel-frame skyscraper among those already reconfiguring Manhattan's cityscape.[7]

There were some reservations concerning the new building. Frank A. Vanderlip (fig. I.2), who replaced Stillman as City Bank president three weeks after the opening (and who took the doors of the old Customs House to "Beechwood," his Scarborough-on-Hudson estate), had wanted a large, modern structure.[8] He anticipated that the fast-growing bank would soon face a crisis of office space, and had gone as far as having plans drafted for a multistory tower.[9] Others were bothered by less practical concerns. They were bewildered by the decision to stack a second colonnade on top of the first. They viewed the renovation as an aesthetic aberration, a vulgar betrayal of the formal perfection of the principles of neoclassical architecture. They saw it as a reflection of the whims and caprices of gauche financiers who wanted to dress up the uncouth and grotesque spaces of modern industrial capitalism with the frills and drapery of Greek and Roman civilization.[10] 55 Wall Street was part of a scourge of neoclassicism found in the factories,

I.1. Irving Underhill, National City Bank, Wall Street, 1909. Library of
Congress Prints and Photographs Division, Washington, DC.

banks, warehouses, and offices whose ersatz evocations of a European clas-
sical past, as social critic Lewis Mumford observed, tried to conceal the labor exploitation, industrial organization, and monopoly combination of
the modern US economy. For Mumford, contemporary business and commercial architecture masked an "imperial enterprise" churning behind an
"imperial façade."[11]

55 Wall Street embodied Mumford's descriptions of a debased imperial architecture. Its neoclassical detailing and Romanesque veneers cloaked
the City Bank's financial labors within the domestic economy, shrouded its
modern office technologies, obscured its ties to the exploitation of oil and

I.2. Frank A. Vanderlip (1924). National Photo Company Collection. Library of
Congress Prints and Photographs Division, Washington, DC.

railroads and cotton and steel, and veiled its connections to the oligopolistic
corporations using the bank as their private financier. But hidden behind
55 Wall Street's façade of neoclassicism was another imperial enterprise: an
enterprise of banking, finance, and empire whose ambitions and expansions
were braided through the US colonial and neocolonial projects of the early
twentieth century. While the City Bank was undergoing a transition from
nineteenth-century merchant bank to twentieth-century commercial and
industrial financier, it was also remaking itself as an international financial

institution. Where it was once jockeying for business and influence among the brokers, merchants, and commission agents of old New York, the City Bank was now muscling its way to a seat at the table of international finance alongside the imperial banking houses of London, Paris, and Berlin. And where it once served the financial needs of a fast-growing domestic economy, it was increasingly involved with the banking, trade finance, and debt issuance of the Caribbean, Latin America, and Asia.

By the time 55 Wall Street's renovations were complete, Stillman and Vanderlip were recasting their institution as an imperial bank. The City Bank's history began to be written overseas, and it increasingly grappled with the conundrums of law and regulation governing international commerce, banking, and finance, as well with the questions of racism and militarism underwriting US imperialism and finance capitalism. 55 Wall Street's neoclassical façade obscured the modern economic aspects of empire and simultaneously expressed imperialism's racial and cultural orders.[12] For Stillman, for Vanderlip, and for other members of Wall Street's white financial elite, neoclassical architecture represented the transmission and transplantation of an Anglo-Saxon heritage to US soil. The evocations of the Pantheon embedded the bank within a European civilizational tradition and joined that tradition to the United States' bloody annals of imperial expansion.[13] Summoning the interlaced history of finance capitalism with *racial* capitalism, 55 Wall Street stood as an elegant monument to the City Bank's cruel imperial history.

The early history of US imperial banking and the internationalization of Wall Street began alongside the project of US colonial expansion at the turn of the nineteenth century and ended amid the financial and economic crises of the 1930s. It was fueled by the capital accumulations reaped from the industrial development, corporate consolidation, and economic expansion that followed the grim history of territorial dispossession that marked the settling of the US West. New York City was its engine. New York's bankers reaped the rewards of this growth as both the financiers of industrialization and as the representatives of a banker's bank serving regional financial institutions and the federal government. Buoyed by this newfound wealth, New York City's financial institutions began to look overseas, searching for outlets for their swelling accumulations of unproductive capital. They also sought to consolidate Wall Street's international position in finance, trade, and commerce. They viewed the organization of an imperial banking system as a critical component in the rise of New York and the westward traverse of the "star of financial supremacy," as imperial theorist and financial reformer Charles A. Conant referred to it, from Europe to the United States.[14]

With these ambitions, bankers and businesspeople set their sights on asserting control over the trade and finance of the Americas. They looked to displace the European joint-stock banks that had commanded South American trade since the mid-nineteenth-century lending booms as well as the Canadian chartered banks that dominated the financing of North American trade in the British West Indies and the Spanish-speaking islands. US bankers had lagged behind. Their European and Canadian competitors were quick to seize on the region's shifting needs for capital, brought on by both the end of slavery and the emergence of nominally free populations of African and indigenous workers and peasants, and by demands for capital by independent postcolonial states seeking to fund their modernization projects. Wall Street's expansion into the Caribbean and Latin America was grafted onto this postemancipation history of economics and finance as it intersected with questions of national sovereignty, political governance, and the political economy of race, labor, and citizenship.

The US government encouraged and supported the internationalization of US banking. The War and State departments required fiscal agencies to support the infrastructure of US colonialism, and financial institutions were an important conduit of colonial policy and financial and commercial diplomacy. Bankers, however, needed little prodding to move overseas and the relations between Wall Street and Washington were contested and contentious. Although foreign policy was often dictated from lower Manhattan and the federal government, alongside the US military, came to protect US banking and investment abroad, Wall Street often clashed with Washington. Similarly, as US bankers exerted their influence in the national palaces of Port-au-Prince and Havana and other capitals of the Caribbean and Central America, local elites sought to use Wall Street for their own ends. And bankers fought among themselves. While they often formed alliances, cartels, and consortiums, competition and rivalry created friction between Wall Street's banking houses—and sometimes *within* institutions as enmity, ambition, and the caprices of personality played no small part in shaping banking policy.

The City Bank was at the center of the history of banking internationalization and imperialism. A federally chartered commercial bank, it emerged as the largest and the most important imperial financier in the United States. Under Stillman and Vanderlip, the City Bank adopted an aggressive, entrepreneurial, and activist strategy for expansion and growth. Their strategy was in part an attempt to modernize the domestic operations of their institution through a process of internal organizational reconstruction and managerial reform that included the diversification of its domestic financial activities, the decentralization of its management and operations, and a push for the reform of banking regulations. Foreign expansion played a substantial part in the bank's modernization, and the most important theater of internationalization was the "American Mediterranean," as one City Banker described the countries and colonies ringing the Caribbean Sea and the Gulf of Mexico.[15] There, the City Bank experimented with the issuance of sovereign debt, the financing of international trade, the funding of industrial infrastructure, and the organization of regional state banks and currency systems. The City Bank also made the Caribbean the centerpiece of the largest foreign branch bank system of any US financial institution as it pushed for a share in a market long dominated by Europe and Canada. As part of its efforts of internationalization and in the attempts to create an institution for imperial accumulation, the City Bank hammered away at the banking regulations shackling its activities and pushed for regulatory reform. In its encounters with the peoples, nations, and colonies of the Caribbean and Latin America, it participated in the creation, replication, and reordering of Caribbean economies on racial lines while helping to reproduce the racist imaginaries and cultures in which finance capital was embedded and through which bankers functioned.

The City Bank was not the only US financial institution charting an imperial turn. It was joined by its neighbors on Wall Street, sometimes as collaborators involved in a collective project to consolidate the financial realms of the US imperium, sometimes as rivals embroiled in bitter intraimperial competition. The City Bank's efforts were preceded by a small group of unheralded entrepreneurs and institutions that emerged as the pioneers of the internationalization of US banking. These overlooked institutions established US banks abroad and provided financial services for US colonial administrations in the Caribbean and Pacific regions during an era from the 1870s to the 1910s that is largely neglected in the history of the foreign expansion of US banking and business. This era is often seen as an interregnum between the closing of a capital-saturated West at the end of the nineteenth century and the emergence of the United States as a global creditor during World War I.[16] But it is a period that is important on its own terms, not simply as a precursor of later events. Although fueled by the rhetoric of nineteenth-century Pan-Americanism, by the commercial boosterism of New York City, and by the euphoric proimperialist mood following the US victory over Spain in 1898, the success of these institutions rarely matched their ambitions, and their histories read as an archive of experimentation, missteps, and mistakes. The most successful and historically the most important of these institutions were those organized in Cuba and the Dominican Republic by private financier Samuel M. Jarvis. Significant, too, is the International Banking Corporation (IBC), an institution whose pioneering branch network in the Caribbean and Asia was long coveted by the City Bank. Both the Jarvis institutions and the IBC were important for their experimental, exploratory institutional histories, as well as for their role as training grounds for an emergent generation of international bankers.

At the same time, from the end of the nineteenth century, Wall Street's unincorporated and private investment banks, including J. P. Morgan and Co., Speyer and Co., and Kuhn, Loeb and Co., began floating the public debt of Caribbean, Latin American, and Asian countries, states, and municipalities and financing railroad and port projects.[17] Where they had grown in prominence by using their strong European networks and their close family ties as the conduit to market US government bonds and corporate securities across the Atlantic, they increasingly sold Caribbean and Latin American debt in the United States. These private bankers came to play an important role in the policy of "dollar diplomacy" initiated by William Howard Taft and his secretary of state, Philander Knox, in the 1910s. In the attempt to displace European influence and extend US capitalism in the Caribbean region, purporting to replace military intervention with financial diplomacy, private bankers worked with financial experts and local governments to refund sovereign debt, reorganize customs collection and currency systems, and organize nominally national government banks.[18]

The disordered global financial and economic conditions unleashed by the First World War accelerated the internationalization of Wall Street and intensified the relationship between banking, bankers, and imperialism. More than any other institution, the City Bank under Vanderlip took advantage of the opportunities provided by the war and ran with the new banking legislation of the Federal Reserve Act (1913), the federal legislation that modernized the US financial system and created the legal platform for foreign branch and commercial expansion. But the European war also roused other New York City commercial banks, trust companies, and private banks to action, especially in the Americas where European credits, once abundant, were now suddenly scarce. Enabled by new, permissive banking legislation, they partnered with the United States' regional and country banks in the formation of foreign finance corporations that rapidly created overseas branch networks and rushed to finance trade in foreign commodities— especially Cuban sugar. The most important of these corporations were the Mercantile Bank of the Americas (organized by Brown Brothers and Co., the J. P. Morgan–controlled Guaranty Trust Company, and J. & W. Seligman and Co.), and the American Foreign Banking Corporation, organized by the Chase National Bank of the City of New York.

This expansion of foreign branches and trade financing was short-lived. Commodity prices soared in the immediate postwar years, sparking a period of speculation and inflation. The period was most pronounced in Cuba, where it is remembered as a dazzling but abbreviated time of prosperity and wealth known as the *danza de los millones*, or the "dance of millions." But the global drop of commodity prices that marked the end of the dance of millions dealt a severe blow to US international banking. It prompted a retreat from branch banking and the dissolution of many of the foreign financial corporations organized to take advantage of the wartime and postwar trade conditions. Meanwhile, the Caribbean's local banking sector, having expanded during the war years, was gutted. North American financial institutions took over the assets and accounts of their vulnerable local rivals, consolidating their dominance in the Caribbean. Cuba, again, was devastated. Neither its financial sector nor its economy would recover from the crisis.

As a result of the crisis of 1920–21, banking internationalization and the organization of finance capitalism began to change in form and practice. Sovereign debt financing and the marketing of corporate bond issues superseded commercial trade financing. "Thrift" emerged as a strategy of expansion and as a new mode of imperial governance. Branch banking gave way to the use of "securities affiliates" as vehicles for imperial accumulation. Securities affiliates, sometimes called "bastard" affiliates, were parallel institutions of dubious legality organized by national banking associations for investment and the marketing of foreign and corporate debt. They helped facilitate the credit boom of the second half of the 1920s, with its unhinged speculation, deranged financing, and massive exportation of capital abroad. The National City Company and the Chase Securities Corporation were the two most important and prominent affiliates. The National City Company was organized by the City Bank, by that time led by a charismatic former bond salesman named Charles E. Mitchell. The Chase Securities Corporation was organized by the City Bank's emergent and ambitious rival the Albert H. Wiggin–led Chase National Bank of the City of New York. Through their securities affiliates, their respective parent banks took over the financing of sugar plantations and government banks and the funding of the sovereign debt of the Caribbean and Latin America.

The era of internationalization ended in the 1930s. Black Friday and the stock market crash of 1929 led to a crisis of finance capitalism. The crisis sparked a wave of both antibanking and anti-imperialist sentiment in the

United States and the Caribbean. It drew attention to the usurious interest rates and suffocating fiscal conditions imposed by bankers on sovereign nations, the strong personal and financial ties between Wall Street and despotic and dictatorial regimes in the Caribbean, the ongoing support for US military occupation by finance capital, and the virtual control of Caribbean industry and agriculture by banking houses. In addition to an outcry over odious debt and calls for the repudiation of loans by Caribbean countries, there were soon demands for both the regulation and reform of banking practices and the nationalization or "indigenization" of US banks operating in the region. New Deal banking legislation accomplished the former; the securities affiliates of the City Bank and the Chase Bank were dissolved as part of a broader deceleration of international activities and a partial retreat from US imperial banking.

A financial crisis sparked the regulatory reform that curtailed the history of Wall Street's internationalization and the expansion of imperial banking. A financial crisis had also enabled internationalization in the first place. Financial crises forced the geographical reorganization of capital accumulation and the territorialization of banking power, initiating the search for new markets and the shift overseas. The response to crisis also came in the calls for the rewriting of the legal underpinnings of the organization of banking institutions. Bankers placed the blame for economic and financial crisis at the feet of outmoded, cumbersome, and restrictive banking legislation and demanded regulatory reform and the modernization of banking law. They called not for the repeal of regulation, but for its extension: for the organization by the state of a stronger and more efficient regulatory structure to facilitate banking internationalization and global capital accumulation. In fact, the history of the internationalization of US finance and the imperial turn in US banking is in part a history of the transformations and challenges to banking law and the regulation of financial institutions in the national and international contexts.

At the most basic, apolitical, and historically sanitized level, banks are "financial intermediaries" whose social function is to link savers with borrowers or investors. Banks are legal entities organized to promote efficiencies of transaction and exchange while enabling the transformation of unproductive, hoarded money into active, productive capital.[19] Economic expansion and innovation have led to increasingly arcane forms of finance, but they have also led, on the one hand, to specialization—spawning, over time, a range of institutions whose names denote their primary activity, be they commercial banks, government central banks, trust companies, investment banks, or development banks—and on the other hand, to the consolidation and organization of integrated "financial department stores" and vast, multiunit, financial conglomerates.

International, multinational, and global banking spatializes specialization. At the heart of the theory and practice of international banking are the problems of geography and law as well as a question concerning the intermediation of capital across political borders and across sovereign jurisdictions. Bankers were faced with the problem of creating an entity chartered under one jurisdiction that could operate in another sovereign jurisdiction, a jurisdiction governed by a different, autonomous set of laws and under a different legal authority. They sought to organize financial institutions that could work across these distinct jurisdictions and apprehend a territory whose monetary and financial systems were shaped by incommensurable legal codes—although, in many cases, bankers saw themselves as above the law and beyond the sovereign authority of individual states, especially in the Caribbean.[20]

For US bankers, this was a particularly difficult problem given the "dual" nature of the country's banking system. The 1863 National Bank Act created two legal categories of financial institutions existing within two different spheres of regulation.[21] "National banking associations," joint-stock commercial banks such as the City Bank (the "national" in its name signifying its legal status), were chartered under the act and supervised by the comptroller of the currency. As federal depositories they could issue national currency, but they were "unit" banks that were limited to a solitary venue of operation and barred from branch or "chain" banking. The injunctions against branch banking dated back to fears of territorial monopoly and the nineteenth-century "bank wars" over Andrew Jackson's Bank of the United States. For Stillman, Vanderlip, and others seeking to move overseas, the restrictions on branch banking proved to be a major obstacle in the internationalization of national banking associations. State banks, on the other hand, did not have access to the monetary reserves of the federal government and could not issue currency. They were allowed to organize branches, although only within the state of incorporation. That said, some bankers found loopholes in the permissive banking laws of states like Delaware, West Virginia, and Connecticut permitting them to experiment with overseas branch banking.

The reorganization of the national banking system through the Federal Reserve Act, signed late in 1913 and operationalized the following year, maintained the dual system and provided the legal infrastructure for foreign branch expansion and the expansion of international commerce and trade. The organization of the Federal Reserve System occurred in part because of the desire to create a domestic financial system with a liquid currency that could attend to seasonal fluctuations in credit demand and stave off the kind of monetary crisis created by the Panic of 1907, when private bankers, led by J. P. Morgan, were forced to intervene to save the financial system from collapse. Proponents of a federal reserve system argued that a "banker's bank" or a "banker of last resort" was needed to regulate the country's economy through control of the monetary supply. Their plan was to decentralize capital reserves to better mobilize credit in response to fluctuations in demand, to expedite the clearance of various forms of securities within a geographically expansive domestic market, and to protect the gold reserve so as to maintain the United States' ascendant favorable balance of trade.[22] The system was also set up as a way of enhancing the dollar's international standing and to promote it as an international currency.[23]

The Federal Reserve Act also contained a number of provisions crucial to the expansion of US banking and markets abroad. It created an international system of discount that facilitated the financing of international trade by national banking associations, and provided for the establishment of foreign branch banks. Even with the organization of the Federal Reserve, the difficulties of the dual system were compounded the moment US bankers considered overseas expansion. Jurisdictional authority beyond the United States was often ill defined, occasionally contradictory, and sometimes nonexistent, and the legal regimes in which international bankers operated were disorganized, uneven, and plural.[24] For the US imperial banks, a quasi- or extralegal modality was the rule not the exception. They sought to evade the scrutiny of regulators by operating in the seams between legal jurisdictions, in the regulatory black holes beyond the reach of sovereign nations, and in regions where oversight from creditors, investors, and regulators was obscured and financial regulation was weak. US financial institutions created parallel institutions that could operate within the jurisdictions from which the parent bank was barred—shadow organizations unknown to regulators that existed outside or in between the normative boundaries of legal authority. Critical to the history of imperial accumulation and finance capitalism, these shadow organizations were created in consultation with Wall Street's most powerful corporate law firms and its infernally brilliant corporate lawyers: Sullivan & Cromwell; Shearman & Sterling; Curtis, Mallet-Prevost; Rushmore, Bisbee & Stern; and Cravath, Swaine & Moore. Prized for their skill and agility in interpreting and rewriting corporate and regulatory code, these firms were retained by New York's banking institutions and oftentimes shared in the spoils and rewards of Wall Street's Caribbean ventures.

As bankers like James Stillman and Frank A. Vanderlip and lawyers like William Nelson Cromwell and John Sterling slouched in their mahogany-paneled offices and ersatz renaissance parlors—sipping scotch amid over-stuffed furniture, marble statues, and velvet curtains suffused by the smoke of Cuban cigars—and outlined the notional visions of imperial finance, on the ground in the Caribbean and Latin America, another set of white men were turning the financial abstractions into monetary reality and performing the dirty labors of international banking and empire. These men, individuals like the City Bank's Roger L. Farnham, John H. Allen, and Joseph H. Durrell, have dwelt in the shadows of the larger-than-life robber barons and "wizards" of modern finance who have dominated the lore and historiography of US banking. These unheralded and lesser-known figures were curious individuals. With their knowledge of foreign languages and extensive travel experience, they were cosmopolitan in a way most Americans of the time were not—even as they were still shaped by many of the racial and cultural prejudices of their compatriots. Always white, always male, half frontiersman, half accountant, more hardened than the gentlemanly capitalists of the City of London, less knowing than the economic hit-men of popular literature, they were rogue bankers who entered the profession with little formal experience and often with no formal training.[25] Some began as journalists and reporters. Others started as the managers of country banks on the US frontiers. Most eventually drifted to New York City and on to the Caribbean and Latin America and back again, finding employment in the US imperial banks operating throughout the region. In the case of Durrell, he left behind a set of private papers that provides unparalleled access and insight into the history of US imperial banking in the first decades of the twentieth century.

Rogue bankers shouldered the burdens of internationalization and imperial banking. Through their labors the tattered and frayed legal geography of early twentieth-century international finance was sutured together, the abstraction of finance capital was rendered in material form, and the economies of the Caribbean were inscribed in the account ledgers of Wall Street. Through these bankers, the intimacy of finance capital and racial capitalism in the US-Caribbean encounter can be most clearly discerned. Racial capitalism suggests both the simultaneous historical emergence of racism and capitalism in the modern world and their mutual dependence.[26]

White rogue bankers not only carried US racial prejudice to the Caribbean but instrumentalized white racism in imperial banking policy and practice through their everyday encounters and transactions with Caribbean peoples, whether they were Spanish-descended businesspeople in Havana, black and mulatto elites in Port-au-Prince, African *braceros* and *jornaleros* in Santiago de Cuba and Colón, Indian peasants in Managua—or even the white Canadians and Europeans that often staffed the overseas branches of US banks. Importantly, the question of racism here is not merely one of individual beliefs but one of institutional policy, not simply one of personal sentiment but one of political-economic structure. As institutions like the City Bank and the Chase Bank established Caribbean branches and agencies, lent money to sugar planters and commercial exporters, funded sovereign debt, and took over central banking functions, their actions were shaped and structured by domestic patterns of racial thinking and racist perception. Their "profits" came in the form of both shareholder dividends and the reproduction of global white supremacy.[27]

Racial capitalism's representations often appeared in strange forms within the banking community. Take, for instance, its appearance in the City Bank Minstrel Show. Organized by the City Bank Club, the educational and social organization for the bank's white employees, the City Bank Minstrel Show saw members of the bank's staff donning blackface and "coon" outfits and performing musical and comedic skits for their peers. From 1911 until the late 1920s, the show was held at 55 Wall Street. During one performance, on Saturday evening, March 28, 1914, an enraptured audience of almost 2,000 people witnessed the transformation of the main banking room, so carefully renovated to replicate the Pantheon, into a southern plantation. They saw an opening scene of "several darkies"—their coworkers at the City Bank, their white faces blackened with burnt cork—"gathered on the shore of a river engaging in the colored man's national pastime, shooting craps," followed by a program of skits and songs. The City Bank staff performed songs such as "Down in Monkeyville" and "That's Plenty" as well as popular tunes including "The Gibson Coon," "Oh, You Coon!," "Go Away, Mistah Moon," "There's a Little Bit of Monkey in You and Me," "The Arrival of That Emerald Pair from Ethiopia," "Come Back to Alabam,'" and "How's Every Little Thing in Dixie?" in what was described as "true darkey style." They were joined over the years by a roster of black caricatures—"pink-costumed coons," "beautiful dusky queens in black and yellow watermelon costume" wearing "real ninety-carat, one-beet, two-parsnip, three-potato diamonds," and a vainglorious and flamboyant figure called "the darktown multi-millionaire."[28]

The City Bank Minstrel Show was in many ways an unremarkable product of its era.[29] It was a sign of the ubiquity of such performances that other Wall Street institutions—from the National Bank of Commerce to the Chase Bank—also organized minstrel shows. These institutions also used blackface waiters and performers at social events. A blackface troupe called the Darktown Agony Quartette performed at the Guaranty Trust Company's Second Annual Dinner and blackface waiters served at a banquet held by the National Bank of Commerce at the Brooklyn Academy of Music.[30] Bankers also staged Orientalist pageants, like "Chin Chin China Maid," and performed ostentatious rituals for staffers initiated into make-believe Asian lodges.[31] Racist stories, jokes, and anecdotes about Asians, Jews, Native Americans, and African Americans regularly appeared within the pages of bank publications, as well as in the trade and professional journals of the time.[32] Often, as in the story "Dark Finance," their humor came from casting black people as economic illiterates whose engagements with modern banking and finance were marked by repeated incomprehension, befuddlement, and vexation. Published in *The Chase*, the house organ of the Chase Bank, "Dark Finance" depicted two African Americans fighting over the meaning and value of a promissory note. Its punch line rested on the assumption of black financial illiteracy.[33] In the malformed worlds of race and money—in the worlds of "dark finance"—Wall Street rendered African Americans muddling their way through the everyday economic situations that most whites apparently took for granted.

These signs and figures traveled far beyond Wall Street. As they moved into the Caribbean, bankers rendered the region within the same racist tropes and narratives in which African Americans were cast. White representations of African Americans were exported to the West Indies and inscribed in a vast archive of pamphlets, reports, circulars, press releases, prospectuses, and journal articles produced by Wall Street about the Caribbean and Latin America. Furthermore, in their dispatches back to the United States, published in the journals, monographs, and pamphlets issued by Wall Street, bankers translated the Caribbean to US businesspeople, investors, and the general public—in some cases debunking stereotypes as a means to encourage investment, in others replicating and reconstituting racial stereotypes to further the expansion of white supremacist control of the region, its returns and accounting found not in the rational extraction of values, but in the ledger of white racial dominance.

The City Bank's John H. Allen offers but one example of this practice of racial capitalism's representation, circulation, and reproduction. Allen aided the bank's expansion into Cuba and Argentina and was the manager of the City Bank–controlled Banque Nationale de la République d'Haiti in the 1910s. He is perhaps best known for his 1930 article recounting William Jennings Bryan's decision making in the lead-up to the landing of US Marines in Haiti in 1915. In the article, Allen describes briefing Bryan on Haiti's history and politics. After listening carefully to Allen's comments, Bryan responded, "Dear me, think of it! Niggers speaking French."[34] Years earlier, in the City Bank's foreign trade journal *The Americas*, Allen evoked a picture of Haiti that would have been recognizable to white US audiences but for its tropical difference. Allen asserted that "cock-fighting and card playing are the [Haitian] national pastimes, and these, together with a supply of Haitian rum, are all that is necessary for a Haitian citizen's perfect day." He claimed that during his visits to Haiti he found that "humorous incidents were of almost daily occurrences." For Allen, such incidents "showed the naivete and also the restricted mentality of the [Haitian] people, which latter was plainly noticeable even among the more highly educated." He supported his claims with anecdotal evidence gleaned from his interactions with one of the employees of the Banque Nationale de la République d'Haiti:

> One day [the employee] stated that after careful thought he was convinced that if he continued working as previously he would not survive the strain many months longer. That he had a large family who would be left penniless and therefore he was not justified any longer in running the risk. If, however, his salary were increased he would be warranted in continuing the risk. I told him that I was sure he was mistaken and suggested he continue as before as no salary increase was possible; that if he tried it and it proved to be fatal, he would have the satisfaction of knowing he was right. If, however, he did not die, he would know his apprehension was unfounded and therefore the increase requested not warranted. He came back the next day, saying that he had thought it over and concluded my suggestion was a fair one.[35]

Such anecdotes, stories, narratives, and representations did not exist in a vacuum—and they were not merely an incidental cultural membrane stretched over the inner workings of banking, racial capitalism, and imperialism. They contributed to the ideological and cultural rationales through which the Caribbean became the subject of the internationalizing and imperial efforts of Wall Street's banks and at the same time fashioned the racial, economic, legal, and governmental terms through which the Caribbean was encountered. These representations were underwritten by the direct and indirect forms of violence that brought the Caribbean under Wall Street's imperial sway: by coercive diplomacy, military force, and labor impressment, as well as by the terms and conditions of credit and debt, the imbalanced application of law and legal regulation, and the imposition of modern forms of postemancipation financial governance.

As the Darktown Agony Quartette was entertaining the staff of the Guaranty Trust Company, the Guaranty's subsidiary, the Mercantile Bank of the Americas, rushed to build a Caribbean-wide chain of agencies and branches. At the same time "Dark Finance" appeared in *The Chase*, the Chase Bank's American Foreign Banking Corporation had just ended a disastrous experiment in foreign trade financing and banking operation in Cuba, Panama, the Dominican Republic, and Haiti and the Chase Bank itself was about to embark on a spectacularly calamitous period of sovereign debt financing in Cuba. As plantation scenes were staged on the marble floors of 55 Wall Street and the City Bank minstrels played in the shadows of the steel vault and jigged under the Romanesque dome, Roger L. Farnham, John H. Allen, Joseph H. Durrell, and other rogue bankers fought for the City Bank's control of the banking and finances of Cuba, Haiti, Puerto Rico, and the Dominican Republic. The following chapters recount this dark history of bankers and empire.

ONE

Colonial Methods

Samuel Miller Jarvis landed at Santiago de Cuba on July 28, 1898, and discovered a squalid, broken city, a somnambulant frontier town seemingly stuck in a fast-retreating Spanish colonial past. What others found picturesque—the narrow lanes and low houses, the rouge-tiled roofs rising sharply from the sheltered bay, their ceramic patchwork broken only by the twinned cupola of the town's cathedral, the narcotic murmur and lull of daily life—Jarvis found disappointing, unattractive, and backward. Santiago, for Jarvis, was architecturally unimpressive, its streets were squalid and unhygienic, and its citizens, Cuban and Spaniard alike, appeared to be of a lowly character. "The town is very old, the style of architecture primitive, there is not a modern residence or business building in the town," Jarvis complained. "There has been no consideration given to sanitary engineering or conditions. The streets are narrow, badly paved where paved at all and at present in a bad state of repair, as well as being very dirty, and the sidewalks are very bad. It is very difficult to get around the town during this hot weather as it seems to be a succession of hills, and what carriages there are are rather heavy, without brakes and the horses are small and poor Cuban ponies."[1]

Jarvis was a New York City businessman and banker, a board member of half a dozen corporate concerns, and a founder and vice president of the North American Trust Company (NATC) (fig. 1.1). He had traveled to Santiago de Cuba to open a branch of the NATC but, upon his arrival, found that after decades of insurrection and war, Santiago's underdevelopment mirrored Cuba's banking and financial organization. He discovered that in Cuba, banking, as US capitalists understood the term, was an "incidental" business, a secondary activity of commission houses and merchants whose specialty was the distribution and sale of cigars and cigarettes and other items. There were but two proper banks on the island: the Banco Español de la Isla de Cuba, fiscal agent of the Spanish colonial government, and the Banco Comercio, a private commercial bank in the process of liquidation; neither institution did much to stimulate economic growth. The merchant banks acted as resolutely private, even personal, concerns. Money was hoarded in fireproof safes, few people had bank accounts, there was little capital in circulation, and commercial transactions were settled not through drafts, but by the cumbersome movement of Spanish and French gold from creditor to debtor and back using a horse-drawn carriage accompanied by armed guards.[2]

Yet Jarvis saw promise and possibility in Santiago de Cuba. Two hours after presenting his credentials to Major General William R. Shafter, the US commanding officer in Cuba, at Santiago's Municipal Palace, Jarvis was searching for an office for the NATC. Two days later, the NATC was opened for business at 10 Marina Street.[3] "It was the first and is at present the only American banking institution in Santiago," Jarvis later stated, "and I was the first civilian to raise the American flag on the island after the commencement of the war."[4]

Samuel Jarvis is among the most important if enigmatic figures in the early history of US imperial banking. Over nearly fifty energetic but peripatetic years, he created a series of financial institutions that, though oftentimes ill starred, contributed to the construction of the platform required for the international expansion of US finance and the development of the fiscal infrastructure of the US colonial state. The institutions Jarvis organized were at the nexus of the geographic imperatives and regulatory issues that plagued the foreign expansion of US banking and finance, and the clerks, accountants, managers, and auditors whom he employed were critical to the foreign management and internationalization of later, more established, and well-known US international banking institutions. Shrewd and entrepreneurial, Jarvis was quick to recognize the profit potential of the frontiers of US capitalism. He saw the promise of regions on the cusp of development and territories not yet strafed and exhausted by investment, and he saw the possibilities of industries and projects still nascent. Jarvis had a lawyer's mind and an assessor's eye, but he also had a politician's wiles and was able to mobilize both the law and the state for his own accumulative ends.

Jarvis's vision led him to Cuba. There, his North American Trust Company quickly took advantage of the financial possibilities of the US occupation (1898–1902) while his Banco Nacional de Cuba, organized in 1902,

1.1. Engraving of Samuel Miller Jarvis. From Theodore S. Case, ed., *History of Kansas City, Missouri, with Illustrations and Biographical Sketches of Some of Its Prominent Men and Pioneers* (Syracuse, NY: D. Mason & Co., 1888). Archive.org.

emerged as among the most important banking institutions in the early years of the *república neocolonial*, in which the Cuban economy and political system was increasingly dominated by the United States. In a similar fashion, a decade later, Jarvis turned to the Dominican Republic, organizing the Banco Nacional de Santo Domingo in an attempt to profit from US fiscal control of the country by taking advantage of the State Department's policies of dollar diplomacy in the Caribbean and Central America.

However, the roots of the Jarvis project were not in the West Indies, but in the US Midwest. Before Jarvis grafted his organizations onto the project of US colonialism in the Caribbean archipelago, he profited from the history of white settler colonialism in the Missouri Valley. Two decades before Jarvis reached Santiago de Cuba, he began as a mortgage broker in frontier Kansas. There, he organized a slate of corporations and banks, the most important being the Jarvis-Conklin Mortgage Trust Company, an institution launched with his erstwhile business partner Roland Ray Conklin. Jarvis-Conklin emerged as the preeminent institution serving as the intermediary for the capital "irrigating," to use the parlance of the time, the US West. It lent Atlantic capital, the savings of the middle classes of England and the eastern United States, to the white farmers, drovers, and ranchers settling the states and territories west of the Missouri River. Jarvis-Conklin offered mortgages on farms and ranches and financed the street railroads, residential plats, and waterworks for the growing urban populations of Kansas City and Baltimore.

In Cuba and the Dominican Republic, Jarvis's ventures were guaranteed by force: protocols and agreements between the United States and the two countries enshrined financial stability through the threat of military intervention; in the US West Jarvis's companies were underwritten by the historical violence of white settler colonialism: territorial dispossession enabled both the financialization of the West and the expansion of racial capitalism.[5] But both territories were governed by an expansionist state eager to encourage investment but whose actual regulatory footprint was weak. Drawing on a reservoir of colonial capital to finance his projects, Jarvis profited from the inefficiencies, oversights, and ambiguities of a state bureaucracy still in formation and encumbered by problems of distance and geography. He worked in regions where jurisdictional boundaries were unclear and fuzzy and where local sovereignty and authority were difficult and transitional.

Jarvis proved an adept navigator of these regulatory spaces, walking the thin lines between legality and illegality, sound and unsound banking practice, and ethical and dubious business pursuits. Such an approach to business did not come without criticism. The *Investors' Review* derisively evoked "the methods of Messrs. Jarvis and Conklin" as a prime example of the suspect business and financial practices prevalent in the US West. These methods prompted lawsuits, investigations, and legal proceedings and generated an aura of impropriety, chicanery, crookedness, and corruption that enveloped all of Jarvis's enterprises and followed him from Kansas to the Caribbean. In the Missouri basin Jarvis and Conklin were accused of patronage, graft, and fraud. In Cuba, a former employee described the Jarvis crowd as a "gang of crooks" who had come to the island "to plunder, exploit, not for any good purpose."[6] In the Dominican Republic, the associates of Jarvis threatened rivals with violence, fell afoul of the US State Department, and became pariahs in the local business community. Despite the criticisms, Jarvis's methods, honed in Kansas and perfected in the Caribbean, were essential to the history and growth of US imperial banking and the training of its bankers. Long after Jarvis's institutions had collapsed, the bankers he employed continued to shape the terms and history of the internationalization of Wall Street.

Samuel Miller Jarvis was born in McDonough County, Illinois, in 1853.[7] He spent his early years on his father's farm, attended local schools, and upon his graduation in 1871, married and moved to Winfield, Kansas, a small township in the southern part of the state. Taking advantage of the federal government's preemption statues allowing white settlers to take over surveyed, "un-occupied" land, he appropriated and worked an acreage. Jarvis also taught school, traded in land, and made mortgage loans for friends back in Illinois. He began editing and publishing the *Cedar Vale Blade* in nearby Chautauqua County in August 1877 but finding it unprofitable sold it by December.[8] He read law in his spare time, and in 1878, he was admitted to the bar. He formed Gilbert, Jarvis & Co., with Stanley L. Gilbert, a local notary. The company loaned money on improved farmland in Cowley and surrounding counties. Jarvis combined his knowledge of real estate law with his skills in appraising farmland. The company proved a success.

When Gilbert retired in 1881, Jarvis reconstituted the business as Jarvis, Conklin Co. His new partner, Roland Ray Conklin, was born in Urbana, Illinois, in 1858. Conklin left school at fourteen and worked for two years as a clerk and a bookkeeper before applying for admission to the University of Illinois.[9] To pay his tuition, Conklin worked as a clerk for a local merchant and spent his summers traveling up and down the Missouri and Mississippi rivers and taking temporary employment. He took jobs as a ship hand, a baker, and a traveling salesman in Sioux City, Kansas, and St. Paul. At one time in St. Louis, he hawked primitive telephones, foreshadowing some of his later enterprises. He was forced to drop out of school because of his inability to pay tuition, and in 1878, he moved to Winfield, Kansas, where his brother was already established as a newspaper publisher. Conklin was hired as the bookkeeper for Gilbert, Jarvis and when Gilbert retired, formed a partnership with Jarvis. It would last nearly forty years.

Within a year the business of Jarvis, Conklin had outgrown Winfield, and they relocated to Kansas City, Missouri. Kansas City was emerging as a regional financial and commercial hub.[10] Its population was swelling with white settlers. Telegraph and railway lines converged on the city, and its financial institutions acted as the clearing house for investment capital: money from the northeastern states and England passed through it on its way for public improvements, urban expansion, and the development of the West.[11] In November 1886 Jarvis and Conklin dissolved their partnership, reconstituting it as the Jarvis-Conklin Mortgage Trust Company, releasing them from individual liability and positioning them to take advantage of the booming economy of Kansas City and its environs.[12]

The Jarvis-Conklin Mortgage Trust Company became the most important financial institution in the region, amassing a large portfolio of five- and ten-year mortgages on city and farm real estate.[13] The headquarters of the company was staffed by almost thirty clerks who issued its paper and a team of traveling inspectors who examined securities and assessed property values. They had a network of agents and inspectors in nearly all of the western states and territories. They opened agencies in New York, Providence, Philadelphia, Boston, Dallas, Portland, Denver, and Memphis, through which mortgages and securities were marketed. They also developed an extensive branch network. The headquarters were responsible for loans in Missouri, Kansas, and Nebraska, the branch in Memphis presided over Tennessee, Arkansas, Texas, and Alabama; the Portland office covered Washington, Idaho, and Montana; and Denver covered Colorado. In addition, in 1887 they established an office in London, England, the first branch of a US trust company to be set up overseas. The London office was soon their busiest, employing the largest number of staff and selling almost as many securities as the other branches combined.[14] Jarvis-Conklin also contracted as the sole fiduciary agent in the United States for the Yorkshire Investment and American Mortgage Company, Ltd., founded by Bradford, England, investors.[15]

By 1888, Jarvis-Conklin had negotiated almost 15,000 mortgages valued at more than $14 million and paid out close to $4 million in interest to its investors and shareholders. Its success led it into enterprises beyond western farm mortgages. Jarvis-Conklin acted as the developer for the Roland Park Company, a corporation formed by London's Land Trust Company in 1891 to oversee the development of a Baltimore suburb. The suburb displaced a long-standing African American community and included covenants against blacks and Jews in the purchase agreements. They platted and developed Kansas City's tony Hyde Park neighborhood, another racially segregated neighborhood, where both men owned large homes. They formed the Bear Lake and River Water Works and Irrigation Co. The prospectus of the company outlined far-reaching plans for a hydrological system that would irrigate much of the Utah Territory.[16] They also founded local banks, including the Farmers and Drovers' Bank, at Kingman, Kansas, and the Bank of Columbus, in Kansas City, and railroad and utility companies, including the Kansas Elevated Railway, the Augusta Railway Company, the North-East Street Railway Company, the Augusta Electric Company, the Ogden Street Railway Company, and Waukesha Hygeia Mineral Springs.[17]

The success of Jarvis-Conklin was based on the possibilities of both land and the law. First, the availability of free, unencumbered, and uninhabited land in the West was the precondition for accumulation; settlement was only possible by prior displacement, and the financial abstractions of land mortgages were underwritten by the historical violence of indigenous expulsion. Jarvis-Conklin issued a publicity tract titled *The Great Loan Land* that inadvertently illuminated this history. The title of the volume played on the trope of empty but financialized space, as its text evoked Kansas and Missouri as lands wherein every square inch was being energized by investment capital.[18] But it was accumulation based on dispossession: they did not settle empty land but *emptied* land, land in which the aboriginal populations had been killed or removed.[19]

The success of Jarvis-Conklin was also facilitated by the regulatory context of the period and the region. Restrictions governing other types of intermediaries that might have otherwise entered the market in western mortgages enabled its expansion. The New England savings banks that had invested their capital in Jarvis-Conklin were strictly local in their operations. They did not have a network of agents that could inspect properties, verify mortgages, or collect charges and payments, and so relied on brokers like Jarvis-Conklin to do this work. Similarly, although under the National Bank Act, New York City's financial institutions were becoming increasingly powerful, they were also restricted from operating beyond their state of incorporation. Only insurance companies offered any competition to the land mortgage companies.[20]

Yet even in the context of this loose regulatory environment, Jarvis-Conklin's geographical expansion raised concerns over its authority to operate in certain jurisdictions. In 1890, the superintendent of the New York State Banking Department asked the attorney general for an opinion on whether or not Jarvis-Conklin had the legal right to accept deposits and borrow money in New York while issuing its debentures as security in Kansas. The attorney general affirmed the right of the company to do so, but stressed that it was restrained by law depending on the material form of the issue: it could issue debentures as security, but was expressly forbidden to issue debentures as circulating currency or banknotes. It was noted that Jarvis-Conklin bonds were of similar material form to banknotes and that such issues were forbidden according to its charter. The attorney general stated that the company was liable to a $1,000 penalty if it began issuing banknotes.[21] Such legal questions and doubts would dog the company.

So long as the farms were productive and profitable, dividends were paid out and investment capital coursed in. Yet for some, there was a nagging fear that this exuberant expansion of credit and the limitless possibilities of western growth could be undermined by the very settlers whose energy it depended on. A letter to the editor of the Quaker publication *Friends' Intelligencer* in 1888 typified this concern:

> Are you aware what these advertisements mean? If the poor emigrant settler in the Far West, who has to earn a scanty subsistence by the labor of his own hands, only paid 7 per cent interest, and no more, I should have nothing to say. But before he can get the money he has to pay a bonus or premium to these wealthy companies. In case of a mortgage for $1,000, he receives only $900, but he pays interest on the whole amount. If the mortgage runs for five years, he pays $35 interest on the $100 which he never received. Is this right and honest? Have you never thought of this?[22]

Jarvis responded on behalf of his company. He acknowledged that the rate of return had fallen, naturally, considering the availability of money, but dismissed the suggestion that the mortgages burdened western settlers and posed a risk to eastern investors. Furthermore, Jarvis continued, the great fertility of the land, tied to the industry of the settlers, promised profits of a size and longevity that were greater than anything offered from the East.[23] Yet signs of distress were emerging. When Jarvis-Conklin agents evicted tenants from properties in default, they clashed with Farmer's Alliance posses who decried the "mortgage company dogs" and expressed an agrarian, populist disgust with the company's cosmopolitan finance. The posses attempted to evict the Jarvis-Conklin representatives from repossessed farms to return them to the mortgage holders.[24]

In the short term, the apparent risks to investors in the Jarvis-Conklin debentures came not from the weight of western mortgages, but from a source inside the company. In 1892, Jarvis-Conklin was caught up in a spectacle of adverse publicity involving a Canadian clerk and gambling addict, Augustus Theophilus Kerr, a figure later dubbed "Embezzler Kerr" and the "Kansas City Swindler." After inheriting a fortune estimated at $150,000, which he lost through stock and grain speculation in Ontario, Kerr opened a number of bucket shops (unregistered brokerage houses that used their customers' capital to gamble on the stock exchange) in Toronto and then drifted to Kansas City, where he became the head bookkeeper of Jarvis-Conklin. In April 1892, a routine audit of his books revealed $12,000 in missing securities. Further investigation by the American Surety Company revealed that Kerr had been using company money both to fund a lavish lifestyle and to support his penchant for stock speculation through a dummy company, the Missouri Commission Company, which he had opened directly across the street from the offices of Jarvis-Conklin.[25] He fled to Canada, then to Europe, where he lost most of his newfound fortune gambling at Monte Carlo, and then to England, where he gained confidence with the locals by, as one report noted, "proclaiming himself an American capitalist." Kerr was eventually tracked to Liverpool, where he was caught trying to cash securities belonging to Jarvis-Conklin. At the end of November 1892, he declared that he was being persecuted for the information he had regarding the company's illicit business practices, and claimed he had written an exposé of the company.

Kerr did not have the opportunity to reveal the details of his accusations. He was convicted on March 22, 1893, and sentenced to two years and six months in the penitentiary at Jefferson City, Missouri.[26] Kerr's replacement at Jarvis-Conklin, Frank W. Black, came with his own reputation tainted by scandal and rumors of fraud. Frank was born in Calais, Maine, about 1865. He began his banking career at the Calais National Bank and then made his way to Kansas City, Missouri, where he worked as the collector for the American National Bank of Kansas City. In 1892, Black and two other employees of the bank were arrested after a bank examiner found that figures in the bank's books had been altered. The trio was charged with embezzlement—some $12,118 had been taken—but Black avoided prosecution after confessing and returning the stolen funds.[27] Black joined Jarvis-Conklin in 1893 and remained with the pair over the next decade.

The drama of Embezzler Kerr and Jarvis-Conklin was overshadowed by a crisis that had a much greater impact on the firm, and on the US economy as a whole. By the early 1890s, the western boom was coming to an end. Overbuilding of railways and oversaturation of capital triggered a decline in interest rates and a retreat by investors from railroad mortgages. Combined with the low prices of produce from the midwestern farms and a glut of silver on the market, investor confidence in the US economy plummeted. Depositors began withdrawing their funds from financial institutions across the West, leading to bank runs, a cascade of suspensions, and in May 1893, a full-blown banking panic. More than 500 financial institutions across the United States suspended during this period, the majority in the newly mortgaged territories of the West.[28]

By August, as mortgage holders were unable to make their amortization payments, Jarvis-Conklin found it was overloaded with debt and would be unable to make its upcoming schedule of fixed payments to investors. The company sent out a fresh call for money. A month later, it was on the verge of bankruptcy. On September 28, 1893, the US District Court for the Southern District of New York initiated receivership proceedings to protect the assets of and preserve their interests in the company. Jarvis and Conklin were appointed the receivers of the company they had created.

When news of the appointment reached Jarvis-Conklin's English investors they were enraged. They argued that not only was it irresponsible for the courts to appoint as receivers the same individuals that drove the company into bankruptcy, but that the company's failure was due to Jarvis and Conklin's reckless management and fraudulent accounting practices. They petitioned the courts to force Jarvis and Conklin to open the trust company's account books—books that had been prepared by the already suspect figure of Frank W. Black. What they found suggested that Jarvis and Conklin had taken both the initial investments in the company and the amortization of properties for their own profits. Money that should have gone toward interest payments due investors was redirected toward the duo's other speculative ventures, from the Kansas Elevated Railway to the Bear Lake and River Water Works—all of which were abandoned before commencing operations. Long before the company failed, Jarvis and Conklin had bamboozled both shareholders and investors, and the receivership plan that they put in place simply continued these practices. The English investors asserted that the company "stuffed" their mortgages: they devalued the assets of the company and later purchased them at below-market prices through straw men, in-laws and associates—and sometimes people on the street who received a small commission for their signature—who then transferred the mortgages back to the duo through a corporate façade, the Western Improvement Company.[29] The mortgages were then resold at more than double their actual worth to investors unaware of the behind-the-scenes dealings.[30] According to the shareholders, when Jarvis and Conklin realized the corporation was on the verge of collapse, they methodically raided its coffers.

At the end of 1894, as the receivership proceedings were unfolding, London's *Investors' Review* published a damning article on the activities of the company. It had long been critical of the activities and practices of Jarvis-Conklin. "We do not like the issuing Company," it wrote of Jarvis-Conklin's prospectus for their Lake Roland Elevated Railroad Company, "and we cannot say that the information given in the prospectus of this issue causes us to put much confidence in this bond."[31] Before the crisis broke, *Investors' Review* had voiced caution and skepticism concerning the sustainability and safety of midwestern farm mortgages. With the onset of the receivership proceedings, its fears were affirmed. The proceedings gave it an opportunity to expose what it had suspected. *Investors' Review* outlined the financial practices of the trust company at the threshold of its collapse:

Thus on August 12, 1893, Jarvis had $19,686 on deposit, R.R. Conklin had $9,452 on deposit, and S.L. Conklin had $4,185 on deposit, making a total of $33,323. On this date promissory notes payable on demand were given for $32,000, which notes were paid on September 22 and 23 following, together with interest, by a cheque for $20,000 drawn in favor of Messrs. Jarvis and Conklin's private secretary, and the balance by a cheque in favor of Mr. Jarvis. And this was done with the full knowledge that that Company was insolvent! Nor did these careful managers stop here. On September 28, 1893, the actual day when failure was acknowledged, the following amounts were paid off: F. R. Conklin $10, Mrs. Priscilla Jarvis $796, Elenora Jarvis $3, Hugh Jarvis $3, and Pamelia Jarvis $3.[32]

Investors' Review asserted that the point of such an enumeration was not the size of the payments but the absolute thoroughness with which Jarvis and Conklin fleeced the company and their investors. It concluded that "land-mortgage business, in the proper sense of the term, appears to have played a poor part in its transactions, and more attention seems to have been devoted to the most vulgar form of commission shearing, and the propping up and working of wild-cat undertakings." It continued, "Had any decent supervision been exercised over its operations, the concern would have defaulted long before it did, much to the benefit of its creditors. . . . The methods of its managers . . . have cast a slur upon a form of capital investment which, when carried on honestly and faithfully, should prove profitable to the English creditor and the American investor alike."[33]

Despite the criticism, the protests, and the negative publicity, the efforts to have Jarvis and Conklin removed as receivers were unsuccessful. Jarvis eventually resigned for business purposes, but Conklin remained. On December 13, 1895, the securities and assets of Jarvis-Conklin were auctioned in Manhattan. The face value of the securities it held amounted to $1,775,000; they were sold for $236,000. The purchaser was the North American Trust Company (NATC). The NATC emerged out of the Citizens' Loan Agency and Guarantee Company, a corporation chartered by the state of New York in 1885. Its charter had remained dormant and inactive until September 1, 1894, when it was revived, and the name of the company changed to the North American Trust Company.[34] Samuel Jarvis and Roland Conklin were both the founders and the president and vice president of the new trust company. "This sale," the New York *Times* noted of the NATC's purchase of the Jarvis-Conklin assets, "is practically a reorganization of the old company."[35]

The first task of the NATC was to preside over the liquidation of Jarvis-Conklin, but it soon embarked on another order of business in a new field of operation. By the end of the century, Jarvis was mobilizing the NATC to take advantage of the possibilities of commercial and governmental financing and banking in the Caribbean, in particular in Cuba, the island having fallen into the hands of the United States following the defeat of Spain in 1898. Where Jarvis-Conklin had emerged as the preeminent institution serving as a conduit for the capital financing white settler colonialism in the US West, the NATC emerged as one of the most important financial institutions aiding the project of US colonialism in Cuba. Jarvis's geographic focus had changed. His methods had not. As in Kansas, in Cuba regulatory ambiguity and legal plurality offered the possibilities of expansion and profits. Jarvis worked the jurisdictional gaps in the landscape of US governance of Cuba while preempting Cuban sovereignty by commencing business during the ungoverned time zones between the period of US occupation and Cuban independence. Furthermore, the reorganization of Jarvis-Conklin as the NATC continued the shell game that contributed to the bankrupting of Jarvis-Conkin and its post-mortem pillaging. In Cuba, Jarvis proved more than willing to extend the operations of the trust company through patronage and graft. Not long after arriving on the island, the NATC was accused of extracting illegal profits from US military governance. It quickly became a symbol of the problems of nepotism and corruption in the years preceding the transition to Cuban self-rule. With the coming of Cuban independence in 1902, Jarvis's Banco Nacional de Cuba emerged as the most important financial institution contributing to the formation of the neocolonial republic. It too would be plagued by scandal, and its history would be overburdened by the kinds of financial manipulation and graft in which Jarvis had become an expert.

How Jarvis came to the decision to embark on a new venture in the Caribbean is uncertain. Both Jarvis and Conklin had followed the developments in the Cuban struggle against Spain at the end of the century alongside the rest of Wall Street.[36] Both men were neutral regarding the conflict. As late as 1897, Jarvis stated in an interview that he was "confident that the McKinley Administration will assume a pacific disposition" regarding Cuba.[37] Certainly, when they had relocated their offices from Kansas City to New York, they were looking for new opportunities for financing and business, but, even with their experience in international financing with Jarvis-Conklin, there is no indication that either the "closing" of the West or the reverberations of the crash of 1893 provided an immediate spark igniting the internationalization that followed.

Even so, by the time the USS Maine was sunk in Havana's harbor and President McKinley moved to intervene on both the Caribbean and the Pacific fronts, the NATC was poised for international expansion. Jarvis converted the London branch of Jarvis-Conklin into a branch of the NATC and created a board of directors with an impressively cosmopolitan outlook, an abiding interest in expanding the United States' foreign trade and commerce, and in many cases, ties to the McKinley administration. The directors included Charleston businessman and banker Wager Swayne; William I. Buchanan, United States minister to Argentina under both the Cleveland and McKinley administrations; and John G. Carlisle, former secretary of the treasury under Cleveland.[38] Former vice president Adlai Stevenson joined as the NATC's counsel.[39] William Lee Trenholm, a Southern banker and former comptroller of the currency (who for some time worked for his father's firm, the cotton brokers and Confederate financiers Fraser, Trenholm and Co.), was appointed as the NATC's president. At the time of Trenholm's appointment, Jarvis resigned the NATC presidency. He remained as a director of the trust company while beginning to focus on the trust company's "international work."[40]

The NATC's international work began the summer of 1898. That July, the NATC announced it would offer subscriptions for the purchase of up to $500 in war bonds by individuals associated with the New York Soldiers' and Sailors' Families' Protective Association, a support organization for US combatants. The NATC offered to advance the capital required for the initial purchase of the bonds to the families, while paying them the interest.[41] The NATC accepted approximately 1,000 subscriptions for $500,000. It paid nearly $24,000 in interest to the families.[42] The total subscription number was misleading, however. After a government investigation, it came to light that the NATC had falsified hundreds of subscription forms in an attempt to claim the interest amounts for its own account.

The revelations concerning the fraud did not emerge until later in the fall of 1898. Neither Jarvis nor the directors of the NATC were directly implicated. Instead, the NATC's subscription efforts were praised in the press, and both Jarvis and the NATC were lauded for their patriotic inclinations and humanitarian efforts in support of the troops. Fraudulent or not, the subscription scheme brought a quick and tangible reward to the trust company beyond the interest income. As a result of the NATC's work, McKinley offered Jarvis something of the spoils of war: the position as US fiscal agent in Cuba. It was a potentially lucrative contract. By its terms, Jarvis would serve an intermediary between the Treasury Department and US colonial bureaucracy and the military administration in Cuba, reaping a commission on transactions and having access to government deposits.[43] Jarvis, however, declined the offer and asked that the contract be given to the NATC instead.[44] On July 20, 1898, McKinley obliged. The NATC became the first financial institution serving the new US empire.[45]

The following week, Jarvis chartered the *Baracoa* and set out from New York City to Santiago de Cuba. He was accompanied on the voyage by five bank clerks, including Frank W. Black, the Jarvis-Conklin accountant, and a heavy cargo of accounting ledgers, office furniture, and barrels and boxes packed with United States coin.[46] Within days of arriving in Santiago de Cuba, Jarvis established a branch of the NATC in the offices of the Banco Español de la Isla de Cuba. He planned to travel to Havana and then onward to Puerto Rico on behalf of the NATC. Farther afield, the NATC established correspondent relations with the Chartered Bank of India, Australia, and China in Manila. The yellow fever quarantine scuttled Jarvis's efforts to reach Havana in the short term, and the plans for a branch in Puerto Rico were abandoned as Jarvis decided to concentrate his efforts on Cuba. The contracts for the fiscal agencies in Puerto Rico were taken up by Boston financier Henry de Ford as well as the American Colonial Bank, chartered in West Virginia by the New York merchants Muller, Schalle and Co. and Cuban-American banker Juan Ceballos.[47] Jarvis arrived in Havana in the fall of 1898 after a short trip to New York City. At that time, he organized a branch of the NATC and participated in the founding of the American Chamber of Commerce of Cuba.[48]

The commercial banking business of both the Santiago de Cuba and Havana branches of the NATC was initially of a limited nature. In Santiago, the NATC sold drafts to US soldiers and officers remitting money to their families in the United States, opened a savings department, and began handling commercial paper, foreign exchange, and bills of lading and exchange. The NATC was an important conduit for the introduction of US currency to eastern Cuba, a process aided by the purchase of relics, presents, and souvenirs by US soldiers.[49] Jarvis also worked to establish a system enabling the telegraphic transfer of money within Cuba.[50] In Havana, the refusal of many Cuban and Spanish merchant-banks to handle US money boosted the NATC's popularity and importance; it was the only financial institution making dollar payments to laborers at the docks, the engineer corps, and the street cleaners.[51] Jarvis was critical of the Cuban merchant-banks for their lending policies, arguing that they inhibited the circulation of capital. "The Cuban banks have amounted to practically nothing," Jarvis stated, "because every man has preferred to be his own banker, and to keep what cash he had on hand. The result of this has been that the banking business of Cuba has furnished no idea of the financial transactions of the island."[52] But the NATC's lending policy was little better than that of the Cuban merchant-banks. It had a conservative policy regarding issuing credits. It refused to lend on real estate. It did little actual banking beyond exchange operations. The Havana branch manager suggested that such policy was dictated by the uncertainty of Cuba's future and claimed that the NATC might shut down and abandon the island if Cuba was granted independence.[53]

The main banking business of the NATC in both Santiago de Cuba and Havana was governmental and colonial. From the time of the NATC's appointment by McKinley as the fiscal agent in Santiago de Cuba in July 1898, Jarvis aggressively pursued other government contracts for the trust company, lobbying for additional government deposits and for the right to collect customs and tax revenues from Cuba's ports and cities. Indeed, despite the initial contract as fiscal agent, Jarvis was disappointed with the size of the US government's deposits bequeathed to the NATC. In a letter to NATC director Wager Swayne, Jarvis complained that he had been told when he left New York City that the trust company would receive sizable deposits from the US Army's paymaster. These deposits were not forthcoming, and, in fact, some of the promised money had actually been shipped back to the United States. "This you will see does not give us any good deposit," Jarvis wrote, "but I presume that this will be arranged in a few days. We are doing all we can to assist the Government and officers and I know that when the matter is properly represented at Washington it will be appreciated and the difficulties remedied."[54] Swayne acted promptly. Three days later, the NATC was appointed the depository for the customs revenue of Santiago and its surrounding ports and was handling War Department disbursements to US military personnel.[55]

Similar circumstances occurred in Havana. Jarvis was frustrated with the speed at which the NATC was receiving government commissions. He wanted the War Department contract for the collection of Cuban taxes with its promises of a lucrative 5 percent commission on monies collected. To Jarvis's surprise, the War Department awarded it to the Banco Español de la Isla de Cuba, an institution largely despised by Cubans for the role it had played in the financing of Spanish colonial rule.[56] Jarvis wrote to Abner McKinley, the president's brother, complaining about the administration's treatment of the NATC. He noted the good work that the NATC was doing for the United States in Havana, pointing out that the officers of the NATC were in charge of the finances of city. But, Jarvis cautioned, "it is not a necessity, and it will greatly facilitate the Government if these respective departments can keep their accounts here, have the money deposited to their credit, the same as at Santiago, and give their checks on the North American Trust Company." "I trust," Jarvis wrote, "that the appointment can be made on Monday, unless the appointment should be made before you receive this letter."[57] Jarvis attempted to grease the interaction by sending a box of Cuban cigars alongside the letter. They were a gift for the president, Jarvis wrote to Abner, with the promise of more to come if he so desired. The intervention worked. The NATC was appointed fiscal agent by the end of the month. By May, the contract for the Banco Español was rescinded and the NATC was appointed the collector of Cuban taxes after posting a $750,000 bond.[58] The NATC's association with Abner McKinley would soon prove to be a liability.

The arrival of the NATC in Cuba was at first greeted with excitement and enthusiasm by the business communities of both the United States and Cuba. When news broke in New York City in the summer of 1898 that the NATC had opened in Santiago de Cuba, its Broadway offices were besieged with inquiries from US capitalists concerning the business possibilities on the island. Businesspeople hoped that the NATC officials could offer advice on how to invest the "enormous superfluous capital," as Roland Conklin put it, that had accumulated in the wake of the recovery following the crash of 1893.[59] They looked for opportunities to provide financing for Cuban street and steam railways and tobacco and sugar plantations. Conklin assured potential investors that the company's experts were scouring the island in search of investment possibilities. In Havana, many in the business community welcomed the NATC, as its presence was viewed as a sign of the normalization of the money market after the instability of the war years and economic suffocation of Spanish rule.[60]

Despite the accolades, there was a growing unease about the operations of the NATC in Cuba. There was increasing concern about both the ways in which the NATC conducted business and the means through which the NATC obtained the business it conducted. In March 1899, less than a year after arriving in Cuba, the comptroller of the currency began an investigation into the activities of the NATC following press accusations that the trust company was profiteering from the rate charged US soldiers and civilians for discounting government bills. Jarvis dismissed the charges, arguing that high fees were necessary to cover the costs of shipping, insurance, and arbitrage.[61] The comptroller of the currency disagreed with Jarvis's explanations and found that such charges were unauthorized by the terms of their contract. The comptroller ordered the bank to immediately quit the practice and to reimburse anyone who had paid the extra fees.[62] Months later, after Jarvis had successfully petitioned Abner McKinley for the War Department contract for tax collection, the NATC was again criticized in the US press. The *Washington Post* claimed that the NATC was now merely replicating the colonial function once performed by the Banco Español de la Isla de Cuba.[63] That summer, the *St. Louis Republic* charged that Abner McKinley was actually the NATC's representative in Cuba, alleging that the contracts the NATC received were based on "favors and privileges" granted through "military channels."[64] When the NATC received the accounts for the Cuban postal service the following month, such favoritism and nepotism seemed confirmed. Perry Heath, the first assistant postmaster general, was the brother of NATC director Fletcher S. Heath. While there were erroneous newspaper reports claiming that the Heath brothers had created the NATC to exploit Cuba, it was later revealed that the NATC was used to redirect postal funds for the personal purposes of US administrators.[65]

The following May, the *New York Journal* accused the NATC of holding a banking monopoly in Cuba. The paper argued that through the operation of the NATC "a comparatively small coterie of politicians and public officials are making fortunes out of the Government's financial department in Cuba." The accusations were brought in the US Senate, forcing Secretary of War Elihu Root to report to the US Congress on the activities of the trust company and the nature of its activities in Cuba. Officials of the

NATC claimed it had never collected any revenue from its employment as the government's depository in Cuba. They argued that it was costing the trust company to provide the service because of the expense of shipping and insuring the millions of dollars that had already been transferred. They also pointed out that no other institution had applied for the $1.5 million deposit fund because they did not want their books subjected to examination or because they did not have the funds to do so.[66] Nothing came of the charges against the NATC, and it continued to operate in Cuba unsanctioned and unimpeded.

Despite the accusations and allegations and the gray cloud of scandal and impropriety gathering over NATC's operations in Cuba, Jarvis was not above criticizing both the Cubans and the US administration for their business practices. For Jarvis, the Cuban was a strange creature, whose business habits grew out of an archaic and outmoded Spanish culture. According to Jarvis, the Cuban was noted for his emotionalism, vanity, and pride—and these factors, more than anything else, hampered the development of the Cuban credit system. The Cuban, according to Jarvis, saw the systemized inquiry into and collection of data on a person's creditworthiness as an affront to his word and his honor. At the same time, Jarvis claimed that many Cubans resorted to petty, dishonorable tactics in business. Not only did merchants resist inquiries into their creditworthiness, they misrepresented the credit of their rivals, especially if a personal vendetta existed between businesspeople. If US merchants wanted to use Cuban retailers to sell their goods, they would have to conduct their own personal investigations to figure out which businesses were sound. "Beware of the Cuban middleman," warned Jarvis. "I do not say that he is dishonest, but his sympathies are with the people he lives among, those he has known for many years. Even if he wishes to act in the interest of his American connections and against his local associates, he will unconsciously be biased in local favor."[67] Jarvis did not mention his own complicity in such bias. The manager of the Havana branch of the NATC was Alfred H. Swayne, a lawyer and the son of NATC director Wager Swayne, while in New York City, Roland Conklin's brother Stanley was the NATC's secretary.[68]

In an 1899 issue of the *Chicago Banker*, Jarvis contributed an article discussing the prospects of Cuban self rule. Drawing on editorials and letters printed in the Havana journal *La Discusión*, he argued for the necessity of a quick transition from colonial rule to self-government. Undoubtedly, Jarvis wrote, the fact of US occupation brought a measure of stability to the island and was appreciated by US business. But for the Cubans, the occupation represented the kinds of patronage and graft that they had witnessed under Spanish rule, where the state was merely a cash register for colonial functionaries and their friends and relations. This time, of course, it was the US officials who had found in Cuba a rich vein of personal wealth. He provided as an example a long list of individuals working for the War Department. "Below the military collector, Col. Bliss, and Mr. Walter A. Donaldson, the special deputy, who draw their compensation from the United States," Jarvis wrote, "are enumerated"

> Captain Ladd, cashier, $3,000; W.P. Watson, auditor, $3,000; R.P. Davis, assistant cashier, $2,400; W.M. Shuster, statistician, $2,000; Wyron C. Wheeler, chief of division, $2,000; Edward R. Sizen, chief of correspondence, $2,000; F.J. Rafferty, Alfred W. Gumaer, P.J. O'Neill, and Roy H. Chamberlin, inspectors, $1,800 each; J. Richmond, special agent, $1,800; G. Bulle, projector, $1,800; W. Bagley, appointment checker, $1,800; A.J. Bumjarner, typewriter, $1,800; C.C. Barton, typewriter, $1,800; A.H. Whilpley, J.C. Kujer, and B.J. Ulmer, typewriters, $1,400 each; B. Brum, typewriter, $1,200; P.L. Craycraft and C.E. Athey, auxiliary typewriters, $900 each; and B.J. Vlayten, employee of the cashier, $1,200. These compensations do not begin to be all that are paid to the persons named. Almost without exception they have per diem allowances, like those of special agents and post office inspectors, ranging from $3 to $5 per day.[69]

In light of a "top-heavy and highly-paid official force of Americans," Jarvis wrote, it is unsurprising that *La Discusión* complained that "the customs of Cuba in the power of Yankee functionaries, in large part the favorites of American political personages, sadly resemble the Cuban customs in the hands of Spanish employees, the pets of influential men in Spain." Jarvis wrote that "civil service reform has obtained no footing under the authority of the War Department," and noted that "these resplendent drawers of salaries," as he described the gang of US employees working for the War Department, mostly came from Nebraska, "the country of the Yankee Deputy-Secretary of War, Mr. Meiklejohn." Mieklejohn, Jarvis continued, "shows himself a good friend to his neighbors."[70] The obvious irony in Jarvis's statement is evident in the parallels between his critique of the War Department and the *Investors' Review*'s critiques of him—especially when it came down to the pettiness and thoroughness with which he and Conklin allegedly fleeced the shareholders of Jarvis-Conklin, doling out small amounts to Elenora, Hugh, Priscilla, and Pamelia. Moreover, when Jarvis and Conklin organized the Banco Nacional de Cuba in 1901 as a successor to the NATC, it, too, would become a symbol of neocolonial graft.

———————————

At the turn of the century, changes to the organization and ownership of the NATC were occurring in New York City that would lead to its abandonment of Cuba and the severing of Jarvis and Conklin from the institution they had created. The broader context of corporate and financial mergers and consolidations occurring in the United States at the time provided the backdrop for the changes in the NATC.[71] The NATC had absorbed the International Banking and Trust Company in 1901, and the following year merged with the larger and more powerful Trust Company of America.[72] During the consolidation, Jarvis and Conklin were not reelected as trustees, and they sold most of their stockholdings. They did not, however, end their relationship with Cuba. Instead, they took over the NATC's Cuban operations via the North American Trust Company of Cuba, a new institution they had chartered in Hartford, Connecticut, in January 1899. They transferred its base of operations from New York City to Havana, taking over a residential building on Cuba Street.[73] On February 11, 1900, they had registered a *sociedad anónima* in Havana called the Banco Nacional de Cuba (BNC) (fig. 1.2). The business of the NATC in Cuba was transferred to the BNC in July. With the transfer the BNC assumed the fiscal responsibilities previously held by the NATC. It was designated the official depository of the insular funds in Cuba and fiscal agent of the US government after depositing $1,725,000 in bonds as collateral security with the Cuban treasury.[74]

Following the withdrawal of the United States from Cuba, the transition to Cuban self-government on May 20, 1902, and the election of Tomás Estrada Palma as Cuba's first president, the BNC emerged as an important force in the financial affairs of independent Cuba. The BNC also became an ambivalent figure of the state of Cuban sovereignty. While the Platt Amendment to the Cuban constitution created the legal framework of US neocolonial political-economic control over the republic—the amendment ensured that the United States had the right to intervene in the country's affairs and regulated Cuba's ability to contract foreign debt—the BNC provided the organizational and institutional structure for the development of neocolonial finance in Cuba.[75] In the absence of codified legislation governing banking and financial institutions and without the organization of a proper state bank, the BNC became, in practice, a government bank, serving as the depository and fiscal agent of the Cuban state.[76] However, the "national"

1.2. Exterior of Banco Nacional de Cuba, Havana, Cuba, ca. 1910s. Manuel R. Bustamante Photograph Collection, Cuban Heritage Collection, University of Miami. Used with permission.

of the BNC's name was meaningless. It was an empty appellation that reflected neither the BNC's relation to the US national banking system nor to the Cuban state. The bank's activities were geared solely to the interests of private capital, and it did little to aid in the development of the republic.[77] The BNC remained privately owned, and the majority of its stock was held outside of the island by investors in the United States, Canada, and Europe. Large blocks of shares were held by both J. P. Morgan and Co. and Canadian railroad magnate William Van Horne, the financier behind the Canadian Pacific Railroad who was then embarking on an ambitious development plan through his Cuba Railroad. Cuban and Spanish businesspeople were present on the board as directors, but they served a largely cosmetic function, and their ownership of shares was limited.[78] A Cuban was initially appointed president of the BNC. He was soon replaced by an American, Edmund Gustave Vaughan.[79]

Questions of banking and national sovereignty were raised early on in the BNC's history, and such questions were tied to the issue of the lack of monetary and banking legislation in the Cuban republic. This absence of regulation had an everyday impact on the operation of the BNC. Without a uniform national currency in the republic, the BNC's clerks suffered through daily "trials," as the bank's Henry C. Niese described it, in settling accounts and calculating payments across currencies.[80] But the problem of banking, regulation, and sovereignty also arose in January 1905 when the BNC increased its capital and announced it would emit 1 million pesos in Cuban national currency. The new currency was printed by the American Bank Note Company, shipped to Cuba, and stored in the BNC's vaults at their Havana headquarters. On January 20, facsimiles of the currency were printed on the front page of *La Discusión*. The ten-peso note was emblazoned with an image of Estrada Palma, and lesser denominations displayed representations of members of the Cuban president's cabinet.[81] The authorizing signatures on the currency were of BNC president Edmund Vaughan and bank secretary William H. Morales. The BNC was acting independently and did not have explicit authorization from the Cuban authorities for the currency issue. When they learned of the BNC's plans, members of the Cuban Congress argued the issue was a violation of the Spanish commercial code. The BNC's Vaughan asserted that the issue was within its charter as approved by the government of intervention, that it did not violate the Spanish Commercial Code, that the conditions under which the Banco Español issued banknotes had been removed by the change in government, and that no formal consent of the government was necessary for the proposed issue.[82] The BNC was forced to halt the issue, the currency was destroyed, and the incident generated calls by Cuban politicians for the passage of proper banking legislation.

The BNC was a neocolonial intermediary in Cuba, a conduit for the private exploitation of Cuban resources and for the tightening of the financial tethers linking Cuba to North America. Van Horne's Cuba Company used the BNC for its deposits, as did other large North American corporations. J. P. Morgan and Co. was appointed as a correspondent to facilitate the transactions and trade between Havana and New York City.[83] The BNC undercut Cuba's local merchant-banks by offering sugar planters credit at competitive rates of interest and loosened the tight lending policy of the NATC.[84] At the same time, Jarvis and Conklin used the authority and networks of the bank to secure industrial concessions in Cuba. They leveraged the Cuban government deposits to finance personal enterprises. Government deposits funded their organization of the Compañía de Gas y Electricidad de la Habana, the Havana Telephone Company, the Havana Subway Company, and the United Construction and Supply Company, the latter organized to build the lines and networks for the other companies.[85] Once these companies were capitalized, their stock was transferred into the hands of Jarvis and Conklin. It was an elegantly simple strategy of accumulation. And it was not only limited to Jarvis and Conklin. W. Bundy Cole, an English employee who served as the branch manager of the NATC and the BNC in Santiago de Cuba between 1899 and 1903, secured the contract for the paving of the city's streets.[86] A concession for a monopoly on the installation of advertising hoardings and signboards throughout Cuba was secured by the West Indies Advertising Company, a company partly controlled by Havana branch manager Alfred H. Swayne.[87]

As with the NATC, the hiring practices of the BNC were based less on competency then on family ties and nepotism. Edmund G. Vaughan, the BNC president, was a Kansas City attorney—"a sort of pettifogging lawyer," as J. P. Morgan and Co.'s Dwight Morrow described him—who had indifferent business skills at best.[88] Not only had he acted as counsel to a number of Jarvis's street railroad projects in the US West, he was also married to Samuel Jarvis's daughter, Permelia.[89] Vaughan's brother, William A. M. Vaughan, was appointed the BNC's assistant cashier.[90] It was said that neither brother knew much about banking or, for that matter, Cuba, and that they were despised in the Cuban business community because they refused to learn Spanish. Rumors also circulated in Havana that Edmund Vaughan had defalcated money from a Salt Lake City bank.[91]

On the surface, the BNC appeared successful. Jarvis and the directors commissioned a handsome, neoclassical building in the heart of Cuba's financial district, on Lamparilla Street, designed by the US contractors Purdy and Henderson at a cost of $300,000. Branches were added in Cienfuegos, Matanzas, Cardenas, Manzanillo, and Sagua la Grande to those already in Havana and Santiago de Cuba.[92] The capital of the BNC increased from $1 million to $5 million between 1901 and 1907. A 3 percent dividend was paid to shareholders after the first six months in operation; by 1907, the dividend was 8 percent. The number of individual account holders with the BNC swelled from 6,000 to more than 11,000–16,000 by 1908, and to 21,670 by 1910. In 1902, total deposits held by the BNC amounted to $4,294,993.40. By 1904 that figure grew to $7,825,820.75, to $14,604,270.00 by 1907, and to $24,147,929.73 by 1912.[93] The strength of the BNC's published statistics and its visible signs of expansion were belied by rumors of its structural instability and its crooked management. Contemporary observers suspected that the success of the bank was only possible because of the government deposits it received—and, even then, they were inflated.[94]

The BNC's position in Cuban banking and finance did not go unchallenged. Many of the merchant banks on the island began to reorganize and expand their operations, and North American institutions increasingly saw the island as an opportunity for profit. The Banco Español de la Isla de Cuba was successfully converted from a Spanish colonial bank into a Cuban commercial bank, and the older merchant-banks that had financed Cuba's trade and commerce continued their operations, many of them growing in strength as Cuba's economy stabilized and recovered after 1898.[95] In 1904, New York private investment bankers Speyer and Co. led a syndicate that secured a $35 million 5 percent, forty-year loan to the Cuban government; it was the beginning of North American sovereign debt financing of Cuba. In 1905, the Trust Company of Cuba arrived in Havana, and the short-lived Isle of Pines Bank was also established. The former was headed by Tennessee capitalist Norman H. Davis and backed by J. P. Morgan and Co., and other US, Cuban, and Canadian financiers; the latter was organized to serve the US settlers and colonists flocking to Cuba with the hope of capitalizing on the citrus craze.[96]

The most important foreign institution to arrive in the early years of the republic was the Royal Bank of Canada (RBC).[97] Chartered in Nova Scotia in 1864 as the Merchants Bank of Halifax, the RBC relocated to Montreal at the end of the nineteenth century, changed its name, and forged links with a powerful cabal of Chicago and New York capitalists including George F. Baker of the First National Bank of New York and J. J. Mitchell of the Illinois Trust & Savings Bank. Edson Loy Pease, the RBC's president, traveled to Cuba early in 1899. Seeing the economic potential of the country, he established a branch in Havana later that year. It was supplemented by an agency in New York City organized at about the same time. In 1903, the RBC took over the Banco de Oriente in Santiago de Cuba, a Spanish merchant-bank founded in Havana in 1845 whose directors owned a major share of the United Railways of Havana, one of the largest railroads in the republic.[98] The merger positioned them to handle the accounts of the North American railroad and sugar companies expanding in eastern Cuba. Also in 1903, the Cuban government awarded the RBC the commission to distribute half of $56 million being paid to the veterans of the Cuban Army of Liberation.[99] The bank received a small payment on each disbursement while the commission itself enabled the RBC to open hundreds of new Cuban deposit accounts (even though it complained that many of the soldiers, suspicious of banks, sold the scrip at a heavy discount to American speculators), increasing its accumulation of local capital.[100] In 1904 the RBC purchased the Banco del Comercio in Havana, and in the same year it established a branch in Camagüey. Branches in Matanzas and Cardenas followed in 1905. The RBC emerged as the strongest competitor of the US banks operating in Cuba—and in the Caribbean region as a whole.

With the onset of the second US occupation of Cuba in 1906, the BNC's position was further challenged. Justified under the Platt Amendment, the second occupation came about because of a political crisis precipitated by Estrada Palma's engineering of an electoral victory during the September 1905 presidential elections and the subsequent repression of a revolt against Palma by Quintín Bandera and other Cuban veterans.[101] The occupation lasted four years, with Charles Magoon installed as provisional governor in 1908. Magoon advocated the establishment of a Cuban government bank and the organization of effective banking legislation, but the occupation served to expedite the presence of foreign banks in Cuba while placing competitive pressure on the BNC.[102] In 1906, the BNC was joined in Havana by the Bank of Nova Scotia and the Banco de la Habana. The former already had a strong presence in the Caribbean and worked closely with the United Fruit Company and Van Horne's Havana Electric Railway; the latter was organized by a consortium of US and European bankers, led by the National City Bank of New York.[103] The Banco de la Habana also successfully petitioned the occupation authorities for the privilege of sharing the handling of US Treasury Department funds during the occupation, posing a direct challenge to the role of both the BNC and the RBC, which had also sought out the accounts.[104]

After the withdrawal of US troops in 1909 and the return to Cuban self-rule, the ownership of the BNC underwent a major shift—one that chafed against an apparent tendency toward consolidation and control of Caribbean banking by North American interests and actually strengthened the BNC's Cuban affiliations. The shift also precipitated the decline of Jarvis in its operations. In 1909, J. P. Morgan and Co. considered taking over the BNC as part of a broad project to consolidate Cuba's banking industry. The firm sought to purchase a controlling interest in the BNC and planned to merge it with the Banco de la Habana and the Banco Español de la Isla de Cuba. But in their investigations into the BNC, the firm found that the BNC's accounts were of dubious standing and the reputation and character of its directors and managers of a questionable nature. Norman H. Davis of the Trust Company of Cuba conferenced with Morgan's London affiliate and let them know that although the governmental accounts were valuable, the BNC held mortgages on properties that were inactive or nonperforming. Furthermore, many in the Cuban business community looked upon the BNC directors with skepticism. Davis singled out merchant Pedro Gómez Mena, a figure who he said was viewed with "great suspicion." It was also said that many merchants would not use the bank as long as Jarvis and Conklin were associated with it.[105] Morgan abandoned the Cuban project soon thereafter and sold his approximately 10,000 shares in the BNC.[106]

The purchaser of the Morgan shares was José "Pote" López Rodríguez, a businessman who became a legendary figure in the history of Cuban banking. Born in the Spanish province of Galicia, Rodríguez immigrated to Cuba as a youth and worked as a shoe-shine boy before finding employment at La Moderna Poesía, a printing house and bookshop, despite his reported illiteracy. When the owner of the La Moderna Poesía died, followed soon after by his wife, Rodríguez took over the company. By 1898, he was wealthy; by 1908 he was emerging as a silent power behind the throne of Cuban politics. He secured lucrative government contracts for his business, reportedly through graft and patronage, and it was rumored that he boasted to his associates that any law passed by the Cuban Congress was first submitted to him for approval.[107] For some time, Rodríguez had been quietly acquiring BNC stock held in New York, Paris, and London with the aim of seizing control of the institution. He purchased the Morgan holdings in 1909 and in 1911 acquired a controlling share, using a reported $5 million overdraft on the bank itself for the purchase.

Once Rodríguez gained control of the BNC, he forced changes in the management. He began a purge of Samuel Jarvis's appointees. He targeted the Vaughan brothers, whom he had long disliked, and he sided with W. A. Merchant over bank policies.[108] The Vaughans tried to isolate Merchant and push him out of the bank. Rodríguez intervened. He threatened to start a rival institution unless the Vaughans tendered their resignation.[109] They resigned at the February 1913 annual general meeting. Both men left Cuba soon thereafter. Rodríguez maintained a core group of US managers within the BNC. Merchant was installed as president, and two Iowa bankers who had previously worked for the Isle of Pines Bank, Charles M. Lewis and Joseph H. Durrell stayed on as cashier and branch manager, respectively. Rodríguez also began an explicit policy of hiring Cuban staff for both the Havana branch and the BNC's growing network of country branches, recruiting on the basis of personality, and determining salaries through appeals to vanity. Despite the vagaries of his management, under Rodríguez the BNC had become a Cuban institution for the first time in its history.[110]

Jarvis and Conklin remained directors of the BNC through much of this period of transformation, although their everyday involvement in its operation had long since waned. During the same period, the relationship between the two men began to fray. Their business partnership, by then almost forty years old, unraveled in a bitter tangle of rivalry and acrimony with the two men accusing each other of dishonesty and fraudulent behavior and attempting to block and sabotage each other's ventures. In May 1912, Conklin filed suit against Jarvis and the United Construction and Supply Company, the firm they had jointly organized in 1901 for the construction of Cuban telephone lines. Conklin claimed that Jarvis had severed Conklin's financial stakes in the company by illegally selling his stock, working behind Conklin's back while he was in Europe in an attempt to gain "complete domination of control" of the Cuban company.[111] Conklin, meanwhile, had formed an alliance with Cuban businessman José Miguel Tarafa de Armas, a figure legendary for his corruption. Tarafa was born in Matanzas in 1870 and educated in US business colleges. He had fought alongside Calixto García in the Cuban war of independence and, with his ability to speak English, proved an astute intermediary between the US occupation forces and the emerging Cuban government. After the war, Tarafa reportedly profited from payments to the Army of Liberation and secured concessions for Cuban industries.[112] Together, Conklin and Tarafa attempted to gain hold of a monopoly on Cuba's railway lines by purchasing and consolidating the Puerto Principe and Nuevitas Railway with the Júcaro and Morón lines with the blessing of a government concession.[113]

When Jarvis learned of the Conklin-Tarafa alliance and their move to consolidate the railroads, he attempted to thwart their efforts. He wrote to Sir William Van Horne, a business acquaintance since the early days of the BNC, warning him that Conklin-Tarafa had made plans that were the "basis for [a] comprehensive scheme" through which control of all remaining lines "must fall into their lap." "They now have a scheme on foot which will give Tarafa and his crowd the control of everything in Cuba outside of the United [Railway]," Jarvis wrote. He suggested that Van Horne lodge a protest with both the US State Department and the British Foreign Office in an attempt to hold up the granting of the concession.[114] Van Horne was nonplussed, confidently assuring Jarvis that control would be impossible.[115] Regardless, at the time he wrote to Van Horne, Jarvis was looking beyond Cuba and seeking business opportunities elsewhere in the Caribbean, this time in the Dominican Republic.

In the Dominican Republic, the rumors of corruption and graft that had followed Jarvis throughout his career would catch up with him—destroying his new institution in the process. Events in the republic signaled a chastening critique of his methods and marked an ignominious end to Jarvis's long career in imperial banking and finance. In April 1911, Jarvis chartered a steam yacht, *The Norman*, and sailed on a recreational trip to the Caribbean with a small group of friends. They ended up in the Dominican Republic, visiting the cities of Monte Cristi, Puerto Plata, Sánchez, and Santo

Domingo, the capital, where they spent three days. Jarvis was intrigued by what he saw there. Banking-wise, the country recalled what he had found on his first excursion to Cuba in 1898, more than a decade earlier: commercial banking was limited, there were no US banks operating in the country, and there was no government bank. In addition, the rural areas, planted with sugar, cocoa, tobacco, coffee, and bananas, were not only lacking in formally organized financial institutions, but maintained a general distrust of banks and bankers and, as a result, often practiced hoarding, keeping capital out of circulation.[116]

However, there was a significant difference between Cuba in 1898 and the Dominican Republic in 1911. In 1898, banking served as a practical adjunct of US colonial administration. It was on this basis that the NATC began its operations in Santiago de Cuba. By 1911, banking was an instrument of neocolonial policy itself. Under Secretary of State Philander Knox the political stability of Caribbean and Central American republics was guaranteed through their financial stability, and US bankers, alongside private financial advisers, were tasked with reforming and rehabilitating the financial systems of the Caribbean and Central America through the control of customs revenue, the refunding of foreign debt, and the organization and operation of government banks.

The policy of "dollar diplomacy," as it became known, of substituting dollars for bullets, had its origins in Cuba but was extended and formalized in the Dominican Republic. In the Dominican Republic, the Platt Amendment's legal strictures were operationalized as a mode of imperial governance. The Dominican Republic had entered the twentieth century overburdened with sovereign debt because of a number of disastrous financing plans contracted between corrupt governments and unscrupulous North American and European financiers. The New York–based Santo Domingo Improvement Corporation emerged as the most active financier in the republic; it began pressing the US State Department for military intervention to reclaim its Dominican investments, after it had been expelled from the country and its debts repudiated.[117] The State Department refused to intervene, and the matter was settled through arbitration, but the settlement angered the Dominican Republic's European creditors, who felt that their interests were not given priority.

To settle the matter, Theodore Roosevelt outlined a proposal in 1904, the Roosevelt Corollary to the Monroe Doctrine, wherein the United States would assume fiscal control of the country, taking over the collection and distribution of the republic's customs revenue while reserving the right of military intervention and the seizure of customs houses in the case of default. Two years later, the US and the Dominican governments signed a convention largely based on Roosevelt's proposal. Between 1905 and 1907, as the agreements were being worked out, the City Bank had served as the depository for the Dominican customs receipts. After 1907, these funds were transferred to the Morton Trust Company, where they were held until Morton was absorbed by the Guaranty Trust Company.[118] Roosevelt's plan for the Dominican Republic became the template for a policy of financial diplomacy applied throughout the region as private bankers J. P. Morgan, Kuhn, Loeb, Brown Brothers, and Seligman sought to control the banking and finances of Honduras, Costa Rica, and Nicaragua—often with the collaboration of national banking associations, including the City Bank and the First National Bank of New York.

Jarvis sought to capitalize on the Dominican situation. Upon returning to New York City, he embarked on the organization of a new institution, the Banco Nacional de Santo Domingo (BNSD), that could offer a general banking business and also compete for the receivership and depository accounts under the US-Dominican convention. He also hoped that the new bank, like the Banco Nacional de Cuba, could be used as an intermediary to gain contracts and concessions in the Dominican Republic.[119] By August, he had interested a group of financiers in the project, including department store magnate Henry Siegel of Siegel-Cooper Company, and had created a management team that included the BNC's Henry C. Niese. The new institution, named the Banco Nacional de Santo Domingo, was incorporated under the laws of the Dominican Republic as a *sociedad anónima bancaria*. It was capitalized at $2 million and authorized to act as a government depository, to issue circulating notes, and to set up a branch network for commercial operations. Its contract was for thirty years.[120] Francis (Frank) J. R. Mitchell was installed as president of the new organization. A relative of Jarvis, Mitchell was a corporate attorney from Paris, Illinois, and graduate of Northwestern University who had published on the legal ramifications of US acquisition of the Philippines.[121] He practiced law in Chicago and had worked for John G. Carlisle, the former secretary of the treasury and an original director of the NATC. The board of directors included Dominican minister Jaime R. Vidal, merchants Angelo Porcella and Pedro L. Nadal, and Arturo Pellerano Alfáu, a businessperson and editor of the Dominican newspaper *Listín Diario*.

The BNSD was opened in Santo Domingo on January 31, 1912.[122] Branches were organized in San Pedro de Macorís, Puerto Plata, Santiago de los Caballeros, and Sánchez; an agency was established at 69 Broadway in New York City, and correspondent accounts were opened in London,

Hamburg, and Paris.[123] In an attempt to draw as many customers as possible, accounts with the bank were available with a minimum deposit of a peso. Yet business was slow for the BNSD during its first year in operation. From its opening, its capital was not fully subscribed, and it gained few commercial customers. The BNSD found itself competing with the RBC, an institution that had maintained an agency in the republic for years, and had opened a branch there once it learned of Jarvis's plans.

By the end of the BNSD's first year in operation, Jarvis and Mitchell saw an opportunity that they hoped would change the fortunes of their institution. On December 14, the government of Dominican president Adolfo A. Nouel was authorized by the US State Department and the Dominican Congress to contract for a short-term loan of $1.5 million. A call for bids went out, and Nouel met with Mitchell to discuss the terms of the loan, telling Mitchell that he preferred it go to a Dominican institution. For Mitchell, this meant the BNSD. At the same time, the lawyer for the BNSD, William C. Beer, called on the Latin American Division of the State Department in Washington, presenting his case that his clients should receive the contract for the loan. Three proposals were submitted, from the BNSD, the Guaranty Trust Company, and the City Bank. According to Roger L. Farnham, a recent appointee to the City Bank who was in charge of its foreign operations, the City Bank bid was submitted only after the bank had been approached by the State Department and encouraged to join the competition. They did so reluctantly.[124]

To their surprise, on January 22 Jarvis and Mitchell received a letter informing them that they had not been awarded the contract. Instead, the loan had gone to the City Bank.[125] Jarvis and Mitchell were incensed by the decision. They felt cheated, and probably also saw the loss of the accounts as a serious blow to the ability of the BNSD to do business. In response to the decision, Jarvis complained to the State Department, and Beer, the BNSD's lawyer, petitioned to have the decision reversed and the loan awarded to the bank. Mitchell, meanwhile, attacked the decision in the Dominican press. He used the *Listín Diario*, whose editor, Arturo Pellerano Alfáu, was a BNSD board member, as a platform, and he published two Spanish-language booklets that compared the competing bids. Mitchell argued not only that the City Bank bid had been submitted after the deadline, but that it was actually illegal, as the interest rate on the City Bank loan exceeded the maximum 7 percent stipulated by the State Department once its amortization had been calculated. One of the booklets contained a series of statements on the illegality of the decision by prominent Dominican jurists. Mitchell had paid them for their opinions.[126]

Philander Knox investigated the complaints and found them baseless. The awarding of the loan to the City Bank was affirmed on February 22, 1913. Secured by a second mortgage on the customs of the republic, the loan saw the country's receiver general pay $30,000 a month for interest and amortization to the City Bank.[127] As it did not have a branch or agency in the Dominican Republic, the City Bank contracted with S. Michelena y Cia., a local merchant bank run by Puerto Rico–born businessperson Santiago Michelena. Michelena had made a fortune through his alliances with former Dominican president Ulises Heureaux. His bank was founded about 1890, and he had formed a company with Heureaux in 1896 to lend money to the Dominican state.[128]

For Jarvis, Mitchell, and Beer, the matter was not settled. Beer filed briefs with the State Department suggesting that Santiago Michelena was crooked, and, without naming them, he asserted that an investigation of Michelena's account books would lead to information on the improper practices of the City Bank. He argued that the State Department needed to "clean house" in the Dominican Republic and get rid of Michelena. With the coming transition in the US diplomatic personnel in the Dominican Republic following the election of Woodrow Wilson, Jarvis's people sought to promote a candidate for the Dominican consular post who could actively promote the BNSD's interests. Mitchell publicly announced that there would be a "general house cleaning" of the US diplomatic offices and suggested that he knew in advance who would get the new appointment.[129] The new consul was James M. Sullivan, an inexperienced, completely incompetent individual with little to no experience in politics, a proclivity to patronage, if not outright graft, no knowledge of Spanish, and profoundly racist views of the Dominicans. "The trouble with the Dominican Republic," Sullivan wrote during his tenure as minister, "is that many of the people are unmoral [sic]. Religion . . . is unable to cope with the savage, brutal tendencies of a semi-civilization—a constant predisposition to immorality and spoliation . . . and no moral fiber or stability, and a gross and crass ignorance prevails throughout the land . . . The men of this generation are hopeless, the highest aspiration of the best being to make public office the means for private plunder."[130] For the organizers of the BNSD, Sullivan's appointment was viewed as a coup. "It was taken as understood that he . . . was going to do all he could to take all the government funds from the hands of Michelena," Mitchell later stated.[131]

Sullivan arrived on the USS *Nashville* in the Dominican Republic to assume his ministerial duties on September 21, 1913.[132] Mitchell was his first caller, and Sullivan quickly developed a conspicuous intimacy with the BNSD that was noted in diplomatic and business circles. Sullivan used Mitchell's Chinese cook and his chauffeur, and Mitchell often took meals at the legation. When Sullivan's cousin arrived, he slept at Mitchell's home. The Santo Domingo quarters of the BNSD became Sullivan's downtown office instead of the US consulate. Sullivan maintained an overdraft on the bank, and a cousin was given a $1,000 loan from the bank secured only by Sullivan's signature. His interpreter was the BNSD's Henry C. Niese.[133] Sullivan soon came to rely on Mitchell for advice on State Department matters, and they jointly authored a report for the State Department on political conditions in the Dominican Republic. Bank officers were enlisted as observers during the national elections, and they pushed for the victory of José Bordas Valdez, at the time the provisional president. "Just lounge around the town and after the election is over, come back and everything is all right," they were told. "You don't have to see what you don't see."[134] Niese financed the purchase of arms for the administration through Niese, Rojas, and Co., a venture that was said to be an "adjunct" of the BNSD.[135]

By October 1913, the BNSD was in trouble. Its capital never fully subscribed, its chief business consisted in making political loans to Dominican politicians against their future salaries. To obtain working capital, it had to solicit drafts from its rivals, the RBC and Michelena, drawn against Jarvis's accounts in New York. Jarvis, who earlier in the year had approached the City Bank's Roger Farnham concerning a joint financing operation in the republic worth $1.5 million, was forced to make a personal loan of $100,000 to the bank so it could function. Mitchell told Sullivan of the many "injustices" done to the BNSD and asked him to provide favors for the bank. Sullivan was sympathetic and argued that Secretary of State Bryan wanted the BNSD to have the receivership contracts and was friendly to Jarvis interests. (Indeed, Bryan had gone so far as to support Jarvis's proposed $1.5 million loan to Nicaragua—in part to dispel any sense of the insolvency of the BNSD).[136] "Under the previous American administration in Santo Domingo," Sullivan reportedly stated during a dinner-party toast, "honest people could not get their rights, and the best and straightest men, Mr. Jarvis and Mr. Mitchell, had fought night and day without success; but now the American Minister has his fist on the throat of Michelena, and if he does not come across, the fist is going to close tighter and tighter until he suffocates."[137]

Sullivan proved true to his word. He threatened Michelena with an investigation into his financial connections to the Dominican government, with imprisonment, and, on at least one occasion, with physical violence. Michelena was accused of "grafting, controlling the government, with having illegitimate financial schemes which controlled everything, of milking the public, doing everything that was criminal in banking."[138] Sullivan ordered the transfer of a public works fund from Michelena to the BNSD, stating that "he had taken financial affairs away from the guilty of questionable conducting and of inflicting usurious rates" and given it to "a legitimate bank which is subject to the laws of the land."[139] Sullivan also pressed the receiver general, Walker W. Vick, to switch the receivership account from Michelena to BNSD, claiming the BNSD was preferred by the US government and the State Department.

Vick refused to switch the account to the BNSD. But he was also becoming increasingly frustrated with the conduct of Sullivan regarding the depository accounts and for what he viewed as Sullivan's generally incompetent and unscrupulous behavior as minister. Sullivan would appear at diplomatic functions without a coat and vest, sometimes in an undershirt, and his personal appearance was unkempt and sloppy. It contributed to his unpopularity among the Dominicans. When he appeared in the streets, he was hissed at, and bricks were thown at him. Vick complained to the State Department about Sullivan's conduct on numerous occasions. While Vick's claims were initially ignored by the State Department, they did eventually prompt an inquiry into Sullivan's actions. Led by California senator James D. Phelan, the investigation was held in New York, Philadelphia, Washington, DC, and Santo Domingo from January 5 to April 15, 1915. A former clerk at the BNSD was among the first to testify. He was followed by a roll call of witnesses from the US and Dominican business and banking community, including the BNSD's Frank J. R. Mitchell and the City Bank's Roger Farnham.

Although Sullivan's actions—including his relations with the BNSD— were now being publicly scrutinized during the inquiry, the investigation did not restrain the activities of Mitchell and his cronies on behalf of the BNSD. Instead, they tried to use the investigation as a forum to assassinate Vick's character and defame Santiago Michelena and the City Bank while continuing to plead the cause of their bank. They produced affidavits accusing Vick of getting drunk on champagne at the Shanghai Hotel in Santo Domingo in September 1913. He was accused of soliciting prostitutes, of committing "indecent acts," including rubbing Dominican currency on his buttocks before paying a restaurant bill, and of participating in a "Bac[c]hanalian orgy."[140] The individual who signed the affidavit was the son of Arturo Pellerano Alfáu, the owner of the *Listín Diario* and a BNSD director. The affidavit was notarized by a BNSD bookkeeper who was also the brother of the minister of public works. Associates of the BNSD were suspected of staging a series of shooting incidents apparently designed to intimidate Vick—at one point, Vick produced as evidence a shell casing found in his bedroom. When Mitchell testified, he appeared unhinged and paranoid. He spoke of a conspiracy against his bank by the Royal Bank of Canada and claimed that the City Bank was part of a "Money Trust" aiming to control the economy of the Dominican Republic. The City Bank's Roger Farnham dismissed such claims of conspiracy during his testimony, asserting that the City Bank had little interest in the Dominican Republic besides the loan. Phelan and the investigators took Farnham at his word.

Mitchell's strategy backfired. The testimony of witnesses painted a harsh picture of the standing of the BNSD in the Dominican Republic. It was said the BNSD had developed a reputation in the Dominican Republic as a "joke."[141] It was avoided by Dominicans and only survived by taking cash from the receivership accounts. Few had confidence in the institution, and it was claimed that "nobody would accept their notes of issue except as handbills on the street."[142] At the same time, Jarvis's reputation proceded him; one businessperson stated that in both Santo Domingo and New York his name "was far from A1, to be as charitable as possible."[143] When the Phelan investigation was concluded and its official report was published, it addressed the concerns and allegations of Mitchell against Michelena. Phelan dismissed Mitchell's assertions of a conspiratorial money trust, led by the City Bank, asserting its control over the Dominican Republic, and he quashed the assertions that the BNSD's actions were made in the interests of patriotism. Phelan pointed out that in legal terms the Puerto Rico–chartered Michelena bank had more of a claim to US corporate citizenship than did the BNSD, which was incorporated in the Dominican Republic and counted a large share of English nationals as shareholders. The legal orders that Jarvis had been so adept at manipulating returned to haunt him, and for once, the methods his institutions had deployed had failed. The Phelan report recommended that Sullivan resign his post; he left the Dominican Republic soon thereafter. With his departure, the BNSD lost its biggest advocate and its only source of revenue. While it remained open until 1920, its business never reached the volume of Jarvis's North American Trust Company or his Banco Nacional de Cuba.

Samuel M. Jarvis did not testify during the Phelan investigation. He had died in New York City on December 26, 1913, before the Phelan investigation was initiated—and just as the lawsuit filed against him by his old partner, Roland Conklin, was being settled in favor of the Jarvis estate. His death marked the passing of an era in the internationalization of US banking. An age of individualism and entrepreneurialism was coming to an end. A new order of banking and empire was emerging, one of regulation and explicit legal support. On December 23, 1913, three days before Jarvis's death, the Federal Reserve Act was signed. It inaugurated a period that privileged the large and powerful federally chartered national banking associations—like the City Bank, Jarvis's bitter rival in the Dominican Republic—over small and medium-sized private institutions and the ambitious, adventuring individuals behind them. The London branch of Jarvis-Conklin became a branch of the Chase National Bank of the City of New York, an institution emerging as a great competitor to the City Bank.[144] The Banco Nacional de Santo Domingo was absorbed by the Chase Bank's subsidiary, the American Foreign Banking Corporation. The assets and business of the Banco Nacional de Cuba would be absorbed by the City Bank and the Royal Bank of Canada.

Jarvis left a legacy of corporations and banking houses in the Midwest and the West Indies, many of which survived longer than their partnership, while neighborhoods such as Baltimore's Roland Park and Hyde Park remain as testaments to their endeavors. More importantly, Jarvis's institutions produced what was effectively a banking diaspora, a group of bankers who played a critical role in the organization and expansion of Wall Street during the era of internationalization after Jarvis's death. Frank J. R. Mitchell joined the New York office of the Mercantile Bank of the Americas, an ambitious foreign banking corporation organized by Brown Brothers and Co., J. & W. Seligman and Co., and J. P. Morgan's Guaranty Trust Company. W. Bundy Cole, who joined the NATC in Santiago de Cuba, managed the Mexico and Panama branches of the International Banking Corporation before working at the Managua branch of the Banco Nacional de Nicaragua, an institution also controlled by Brown Brothers and Seligman. Henry C. Niese managed the Buenos Aires branch of the Chase Bank's American Foreign Banking Corporation. Frank W. Black, the Jarvis-Conklin Mortgage Trust Company accountant and the auditor for the NATC's Santiago and Havana branches, also joined the AFBC, working for its Havana branch. Black was later both a manager of the foreign department of the Equitable Trust Company and a vice president of the Chase Bank.[145] John H. Durland, who joined the NATC in Cuba and organized and managed the Matanzas branch of the BNC, worked for the City Bank–controlled Banco de la Habana and managed the City Bank's Valparaiso, Chile, branch.[146] Joseph H. Durrell spent almost a decade with the Banco Nacional de Cuba, until he resigned in 1918 to join the City Bank as its superintendent of Cuban branches. Durrell spent the rest of his career with the City Bank and would become the most important figure in its international expansion in the late 1920s and early 1930s. All told, the Jarvis-Conklin Mortgage Trust Company, the North American Trust Company, the Banco Nacional de Cuba, and the Banco Nacional de Santo Domingo gave a later generation of rogue bankers their earliest experience in the management of foreign branches and their initial encounters with the legal orders of international trade and finance. Jarvis's institutions offered bankers the first contact with the people and markets beyond the borders of the United States and introduced them to the methods of imperial banking.

TWO

Rogue Bankers

When rumors of an impending revolution on the Isthmus of Panama reached the directors of the International Banking Corporation (IBC) in the fall of 1903, they immediately saw a financial opportunity and quickly mobilized to seize it. They gathered in the boardroom of their leased offices at 1 Wall Street—cramped, unpresuming quarters at the top of a rickety wooden staircase above a drugstore—and there, as James Morris Morgan tells it, they resolved "to spy out the land and report as to the advisability of establishing branches [on the isthmus]."[1] Morgan was the assistant manager of the IBC's Washington, DC bureau. The "high officials of the bank" decided to send him to Panama to investigate, though he claimed they chose him less for any inherent skills he had as a banker than because the "universal fear of the dreaded yellow fever" saw all the other IBC employees "sidestep" the detail. Morgan reluctantly accepted the assignment, expecting to return to his desk at the IBC's G Street offices within a few months, "unless," he stated, "the yellow fever gathers me in and I stay permanently."[2]

On December 1, 1903, a month after Panama seceded from Colombia following a brief, US-supported revolution, Morgan boarded the Panama Railroad–owned steamship *Segurança* and embarked for the newborn republic.[3] His investigations on behalf of the IBC began the moment the *Segurança* set sail. Members of the Panamanian junta were among Morgan's shipmates. They were suspicious of his presence on the steamer and followed his every move during the voyage. Philippe-Jean Bunau-Varilla, the French engineer who was Panamanian minister to the United States, keenly watched Morgan whenever Morgan appeared on deck. After three days at sea, Pablo Arosemena, future vice president of the republic, approached Morgan. Arosemena discreetly inquired after Morgan's reasons for traveling to Panama. Morgan blurted out the nature of his mission and admitted to the IBC's interest in opening a bank in Panama. Taken aback by Morgan's frankness and candor, Arosemena gasped and quickly exited the room. Federico Boyd, another member of the junta, appeared at Morgan's door, entered his quarters, and testily told him that "under no circumstances would [Morgan] be permitted to open a bank on the Isthmus." In a flash of anger, Boyd left Morgan's quarters. When Arosemena returned to suss out how Morgan fared in his interview with Boyd, an irritated Morgan drew on the powers of the IBC and of the US government to let Boyd know that the bank would get its branch, no matter the desires of the Panamanians. "I told him," Morgan recalled,

> that General Thomas H. Hubbard, President of the International Banking Corporation, was not only a man of great wealth and social prominence, but that he was a man of great influence in the councils of the Republican party, and that as soon as the ship reached the dock in Colón I was going to cable him that no American would be allowed to do a banking business in the country, and that of course he would make the contents of my cablegram public and that I did not believe any United States Senator would have the courage to vote for the recognition of a country which would not allow a reputable American banker to do business within its limits.[4]

Chagrined, Arosemena left the boardroom. Soon thereafter, Panamanian president Manuel Amador Guerrero made his entrance. In a conciliatory tone he suggested that Morgan misunderstood Boyd's comments: what Boyd had actually meant was "that no *foreign* bank would be permitted to flood the country with its notes." As the IBC was not a bank of issue, its presence would be welcomed so long as Morgan was aware that its business would be unprofitable and that its directors were prepared to suffer heavy losses.

Disembarking at Colón, Morgan traveled by train to Panama City, passing along the way settlements of "Chinamen and Jamaica negroes" and the open graves of abandoned and broken machinery lining the banks of the Chagres River.[5] Still celebrating Panama's independence, Panama City was papered with flags and bunting, and the entire Panamanian army, a ragtag bunch, "mostly negroes," attired in threadbare and ill-fitting uniforms and armed with vintage muskets, greeted the arrival of the president and the junta. Upon arrival, although discomfited by the heat and humidity, Morgan immediately began inquiring into the banking possibilities of the IBC. His inquiries continued to be stifled. Panama's US merchant community practically begged him to establish a branch of the IBC, but the local business elite—disappointed that Morgan did not personally know corporation lawyer William Nelson Cromwell, vexed that the former's namesake had sacked, looted, and burned the city to the ground in 1671—tried to dissuade him from his plans. Morgan met with José Gabriel Duque, a naturalized US citizen born in Cuba, who owned the *Panama Star and Herald* and controlled the lucrative national lottery. Duque (or "Dukey," as Morgan referred to him) told him that the IBC would be "ruined" if it set up shop in Panama. Morgan called on Isaac Brandon, head of Isaac Brandon & Bros., merchant bankers in business on the isthmus since 1878. Brandon asserted that the establishment of a branch of the IBC on the isthmus would signal the institution's "death-knell."

Henry Ehrman agreed. A one-time peddler in Louisiana who had established himself on the isthmus in 1865, Ehrman had emerged as what Morgan described as "the local king of finance." His bank doubled as a dry goods store, and coils of rope, bolts of silk, and other merchandise tumbled from boxes and crates stockpiled in his office. During their conversation, two men pushed a cart piled high with silver pesos to the front of Ehrman's premises. Morgan watched as they dumped the silver on the sidewalk, and clerks came out and began counting the species. When Morgan asked Ehrman the going rate of interest, Ehrman paused for a moment before replying, "Whatever I choose to make it!" When Morgan asked him how much interest he paid depositors, Ehrman grinned and laughed and told Morgan that he "charged them two per cent for taking care of their money!" Morgan had seen enough. "I decided then and there," he wrote, "that Panama was a good place for a bank."[6]

Based on Morgan's positive report to the directors, the IBC opened a branch in Panama City in 1904 (fig. 2.1) and followed with agencies in Colón in 1906 and two years later at Empire, a town in the Canal Zone where the headquarters of the Isthmian Canal Commission was located. The Panamanian branches and agencies, Morgan "was happy to say, proved great successes."[7] But the IBC's operations were not limited to Panama. Its Panama branches were but a part of an expansive and ambitious project of imperial banking conceived of by lawyer and industrialist Thomas H. Hubbard—Morgan's man of great wealth, social prominence, and influence. Hubbard had envisioned a "world-encircling banking corporation," a financial institution that would herald the arrival of the United States on the stage of global banking, finance, and commerce while supporting the country's colonial ventures in the Caribbean and the Pacific.[8] "Heretofore there has been no particular

2.1. Man standing in front of International Banking Corporation, ca. 1900–1914. John Barrett Papers, 1861–1843. Library of Congress Prints and Photographs Division, Washington, DC.

need in the US for a banking institution doing an international business," Hubbard told the *New York Times* soon after the IBC was organized in 1901,

> but since the Spanish war and the tremendous trade of recent years with South America and the promise of a constantly increasing commerce with China and the Orient, the necessity for just such an institution as this has developed.

Heretofore all of the exchange with foreign countries has been handled by the banks of Berlin and London. There are a number of international banks in these cities. It will be the purposes of the IBC to secure as much as possible of the exchange business heretofore handled by these foreign banks with which this country is concerned.

Hubbard linked the IBC's organization to the triumphalist energies of American mission and destiny, claiming its organization was "but the natural outgrowth of the commercial and territorial expansion of the United States."[9] *The Washington Post* concurred. It stated that the birth of the IBC was the "first step toward the transfer from London to New York of the financial supremacy of the world."[10] The IBC's corporate seal evoked these ambitions; it depicted an American eagle astride a Greek temple that fused the two hemispheres of the globe. From the moment the IBC was chartered in 1901, it followed the example set by Samuel Jarvis and the North American Trust Company in Cuba and rushed to take advantage of the governmental and commercial opportunities opened up by US military and diplomatic interventions.

The IBC emerged both from the visions of empire and global commerce floated by the Pan-American Financial Conferences at the end of the century, with their calls for an "American International" or a "Pan-American" bank, and from the nationalist bluster and chest thumping that followed the US victory over Spain. A handful of institutions, including the Pan-American Bank, the Pan-American Bank and Trust Company, and the Mexican Trust Company, sought to capitalize on this robustly imperialist mood. However, these institutions were little more than fly-by-night operations: wildcat banks and bucket shops with global pretensions run by con men, swindlers, hustlers, and fraudsters that often survived only long enough to dupe their investors and depositors. The IBC was different. Attempting to find an institutional form that could overcome the transnational jurisdictional morass of early twentieth-century global commerce and at the same time serve as an intermediary for the US colonial bureaucracy, the IBC grew to become the staid, patrician aberration among these early international banks. Later dubbed the United States' first international bank, it became a venerable elder statesperson in the field.

Yet the history of the IBC was fraught. Imperialism did not come easy, and the IBC was not entirely successful in its operations. Instead, the IBC's much vaunted "internationality,"[11] to borrow a phrase that appeared in the bank's promotional material, was experimental and disorganized. The IBC's innovative charter and its worldwide branch network were coveted by other banking institutions, especially by national banking associations such as the City Bank that were restricted from organizing branches. But it was seen as operating far below its potential. The IBC remained an institution in progress through its entire history. It was a pioneer in the foreign field, and as a pioneer it often advanced blindly or haphazardly, inventing itself as it went, learning the terrain as it proceeded. The bank found itself fighting for business with both the imperial banks of Europe and its own brethren on Wall Street, and it was confronted with a problem of staffing and management and the fact that at the beginning of the twentieth century, the US international banker was an anomaly, a profession that was still being devised. The international vision of the IBC was Hubbard's. The work of realizing that vision was carried out by rogue bankers like James Morris Morgan: white men of varied and checkered international experience, who, with little to no banking background, became the foot soldiers of the IBC's imperial expansion and provided the IBC's working ties between racial capitalism and finance capitalism in Panama, and around the world. Morgan and his ilk were tasked with making the IBC work in the face of disorganization, cultural difference, competition, and incompetence. His arrogance, his roguish methods, his assumption of American superiority, and his easy, naturalized sense of white supremacy made him a perfect candidate for the job.

The institutional predecessors of the IBC are found in the nineteenth-century debates concerning the commercial and monetary unification of the Americas, especially through the Pan-American Conferences and the often ill-fated attempts to organize banks as a result.[12] The first of these conferences was held in Panama City in 1826 and convened by Simón Bolívar as a check on US hegemony in the hemisphere. Subsequent conferences attempted to promote trade relations, encourage the standardization of commercial protocols, and assert US economic supremacy. During the First International American Conference, convened in Philadelphia on October 2, 1889, and continued in Washington from November 19, 1889, to April 19, 1890, the earliest calls for the development of an international US banking institution were raised.[13] Delegates pointed to the growing trade figures of the Americas as both a sign of the great strength of the bonds between the American republics, and symptomatic of its primary weakness, its domination by European financiers.

In the fiscal year ending on June 30, 1889, the total foreign commerce of the Caribbean, Mexico, and South and Central America amounted to some $1.2 billion in United States gold; during the same period, almost $300 million in goods was exchanged between the United States and South and Central America. European banks financed the bulk of this trade. A US merchant importing or exporting goods to or from Latin America had to present a letter of credit, secured from a European bank established in the region, to a Latin American merchant for an advance on agricultural products or manufactured goods, remitting funds to Europe to cover the cost of the transaction. In the process, merchants were charged three-quarters of 1 percent of the total cost of the shipped goods, as well as the fees for exchanging US gold for Mexican silver or Spanish gold for sterling and back again for US gold. European banks, noted the delegates, "reap this great profit at a minimum risk."[14] Besides using the shipped goods as collateral, American merchants often had to deposit cash with European bankers before their drafts reached maturity—causing a great problem of capital liquidity. This problem of liquidity hindered the growth of commerce by retarding the expansion of credit.

The report from the conference's Committee on Banking argued that the future development of the hemisphere was contingent upon breaking a regional dependence on European banking institutions, especially the powerful, British imperial banks, including the London and River Plate Bank and the London Bank of Mexico and South America.[15] To staunch the loss of commissions to European bankers, and to help promote not only the efficiency of financial transactions within the hemisphere but also the region's very economic independence, delegates to the conference passed a resolution calling for the chartering of a Pan-American or American International Bank. The bank would be authorized by the US Congress to instill public confidence in its stability and liquidity. Shares would be issued to the other American republics taking part, and branches or agencies would also be established beyond Washington. The bank would have no power of note issuance but could issue letters of credit and make loans.

The American International Bank was endorsed by President Benjamin Harrison, Secretary of State James G. Blaine, and a subcommittee of the Committee on Banking and Currency, as well as by industry journals.[16] No headway was made with its organization. In 1897, during the fall convention of the New York Board of Trade and Transportation, the idea of an American International Bank was again raised. Delegates cited its importance in facilitating hemispheric trade and, furthermore, in promoting the international financial supremacy of New York City. "Why may not Greater New York become first the Clearing House of the business of this hemisphere," asked one delegate, "and later on the Clearing House of the commerce of the world?"[17] That year Congress passed a bill authorizing the charter for the American

International Bank. Initially, it would be capitalized at $5 million, though this sum could be increased to a maximum of $25 million. The comptroller of the currency would supervise it. After some senators complained of its potential monopoly on international banking, the bill was amended, allowing any group of citizens complying with the requirements of the charter to organize a similar institution.[18]

The plan for the bank received strong editorial endorsements from the *Washington Post* and the *New York Times*. The latter linked the bank's importance to gendered discourses of national development and imperial virility, claiming that the lack of an American international bank was an affront to the United States' manliness.[19] "This nation combines in a singular degree the powers of stalwart manhood with the weakness of infancy," the *New York Times* wrote. Contrasting the manufacturing strength of the country with its dependence on European exchanges, it saw the current US approach to commerce as "a preposterously childish way of doing business."[20] The bank remained an idea only, a vision sketched on paper. The following year, commenting on the lack of movement in the bank's realization, the *Bankers' Magazine* reversed its position from earlier in the decade and claimed that there was no need for a federal institution whose business could be handled by existing private, state, and national banking institutions. The editors evoked a populist suspicion of federally organized banking institutions with monopoly privileges that was a holdover of the Bank Wars of the Jackson era. "Naturally," they wrote, "it is suspected that the extraordinary powers are desired to enable the incorporators to exercise a sinister competition in other branches of the banking business."[21] They also argued that the nation's existing banking infrastructure could, quite simply, do the job. Delegates to the Second International American Conference, held in Mexico City in 1902, returned to the question of an American international bank and voted in support of the organization of a "Pan-American Bank" similar in form to those of the previous conferences.[22] But again, nothing happened. Plans for a federally chartered international financial institution stalled, dissipated, and eventually disappeared.

However, a number of private bankers—rogue bankers—stepped into the arena, taking up the cloak of Pan-Americanism and the mantle of Pan-American banking. They found their way around legislation restricting branch banking and international banking by chartering in states with liberal banking laws like Delaware and West Virginia. They operated unsupervised across national borders and in the lax (or nonexistent) regulatory environments in the Caribbean and Central America where weak governments had little power to curb their activities. Although publicists hyped these institutions when they were first chartered, their actual activities remain obscured to historians. The Pan-American Bank and Trust Company (PABTC), for instance, was chartered in 1903 by a syndicate of northeastern banking and industrial interests. Journalists claimed the PABTC would eventually "have control practically of the finances of [Mexico]" after being granted a liberal concession by the Mexican government.[23] There are no records of this bank's achievements—or of its failure. Still other banks, like the West Virginia–chartered, Illinois-based American International Bank, were found to have depositors, but no assets. When the American International Bank went into receivership in 1905, all the Chicago police could claim was its furniture. Its dissolution prompted calls for more stringent regulations of institutions using the word "bank" in their name.[24]

William H. Hunt's Pan-American Bank was the most notorious example of this species of US international financial institution, and Hunt himself perhaps typified the personality of these bankers.[25] Born in Alabama, Hunt had organized financial institutions in Selma before moving to the Northeast. He traveled to Mexico and studied its financial organization, coming to the conclusion that while it was silver-based, had archaic banking laws based on the Code Napoléon, and employed crude business methods, a US bank could be successful there—and could potentially break the European monopoly on banking. Seeing the possibility of diverting remittance income from European banks in Mexico and undoubtedly encouraged by the political and economic climate created by Porfirio Díaz and his finance minister José Yves Limantour, both of whom maintained liberal economic policies that encouraged foreign investors, Hunt looked into the possibilities of banking and finance in Mexico.[26]

In 1901, Hunt organized the Mexican Trust Company (MTC) in Mexico City. Seven branches of the MTC were established thoughout Mexico, agencies were established in New York City and Chicago, and Hunt further planned to expand the trust company throughout the United States, South America, and Europe.[27] After only six months, the MTC was turning a profit and attracting interest from US investors. Hunt decided to expand the company, merging it with the Corporation Trust Company of Delaware to create the International Banking and Corporation Trust Company (IBCTC).[28] A circular released by the bank claimed that under Mexican corporation laws the combined charter of the new company allowed it to engage in "any and all lawful business, whatsoever, wheresoever, and whensover"—including the power "to undertake the management of a sovereign government." "Well might the prospectus of the IBCTC remark in closing," quipped the *New York Times*, "under this charter no opportunity for profit need be neglected, for there is practically no limit whatsoever to the scope of the operations allowed."[29] It continued to operate the branches in Mexico and announced plans for branches in Nicaragua, Cuba, Argentina, Brazil, and Chile.

Less than a year after its merger the IBCTC was in crisis. On October 18, 1903, the Mexico City branch of the IBCTC closed its doors, and the Mexican courts appointed a receiver to preside over its liquidation. The bank's cashier claimed he had received a telegram from Hunt instructing him to forward all deposits to the New York parent, draining the bank of funds. Hunt denied the cashier's accusations and blamed the insolvency on a sudden bank run by panicking Mexican depositors who withdrew more than $600,000, wiping out the company's reserve.[30] Following the IBCTC's collapse, Hunt set about reorganizing the bank by forming a new company, the Pan-American Bank (PAB). IBCTC depositors were offered stock options in the new institution at the par value of their deposits. But during the reorganization, it emerged that the new underwriters were barely solvent and that the stockholders of the bank directed deposits to personal accounts despite knowing of the bank's insolvency. The company's underwriters had marginal credit, at best, and the directors appeared to be reorganizing for their own benefit.[31] Hunt was arrested in New York on January 21, 1905, and extradited to Chicago—the press reporting on his every move—where proceedings were instigated against him for what was described as "collusion, trickery and fraud." Hunt initially pleaded not guilty to the charges, claiming securities he possessed would cover depositors' losses. Two weeks later, however, apparently realizing he was caught, he admitted his culpability and, in September 1905, was found guilty of embezzlement, ordered to pay a fine of $298, and sentenced to a one- to three-year prison term in the Joliet prison.[32] He was paroled largely because of the efforts of his wife; she maintained his innocence during his trial and imprisonment, eventually securing both a pardon and financial backing from her father to allow Hunt to reenter business. She would divorce him soon afterward. Hunt was caught frequenting the brothels of New York while his repute with prostitutes in both Havana and Santo Domingo was described as "notorious."[33]

The International Banking Corporation emerged from the failures and false starts of turn-of-the-century Pan-American banking. Yet its origins were in Asia, not the Americas, and before it was established in Panama and Mexico, it was participating in the US imperial projects in China and the Philippines. The IBC was organized by Colonel Thomas H. Hubbard, a Union veteran and a corporate attorney who had been a partner in the law firm

Butler, Stillman, and Hubbard since 1888 (the Stillman in question was the brother of the City Bank's James Stillman). Hubbard was well known for his corporate litigation and was involved in corporate reorganization and trust management. He was a director or trustee of financial institutions, insurance firms, and railroad companies, including the Southern Pacific Railroad, the Mexican International Railroad, and the Guatemala Central Railroad.[34] Marcellus Hartley, the Connecticut industrialist and arms dealer in charge of the Remington Arms Company and the Union Metallic Cartridge Company, was the IBC's first president. After Hartley's sudden death, he was replaced by Valentine P. Snyder, president of the Equitable Life Assurance Company, among the largest and most powerful insurance companies in the United States. The IBC was closely connected to Equitable. Directors of the Equitable Company originally sat on the board of directors of the IBC but resigned when Snyder decided it would make operations difficult—especially as they had a controlling interest in the Western National Bank of the City of New York, an institution that they thought would compete with the IBC. The Equitable sold many of its shares to Hubbard but remained one of the IBC's larger shareholders. Its rival, the Metropolitan Life Insurance Company, was also an initial subscriber to the IBC stock.[35]

Hubbard and the directors wanted to use the IBC to create a US-controlled international branch-bank network that could support the extension of US commerce overseas while profiting from the business of US colonial finance in the insular territories and China.[36] But the IBC was faced with a practical problem of legality. It realized that to create an international institution it had to find a way around a set of legal and regulatory roadblocks governing the organization of both domestic and international banking and create an entity that could navigate the plural, transnational legal environment of global finance. The National Bank Act's explicit injunctions against branch banking created a legal impediment to the foreign expansion of federally chartered national banking associations, such as the National City Bank of New York. At the same time, within the banking community, there were questions concerning whether or not the authority of the Act extended to the insular territories. From 1898, Charles Dawes, the comptroller of the currency, was receiving requests and queries regarding the possibilities of incorporating national banking associations in Puerto Rico and Hawaii. Dawes surmised that the authority of the Act was limited to the continental United States, and he urged the US Congress to enact legislation regulating banking in the insular territories and setting out the legal relations of domestic banks to the US colonies.[37] Like the delegates to the 1889 International American Conference, whose report he cited, he argued that without its own international (or what he called "intercolonial") banking institutions, US foreign trade would be impaired, as would the development of the colonies themselves.[38]

The extension was not forthcoming. Wall Street found the US government reluctant to support the internationalization of banking and indifferent to its demands for the regulatory reform to enable foreign expansion. Instead, governmental requirements were privileged over commercial ones in the US colonies. The state's immediate financial needs were for depositories and fiscal agents who could collect and disburse insular revenues and Treasury Department funds. Private banks and trust companies were authorized to do so, leading to the establishment of Samuel Jarvis's North American Trust Company in Cuba and to both Henry de Ford and Company and the American Colonial Bank in Puerto Rico.

In light of these regulatory constraints, the IBC found a way to combine the banking functions of colonial governance with those of commercial finance. It was also able to manipulate both the domestic dual system of regulation and the discrepant and plural geographies of international jurisdiction and legal authority. Chartered in January 1901 as the International Company, the directors changed its name to the International Banking Corporation two months later. Connecticut was chosen as the state of incorporation because of its liberal banking laws. Provisions on the supervision and inspection of banking institutions were lax, and the state had no specific injunctions against branch banking, foreign or otherwise.[39] The charter was written by John Randolph Dos Passos, a specialist in corporation and banking law who organized H. O. Havemeyer's American Sugar Refining Company (and who was both an advocate for the expansion of corporate capitalism and a defender of Anglo-Saxon racial purity).[40] It was broad and capacious—indeed, nearly limitless in its scope. It allowed the IBC "to undertake and execute any and every kind of contract, and to transact and engage in any other lawful business whatsoever" without regard for geographic restriction. "The corporation hereby created is authorized and empowered to have one or more offices, to carry on all or any of its operations and business in any state, territory, dependency, or possession of the United States, or in any foreign country, as aforesaid," read the charter, "and without restriction to the same extent as natural persons might or could do, in any foreign place." Configuring the IBC as a "natural person," the charter imbued the institution with the authority and power to conduct business without any restriction "in any foreign place." This created a conceit that gave the IBC the power to operate in the absence of legal authority, assuming that "foreign places" did not have their own internal systems of jurisdiction that constrained the activities of US businesses. Furthermore, among the IBC's powers was the ability "to establish branches in any part or parts of the world." With the stroke of a lawyer's pen, the IBC was able to evade legal restrictions on foreign branch banking. It immediately became a coveted organization within the Wall Street community.[41]

There was more to the IBC's organization. Recognizing that as a Connecticut-chartered and, hence, "foreign" bank in the state of New York, the IBC could not accept deposits under New York State banking law, the directors organized another, parallel institution designed to complement the IBC's work. As a means of extending the orbit of the IBC's activities, the directors created a second institution, the International Bank, in 1903. The IBC operated under a Connecticut charter, and the International Bank was chartered under the banking laws of New York State. As a legally separate entity from the IBC, the International Bank could accept deposits in New York City and engage in activities prohibited for the parent institution according to New York State banking laws. The IBC's New York address would also become as important to its operations as the overseas branches. It processed foreign exchange and acted as a clearinghouse for its international branches while the other branches transferred funds through direct wire, issued letters of credit, and offered interest-bearing checking accounts and high-interest, fixed-term deposit certificates. Both the IBC and the International Bank shared premises at 1 Wall Street. The directorship of the International Bank was identical to that of the International Banking Corporation.[42] Other than in name and by charter, there was no distinction between the two institutions. By settling on this dual structure the directors of the IBC were able to skirt the regulatory restrictions that had hampered the development of American foreign banking up to that point. The importance of this dual structure for the history of US foreign banking cannot be understated.

Within months of its organization in 1901, Hubbard and the IBC began pursuing the kinds of colonial contracts that Samuel Jarvis secured in Cuba, but in the Pacific region, not the Caribbean. The first contract was in China. The United States was part of the interimperial coalition forcing the Qing government to make indemnity payments to foreigners for losses sustained during the Boxer Rebellion. Totaling $335 million, the indemnity amount was greater than the total claims submitted by foreign governments, and far in excess of the ability of the Chinese to pay. The indemnity served to cripple the Qing government, saddling it with a debt generated by the advance required to initiate the settlement of the indemnity amount. For the IBC, the the advance on the indemnity payments provided a foothold in the region and a quick injection of capital.[43] IBC counsel Frederick W. Holls successfully petitioned the US government for the contract as agencies for the disbursement of the US share, totaling some $25 million.[44] After posting a half-million dollar bond with the secretary of the treasury, the IBC appointed as its agent in Shanghai James S. Fearon. Fearon was an Australia-born merchant with the import-export firm Fearon, Daniels who was a member of the American Asiatic Society, a militant trade organization that had long advocated an aggressive stance on the part of the United States toward markets in Asia.[45] For its services as fiscal agent, the IBC received a commission of one-half of 1 percent for the amounts collected and remitted to the United States. (It was later found that it had overcharged the US government for its services.) A branch in Shanghai soon followed, opening on May 15, 1902. The Shanghai branch eventually became involved in trade financing, foreign investment, and currency issue, and as the first international branch of the IBC, represented the beginning of an ambitious project of imperial banking in Asia.[46]

As in China, the IBC waded into the Philippines in the wake of a flurry of US colonial violence and grafted itself onto a project of colonial finance. Although the Philippines, like Cuba and Puerto Rico, had been ceded by Spain to the United States with the signing of the Treaty of Paris in 1898, the Filipinos objected to the terms of the treaty and on February 4, 1899, launched an insurrection against the United States. With the US suppression of the insurgency—after a bloody war that ravaged both soldiers and civilians—McKinley inaugurated a policy of "benevolent assimilation" and colonial occupation whose aim was to prepare the Filipinos for self-rule. In the immediate aftermath of the counterinsurgency campaign and at the beginning of the US occupation, US authorities commissioned as depositories in the Philippines the Hongkong and Shanghai Banking Corporation (HSBC) and the Chartered Bank of India, Australia and China (CBIAC).[47] Both banks had long histories in the region. The HSBC had been chartered in British Hong Kong in 1865 and had opened its first branch in Manila in 1876. The CBIAC (which was tapped by the North American Trust Company as its Philippine correspondent in 1898) was founded in Karachi in 1853 and opened a Manila agency in 1872.[48] Alongside the Banco Español de Filipino, chartered by royal decree in 1851 with the authority to issue notes, the British banks were the dominant institutions in the archipelago.[49]

The exorbitant exchange rates charged by the British banks, as well as the "many opportunities [that] arose for them seriously to hamper the fiscal operations of the government," as one journal noted, prompted the US authorities to drop them and search instead for US institutions.[50] They received applications from both the IBC and the Guaranty Trust Company of New

York (GTC). The GTC was founded in 1864 as the New York Guaranty and Indemnity Company. It was purchased in 1891 by the Mutual Life Insurance Company, a rival company of many of the insurance interests behind the IBC, as part of an aggressive and profitable policy of acquiring bank stock. The Mutual's directors changed its name in 1896 to the Guaranty Trust Company, and began using it both as an outlet for its accumulation of insurance funds and as a source for additional working capital.[51] The GTC also became the vehicle for foreign expansion. It established a foreign department in 1892. A London agent was appointed the same year, and a permanent branch office followed in 1897. The GTC soon had eight offices in Europe, three in London and one each in Paris, Brussels, Liverpool, Le Havre, and Antwerp.[52]

Faced with competition between the IBC and the GTC for the contracts for the fiscal agency in the Philippines, the secretary of the treasury reached a compromise. The GTC was made the government's fiscal agent at Manila and given control of the Philippines; the IBC was made fiscal agent at Hong Kong and offered China and, in the future, all the other countries of the region.[53] Yet by 1904, finding banking in Asia unprofitable, the GTC decided to leave the Philippines.[54] It transferred its business and goodwill to the IBC and would not return to the region for almost twenty years, until the wartime organization of the Asia Banking Corporation in 1918.[55] Once the GTC departed, the IBC was made fiscal agent and depository for the United States in the Philippines and was the only US financial institution operating in Asia.

The IBC had opened a branch in Manila in June 1902, and a second branch followed in the regional commercial hub of Cebu in 1903.[56] The IBC performed a strictly colonial function in the Philippines. Beyond its role as a US fiscal agent, it did little to aid the internal circulation of capital in the islands. The IBC's savings account balances were modest, and did not compete with those of the Monte de Piedad, a savings institution established for workers during the period of Spanish rule and run by the Catholic Church. Like the North American Trust Company in Cuba, the IBC was extremely constricted in issuing credit. Instead, it served as an intermediary for US finance capital and the development of industrial development projects whose profits were repatriated to the United States. In 1903, for example, the IBC joined the "Manila syndicate," a consortium of US banks and financiers, including William Salomon & Co., Cornelius Vanderbilt, J. G. White & Co., and Heidelbach, Ickelheimer & Co., that was put together by Cravath, Swaine & Moore partner Carl August de Gersdorff for the development and exploitation of Philippine resources. De Gersdorff organized a number of companies for the syndicate, including the Manila Construction Company and the Manila Electric Railways & Light Company of New Jersey, as well as a holding company, the Electric & Lighting Corporation of Connecticut, that both managed the syndicate's bond issues and acquired properties in Manila. The syndicate secured monopoly concessions to build electric railway lines in Manila, for the city's first electric light and power plant, and for transportation and trucking. By 1907, the syndicate had added to its portfolio the Manila Suburban Railways Company and the Philippine Railway Company. The latter company was contracted to build 300 miles of railroad within the archipelago, all financed by bonds guaranteed by the Philippine government.[57] Through its participation in the Manila syndicate, the IBC was effectively involved in a project of US colonial control in the Philippines.

As Hubbard and the IBC directors were angling for a foothold in Asia, they were also pushing for another in a corner of the US colonial and neo-colonial world: the Caribbean and Latin America. On January 26, 1903, the IBC opened a branch, its first in the Americas, at Coliseo Nuevo No. 4 in Mexico City.[58] In Mexico, the IBC began operations as a commercial bank serving the industrial interests of the corporations and businesses controlled by its directors. It emerged as an important intermediary for US business operating in the country, accepting corporate deposits and collecting on local commercial accounts. The IBC used its directors' involvement in railroads, timber, steel, oil, mining, and insurance to expand in the region. The IBC entered what was already a crowded landscape in Mexico, where the British banks were well established, and US private bankers and trust companies were jockeying for influence. In its early years, the Mexico City branch was managed by John Clausen and W. Bundy Cole, former employees of Samuel Jarvis's North American Trust Company / Banco Nacional de Cuba.[59] Clausen had joined the Matanzas branch of the NATC in December 1899 and stayed on during its transition into the BNC, working as a bookkeeper, cashier, and branch manager in Matanzas, Cardenas, Manzanillo, Santiago de Cuba, and Havana before leaving to join the IBC in Mexico City.[60] Cole was an auditor for the Banco Internacional de Guatemala before moving to Cuba where he found employment in the NATC's Santiago de Cuba and Matanzas branches.[61] He joined the International Banking Corporation as an assistant to Hubbard and was sent to work in the Mexico City branch and later the Panama and Colón branches.[62] The organization of these latter branches was initiated in 1903, when the IBC's Washington manager James Morris Morgan traveled to Panama. The following year, an IBC branch was opened in Panama City.[63]

In Panama, the IBC was as interested in commercial banking as it was in governmental finance. Hubbard recognized that the building of the canal by the United States would require financial and banking support, especially to pay laborers. Soon after the Panama City branch was opened, Hubbard wrote to both Theodore Roosevelt and Secretary of the Treasury Leslie M. Shaw requesting that the IBC be appointed fiscal agent for the United States in Panama.[64] Roosevelt was willing to oblige. He was sympathetic to Hubbard's request and saw that Hubbard was "anxious" to get the fiscal agent contract for the IBC. But Secretary of War William Howard Taft was reluctant to grant the IBC a monopoly.[65] Although Taft recognized the fiscal work the IBC had performed for the War Department in the Philippines, he initially declined the IBC's request, citing two factors. First, he believed that granting this concession to a US bank would lead to protests by established Panamanian institutions. Second, he doubted that the IBC alone would be able to handle the business. The contract required the IBC to issue some $500,000 in silver every two weeks to pay the laborers on the canal project. Taft feared that such demand for silver could lead to scarcity and a sharp increase in the price of the metal, which would, in turn, inflate the salaries of the workers.[66] "The strain of supplying that currency, concentrating on the Isthmus, was more than the new American bank could carry," Taft commented. "Therefore I was exceedingly anxious that we should have the assistance of all the old local banks to gather together enough silver to enable us to make these very large payments—I say very large; very large for a country like that which does very little business of its own—in order that the price of the coin which we wished to use should not increase."[67]

As a result of Taft's assessment, the IBC was one of four financial institutions contracted for disbursement operations of the US government in the Canal Zone. Two of the other three—Ehrman and Co. and Isaac Brandon & Bros. (reorganized as the Panama Banking Company in 1907[68])—were run by the individuals Morgan encountered during his exploratory mission to the isthmus and had their origins in the development of nineteenth-century interoceanic commerce.[69] The third, the American Trade Developing Company (ATDS), was a New Jersey corporation owned by Panamanian merchant banker Ramón Arias Feraud. The IBC's share was less than it had wished for. Morgan's erstwhile rivals in Ehrman and Brandon were each given a 30 percent cut, the IBC received 25, the ATDS 15.[70] The IBC opened subbranches in Colón in 1906 and in Empire, in the Canal Zone, in 1908, to handle the payments. The latter branch handled the payroll of the managers and laborers employed in the construction of the canal.

The IBC's Panama accounts mirrored the racial division of labor established by the US authorities in the Canal Zone, with white Americans performing the skilled, managerial duties paid in gold, and black, African-descent West Indians from Jamaica and Barbados paid in silver.[71] Gold and silver became a euphemism for the segregation of white and black labor on the isthmus. For the black "silver men," as they were called, the system of payments also became a source of difficulty.[72] Though paid in silver, those who did not send currency in parcels or via registered letters would remit their earnings in gold, and their wages would be devalued because of the fluctuations in exchange and the usurious exchange rates offered by the banks.[73] In the case of the IBC in Panama, financial intermediation was explicitly racialized. It did not create the dual monetary system, but as one of the four banks dispersing payments to the canal workers, it was critical in the maintenance of the racial division of labor and finance on the isthmus. It also profited from the arbitrage and the usurious rates of exchange until the US government established a postal money order bureau in the Zone for black workers.[74] Years later, the IBC in Panama City was known as the "Nigger Bank" because of its use by Caribbean laborers.[75]

By 1905, the IBC had left its leased quarters at 1 Wall Street for a new building at 60 Wall Street. It moved into new premises in Washington, DC, and opened a branch in San Francisco. The IBC had a global network of branches that was unparalleled in US banking history, with offices in London, Mexico City, Manila, Hong Kong, Yokohama, Shanghai, and Sinagpore, supplemented by agencies in Colombia and throughout Asia: Yokohama, Shanghai, Bombay, Calcutta, Madras, Penang, Rangoon, Amey, Hankow, Canton, Tientsin.[76] The IBC both served US business abroad and aided the US colonial bureaucracy in Panama, the Philippines, and China. Yet despite the IBC's spectacular expansion and its apparent success, five years into its operation, its directors complained that its management had not pursued lines of business as aggressively as it should have and that its profits were subsequently depressed. IBC vice president James Fearon responded to the criticism in a letter to the directors.[77] He argued that although the bank had had early losses at its branches in Manila, Singapore, and Mexico, its business was actually undergoing a "gradual and healthful increase." "It is . . . satisfactory to note that in the five years of our existence we have succeeded in obtaining a firm foothold in the Far Eastern trade," he wrote, "and are now an important factor in the Far Eastern business." He argued that the IBC "occupies the foremost place amongst banks in the Philippines."

Yet Fearon also conceded in the letter that the IBC's growth was hampered by a number of factors. He pointed out that the Shanghai market was glutted with goods and the value of exports had been reduced, curtailing the IBC's profits from the issuance of commercial credits. Because of the volatility of exchange rates in the silver-based countries in which the IBC operated, to minimize the risk of losses from currency speculation, the IBC's managers were instructed to not overexpose their exchange positions and told to curtail their extension of credit. Fearon stated that the IBC's size was a problem. The IBC was undercapitalized and because of this, had to limit the volume of business it could take on as it needed to keep its accounts liquid. The New York office had to get advances from other banks to discount commercial acceptances, and the London bank often jointly handled its discounts, sharing commissions with its British rivals and losing potential profits in the process. The IBC was simply too small to compete in any meaningful way with the British banks. And it was simply too new. The Hongkong and Shanghai Banking Corporation and the Chartered Bank of India, Australia and China had an advantage because of size and history. The IBC barely posed a challenge to their monopoly on foreign trade, and their reputation preceded them, making it, as Fearon noted, "a difficult task to firmly establish [the IBC's] credit and standing."

Furthermore, in some cases, the IBC found itself fighting against its better-known and better-capitalized rivals on Wall Street. Indeed, when, in late 1907, the IBC's directors sought to finance the Hankow-Canton railroad project, their bid for the contract was dismissed by the State Department and displaced by the American Group—a consortium of powerful financial interests composed of J. P. Morgan and Co., the City Bank, Kuhn, Loeb and Co., the First National Bank, and E. H. Harriman. J. Selwyn Tait, the IBC's Washington, DC, branch manager and a vice president, had returned from China in the fall of 1908 and believed that the European scramble for Chinese railroad loans could provide an opportunity for the IBC, and for any US bank that was competing with European financiers for the loan contracts.[78] Embittered and humiliated after its efforts to secure the contracts were dismissed by the Europeans, the IBC approached Morgan and the City Bank with the hopes of joining a consortium. However, the State Department ignored the IBC's entreaties and secured a railroad contract for the American Group. The IBC tried again, this time, hoping to act as the American Group's agent for the administration of the loan in China. Morgan declined the suggestion. Hubbard was furious. He denounced the

American Group and accused the State Department of acting as Morgan's personal commercial representative and supporting what he described as a monopoly on American banking in China. Tait was more circumspect than Hubbard in his assessment of the situation. "We certainly do appear in our own eyes in this instance," he wrote, "to have simply been the jackals of the lions of Wall Street."[79]

The IBC's profitability problems were compounded by the nature of the markets it found overseas and its perceptions of those markets. James Morgan's account of Panama was revealing in this regard. "There was nothing much to see, all tropical countries look alike," Morgan wrote of Panama. "Bamboo trees, palm trees, bananas, and dirty people. Heat and heavy rain."[80] Yet his observations in his autobiography, titled *Recollections of a Rebel Reefer*, provide a surprisingly acute account of the culture of banking and money in Panama from the perspective of an US observer. Similar to what Samuel M. Jarvis found in Cuba after 1898, banking conditions were archaic by US standards. Local banking institutions resembled the merchant banks operating in New York, Philadelphia, and Baltimore a century earlier. Actual *banking* was a marginal, ancillary activity, secondary to the role of local banking institutions as commission merchants of the goods warehoused and stocked in port cities for trade. These institutions were unregulated; their activities were governed by an inherited Spanish commercial code that did not encourage inspections or restrictions on activities, or specify reserve requirements. In addition, hoarding, as opposed to saving, was rampant; circulation was limited as a result. The setting of interests rates was entirely arbitrary, and credit was offered based on personal ties, and for periods of time much longer than what US bankers and merchants were used to, often for more than six months with negotiable extensions, whereas Americans usually granted credit at thirty, sixty, and ninety days.[81] Meanwhile, the presence of either a silver or a bimetallic "limping" standard made currency subject to both speculation and drastic fluctuation, creating instability and risk in commerce.[82] Transactions were inefficient, and the velocity of circulation, exchange, and accumulation was seen as languid, mirroring the perceptions that American bankers had of both the temperament of African and Latin peoples generally, and the temporalities of the tropics, writ large.

For the IBC, many of these problems were embodied by the Panamanian elite and in the cultural and racial characteristics of their business methods. This Creole elite was cosmopolitan in origin.[83] They had long held a vision of an independent republic that could serve as an international crossroads of commerce and would be governed by laissez-faire principles of free trade.

At the same time, as perceived by Americans, the Panamanians were still governed by the traditional, backward Spanish modes of commerce, banking, and finance. As with Samuel Jarvis's perceptions of the Cuban businessperson, the view of the Panamanian elite was defined by suspicion, skepticism, paternalism, and an innate sense of the normative quality of US business culture. To some degree, Isaac Brandon & Bros.—one of the merchant bankers that Morgan encountered during his exploratory trip to the isthmus—epitomized this contradiction between cosmopolitanism and perceived backwardness. Brandon and his brothers were descended from Portuguese Jews who had fled the Inquisition to Jamaica. Isaac Brandon had arrived on the isthmus in 1868 from the United States and established an import-export firm that had monopolized trade in tobacco and other products. They had helped to finance the revolution against Colombia, hoping in part to benefit from the economic sovereignty of the isthmus. Brandon founded the Panama Banking Company in 1905. It was one of the firms that had contracted with the Canal Commission to act as its fiscal agent. The parent firm, Isaac Brandon & Bros., though based in Panama, was incorporated in New Jersey. The Panama Banking Company had offices in both New York and Panama, and its charter was from West Virginia. While benefiting from the modern incorporation laws of the United States, the Panama Banking Company drew much of its institutional identity from its family roots. "Back of the Panama Banking Company stands an element of strength that few banks possess," read the text in an advertisement, "the unwritten but powerful guarantee of family pride and honor, dating from 1868 when Isaac Brandon, its president, founded in the Republic of Panama the present business."[84] This reliance on the "guarantee of family pride and honor" often slid into the terrain of kinship, patronage, and outright graft. At the same time that Brandon told Morgan that there was no chance of success for the IBC in Panama, Morgan also alleged that Brandon told him "that he would accept the management of it if the pay was sufficient." Morgan claimed that both Ehrman and Duque offered the same arrangement, and President Amador offered a slightly different proposal. According to Morgan, Amador entered his room in the Hotel Central unannounced during his siesta to discuss "a little business, on the side." He wanted to rent his buildings to the IBC in case Morgan wanted to open a branch in Panama. Morgan also learned that "two of the President's daughters were married to two sons of Ehrman."[85]

The IBC faced other problems in its expansion. In the first instance, there was a problem of staffing. At the time of the IBC's organization, the United States had nothing resembling a cohort of indigenously trained international bankers. Staff for international branches and for international banking when culled from within the profession often had no prior *foreign* experience and when culled from without often had no prior *banking* experience. Many of the IBC's staff "were not people who found it easy to tell the Chinese apart," as one banker put it, and often their contempt for Caribbean, Latin American, and Asian people was barely concealed.[86] The IBC hired a number of employees from Samuel Jarvis's banking institutions, including Clausen and Cole for the Mexico City branch, but more often than not staff were recruited from British, German, and Canadian institutions. J. Selwyn Tait, for instance, James Morris Morgan's superior at the IBC's DC branch learned the ropes of the banking industry as an employee of the British Linen Company Bank and the London & Southwest Bank.[87] John R. Lee, an individual who had previously spent twenty-two years with the Chartered Bank, was brought in to run the New York office. The New York office also hired two Germans from Deutsche Bank, Wilhelm Pannenborg and Bernard Duis, as accountants, and the Manila branch was staffed by R. W. Brown, who had fifteen years of experience with the Chartered Bank.[88]

James Fearon had been involved in Chinese commerce since 1870. He had no previous experience as a banker. Both Fearon and Edward Quelch, the Shanghai branch's unqualified accountant, had to rely on telegraphic instructions from New York City.[89] John R. Lee of the New York office was eventually sent to Shanghai to clean up the mess created by Fearon and Quelch. This lack of experience in banking was also felt in the New York office, where John Hubbard and Charles Palmer were employed. Hubbard's main qualification was that he was the son of the IBC's president. Palmer, a West Point graduate and retired army officer, had even fewer qualifications than Hubbard. Although his only encounter with international banking came from the mere fact of having spent time in the Philippines, he rose through the IBC's ranks, becoming inspector of its Asian branches, branch manager at Manila and Cebu from 1905 to 1909, and manager of the entire bank from 1909 to 1915.[90]

Despite his evident success in establishing the IBC's branches in Panama, James Morris Morgan's résumé as a banker was a short one. When he joined the IBC he was nervous about keeping a desk job and slightly overwhelmed by his prospects as a banker. "I am not accustomed of late years to keep office hours and nine am to five pm comes a little hard at first but I will soon become accustomed to it," Morgan wrote in a letter. "It makes me feel funny sometimes," he continued, "to be sitting amidst great piles of other people's money while signing bills of exchange and checks for hundreds of thousands of dollars and then to think that I have not thirty cents, max to jingle in my pocket that belongs to me. Is it ludicrous or pathetic?"[91]

Although not versed in the practical methods of banking, Morgan brought other skills and other experiences to the IBC. The *Eugenical News* described Morgan as made of "fighting, adventurous stock," and certainly, *Recollections of a Rebel Reefer* presents him as brash and roguish, qualities that were highlighted during his belligerent negotiations with the Panamanians. These qualities made Morgan an ideal figure to patrol the international frontiers of US capitalism.[92] Morgan also lived through the violent crucible of racial capitalism in the nineteeth-century United States. Born on a cotton plantation in New Orleans in 1845, Morgan's earliest memories were of the almost apocalyptic tableaux of Southern life. In the opening pages of *Recollections of a Rebel Reefer* Morgan recounts witnessing an angry crowd of white men and women cursing Seminole prisoners who were being transported from Florida to the Indian Territory. One of Morgan's uncles was killed during the Seminole Wars, and he felt that if given a chance, the crowd would murder the Seminoles. Morgan also recalled the explosion of the steamboat *Princess* on the Mississippi and the chaotic and gruesome scenes of burning cotton bales floating downriver as dazed members of the boat's crew wandered the shore, engulfed in flames. Nearly one hundred people died in the explosion. The shocked Morgan fled to the comforting arms of Katish, "his old black nurse."[93]

Morgan enrolled in the Naval Academy at Annapolis but dropped out at sixteen. He was taken on by merchant, slave owner, and cotton planter George A. Trenholm, whose firm, Fraser, Trenholm and Co., financed the Confederacy. (Trenholm's son, William Lee, was a director of Samuel Jarvis's North American Trust Company.) Morgan joined one of Fraser, Trenholm's ships and ran cotton around the blockades during the Civil War until he joined the Confederate Navy. For Morgan, emancipation and the defeat of the Confederacy brought on a new, horrific racial order whose values were debased and whose hierarchies were upended. "Since emancipation," Morgan commented, "an English bulldog was worth a great deal more money to me than a free nigger." Morgan disdained black self-government and he was disgusted by what he viewed as the decadent "spectacle" of Reconstruction. After the defeat of the Confederacy, Morgan joined a group of former Confederate soldiers serving in the army of the Egyptian Khedive. Upon his return to the United States, he took over one of Trenholm's plantations near Charleston. He described the legislative sessions of South Carolina as a "circus" where both white "carpetbaggers" and black legislators enacted a pretentious and absurd theater of politics. Morgan mocked the language and comportment of black lawmakers and politicians, bristling at their use of "sea island and ricefield pidgin English," and he ridiculed what he saw as the ostentation, extravagance, and gaudiness of free blacks.[94] His contempt for blacks anticipated that for the Panamanians.

The IBC was coveted by other institutions and other bankers despite its ambivalent success. The City Bank and Frank A. Vanderlip, in particular, watched the development of the IBC and, almost from the moment of its organization, considered taking it over. Vanderlip and the City Bank were embarking on a period of expansion and internationalization and had been largely frustrated in their attempts to organize foreign branches. He had long sought a way around the regulatory constraints hampering foreign branch expansion and had long coveted the branch network of the IBC. As early as 1909, Vanderlip looked to purchase the IBC through a consortium of US banks and corporations including Grace and Co. and J. P. Morgan and Co. The City Bank's foreign exchange manager, John E. Gardin, interviewed managers of the Hongkong and Shanghai Banking Corporation and the Chartered Bank of India, Australia, and China regarding the condition and reputation of the IBC. He learned that its headquarters in New York was an impediment to its business in Asia, as it was staffed by men without Asian experience. "As a banking concern in New York, they certainly are a failure as most of their losses have been made right here," Gardin noted. He continued, "Not understanding the Eastern business it is very difficult to imagine how such a function can be carried out in an intelligent manner." Yet Gardin believed that experience could be gained from the losses and that the City Bank should reorient the IBC to its "proper field," the Americas, especially the Atlantic coast of South America. "There is no reason in my mind why the legitimate South American business should not be taken care of by the National City Bank indirectly through this Corporation," Gardin concluded, "and with good management and care there is a good prospect of success in view of the approaching development of the relations between this country and the South American continent."[95] Gardin suggested the City Bank should sell the agencies of the IBC to German banking interests and hold onto the Manila branch because of its ties to the US insular government.

The difficulty was in the acquisition. Hubbard still owned a majority of the IBC shares, the Equitable Company controlled a smaller amount, and the rest were scattered throughout various holdings. Although he encouraged Vanderlip to pick up the stock on the open market as it became available, Hubbard did not want to sell. He was reluctant to relinquish his controlling interest in the institution he had created, and worried that if

Hermann Sielcken, a German-American merchant who held a monopoly on coffee exports, was put in charge of the bank, the IBC's staff would suffer under what was perceived to be Sielcken's efficient and strict regime. Vanderlip mused to Stillman that "a good deal of ruthlessness would be exactly what the present staff would need in order to put it in a good working condition."[96]

By 1914, the International Banking Corporation had sixteen overseas branches in addition to the state-chartered International Bank within its fold. It had the largest foreign branch network of any US banking institution. But its problems of staff and management, of capitalization, and organization had not propelled it into the ranks of the imperial banks in the way in which Thomas Hubbard had envisioned. The branch networks of Canadian institutions such as the Royal Bank of Canada and the Bank of Nova Scotia dwarfed the IBC in size, especially in the Americas, where the IBC's presence was limited to Panama and Mexico. In 1912, the IBC's Washington, DC, operations were sold to the United States Trust Company. The branches in Mexico City and Monterrey were closed in 1914 because of the fear of political-economic instability brought on by the Mexican Revolution.[97] In the Philippines, the IBC lost its role as fiscal agent with the establishment of the state-controlled National Bank of the Philippines in 1916.[98] British banking institutions such as the London and River Plate Bank and the Anglo-South American Bank also maintained a position of dominance in the Americas. In the Asia-Pacific region, the Hongkong and Shanghai Banking Corporation had thirty branches.[99]

The challenge to the competitiveness of the IBC came not only from foreign international banks, but from within the United States. With the signing in late 1913 of the Federal Reserve Act, national banking associations were permitted to establish foreign branches with the approval of the Federal Reserve Board. The legal and regulatory regimes that had constrained institutions like the City Bank and the First National Bank of Boston were dismantled, and the competitive advantage that the IBC once had was removed. The City Bank was quickest off the mark; in the fall of 1914 it established its first foreign branch in Buenos Aires, a location where the IBC was not active. The First National Bank of Boston followed the City Bank into Argentina. In 1914, the Commercial National Bank of Washington, DC (CNB) opened its first foreign branches in Colón and Panama City, establishing itself as a direct competitor to the IBC.

The directors of the CNB were spurred by the opening on August 15, 1914, of the Panama Canal. The onset of maritime travel through the isthmus drastically reduced the time and cost of shipping, collapsing the space of global commerce by bringing Atlantic ports closer to those on the Pacific, and the markets of Asia closer to the merchants and industrialists of New York, Boston, Philadelphia, and New Orleans. The canal's opening encouraged the consolidation of the Caribbean as a military and strategic unit as the need to defend shipping lanes and man coaling stations along its routes demanded regional political stability via increased diplomacy, militarization, and the eviction of European, especially German, commercial and banking interests. It also created the need for a new set of financial and banking services for US imperialism. No longer was the primary demand for a system and infrastructure for the payment of laborers; instead, institutions were needed for the operation of the canal itself and its maritime traffic.

The CNB's directors used its Washington connections to compete with the IBC for the federal deposits for the Canal Zone.[100] The branches of both institutions served a number of purposes. They were involved in canal-related shipping and trade, including the handling of canal tolls and fees and the expenses for fuel, repair work, and other needs, charging owners of vessels one-eighth of 1 percent of the transactions amount. They served as depositories for the US Treasury, the Panama Railroad, the Panama Canal Commission, and the US Army and Navy and acted as the official disbursing agent for the accounts of the latter, as a paymaster for US military personnel stationed on the Atlantic side, and as agent for the accounts of the army and navy's post exchanges and ships service stores.[101] The CNB also was established as a local bank of deposit and discount, offering savings accounts and personal banking services for both the expatriate community and Panamanians.[102]

The passage of the Federal Reserve Act also made the IBC vulnerable to the threat of takeover by the larger Wall Street institutions that it had come up against. When Hubbard died in 1915, the City Bank pounced. It purchased a controlling interest in the IBC, using financier and IBC director Jules S. Bache as an intermediary. Much of the IBC's board was replaced by City Bankers. James Morris Morgan resigned from his post in Washington and retired.[103] A year later, the City Bank's Gardin wrote a report titled "What Shall We Do with the International Banking Corporation?" Gardin likened the purchase of the corporation by the City Bank to the Louisiana Purchase. He argued that the IBC's profitability was not something that the City Bank would look to in the short term, but that, over the long term, given the relatively slow pace at which the City Bank was opening overseas branches since the establishment of the Federal Reserve System, the purchase of the IBC could accelerate this process. In two years, he noted, the City Bank had opened branches in only six cities: Rio de Janiero, Santos, São Paulo,

Montevideo, and Buenos Aires. "At this rate it will take a generation to cover the world as it must be covered within a reasonable time to crush the aspirations of rivals," Gardin wrote, "and to make the City Bank the master of the foreign trade situation so far as banking operations are concerned."[104] Despite Gardin's lament, for the City Bank, that mastery would soon come. It would arrive on the back of the pioneering foreign branch banking network created by the IBC—and the City Bank would inherit many of the IBC's difficulties with staffing, regulation, and racial capitalism.

THREE

Financial Occupations

The Banque Nationale d'Haiti (BNH) was housed in a whitewashed, two-story colonial building at the corner of rues Ferou and Américaine in the downtown business district of Port-au-Prince. On weekday mornings, before the afternoon heat forced the closing of its tall iron shutters for the late-day siestas, the vaulted main banking room sheltered a staff of about sixty clerks, accountants, messengers, and managers nattily outfitted in white linen suit jackets and black bow ties. They worked at mahogany bureaus within a brass-screened banking cage, handling the BNH's everyday transactions and annotating its accounts in the columns of oversized leather-bound ledgers.[1] The BNH's staff was cosmopolitan, international in complexion, and mixed racially, though as William H. Williams, the BNH's manager, noted, "as might be expected, the negro and mulatto" made up the majority of employees. "However," Williams observed, "most, in fact I might say all, important and responsible positions are held by foreigners, thus showing the 'push' of the white man. The general idea among the natives is to do the work allotted and no more."[2]

Williams's racial chain of command had a spatial counterpart. The BNH had a network of branches and agencies throughout Haiti—in Cap-Haïtien, Port-de-Paix, Gonaïves, Saint-Marc, Petit-Goâve, Jérémie, Aux Cayes, Jacmel, Fort-Liberté, Môle-Saint-Nicolas, Miragoâne, and Aquin. The branches and agencies served as tributaries through which the revenues of the republic from the export of coffee, cotton, sisal, and other commodities were carried by mules and peasant messengers up and down country roads from the rural districts to Port-au-Prince.[3] This revenue did not remain in Port-au-Prince, however. Despite its name, from the time it was chartered in 1880, the BNH served a foreign master. Its president and directors were French. Executive decisions were made in Paris at the Société Générale de Crédit Industriel et Commercial. Its profits were repatriated to Europe. And the push of the white man in the BNH's affairs came from France.[4]

From 1910, this began to change. The push in the affairs of the BNH increasingly came not from the boardrooms of the Société Générale at 66 rue de la Chaussée-d'Antin in Paris but from the offices of the National City Bank of New York at 55 Wall Street. For the City Bank, control of the BNH emerged as a core element of a strategy of internationalization that itself was part of a broader project of modernization and organizational reform. Under the leadership of James Stillman and Frank A. Vanderlip, the City Bank sought to diversify and expand its business activities beyond that of a regular commercial bank. Stillman and Vanderlip wanted to decentralize the City Bank's operations by separating the bank's owners from its management. They created specialized internal units within the bank overseen by a growing cohort of managers and technicians. They lobbied for the deregulation of a legal landscape that they saw as constraining the bank's operations.[5] Overseas expansion, and the organization of the City Bank as an imperial institution, were central to this strategy of diversification, decentralization, and deregulation. Stillman and Vanderlip sought increased involvement in the flotation of foreign government bonds and securities, in the establishment of international branches and agencies, and in the control and operation of government banks within the republics, colonies, and dependencies of the Caribbean and Latin America.

Although Haiti has been excised from the City Bank's official histories, the bank's effort to acquire the BNH was arguably its most successful experiment in foreign banking.[6] It was certainly among the most controversial. Its attempts to gain control of the BNH exacerbated the long-standing strife between the BNH and the Haitian government while fomenting the conditions leading to US Marine intervention in Haiti in 1915 and a bloody nineteen-year military occupation. By the fifth year of the US occupation—the tenth year of the City Bank's growing involvement in Haiti's affairs—the bank was being denounced in the US press for its support of US imperial rule in Haiti and its role in the unceremonious suppression of Haiti's hard-fought sovereignty. Members of the growing cohort of City Bank managers were publicly attacked both for their handling of the affairs of the BNH and their intimate role in shaping the terms of occupation and empire. Roger Leslie Farnham, in particular, was singled out. Hired by Vanderlip, Farnham had quickly emerged as one of the most active individuals in the City Bank's affairs in Haiti. But Farnham did not act alone. The City Bank's Haiti policy was shaped by a group of bankers that also included Vanderlip, William H.

Williams, and John H. Allen, all City Bankers, as well as Henry H. Wehrhane of New York investment bankers Hallgarten & Co.

While the City Bank's attempts to take over the BNH were part of a project of modernization, these efforts also emerged from and reproduced a longer history of antiblack racism directed toward the Haitian republic. Indeed, in the context of Haiti, to imagine a history of capitalism scrubbed clean of the stain of racism is impossible. Since its revolutionary founding in 1804, Haiti has been despised and its history degraded and demeaned by racist representations, its sovereignty repeatedly attacked by imperial powers keen to reestablish white supremacy over the country.[7] The actions of Farnham and other City Bankers continued this history of antiblack representation, imperial violence, and racial sovereignty. Their decisions and opinions operationalized notions of racial difference and naturalized ideologies of white supremacy within the bank's Haiti policy. For the City Bank in Haiti, the collapse of financial capitalism into racial capitalism was stark—and the push of the bank into the affairs of the BNH was ruthless.[8]

The City Bank of New York was incorporated in 1812.[9] Its charter was taken up from Alexander Hamilton's Bank of the United States when the federal government decided against renewing Hamilton's bank. Former secretary of the treasury Samuel Osgood was the new bank's first president, and its directors were drawn from New York's mercantile elite. Although organized as a commercial entity, it was soon involved in war financing, loaning the US federal government money to fight the War of 1812. In the late 1830s, the City Bank's capital base grew radically when it became the repository of John Jacob Astor's fortunes. Astor appointed his protégé, Moses Taylor, as a director, and Taylor became the president of the bank in 1856, remaining with it until his death in 1882. Taylor was a sugar merchant who grew wealthy through his financial connections with Cuban planters, whose sugarcane was harvested and processed by the labor of enslaved Africans. He ran the bank as a profitable, if largely personal, institution. Taylor developed important, long-standing ties between the bank and the Farmers Loan and Trust Company, and he invested the City Bank's funds in many of the expanding industries of the US economy: gas lighting, coal, railroads, iron, insurance, and the deposits of Southern cotton planters and slaveholders.[10] Taylor brought the City Bank under a federal charter in 1865, at which point the bank's name was changed to the National City Bank of New York. After Taylor's death, the City Bank was competently run by his business partner and son-in-law, Percy Pyne, until James Stillman was appointed bank president in 1891. Stillman's ties to the bank began early. His father, Charles Stillman, was a director of and major investor in the bank. Born into a Connecticut family of shipowners, the elder Stillman was a cotton merchant, investor, and property developer. He was an antisecessionist Northerner with Southern sympathies and a New Yorker with Texas identifications. Stillman opposed the "abolishing fanatics" and ran a lucrative trade as the dominant cotton runner during the US Civil War. Engaged in a Texan project of settler colonialism, Stillman also annexed, platted, and sold the communal lands in northern Mexico that became the city of Brownsville.[11]

Under the younger Stillman (whose favorite toy as a child, it was said, was a japanned tin City Bank piggy bank) the City Bank entered an extended period of modernization and growth. It transitioned from being a well-capitalized and powerful merchant bank to being one of the largest financial institutions in the United States and the world. Stillman maintained an approach developed under Taylor: building the bank through cautious but astute lending backed by a constant supply of ready cash. It was a policy that had helped the City Bank grow in public prestige, as it was seen as a bulwark of stability against the banking panics that roiled the late nineteenth-century United States. Stillman further strengthened the City Bank's capital base by securing an outsized share of the federal government's balances in New York City. He increased bankers' balances (the deposits of midsized banks throughout the country) by expanding the City Bank's network of correspondent relations, a process accelerated by his 1897 takeover of the Third National Bank.[12] He courted accounts from the United States' largest industrial concerns, including Amalgamated Copper, the Union Pacific Railroad, and, most important, the Standard Oil Company and the Rockefeller fortunes.[13] The ties to the Rockefellers were such that the City Bank became known as "the Standard Oil Bank." Despite the fact that Stillman's two daughters married Rockefeller's two sons, the appellation understates the autonomy of Stillman and the range of the City Bank's financial connections.

Stillman was constantly on the lookout for new avenues of accumulation and recognized the potential profitability of an international bank network organized to support the export of US goods. Stillman worried that US businesspeople were ill prepared for foreign business. He believed racial and cultural differences between Americans and their neighbors were too great, and would thus hamper and frustrate the development of business ties. He recognized that US bankers at the time were largely provincials who did not have the skills, languages, or cosmopolitan instincts to staff a foreign branch network.[14] Stillman also began to see that banking regulation hampered the

City Bank's ability to grow. The National Bank Act prohibited national banking associations from owning stock in other associations or other banks, disallowed them from engaging in the marketing and sales of securities, and forbade them to establish branches, be they domestic or foreign. The logic behind these provisions was to avoid monopoly in banking and the concentration of financial power in a handful of institutions. Stillman began to see the National Bank Act as a relic of an earlier era that could not support the organization and activities of a modern financial institution. He began to search for legal and extralegal ways to skirt the prohibitions of the act.

Gradual steps were taken to assert the City Bank's foreign presence. In 1897, the City Bank opened a foreign exchange department, set up agencies in Berlin, Hamburg, London, Paris, and Brussels, and began participating in the marketing and sale of foreign securities and foreign government bonds. In 1899, the City Bank joined the syndicate behind J. P. Morgan and Co.'s $110 million loan to Mexico, where, decades earlier, he had supported the 1876 revolution that brought Porfirio Díaz to power.[15] It was the first issue of foreign securities payable in New York, instead of London or another European capital, and the beginning of the shift of financial power from those capitals to New York City.[16]

Stillman's vision of the City Bank's internationalization was shepherded into being by Frank A. Vanderlip. Hailing from Chicago, Vanderlip was a former journalist and editor who had been appointed by Lyman Gage as assistant secretary of the treasury.[17] Even before he arrived at the City Bank, Vanderlip was experienced in matters of imperialism and international finance. As a journalist, he had covered the 1890 International American Conference, where the earliest calls for an international US banking institution were raised, and he rubbed shoulders with the most important leaders and businesspeople of the American republics; as assistant secretary of the treasury, he had helped negotiate the indemnity to Spain following the Spanish-American War for Cuba's Independence, had investigated the monetary and currency conditions of Puerto Rico, and had written on the political-economic conditions in the Philippines.[18] Hired by Stillman in 1902, Vanderlip was appointed as City Bank president in 1909, months after the City Bank moved to 55 Wall Street, at which time Stillman became the chairman of the bank's board of directors.

Vanderlip was a liberal, progressive force in the bank whose work continued Stillman's efforts to move the City Bank out of the financial world of the nineteenth century. He transformed the City Bank's internal organization and expanded its financial activities. He further expanded the City Bank's correspondent system by soliciting accounts from the hundreds of regional banks he had had contact with during his stint in the Treasury Department. Between 1902 and 1905 the City Bank's correspondents more than doubled, from 606 to 1,230, while its $44 million in correspondent accounts represented almost 20 percent of its total capital.[19] Vanderlip revolutionized the public engagement of financial institutions, writing signed articles on economic matters for the press, beginning a modest advertising campaign, and, from 1904, writing and distributing a four-page monthly letter on Treasury policy, bond movements and the money market, and other questions of contemporary economy and business. He continued the City Bank's role in the flotation of sovereign debt and foreign corporate securities and solicited a role in US colonial projects. Vanderlip contracted for a portion of the deposit and distribution of the 1904 $35 million Speyer and Co. loan to Cuba and participated in Speyer's 1904 loan to Mexico, and, also with Speyer, the Bolivian railway construction contract of 1907. Vanderlip described the Bolivian contract as the City Bank's "first South American project," financing and building a railroad from La Paz to a Pacific port at the cost of $27 million.[20] (Vanderlip planned to import labor from India, but the Bolivian government objected and, instead, used the army to conscript local peasants.[21]) The bank made about $1 million in profit when it sold the line to a British concern. The City Bank also joined with J. P. Morgan and the First National Bank of New York in 1908 to bid for the entire $30 million worth of US Panama bonds.[22]

As part of an internal reorganization of the bank and in an attempt to separate the City Bank's owners from its management, Vanderlip appointed a group of managers and vice presidents who presided over the portfolios of the City Bank's increasingly specialized internal units. Over the course of his tenure, he recruited a set of ambitious and uniquely skilled individuals who took charge of the City Bank's growing education and publicity programs, its bond retailing and marketing, its statistical and analytical departments, and its foreign exchange and trade departments. Some came from other banking institutions, including Samuel Jarvis's North American Trust Company and Banco Nacional de Cuba, the International Banking Corporation, and the Canadian and British colonial banks; some came from government, and some from corporations. They included John H. Allen, Oscar Phelps Austin, Joseph T. Cosby, Herbert Rucker Eldridge, John E. Gardin, William S. Kies, Samuel McRoberts, George Evans Roberts, Ferdinand C. Schwedtman, W. Morgan Shuster, and Stephen H. Voorhees.[23]

Roger Leslie Farnham was among this group of Vanderlip's managerial appointees. Farnham was born in Washington, DC, in 1864, completed high school, and then traveled to Wyoming, where he worked on a cattle ranch.[24] He drifted from the West, spent years "at sea" and in Mexico, returning to the United States in January 1889, where he joined the United Press Agency (UPA) in New York City as a financial reporter. While working for the UPA, he covered the 1890 International American Conference alongside Vanderlip, then a reporter for the *Chicago Tribune*.[25] After two years with the UPA, Farnham joined Joseph Pulitzer's *New York World* as a reporter and assistant to the financial editor, Jonas Whitley. He remained with the *World* for six years before moving in 1897 to the Manhattan Trust Company, where he worked as a financial assistant. Farnham was courting controversy at this time. He was developing a reputation for his stock market manipulations and was sued by a woman who alleged that he "accomplished her ruin" in New York's Hotel Royal. When the hotel caught fire, Farnham jumped from the room and saved himself; she fell to the ground, broke her spine and legs, and was consequently permanently confined to a wheelchair.[26]

Farnham's work with the Manhattan Trust Company brought him to the attention of William Nelson Cromwell, the powerful corporation lawyer and head of the firm Sullivan and Cromwell. Cromwell admired Farnham's extensive knowledge of business, especially of the shipping industry, and hired him in 1898.[27] Farnham worked for Cromwell for the next decade. Often described as Cromwell's "man Friday," Farnham's position was fluid and malleable. He was a corporate adviser, a purchasing agent, a lobbyist, and a press agent. He worked behind the scenes in Washington, New York, and elsewhere to help push through Cromwell's many projects.[28] When Cromwell was retained by the New Panama Canal Company to sell the concession for the Panama route to the United States, Farnham emerged as a critical figure. Farnham was in charge of the publicity machine attempting to convince Congress of the logic and viability of a Panama route over one through Nicaragua. He hired a team of agents, who, working independently of each other and without exposing their ties to Cromwell, interviewed each senator and congressperson on their opinions on the canal matter. They followed up the interviews by both anonymously sending literature extolling the virtues of the Panama route and sending another group of agents who discreetly pressured the politicians to support the Panama route. He produced and distributed to each senator and congressperson an embossed three-volume report detailing the strengths of the Panama route.[29] A similar team was deployed in Bogotá to convince the Colombian parliament. Farnham's efforts in Washington were successful, but his efforts in Bogotá failed, and the Colombian parliament refused to recognize a treaty giving the United States the canal concession.

As relations between the United States, the Colombians, and the Pana-

manian nationalists broke down, Farnham worked behind the scenes to
help Cromwell foment a secessionist coup and US intervention in Panama.
He was no stranger to appeals to the US government to protect the interests
of Cromwell; on a previous occasion, Farnham had personally appealed to
Secretary of State John Hay requesting warships be sent to protect the property of the Panama Railroad.[30] Now, serving as as an intermediary between
Washington, Cromwell, and the Panamanian junta, Farnham worked to
create the political conditions that would make the Panamanian revolt,
and its success, seem inevitable. Farnham wrote and published an unsigned
article in the *New York World*, his old employer, announcing that if Colombia
refused the treaty, Panama's citizens would revolt. The revolt occurred on
November 3, 1903, the day Farnham's article predicted. With support from
the United States, the Panamanians were successful. Panama declared its
independence on November 4 and the United States recognized the country two days later. On November 18, the United States and Panama signed
the Hay-Bunau-Varilla Treaty, granting the United States possession of the
Canal Zone in exchange for a $10 million payment and a $250,000 annuity.
Farnham traveled with Cromwell and Secretary of War William Howard Taft
to Panama to help hammer out the details of the treaty. In May 1905, Taft
appointed Farnham a director of the Panama Railroad Company, citing both
his knowledge of shipping and his intimacy with the Panamanians, though
it was suspected in financial circles that Farnham served as a proxy for Cromwell's interests.[31] Farnham, who was joined on the board by Charles Taft, the
secretary's brother, traveled to Europe to buy ships for the Panama Railroad
Company.

In March 1911 Farnham was hired by Vanderlip and joined the City Bank.
His importance to Vanderlip and the bank matched what he had done for
Cromwell. "Farnham is growing invaluable to us," Vanderlip wrote to Stillman less than a year after Farnham's hire.[32] Farnham quickly immersed himself in the City Bank's burgeoning imperial operations.

With the aid and expertise of Farnham and the other managers, Vanderlip
initiated a series of tentative, often unsuccessful forays overseas focusing
largely on the Caribbean and Central America. As early as 1904, Vanderlip
had considered opening an affiliated institution, agency, or branch abroad.
In anticipation of the revenue that would flow from Washington toward the
isthmus during the building of the Panama Canal, he considered opening
a bank in Panama. His efforts were stymied by the comptroller's refusal to
extend the National Bank Act to American foreign territories, colonies, and

dependencies.[33] The following year, Vanderlip rejected a proposition to take over the Banco Español de Filipino, the old Spanish colonial institution in the Philippines, because of concerns over both the nature of the privileges of its charter and the prospects of banking in Manila.[34] He did, however, secure the contract to serve as the depository for the customs receipts of the Dominican Republic, and Dominican tax revenue was deposited with the bank in New York.[35] Vanderlip also organized the Banco de la Habana with a number of other US and European financial interests.

The Republic of Haiti also came to the attention of Vanderlip and the City Bank at this time. In February 1909, Speyer and Co. approached Vanderlip with prospects for investments in Haiti and the Domincian Republic.[36] The City Bank had already collaborated with Speyer on its Bolivian railroad project, as well as on government loans to Cuba and Mexico, but Haiti was a new field for Vanderlip. He had little knowledge of the financial prospects of the republic or of the quality of the propositions offered by Speyer. The Haiti business "did not appeal to me particularly," Vanderlip wrote to Stillman, while the Santo Domingo business "look[ed] better."[37] Vanderlip sent Lawrence M. Jacobs to investigate. Jacobs was a recent appointment to the Foreign Department who had graduated from the University of Chicago and had worked as a statistician for the US Department of the Treasury in the Philippines.[38] Speyer shared the expenses. Jacobs's report was enthusiastic. "The trip was very satisfactory," Vanderlip wrote, "and I think there is a good deal of business ahead there."[39] The Speyer proposal consisted of the purchase of stock in a soon-to-be-formed holding company called the Central Railroad of Haiti. The Central Railroad controlled the Compagnie des Chemins de Fer de la Plaine du Cul-de-Sac (the Plain du Cul de Sac, or PCS Railroad), a forty-mile railroad between Gonaïves and Hinche with a branch line to Gros-Morne, and the Compagnie Haitienne du Wharf de Port-au-Prince.[40]

Both the PCS Railroad and the wharf company were originally organized by German and German-American interests based in Port-au-Prince and New York City. The railroad held contracts and concessions with the Haitian government made between 1899 and 1906 that guaranteed 6 percent interest on construction bonds. The wharf contract, dating from 1906, involved the construction of a new steel dock that upon completion would hold a monopoly on all goods entering or leaving Port au Prince while the holder of the concession was free to set lightering rates at its discretion. The City Bank and Speyer and Co. purchased $800,000 of the PCS stock at 80 percent of its par value. They turned a quick profit by selling a $300,000 block of stock at 82 ½ while keeping the rest under option at 85. A substantial block of stock in the wharf company came to the City Bank and Speyer as a "bonus." Much of the investment capital was to be held by the City Bank, with the bank supervising how it would be spent.[41]

The PCS Railroad concession proved, as Vanderlip noted to Stillman, "a small but profitable piece of business" while the wharf company gave "every indication that it will prove very valuable."[42] Yet for Vanderlip, the City Bank's investments in Haiti's railroads were but a stepping-stone to a larger prize: control of Haiti's banking and monetary system. "This stock will give us a foothold there," Vanderlip wrote to Stillman soon after the PCS purchase, "and I think we will perhaps later undertake the reorganization of the Government's currency system which, I believe, I see my way clear to do with practically no monetary risk."[43]

Vanderlip and the City Bank were not the first financiers and financial institutions to set their sights on Haiti's banking and monetary system. The City Bank's interest in Haiti was grafted onto a long history of foreign involvement in Haiti's finances—and the contested, bitter relations therein—dating back to Haiti's independence in 1804. Foreign financiers saw an opportunity to take advantage of Haiti's vulnerable position within the global economy. In the years following the revolution, Haiti's need for foreign exchange was oftentimes desperate and its economic growth was hampered by both its diplomatic isolation and its defense against external political and economic threat.[44] Haiti's external debt, a crippling burden well into the twentieth century, dated back to the *double dette* contracted by President Jean-Pierre Boyer with France in 1825. In order to gain recognition of Haiti's sovereignty, Boyer agreed to pay France a 150 million franc indemnity for French losses of the plantations and the black slaves that had made Saint-Domingue the wealthiest colony in the world. Boyer then contracted with the Banque de France for a 24 million franc loan to pay off the first installment.[45]

There were failed attempts to organize a state bank in Haiti in 1826 and 1859.[46] In 1874, the government of Michel Domingue granted a concession to US speculator Adolph H. Lazare to open a bank, though the concession was rescinded when Lazare could not come up with the stipulated capital. Lazare later charged the Haitian government with arbitrarily canceling the concession and petitioned the US State Department for a claim against the Haitian government. His claim was eventually dismissed by the United States.[47] A government bank was finally chartered in 1880; its organization initiated a new history of conflict between the black republic and white finance. On September 10, 1880, Haiti's president Lysius Salomon granted a concession to the Société Générale de Crédit Industriel et Commercial to create a government bank called the Banque Nationale d'Haiti. Based in Paris, the Société Générale was chartered by decree of Napoleon III in

1859. It had a presence outside of France in central and eastern Europe, but its activities in the Americas were were limited to the organization of the Banque Française du Brasil in 1896. Although based in France, the BNH was granted the rights of a Haitian citizen.[48] Capitalized at 10 million francs, it was given a fifty-year concession to act as the Haitian government's treasurer, and permitted the privilege of note issuance.[49] The BNH was responsible for maintaining the republic's schedule of repayments on its foreign debt, and was expected to stabilize the gourde, Haiti's paper currency, by protecting against speculation. It also handled the deposits of customs revenue generated from exports.

The opening of the BNH in Port-au-Prince was accompanied by marching bands and speeches heralding the republic's grand financial future—as well as by chants of *Aba la banque!*—"Down with the bank!"—by factions opposed to its organization, calling for its destruction, and accusing the government of chartering a dangerous monopoly that would impinge on the country's sovereignty.[50] Rifts between the bank and the government quickly surfaced. In 1887, its foreign clerks and managers were charged with stealing from the Banque and imprisoned.[51] At the turn of the century, Haiti's president Alexis Nord accused the managers of the BNH of taking exorbitant and illegal profits from a bond issue authorized by the previous government during what became known as the "consolidation affair."[52] Nord imprisoned the staff and inaugurated a drawn-out legal battle in Haiti's courts. The BNH's directors reported to their shareholders in France that profits were maintained despite the unsatisfactory conditions in Haiti and the continued fractious relations between the government and the bank. With the ascendancy of François C. Antoine Simon to the presidency of Haiti late in 1908, the BNH's directors hoped the conflict would be resolved. Yet a series of meetings and interviews between Haitian officials and the bank did little to reconcile the differences between the parties. Conditions between the government and the bank remained rocky, and charges against the bank were made in the Haitian courts, which the officers of the bank refused to accept as legitimate.[53]

In 1910 Simon demanded that the Société Générale agree to terminate its contract for the BNH and abandon its rights and privileges, and sent a delegation to Paris to seek out another group of financiers who could take over the contract and concession.[54] US banks were also hoping to get a foothold in Haiti through the republic's banking and finances. A group backed by J. P. Morgan wanted to take over the BNH, and in November 1909, months after Lawrence M. Jacobs's exploratory mission the City Bank and Speyer and Co. sent representatives to Haiti to negotiate with President Simon.[55] Neither group was successful. The Morgan proposition floundered on the demand to establish a US-controlled Dominican-style receivership. The City Bank and Speyer group could not come to an agreement with the Société Générale and the BNH interests.[56]

In the meantime, the Haitian government found another European group willing to take over and renegotiate the concession: a consortium of French and German banking houses, led by the Banque de l'Union Parisienne (BUP). The BUP group wanted to take over the functions of government treasurer and offered to refinance the debt through a 65 million franc loan with a provision for retiring the outstanding circulating currency through a 10 million franc fund. Once the bank was established, the Haitian legislature was to authorize a law enabling the new bank to withdraw the currency and establish and issue a new gold-backed monetary unit with a seventy-five-year privilege of note issue.[57] With the consent of the Haitian government, the BUP and the Société Générale came to an agreement. The Haitian government renounced its claims and charges against the old bank and paid almost half a million gourdes in interest and commission fees to the Société Générale for the contested loan consolidation operations of 1900.[58]

Yet as the new contract between the BUP and the Haitian government was being negotiated, the US State Department intervened. It was displeased with the new banking contract and its conditions. At 72.3 percent of the face amount, or 47 million francs, the price of the loan was horrifically low for the banking consortium and ridiculously high for Haiti. While the loan was guaranteed by a tax of $1 per 100 pounds of coffee exported and a 15 percent surcharge on import duties, the contract was said to have been sealed by a payoff of 5 million francs to the Haitian officials. Furthermore the US officials viewed a clause permitting French military intervention if the republic failed to meet its financial obligations to the new bank as a violation of both the 1823 Monroe Doctrine and their more immediate strategic goals in the region.[59]

Philander Knox pressured the Haitian government and the bank's French directors to include US interests in the new institution. As a result, a portion of the bank's shares were divvied up between a group of US and German-American financial institutions. A new contract was drawn up between the government and a syndicate led by the BUP, and the bank was reconstituted as the Banque Nationale de la République d'Haiti (BNRH).[60] The BUP remained the majority shareholder, owning 80 percent of the BNRH's shares, while 2,000 shares each were acquired by German investment bank Berliner Handels-Gesellschaft, a group of New York–based German-American houses including Speyer, Hallgarten & Co., Ladenburg Thalmann, and, finally, the

City Bank. Hallgarten had been founded in 1850 by German-Jewish immigrant Lazarus Hallgarten and quickly emerged as an investment banking
and bond-dealing force. It maintained strong ties to Germany through the
Berliner Handels-Gesellschaft.[61]

The headquarters of the BNRH remained in Paris, removed to the 55
rue de Châteaudun offices of the BUP, while a New York committee for the
bank operated out of the City Bank's 55 Wall Street offices and the offices of
Hallgarten & Co. Its president was the marquis de Reverseaux, a French ambassador and BUP director, and the vice president was Henry H. Wehrhane
of Hallgarten. Born in Baltimore, Wehrhane studied banking in Europe
before returning to the United States to join Hallgarten, where his father
was a partner. Paul Santallier, who had taken over management of the BNH
when its previous manager died, was a vice president of the new institution;
other directors included the City Bank's Samuel McRoberts, Walter T. Rosen
of Ladenburg Thalmann, and Richard Shuster, a partner of Speyer and Co.
who was a director of the National Railroad of Mexico and had organized
the Banco Mexicano de Comercio e Industria. John H. Allen was appointed
the director of the branch in Port-au-Prince. Allen had studied at Brooklyn
Polytechnic Institute and had worked as an assistant secretary of the Bankers Trust Co. of New York, and he had organized the Sacramento Banking &
Trust Co. before joining the Farmers Loan and Trust Co.[62] In the early days
of the BNRH, Allen, and Henri Desrue, a French citizen, emerged as the most
important people on the ground in Haiti. In New York City, Wehrhane and
Farnham supervised BNRH operations.

In July 1911, Antoine Simon was overthrown and Cincinnatus Leconte
came to power. Leconte was backed by German merchants in Haiti, and he
quickly contracted a loan to repay them for their support.[63] The Leconte
presidency proved a boon to the City Bank and the BNRH. In May 1912,
Leconte's secretary of finance and commerce, Edmund Lespinasse, signed a
contract with the BNRH, represented by John H. Allen and Henri Desrue,
through which the bank performed the treasury services for the government
while receiving in return "special affectations," including the monopoly
rights on the holding of tax deposits and a commission on the exportation
of goods.[64] The City Bank's Roger Farnham later estimated that 90 percent
of Haiti's customs revenue was collected under Leconte's reign—a high
figure considering the problems of graft and the frequent disruptions in
collection—ensuring that the BNRH received high commissions on deposits while maintaining the schedule of repayments to the republic's creditors
for the internal and external debts.[65]

During Leconte's government the City Bank also became a stockholder of the National Railroad of Haiti. The concession for the National Railroad was held by a shady American entrepreneur, James P. MacDonald, who had previously built railroads in the United States, Jamaica, and Ecuador—the latter of which was marred by violent conflicts between its white American foreman and its imported Jamaican laborers.[66] In Haiti, MacDonald reportedly secured the concession for the National Railroad from Philadelphia interests by bribing President Antoine Simon and his daughter Celestine, who, according to US lore, was given a string of fake pearls in exchange for her influence with her father. For MacDonald the exchange was a profitable one: the concession guaranteed 5 percent interest from the government for financing of the construction of a railroad line between Cap-Haïtien and Port-au-Prince up to a total of $33,000 per mile with a guaranty of 2,000 miles per year. The concession also granted MacDonald a fifteen-year monopoly privilege on growing fruit on a swath of land stretching twenty kilometers on either side of the railroad. MacDonald invited W. R. Grace and Co. to participate in the financing. Grace formed a syndicate that included the City Bank and Speyer and Co., and it organized the Caribbean Construction Company (CCC) as a subcontractor to build the railroad. Grace floated $2 million in bonds, borrowing $500,000 from the City Bank for its own purchase and depositing $878,000 in bonds as collateral; the London-based Ethelburga Syndicate, which had previously been involved in Nicaraguan loans, took 50 percent of the company stock. Roger Farnham was the president of the CCC, and MacDonald, the City Bank's McRoberts, and Grace vice president Lawrence H. Shearman were directors. Bonds were purchased by investors in France.[67] The City Bank opened a credit line of $2 million for financing the railroad's construction.[68]

By 1912—three quick years after Speyer initially approached Vanderlip—the City Bank had found an anchor in Haiti through investment in the PCS Railroad, the National Railroad of Haiti, the Port-au-Prince wharf company, and the BNRH. In relation to the aggregate total of the City Bank's domestic and foreign investments at the time, Haiti represented a relatively small amount. But in terms of the total foreign investments in Haiti, the bank had gained an outsized presence in Haiti's economic affairs and emerged as a competitor to the long-standing French and German mercantile presence that had dominated the Haitian economy. At the same time, the City Bank's economic foothold positioned it to make greater demands on both the Haitian government and the US State Department and quickly led to the bank's virtual control of Haiti's finances, just as Vanderlip had hoped.

For the City Bank, the Leconte administration proved a boon for its expanding ventures in Haiti. But his administration was unpopular among

Haitians themselves. According to Farnham, Leconte's efforts to organize and collect the customs duties were resented. Death threats were made against Leconte and his cabinet, and he was allegedly warned to back off from the collection of customs or risk being thrown out of office. The threats were not empty. On August 8, 1912, less than a year after coming to power, Leconte was killed when an ammunition depot at the presidential palace exploded.[69] The presidential transition happened the same day—Tancrède Auguste was quickly appointed—but a period of economic turbulence soon began. Strife between the government and the BNRH reemerged, with the officials of the City Bank and Hallgarten, along with the US State Department increasingly involved in the fracas. Soon after Leconte's death and Auguste's appointment, the value of the gourde increased from about 5 or 6 to the dollar to between 3.10 and 3.50.[70] The initial issue of 10 million francs set aside to retire the outstanding currency was deemed insufficient. Edmund Lespinasse, the Haitian minister of finance, decided to suspend the execution of the law withdrawing the paper money and passed a new law authorizing a plan for a gradual, three-stage withdrawal of the currency, demanding, at the same time, that the bank release the 10 million franc reserve to accomplish it.[71] However, neither Allen nor the Paris directors were willing to abide by the new law and Lespinasse's demands and refused to divert the 10 million francs from its original purpose.[72] They protested against the law as a violation of the bank and loan contracts and claimed it would not help stabilize the currency.[73] They argued that the new plan would quickly drain the republic's gold supply, leaving Haiti without a gold reserve and with an outstanding 5 million gourdes in circulation whose only backing was the credit of the republic.[74]

Lespinasse was furious at the BNRH's refusal. He wrote of his "astonishment" at its attitude and its suggestion that the BNRH had the right to refuse to employ the money of the republic according to the government's wishes. He argued that there was a matter of law at issue—and one of sovereignty. He asserted that the legal provision of the contract did not usurp the laws of the republic, and argued that once the Haitian government had entered into a contract with the bank for both the loan and the bank charter, the 10 million francs became the property of the government and could thus be disposed of according to its desires. In the *Moniteur*, the official publication of the Haitian government, Lespinasse wrote, "If the arguments of the BNRH were correct or well founded, the Government of Haiti would lose the right of regulating its monetary circulation under conditions which the circumstances impose upon it and in a manner which it would deem best for the well being of the people and the prosperity of the nation."[75] In effect,

Lespinasse charged that the bank and its foreign backers were challenging the sovereignty of the Haitian republic.

In November 1912, Henry W. Furniss, the US minister in Port-au-Prince, described the situation between the Haitian government and the BNRH as "chaotic." The chaos stemmed in part from the problems of management that had plagued the bank prior to its reorganization in 1910. While the distance between Port-au-Prince and Paris had made managing the bank cumbersome, especially as ultimate authority for local decisions remained abroad, the splitting of the committee between Paris and New York compounded the BNRH's problems. John H. Allen in Port-au-Prince had to wait on the Paris directorate to approve decisions concerning the bank's management. At the same time, Allen complained to Furniss that the New York committee was not as involved in the affairs of the BNRH as he would like. He expressed the hope that the New York group would "wake up" and that the head office would be transferred there.[76]

The New York committee, represented in 1912 by Roger L. Farnham, the City Bank's Samuel McRoberts, and Hallgarten's Wehrhane, was inconsistent in its policies and obscurantist in its motives. Farnham had traveled to Port-au-Prince to examine the conditions of the City Bank's investments in Haiti and while there, had conferences with both Leger and Lespinasse. To the surprise of the Haitians, Farnham said he sided with them regarding the law on the withdrawal of the currency and promised that, after conferring with the New York committee, he would try to use his influence to convince the BNRH's Paris directors to accept the Haitian proposals. "Both Secretary Leger and the President were sure that they had not misunderstood Mr. Farnham," noted Furniss, "though they stated that from past experience the Government had not much faith in any statements which he made, but await developments."[77] Farnham told Allen that he disagreed with the Haitian government's position. Allen suggested to Farnham that they comply with the government's demands rather than lose the treasury service and risk being subjected to public embarrassment and humiliation by the Haitian government. He worried about the government threatening the BNRH with the withdrawal of the treasury service and the possibility that they might start "a public agitation against the Bank of such character as will probably hereafter make the bank an unprofitable institution."[78] The directors of the BNRH made a strategic decision to agree to accede to the demands of the Haitian government. They released one-third of the gold reserve to initiate the retirement of the currency and at the same issued a public statement rebuking the minister of finance while distancing themselves from his decision and asserting that his actions were a violation of the contract between the bank and the government. As a condition they also asked that the government appoint commissioners to work out the monetary reform so that it could be presented to the Haitian congress for ratification.[79]

The agitation by the Haitian government against the BNRH began to work. Resentment among the Haitian elite against the bank grew, with the latter often referred to as a "bucket shop," according to Furniss, whose profits came from speculating with government funds.[80] Furniss believed the public's opinions concerning the bank were valid. Indeed, after a February 1913 article in *Le Matin* denounced the bank for causing fluctuations in the rate of exchange and destabilizing Haiti's currency, Furniss wrote a dispatch to Secretary of State William Jennings Bryan affirming *Le Matin*'s claims and providing additional evidence regarding the BNRH's activities. He noted that the seasonal demands for money resulting from the natural cycles of Haiti's agricultural economy were exaggerated by the BNRH, which withdrew gold from circulation when it was in high demand, forcing farmers and merchants to borrow money at exceptionally high interest rates. The cost of borrowing was then passed on to Haitian workers and peasants. Furniss described these operations as "stock-jobber intrigues" whose effect was to "demoralize" the Haitian market.[81]

The BNRH accumulated gourdes for the payment of government salaries when its exchange value against gold had fallen, releasing the funds when its value had increased so as to profit off the difference. It charged interest on funds utilized by the government when the government coffers were bare, reimbursing itself as revenues were collected instead of managing state revenues in a fiscally sound fashion.[82] Furthermore, the BNRH was sending gold to Paris before interest payments on the loan were due, starving the government and the country of working capital that could otherwise be used for commercial and agricultural loans. Meanwhile, the bank charged the Haitian government commissions on the return of this money—after it had already paid commissions for having it sent. In 1911, the BNRH sent upward of $800,000 of gold to Paris for the 1910 loan, a figure far in excess of the requirements of the amortization payments.

Furniss also questioned the role of the US State Department in lending diplomatic support to the BNRH, as the institution was not American. He pointed out that when the 1910 contract of transfer was signed, it was assumed that US capital would predominate, and the bank would become a commercial bank. Yet although John H. Allen, the local manager, was an American, as were a number of the clerks—and the institution had been "outfitted with American furniture"—in reality, the BNRH remained a French entity. It was run by the Paris committee and was French "in sentiment." Furthermore, other than those of the City Bank, the US interests were in the hands of German-American investment banks whose "sentiments and interests are more German than American." Furniss concluded the bank merely continued the operations of the previous institution, though because of the "so-called American capital" now involved in the bank, via Hallgarten and the City Bank, there was now an expectation that the State Department would support its endeavors. "The Bank is of little benefit to Haiti," wrote Furniss in summary.

> It is practically of no benefit to commerce as it does not conduct a loan and discount business as is usually done by banks. When it lends money it is usually to parties doing work for the Government under contract and having a guarantee fixed by law for the work, it being stipulated that the Bank is to collect and disburse the money. On such loans the Bank charges from one to two percent a month on the amount certified by the Government as due the contractor. The Bank makes its profit chiefly by manipulating the money which it collects for the Government. Current government fought the Bank contracts when they were before Congress during the Simon administration as they saw the result. They now desire to bring about some change whereby the Bank will be run in the interest of Haiti and the contract conditions will not be so onerous.[83]

"The Haitian Government has some well-founded grounds for complaint," Furniss concluded.

Furniss's dispatch was passed on to New York and the bank's officers for comment. The City Bank's Samuel McRoberts, a director of the BNRH, wrote a terse note in response. McRoberts sent it to Milton Ailes, Vanderlip's man in Washington, who gave it to the secretary of state. "The bank is now engaged in a commercial business as well as a government business," wrote McRoberts. "So it is claimed that our Minister has not taken pains to inform himself."[84]

The relationship between the BNRH and the Haitian government deteriorated further in the fall of 1914 as political conditions in the country worsened. President Tancrède Auguste had died in office on May 2, 1913, of a rumored poisoning, and Michel Oreste assumed power. Oreste's reign was a short one, notable, according to Farnham, for its unprecedented levels of graft and marked by a new inflationary period that pushed the price of staples beyond the reach of the Haitian peasant. By early 1914, discontent with the Oreste administration led to insurrections throughout Haiti and a contest for control of the country between Oreste Zamor, who had returned from exile in Jamaica and was gathering support in the towns around Port-au-Prince, and General Joseph Davilmar Théodore, whose power base was in Cap-Haïtien in the north.[85] For the City Bank, with its interests and investments in the Caribbean Construction Company, the railroads, and the BNRH—and, through the BNRH, the foreign debt of the republic—the insurrection proved a costly interruption of business. Customs collection slowed as rebels seized customs houses, evicted government officials, and appropriated customs duties for their own uses. Railway lines were shut down, train service was disrupted, and construction was suspended.[86] Officials of the National Railroad requested protection from the United States for their life and property, while Allen and other officials of the BNRH protested the seizure of duties to the Haitian government and to the insurrection committee, as well as to the French and US governments, demanding protection of Haiti's creditors. On the verge of collapse and suffocating because of a lack of funds, the Oreste government pledged to use postage and internal revenue stamps—its last remaining asset—to meet the February interest due on the railroad bonds, but the BNRH refused to make the loan as it awaited the outcome of the revolt.[87] Only in Port-au-Prince (where the City Bank had a monopoly on commerce entering and exiting the country through its control of the wharf) were duties from customs being collected. Other ports had paid nothing since January 24, and John H. Allen was drawing up plans to present claims against the government for damages due to lost commissions.[88] By the beginning of Febuary, agents for the BNRH at Saint-Marc requested US gunboats for their protection as Gonaïves burned and Aux Cayes was under siege and many of the towns in Haiti's north were falling into the hands of the insurrectionists.[89]

Oreste was ousted from power by the second week of February, and Oreste Zamor claimed a fragile hold on the Haitian state. Zamor's power was dependent in part on the success or failure of Théodore, who still controlled much of the north, including the customs houses in Cap-Haïtien, and in part on the willingness of the BNRH to lend financial support to his government. The BNRH refused Zamor's requests for funds, placing him in a fiscally precarious position. State funds were dwindling, and the remaining amounts in the reserve were going toward interest charges on the railway.[90] For many Haitians the bank's intransigence stoked a bout of anti-Americanism.[91] There was a sense that the United States was responsible for the government's precarious situation and the political foment roiling the country. John H. Allen described the Zamor government's relation to the bank as "vicious" and claimed that the bank and its staff were under potential threat. "Reports have reached me that the President is so enraged at the Bank's net advancing funds," Allen wrote Farnham, "that not only is my life in danger, but also the lives of other of the foreign employees. Zamor is not of the same class as Leger or Lespinasse or Leconte, but is ignorant and, according to reports, depraved. Is said to be an inebriate and uncontrollable when intoxicated and capable of taking any steps which he believes would result in his obtaining funds. I write you this, not that I am at all alarmed, but may have a better idea of the situation and the class of people with whom we have to deal. The city is full of semi-savages brought here by Zamor as soliders, and life is held here cheaply."[92]

As the political crisis in Haiti deepened, the intimacy between the City Bank and the State Department in involvement in Haiti's affairs increased. Roger Farnham and often his counterpart Henry H. Wehrhane of Hallgarten became the conduit for dispatches from John H. Allen, Henri Desrue, and others for the bank in Port-au-Prince and its branches and agencies in Cap-Haïtien, Saint-Marc, and other cities. Their dispatches often contained more detail on Haitian conditions than those of the US legation. Out of this intimacy, a diplomatic plan for Haiti that drew from the opinions and observations of Farnham and Allen slowly congealed within the State Department. Following the stream of dispatches from Allen via Farnham, Bryan eventually solicited Farnham's thoughts for a long-term solution to the unsettled political and economic conditions in Haiti. Farnham offered Bryan a plan whose ultimate solution was military intervention. But the logic of such a solution was based on ideas of Haitian racial backwardness and civilizational underdevelopment and borrowed from the convention imposed on the Dominican Republic almost a decade prior. Following a telephone conversation with Bryan on the morning of January 22, 1914, Farnham drafted and sent to him a memorandum that outlined the history of Haiti's domestic political strife and proposed a plan for intervention and customs control. Farnham argued that the republic's economic development was hampered by "the almost continuous revolutionary disturbances which are imposed upon the country by a relatively small number of political aspirants." Those aspirants, Farnham continued, tempted their followers with promises of "big pay and the gain of loot" in exchange for support in overthrowing the current government. Often, these movements were funded by foreign merchants, who were rewarded with funds from the Haitian treasury or, if it was empty, "as is sometimes the case," the granting of privileges on coffee, cocoa, and cotton exports if the revolution was successful.[93]

Farnham asserted that the majority of Haitians had little interest in these revolutionary movements, and claimed that military intervention would be a welcome prospect for most Haitians—especially once they realized it would not do anything to degrade their current conditions. Conditions in Haiti, Farnham continued, would remain undisturbed "until such time as some stronger outside power steps in."[94] Farnham concluded that there were few good men in the country and that few would be willing to take on the mantle of political power without a promise of foreign support, especially if faced with an internal threat of revolution. Farnham reiterated his views to Bryan in a later conversation. He argued that any man who came to power in Haiti would welcome "the friendly suggestions" of Wilson and Bryan, especially if it meant it would help that ruler control the country. A new ruler, Farnham claimed, would be willing to allow the United States "to direct the affairs of Government for a year or two without interruption and without being compelled to combat revolutions inspired by those who desire to get control of the country's finances." For Farnham, such a situation "would put the entire country of Haiti and the people as well, in a condition such as has not prevailed since the establishment of the Haitian republic."[95] Farnham's opinions were bolstered by a State Department memo in which Haiti's internal political conflict was seen as an opportunity to capitalize and fulfill many of the US government's long-standing desires with regard to Haiti: the establishment of a coaling station at Môle-Saint-Nicolas, the signing of a protocol designed to settle the outstanding financial claims of US citizens against the Haitian government, and a revision of article 4 of the Haitian constitution barring non-Haitians from owning property in Haiti—a clause that was viewed by US businesspeople as an impediment to investment.[96]

By March 1914, with interest payments on the City Bank's loan for the Central Railroad unpaid, Frank A. Vanderlip's initial optimism concerning Haiti began to take on a measure of ruefulness and despair. "I shall be glad to see the whole Haitian situation cleaned up in some shape," he wrote to Jacobs, "which I trust will be done in due course."[97] Vanderlip's desire slowly found form. On April 8, 1914, John H. Allen requested that the State Department maintain vessels at Port-au-Prince as a warning sign to potential insurrectionists.[98] By the summer, with Farnham and representatives of W. R. Grace and the Caribbean Construction Company visiting Haiti to inspect their properties, Bryan began setting Farnham's plan in motion.[99] He instructed the secretary of the navy to maintain a force of marines close at hand, ready to land to protect US interests, and he cabled Lemuel W. Livingston, the American consul in Cap-Haïtien, that the State Department "earnestly desires successful carrying out" of Farnham's "plan for permanent solution of political and financial unrest" in Haiti. By the end of the month, Bryan requested a statement on the Farnham plan's status and sent a draft of a proposed convention between the United States and Haiti, along with a copy of the Dominican Convention of February 8, 1907, to Arthur Bailly-Blanchard, who had replaced Furniss as the US minister at Port-au-Prince. It differed little from the Dominican Convention, though the new draft included a provision giving the president of the United States the authority to appoint a financial adviser to Haiti to organize its finances.[100] Bailly-Blanchard was instructed to visit President Zamor, accompanied by US Marine Captain John H. Russell, to sound out the government on its amenability to signing the convention.[101] According to Bailly-Blanchard, Zamor was not against the plan but, as with prior administrations, requested that the convention be put in front of the Haitian congress for approval.[102] The State Department's attempts to impose the Farnham plan on Haiti were thwarted. But within the week, the onset of war in Europe pushed the United States and the City Bank closer to their goals in Haiti.

In 1914, as Europe was engulfed in war, John H. Allen, the BNRH manager who had been with the bank in Haiti since 1911 and who had served as a point man for both the bank and the US State Department, was tapped by Frank Vanderlip to establish a new Buenos Aires branch. In the absence of Allen, the French banker Henri Desrue was promoted to manager. He was joined by a new hire, William H. Williams, a Wales-born banker who had lived in the United States since he was eleven years old and had previously worked for Irving National Bank.[103] Meanwhile, the conflict between the BNRH and the Haitian government continued. By August the BNRH was refusing the government's requests for additional monies, and the government in turn pondered a potential issue of paper money as a means of continuing its operations and meeting its obligations. The USS Hancock was deployed to the region in anticipation of further problems.[104] By September, the Haitian government had defaulted on interest payments to the Haitian National Railroad, forcing the line to suspend operations. Railroad officials demanded an indemnity from the government for losses and damages caused by its "hostile attitude."[105] At the end of the first week of November, the Zamor government was overthrown in a coup led by Joseph Davilmar Théodore.[106] His seizure of power precipitated one of the most controversial events during the lead-up to the US military intervention, bringing the conflict of finance capital and sovereignty to a head.

On December 8, 1914, Henry H. Wehrhane sent a note to Bryan stating that it was "very urgent" that the BNRH transfer $110,000 in gold from its vaults in Port-au-Prince to the Hallgarten offices in New York via US naval vessel.[107] Wehrhane and the committee apparently believed that political conditions in Haiti threatened the BNRH's gold reserve, and feared its "theft" by the government. Years later, Farnham claimed that the idea of removing the gold had originated with Bryan, who requested that Farnham and Wehrhane come to Washington to discuss a plan of removal, perhaps to Jamaica.[108] The Paris committee's Maurice Casenave wrote in a memorandum that the bank decided it would be prudent to keep only a minimal reserve in Port-au-Prince, enough to carry on business, and to send the rest to New York for safekeeping during the war.[109] Two days later, Farnham telephoned Bryan, reiterating Wehrhane's instruction and telling Bryan to increase the amount of gold to be shipped to $400,000.[110] The secretary of the navy requested that the USS *Machias* proceed to Port-au-Prince to receive the gold, and the USS *Hancock* was instructed to "land as many marines as necessary to furnish safe escort for gold from bank to *Machias*."[111] In the meantime, with the telegraph cables between the United States and Haiti severed, the Latin American Division of the State Department became the intermediary between the New York committee of the BNRH and its Port-au-Prince managers, with Bryan as a messenger, communicating instructions from Farnham and Wehrhane to Allen and others and vice versa.[112]

Desrue relayed a message that the BNRH could prepare the gold for shipment but worried that its removal could upset the Haitian government.[113] He advised Wehrhane against sending the gold at all, assuring him that it was safe in the bank's vaults. "If you have decided this measure through fear of pillage of the bank," he wrote to Wehrhane, "we consider the gold sufficiently safe in our vaults owing to the presence of American warship." Both Desrue and Bailly-Blanchard also believed that the Haitian government was willing to work with the BNRH regarding the state budget and the status of the disputed funds allocated for monetary reform. They also thought the goverment was more than willing to negotiate a protocol with the United States so long as the protocol did not concern the control of Haiti's customs.[114] The only opposition to a US-Haiti convention came from Rosalvo Bobo, minister of the interior, who published an anti-imperialist tract in defense of Haiti's sovereignty in a Port-au-Prince journal.[115] Bailly-Blanchard reiterated Desrue's point to Bryan. "I respectfully submit that the gold is perfectly safe in the Bank of Haiti while a warship is in the harbor," wrote Bailly-Blanchard. "Its transfer to the *Machias*, whether by means of agents from the Bank or men from the warship will probably bring about serious complications which it seems advisable to avoid at this time in view of possible feeling of the Haitian Government."[116] The captain of the USS

Hancock also doubted the nature of the threat. "Personally I do not believe there is any danger of the Haitians openly attacking or seriously molesting our marines, whether they are armed or unarmed," he wrote. But he added a caveat: "However, as the Haitians are naturally treacherous, it is well not to take chances."[117]

Blanchard's protest, alongside Desrue's caution, was forwarded to Farnham. Farnham forwarded the protest to Wehrhane. The response was swift. "You must carry out our instructions to ship gold on the *Machias* immediately," Wehrhane wrote in a cable to Desrue delivered to the BNRH via the American legation. "These are absolute instructions of both Paris and New York boards and must be obeyed."[118]

On December 16, the *USS Machias* and *USS Marietta* sailed from the Dominican Republic to Port-au-Prince where they joined the *USS Brutus*, which had arrived from Cap-Haïtien, and the *USS Hancock*. The officers of the vessels called on the US legation. With the staff of the BNRH, they worked out a plan to remove the gold from the bank's vault. The following day, they put the plan into action. The staff of the BNRH loaded the half million dollars of gold into seventeen wooden boxes—fifteen boxes containing $30,000 each, and two with $25,000 each. At one o'clock—a time decided on because it was believed that most Haitians would be eating their lunch or taking their "siesta," thus ensuring the streets of Port-au-Prince would be almost empty—eight US Marines, armed with canes and revolvers, landed from the ships, crossed the Place Geffard, and entered the bank. They loaded the gold onto a wagon, and rode with it back to the wharf, all the while watched by additional marines, also in civilian clothing, posted at regular intervals between the wharf and the BNRH. A forty-foot motorboat waited at the wharf at the launch. It was outfitted with a cargo net and buoys and protected by an additional twenty-five marines armed with rifles. Both the *Machias* and the *Wheeling* stood ready, each with a company of marines prepared to go ashore at a moment's danger, while watching the movements of the *Pacifique*, a Haitian gunboat. The marines quickly passed the boxes from the wagon to the motorboat, which then sped through the harbor to the *Machias*. The operation went quickly and smoothly. In less than half an hour, the $500,000 in gold was on board the *Machias*. At two o'clock, the *Machias* sailed for New York. At five, the *Hancock* sailed for Philadelphia and the *Brutus* for Key West. The *Wheeling* remained in Port-au-Prince.[119] Two days later, the *Machias* arrived at the Navy Yard in New York City, where the gold was then transported under armed guard to the vaults of Hallgarten & Co.[120]

The reaction to the removal of the gold was as Bailly-Blanchard predicted. The news quickly spread throughout Port-au-Prince and was greeted with shock and disbelief. Editorials in *Le Nouvelliste* and *Le Matin* immediately speculated over the nature of the incident and its infringement of the sovereignty of the Haitian nation.[121] The Haitian government sent commissioners to the bank to ascertain whether the bank funds were still available. The clerks of the BNRH refused to open the vaults, as ordered by their superiors in New York. Desrue was accused of embezzlement and threatened with imprisonment. He wrote a desperate letter to Wehrhane asking for protection, while the State Department instructed Blanchard to request protection from the Haitian government for the BNRH's employees.[122] The government then began legal proceedings against the bank, initiating a back-and-forth that would continue over the next few months as government officials attempted to both verify the amount remaining in the BNRH's vaults and appropriate portions of it to maintain the functioning of the state. Ministers were called before the Haitian Chamber of Deputies to explain the situation while Solon Ménos, the minister of foreign affairs, sent a formal protest to the US State Department.

In his protest, Ménos pointed out that the fund was property of the Haitian state, not the bank, and could not leave the treasury without consent of the government. Ménos argued that the "good faith of the Deparment of State has been abused," and he sought an explanation. He outlined the history of the BNRH and argued that the bank had "violated its engagements." Ménos declared that the Haitian government "deeply deplores an arbitrary and offensive intervention which carries a flagrant invasion of the sovereignty and independence of the Republic of Haiti," and requested that the State Department "disown" the actions of the bank and order restitution to the Haitian government.[123]

Bryan's response to Ménos was condescending and dismissive. He asserted the BNRH was a private bank, and the gold in question belonged to it with the specific purpose of retiring the paper currency under the 1910 loan agreement. He also claimed that various revolutionary governments had tried to seize the gold for their own purposes, making its status "precarious" and prompting the directors to remove it to a place where it was not only safe, but might draw interest "pending the retirement of the Haitian currency." He further claimed that the *Machias* was deployed only because no other means of transportation was available and that armed US Marines were landed because "American interests" were "gravely menaced." "It is hardly necessary to state that if it had happened that the gold had been taken from the bank by revolutionary authorities, or by irresponsible rioters, the bank, through its negligence to place the gold in safety, might have become liable later on to some duly established government of Haiti for any losses of the specie in its safe keeping," wrote Bryan. Pointing out that $400,000 remained in the bank, he described the entire incident as

> merely a withdrawal of funds by the authorities of a private bank in Port-au-Prince from the [location] of Haiti as a measure of precaution for their security and the placing of such funds on board a gunboat to the United States in the absence of other craft for the transportation to a place of safety. The Department is at a loss to perceive, therefore, how such circumstances constitute "an arbitrary and offensive intervention which carries a flagrant invasion of the sovereignty and independence of the Republic of Haiti," which you call upon this Government "to disown" and "to order such restitutions and amends as may be necessary." Furthermore, it is not clear to the Department upon what practical ground your government bases its objection to the withdrawal of the five hundred thousand dollars; for if it is the desire of your Government to have the retirement of the currency resumed, there are, so the department is advised, now on deposit at Port-au-Prince four hundred thousand dollars ready for that purpose; or, on the other hand, if your government has no intention of continuing the retirement at the present time, the placement of a portion of the funds in a position to draw interest during the period of suspension would seem to be a wise measure.[124]

Ménos was baffled. He was "surprised and pained" that the United States would interfere in Haiti's internal affairs, and pointed out that the BNRH was a French corporation headquartered in Paris, charged with the treasury service of the Haitian state, and bequeathed the rights of Haitian citizenship.[125] Based on these facts, the United States had no right to intervene. This question of the citizenship of the bank was highlighted by the resignation of Henri Desrue because of sickness and his replacement by William H. Williams in early February 1915. The Haitian government was notified via the US legation of the resignation and appointment; according to the contract of the bank, notification should have come from France, and the appointment should have been approved by the Haitian government. It compounded a diplomatic crisis between the United States and Haiti that was already spiraling out of control. Ménos had resigned his post in the government by the time of Williams's appointment, but his replacement, Louis Borno, refused to accept the new manager and wrote a scathing protest to the US State Department.[126]

The crisis continued through the spring as the Haitian government attempted to remove the treasury service from the BNRH, in violation, according to Williams and Wehrhane, of the bank contract and concession, while claiming the disputed funds and issuing currency against treasury bills. Williams attempted to seal the vaults of the bank in order to prevent the removal of currency, and the BNRH executives complained to the State Department, which then issued formal complaints through the US legation. By April, the Paris committee of the BNRH sent a special delegate to break the stalemate with the Haitian government; however, by then, the New York committee and the State Department had begun drafting a plan of their own.

———

"The time to act is now," US president Woodrow Wilson wrote to Bryan on April 5, 1915.[127] Days before, Bryan had conferred with Robert Lansing on the "Haitien [sic] situation" and then solicited the president's opinion. For Bryan, the situation had become an "embarrassment."[128] He felt that Bailly-Blanchard was not doing his job, and that the current Haitian president seemed amenable to signing a convention with the United States, whose terms included the US control of Môle-Saint-Nicolas. Furthermore, he was frustrated with the state of the BNRH. The French still controlled 50 percent of its stock, while the rest was split evenly between US and German interests. While the US bankers wanted to remain in Haiti, they wanted to do so on condition of not only the protection of their interests in the bank and their other investments, but the control of Haiti's customs receivership. Bryan stated that he was unwilling to use force, but he thought other methods—such as the Dutch model of fiscal control in Java or the US control of the Dominican Republic—were possibilities. Wilson agreed. He believed the United States should be assertive in its Haiti policy, assuming control of both the long-desired Môle-Saint-Nicolas and the finances of the country.[129] Bryan quickly summoned Wehrhane and Farnham to Washington to discuss the matter and the possibilities of the "Americanization" of the BNRH, and, as Farnham later put it, "[the elimination], as far as possible, [of] European influences in the island."[130]

Yet as they attempted to work out an agreement, they realized that they were hampered by legal questions. They could not easily transform the BNRH from a French to a US institution because of the exceptional nature of the contract between the Haitian government and the BUP. The Haitian government would consider the transfer illegal, as there was no provision of transfer or secession of rights within the original contract. At the same time, French law prevented the contract from being transferred to a third party without consent from three-quarters of the shareholders. Given the conflict in Europe—and the different nationalities of the shareholders—it was unlikely that a meeting could be held to stage a vote. As a solution, they determined that they could create a US holding company to acquire a majority of the shares in the BNRH once the war was over. With control of the BNRH, they would have absolute authority over the "receipt and disbursement of government revenue," and "would be able to coooperate with the US government in some plan for the reorganization of the finances of Haiti which would include the collection and management of the customs." According to Wehrhane, the government of Haiti had indicated its willingness to work out a supervisiory relationship over control of customs collection. However, he also echoed Farnham's memos to Bryan a year prior and stressed that the arrangement would only work if an outside power protected the bank. "Such an arrangement however if unsupported by some power outside of Haiti could not be maintained against the inevitable attacks from revolutionary bodies desiring to lay hands on the customs houses and income of the Government," he wrote.[131]

Events in Port-au-Prince expedited the State Department's goals for Haiti and for control of the BNRH. The night of July 27, 1915, the BNRH's William H. Williams was startled from his sleep at the Hotel Montaigne. Williams quickly dressed and, joined by the newly appointed American chargé d'affaires, Robert Beale Davis, Jr., went downtown in the direction of the bank as the sound of musket fire and machine guns echoed off the buildings.[132] As dawn broke over the city, they learned that Haitian president Vilbrun Guillaume Sam, whom the United States thought would be amenable to an agreement, had arrested and imprisoned 175 of his political opponents. As talk of a revolt against Sam grew, he ordered the massacre of the prisoners. Crowds filled the streets of Port-au-Prince and descended on the prison to account for their relatives. Fearing his life, Sam sought refuge in the French legation, only for his opponents to drag him into the street, killing him. Amid the upheaval, Davis made his way to the US legation, telegraphed William Caperton, captain of the *USS Washington*, stationed at Cap-Haïtien. The *Washington* quickly sailed to Port-au-Prince, where Caperton disembarked with 500 men, placing soldiers at the BNRH and other locations. The US military occupation of Haiti had begun.

The US occupation of Haiti was brutal in its administration. Haiti's political classes were muzzled, and its assembly was deprived of power. Elections were staged, and a puppet president in the figure of Louis Borno, previously a critic of the politices of the BNRH, was installed. Martial law reigned, and the press was censored. For the Haitian elite, the experience was a humiliating one. Not only were they unceremoniously dethroned from their positions of political power, but the codes and cultures of white US racism demoted them to the status of the black peasant. While at the beginning of the occupation there was a brief insurgency led by peasant insurrectionists, known as Cacos, lasting from July to November 1915, it was quickly crushed.[133] To neutralize the potential threat of future insurrections, US Marines methodically fanned into the countryside destroying villages in a slash-and-burn campaign and arresting or assassinating suspected Cacos. A police state overseen by US Marines was established; rule of law was enforced by a militia force, the Garde d'Haiti, whose lower officers were recruited from the Haitian populace. In 1917, work began on a 170-mile highway connecting Port-au-Prince via Bathon, Gonaïves, Ennery, and Saint-Marc to Cap-Haïtien, and then from Port-au-Prince toward the Dominican border to Hinche. This road-building project had two aims. It was initiated as an attempt to develop a communication and transportation infrastructure that would link the outlying regions of the country to the coastal cities and, following this, open up the country's potential wealth in coal, sugarcane, bananas, and cotton to international markets.[134] The United States also saw the road project as a means of promoting stability and maintaining military control through the surveillance and containment of the Cacos. US officials recognized the isolated regions of the country, especially near the Dominican border, were a major contributor to the historical problem of insurrection. They correctly linked the geographic diffusion of the Maroons of the revolutionary era to the spread of the Caco revolts of the early twentieth century.[135]

Through the activation of the 1864 Haitian corvée law the US Marines found the necessary labor for the road project. According to the corvée, peasants were required to work on local roads in lieu of paying road taxes. ("They had the option," quipped General Smedley D. Butler, the US Marine in command of the project, but "nobody had any money, so they reported for work.") Those who refused to work or who tried to escape were tortured, jailed, or executed.[136] For many Haitians, the corvée appeared to be "a return to racial slavery,"[137] while for the US Marines, it was an extension of the chain gangs of the US South. It sparked another revolt against the United States, led by Charlemagne Péralte, a former schoolteacher who had been conscripted into the road-building project. After his escape from the chain gang, Péralte set up a provisional government in Hinche and planned to seize the town of Grande Riviere. Péralte was betrayed by a Haitian within his camp and assassinated by US Marines the night of October 31, 1919. After Péralte's death, Benoît Batraville took up the leadership of the rebellion and tried to seize the capital. Several hundred Cacos were slaughtered in the attempt, and Batraville, too, was betrayed. He was killed on May 20, 1920. "His death, it is believed, assures complete pacification," a US Navy report concluded.[138] In all, some 3,000 Haitians were killed in the first five years of occupation as hunting Cacos and torturing peasants became a "sport" for the marines.

When the Haitian lawyer and intellectual Dantès Bellegarde, who was then working for the BNRH, traveled to New York in August 1916 as part of a delegation to clean up relations between the bank and its New York authorities, he met with both Roger Farnham and Maurice Casenave of the Banque Française pour le Commerce et l'Industrie Paris. They asked him to assess the results of the US intervention. "L'intervention américaine en Haïti," Bellegarde stated, "est une faillite." ("The US intervention in Haiti is a failure.") Farnham's reply was cool: "Je ne suis pas d'accord avec vous." ("I do not agree with you".)[139] Indeed, for the City Bank, the US occupation of Haiti was good business. While Haiti's sovereignty was extinguished, the treaty forced on Haiti by the occupation authorities meant the regularization of customs collections—and hence regularization of interest payments on both the PCS Railroad and the floating debt—by a US-nominated, Haitian-appointed receiver.[140] John H. Allen believed that if the occupation was to become permanent, the City Bank should acquire the entire stock of the BNRH. He saw the rich possibility of the BNRH, arguing that if it were properly managed, it would "pay 20% or better."[141] Allen used the opportunity of the occupation to extend the City Bank's control of Haitian commerce. He pushed the US financial adviser to rewrite the BNRH's contract to include a clause giving the bank a monopoly on the import and export of currency. The rewriting generated a spate of protests from within Port-au-Prince's banking and business community, led by the Royal Bank of Canada. The Royal Bank had also tried to take advantage of the occupation, opening a branch in Port-au-Prince in 1919 and hoping to challenge the supremacy of the City Bank–controlled gourde and break the bank's monopoly on commercial transactions (fig. 3.1). The Royal Bank hired Louis Borno, former finance minister (and, later, from 1922 to 1930, nominal president of the occupied republic, despite Americans having derided his "anti-Americanism"), as its representative and protested, with the American Foreign Banking Corporation, an institution largely controlled by the Chase Manhattan Bank, and other local and foreign financial institutions, against the monopoly, complaining that the new clause would prevent them from doing business. Their protests were unsuccessful. The financial adviser was forced to rescind the change.[142]

The following spring, articles in the City Bank's The Americas lauded the new regime and the new era in Haiti.[143] At the same time the City Bank bought out the remaining German interests in the BRNH after they were seized by the French government.[144] The bank used its stock-holding affiliate,

3.1. Haiti, Banque Nationale de la République, 1 gourde (1916). Engraved by the American Bank Note Company. Depicting Jean-Jacques Dessalines with signature of Roger L. Farnham. National Numismatic Collection, National Museum of American History at the Smithsonian Institution/Wikipedia.

the National City Company, as the vehicle for the purchase.[145] The following year, the City Bank purchased the shares of Hallgarten, Speyer, and Ladenburg Thalmann.[146] While the French remained the majority stockholders in the bank, control of its everyday operations was slowly shifting to the United States.

During the first five years of the US occupation of Haiti, the City Bank was seen in the United States as an important presence, stabilizing and rehabilitating the finances of a backward, chronically revolutionary country that was ill prepared for self-government. But in 1920 perceptions of the occupation began to change. That fall, *The Nation* published a four-part series titled "Self-Determining Haiti," written by James Weldon Johnson, the field secretary of the National Association for the Advancement of Colored People.

Johnson had traveled to Haiti in the spring to investigate the conditions of the occupation. His assessment was searing. His articles presented a damning history of the occupation that placed the City Bank at its center.[147] "To know the reasons for the present political situation in Haiti," Johnson wrote in the introduction to the series,

> to understand why the United States landed and has for five years maintained military forces in that country, why some three thousand Haitian men, women, and children have been shot down by American rifles and machine guns, it is necessary, among other things, to know that the National City Bank of New York is very much interested in Haiti. It is necessary to know that the National City Bank controls the National Bank of Haiti and is the depository for all of the Haitian national funds that are being collected by American officials, and that Mr. R. L. Farnham, vice-president of the National City Bank, is virtually the representative of the State Department in matters relating to the island republic.[148]

The occupation, Johnson asserted, was "of, by, and for the National City Bank of New York." He argued that the City Bank exercised a force in Haiti that, "because of its deep and varied radications," was "more powerful though less obvious, and more sinister," than the State Department or the US Marines. The City Bank, he claimed, was "constantly working to bring about a condition more suitable and profitable for itself" through its attempts to install a financial adviser and a receiver general who dictated how government revenue was collected and disbursed, by monopolizing access to credit and the importation of specie, by pushing a $30 million loan on the country, and by consolidating control of the BNRH. The City Bank, according to Johnson, tried to effect "a strangle hold on the financial life" of Haiti. Behind this control, and, ultimately, behind the US occupation, was the figure of Roger Farnham. As the point person for both the bank and the State Department in Haitian affairs, Farnham "was effectively instrumental in bringing about American intervention."[149] Johnson's articles, along with others, shocked the US public, a majority of whom had believed in the benevolence of the occupation, and prompted a number of investigations. An internal investigation by the US Marine Corps responded to allegations of marine atrocities by concluding that the marines had acted in a moral manner and that their presence was entirely beneficial to the Haitian people.[150] A congressional investigation was launched the following year, and its conclusions were much the same.

Roger Farnham testified during the congressional hearings on Tuesday, October 4, 1921. He was asked to recount the history of the City Bank's involvement in Haiti and to offer an assessment of the success or failure of the US occupation to date. Farnham lauded the work of the US Marines, praising their road-building efforts, including their use of Haitian conscript labor. Farnham was critical of the US government in Haiti. He suggested that it had gone into Haiti without a definite policy and because of this all parties—the marines, the State Department, the financial adviser, and the Haitians themselves—worked blindly.

Farnham's testimony was also striking for its analysis of the Haitian people. His comments offer a window into the City Bank's ideas and beliefs concerning blacks, its perceptions of racial and cultural difference, its vision of white rule and self-government, and its understanding of racial capitalism in the Caribbean. Farnham's analysis was shaped by a paternalistic view of Haitians and a naturalized sense of Haitian inferiority. He doubted their capacity for self-government and believed in the necessity of white intervention to guide and guarantee Haitian development. In light of these beliefs, Farnham's signature as the authorizing symbol on the Haitian gourde is significant, inscribing paternalism, racism, and ideas about political economy on the currency itself.

Farnham was suspicious of the Haitian elite; his comments echoed those of Samuel Jarvis on the Cuban elite and of the IBC's James Morris Morgan on the Panamanian elite. "They have lived abroad and have acquired the polish of the European," he commented; "they are very well read in literature; they are pretty good diplomats, very cunning, and a considerable number of them are absolutely untrustworthy; I mean they do not stick to what they agree to." Of the Haitian peasant, Farnham mused as to their physicality, their strength, and their ability to perform manual labor. He stated that he had witnessed Haitians cutting sugarcane on Cuban plantations and saw that they did not have the muscular strength or energy of "Gallegos" (Galician laborers), "Jamaican Negroes," or an "Irish track hand." Haitian men, Farnham asserted, were "rather light and small, underfed," "lacking in stamina," and unable to "stand up under hard work." Haitian women, on the other hand, were "on the whole . . . actually stronger," "strong, big, husky," and able to "walk as fast as a good horse will walk."[151]

If for Farnham the underlying ideology of the occupation was based on paternalism, its higher purposes were pedagogical. Disipline and force were needed; so too was education. "I think that the Haitian can be taught to become a good and efficient laborer," Farnham stated. "If let alone by the military chiefs, he is as peaceful as a child, and as harmless. In fact, today they are nothing but grown-up children, ignorant of all agricultural methods, and they know nothing of machinery. They must be taught."[152]

Such statements were not unique to Farnham. John H. Allen, the former manager of the BNRH in Port-au-Prince who had been promoted by Vanderlip to run the City Bank's foreign division, echoed Farnham's comments. Writing in *The Americas*, Allen attempted to dispel the persistent popular racist perceptions of Haiti, arguing, "the stories occasionally heard of recent-year cannibalism and of infant sacrifices are not founded on fact, nor are the stories of attacks upon foreigners."[153] But he too, believed that the Haitian people "must be taught" and would benefit from the paternalistic hand of white men governing their affairs. "Haiti's dark millions can be a decided menace to the United States," Allen wrote, "but under wise and thoughtful guidance can be developed into a self-respecting and dignified nation that could perhaps help in the solution of one of the greatest problems before us today, namely, the future of the colored race." Allen asserted that without the tutelage of white rule Haiti would continue along the path of degeneration that had seen the country return to a primitive state of nature in the absence of slavery.[154]

For Allen, the backwardness of Haiti was based in the racial difference between black and white, but it was exacerbated by the absence of white power over black people. Haiti, according to Allen, had degenerated after the 1804 revolution and the birth of Haitian sovereignty. Allen marveled at the traces of the French colonial society found throughout Haiti, and the ruins of a once thriving civilization hidden in the Haitian bush. "In the old French colonial days, Haiti must have been a garden," Allen wrote. "Records tell of, and ruins show, irrigation work, drainage, boulevards, and other developments, all of which has been allowed to fall into decay, and one cannot help but think what a waste the past hundred or more years have been for that country."[155] For Allen, Haiti's development had been marred by black sovereignty and, as another City Banker put it, "a century of negro rule by emperors, kings, and presidents."[156] Like Farnham, Allen argued that all Haiti needed to regain its former grandeur was white tutelage. "Scarcely any plantations or orchards exist today—all is grown wild," Allen wrote of Haiti. Haiti was, in his words, "truly a virgin territory ready for the white man's guiding mind to help it to get back to the conditions existing when, as history tell us, Haiti was the richest of all of the colonies of France."[157] Allen and Farnham saw the City Bank guiding Haiti's return to history.

Beyond Farnham's testimony, the City Bank made no official statement on the US occupation of Haiti until 1922. In its May *Monthly Letter*, the bank reprinted an excerpt of an essay on the US interventions in Haiti and the Dominican Republic by sociologist Carl Kelsey. It prefaced the excerpt with a note that read:

> The subject [of Haiti] has been in the public prints in a more or less sensational way for several years, and this Bank has figured to some extent, as owner of the Bank of Haiti. The Bank has been much misrepresented, but inasmuch as the charges against it were incidental to charges against the United States Government, as the latter was in possession of full information about the Bank's operations in both countries, we thought it best that statements to the public should come from the authorities at Washington. The article . . . however, is of such an authoritative character that we are moved to give in full that part which relates to the banking situation in Haiti.[158]

Where James Weldon Johnson claimed that the City Bank was responsible for the US occupation, Kelsey asserted the bank was a mere victim of opinion. "Every community has its scapegoat on which the collective sins may be laid and which everyone is at liberty to curse," wrote Kelsey. For Kelsey, the scapegoat was the City Bank. Beyond the bad publicity, the articles in *The Nation* did nothing to change the City Bank's policy in Haiti, and the investigations did little to change US policy. Johnson later lamented that the investigation was "a whitewash."[159] The subsequent report dismissed the testimony of native witnesses, ignored Johnson's charges against the City Bank, and exonerated the marines, while concluding that if the United States withdrew, Haiti would return to "chronic revolution, anarchy, barbarism, and ruin."[160] However, Johnson's efforts spurred the organization of Union Patriotique d'Haiti, a nationalist organization made up of Haiti's elites, who, through the 1920s, protested the occupation through the press and diplomatic channels.[161]

At the same time, under the treaty signed by the United States and Haiti, Haiti's internal and external debts were consolidated, and provision was made to retire the debts through the flotation of a $40 million loan. The conditions of the bond market made it impossible to find buyers for the bonds. However, because of the depreciation of the franc, the Haitian government was able to reduce its outstanding debt, and in 1922 it was decided to issue the bonds in two series: an external series, Series A, amounting to $16 million, and Series B, an internal loan of $5 million. The Series A bonds were taken up by the National City Company and the National City Bank's securities affiliate at 92.137, leaving the Haitian government $14,741,920.

The bonds were sold by the National City Company to the public at 96½. The Series B bonds were marketed internally and not offered outside the republic.[162]

On August 17, 1922, the BNRH had begun operating under a new charter, and its management and supervision were moved from Paris to 55 Wall Street.[163] The City Bank's acquisition and control of the BNRH was complete. "Bank of Haiti Is Ours!" read the title of the cover story of the November 1922 issue of *No. 8*, the City Bank employee journal. The BNRH joined a growing group of City Bank subsidiaries organized as part of Vanderlip's project of modernization and managerial reform. These subsidiaries, what the City Bank referred to as its "allied financial institutions," made up the City Bank "family."[164] They included the National City Company, the National City Realty Corporation, and the National City Safe Deposit Company, the International Banking Corporation, the long-coveted foreign banking firm purchased by the bank in 1915, and an international branch network that was among the largest in the world.[165] The control of the BNRH and the finances of Haiti represented the fulfillment of the vision that Frank A. Vanderlip and the City Bank had had for Haiti as early as 1909, and signified a managerial triumph in attempts at diversifying and expanding the bank's operations. For Haiti, such control represented the end of independence and, as the BNRH and the republic's gold reserve became mere entries on the ledgers of the City Bank, a sign of a return to colonial servitude.

Yet for the City Bank, the successful conquest of the BNRH was tempered by other crises in the Caribbean. By 1922, the City Bank was embroiled in a financial calamity in Cuba, where, at the same time the bank was pushing for control of the BNRH, it had established an extensive branch network and become heavily invested in sugar. The collapse of sugar prices following the armistice dealt the bank a crushing blow. With the Cuban banking system on the brink of collapse, the City Bank was desperately trying to extricate itself from toxic sugar loans while offloading overvalued mortgages on sugar properties. As Farnham was being called to account for the bank's actions in Haiti, he was also trying to rescue its investments in Cuba. His efforts in both Caribbean countries would come to define his career as a banker and would help write the imperial history of the City Bank itself.

FOUR

Foreign Regulation

The City Bank's Roger L. Farnham was a frequent visitor to Cuba in the years before and after his 1921 testimony before the US Congress on the bank's involvement in the US occupation of Haiti. He was a well-known figure in Cuba, having first traveled to the republic on behalf of the City Bank in 1915, when he assisted with the early organization of the Havana branch.[1] In the intervening years Farnham regularly made the steamship journey from New York City to Havana to check in on the small but elegant two-story branch on Cuba Street, located in the concentration of banking houses, insurance companies, and mercantile firms known as the "Wall Street District" of old Havana (fig. 4.1).[2] He was known at the Cuban National Palace and the City Bank's country branches and sugar properties.[3] In May 1920, Farnham's name appeared on the menu for a noonday banquet at Havana's Hotel Telégrafo celebrating the inauguration of the City Bank Club of the Sagua la Grande branch. "Canfaina [sic] de Guinea—à la Farnham," a chicken stew named after the banker, was listed alongside "Variado—à la Stillman" and "Frituras—à la Allen" and other lunch items recalling the City Bank's executives and managers.[4] The goodwill toward Farnham extended to the bank as a whole. For a time, the City Bank was a popular institution in Cuba. It was seen as contributing to the economic growth of the republic during World War I and in the immediate postwar period. Its heavy investments in Cuban sugar were viewed as contributing to an unprecedented period of wealth on the island, an iridescent and delirious dreamworld of speculation and affluence that became known as the dance of millions. Where in Haiti, Farnham was viewed as "a real enemy of the Haitian people," as one observer put it, in Cuba both Farnham and the City Bank were seen as true friends of the republic.[5]

By the fall of 1920, Farnham's status in Cuba, and that of the City Bank

4.1. Interior of the National City Bank of New York, Cuba. From Oscar P. Austin, *Trading with Our Neighbors in the Caribbean* (New York: The City Bank of New York, 1920). Archive.org.

itself, were beginning to change. By then, the sugar boom had collapsed, the dizzying speed of capital circulation had slowed to a tortured creep, money was hard to come by, and the dance of millions was almost over. Soon after the publication of James Weldon Johnson's *Nation* articles excoriated Farnham and the City Bank for their role in the US occupation of Haiti, the City Bank's position in Cuba was becoming precarious. In October 1920 Cuba was wracked by a banking panic sparked by the precipitous slide in the price of sugar since its peak in May. The panic pushed Cuba's banking and financial system to the edge of collapse. Where money was once easy and credit bountiful, both were now tight and constricted. The government and sugar mills found themselves desperately short of cash. North American banking institutions, including the City Bank, were teetering on the edge of crisis as a result of carrying high-priced mortgages on Cuban properties collateralized by sugar stocks that were worthless and in some cases nonexistent. By 1921, Cuba was in the throes of the worst financial and economic crisis in the republic's short history. The crisis threatened to bring the City Bank down with it.

For the City Bank, the Cuban banking crisis of 1920–21—*el crac*, as it was known locally—marked the disastrous culmination of a policy of expansion and imperial banking initiated many years earlier by Frank A. Vanderlip. It was a policy that had its parallel in Haiti but whose impact was felt beyond the Caribbean. In Haiti, the City Bank's expansion came through the control of a government bank, the Banque Nationale de la République d'Haiti (BNRH); in Cuba, expansion occurred through two institutional forms: on the one hand, the organization and development of an international branch network supported by the new legal regimes of the Federal Reserve system; on the other, the early and tentative use of "security affiliates" or stockholding adjuncts as the vehicle for the expansion of foreign investment and international financing. In both cases, both branch banks and security affiliates required the development, training, and hiring of a new group of managers and executives, including Roger Farnham; both emerged from struggles with regulation, banking law, and jurisdictional authority. While the BNRH was limited to a single country, the purview of the branch organization and the investment affiliate was international, organized to compete with institutions like the Royal Bank of Canada and the International Banking Corporation and with the goal of dominating the banking field in the Caribbean and South America.

Farnham was sent to Cuba by the City Bank directors to ensure the stability of the branch network and its Cuban accounts. For some in Cuba, his arrival carried with it the promise of Wall Street and the hope that through him, through the City Bank, the capital necessary to start the grinding of the sugar mills and clear up the horribly clotted credit situation would be released. For others, Farnham's arrival was deserving of scorn. His appearance and the increasing prominence of the City Bank in the affairs of the country signified the death of Cuban sovereignty. The banking crash represented the extension of a new regime of colonialism wherein the country's sugar mills and commercial banks were absorbed by Wall Street, and the country's future was pledged as collateral to US capitalism. For Farnham, his journeys to Cuba marked the final days of a long career as an imperial banker.

The City Bank's involvement in Cuba dated back to the early nineteenth century when the bank was run by Moses Taylor, the Wall Street merchant and bank president with strong ties to Cuban sugar. But it was through the bank's participation in the formation of the Banco de la Habana, an early project of neocolonial finance in Cuba, that it first created a physical footprint on the island. The Banco de la Habana was organized in 1906. It represented a major part of the tentative, early twentieth-century international ventures initiated by Frank A. Vanderlip, who at the time was still vice president of the City Bank. It grew out of the Havana-based private merchant bank Zaldo y Cia., an institution chartered in 1860 by Spanish immigrant Guillermo de Zaldo.[6] The original merchant bank financed sugar and railroads, including the Ferrocarril de la Bahía, a line that stretched from Havana to Santiago de Cuba, and a warehouse and dock company serving the commerce of Havana.[7] De Zaldo's sons, Carlos, Federico, and Teodoro, continued the firm's business while solidifying its international financial connections by becoming local correspondents for Belmont & Co. and the Farmers Loan and Trust Company, both of New York, the Comptoir nationale d'escompte of Paris, and J. Henry Schroder of London, a merchant bank whose interests in Cuban sugar and railroads dated from early in the nineteenth century.[8]

Such international connections provided the foundation for the Banco de la Habana. It was organized through a network of investors in London, Paris, Hamburg, and New York. Its initial shareholders were a group of what Vanderlip described as "a number of our friends," including the four aforementioned institutions and the City Bank, the London Bank of Mexico and South America (Limited), Kuhn, Loeb & Co., Warburg & Co., the Société Générale de Crédit Industriel et Commercial, and the Banque Française pour le Commerce et l'Industrie.[9] The latter two concerns were among the most important of France's international banking houses and helped support its overseas commercial empire. Agents of the London Bank of Mexico and South America had researched investment conditions in Cuba three years previously and already had organized banks along similar lines in Mexico, Peru, Argentina, and Chile.[10] British financier Sir Ernest Cassel was a stockholder and early supporter. US corporate interests involved in the Banco de la Habana included the National Sugar Refining Company and the Equitable Trust Company.[11] The London Bank of Mexico and South America and the Banque Française were the largest shareholders in the new institution, followed by the City Bank and Zaldo y Cia.[12] Shares of the bank sold quickly; sugar magnate Horace Havemeyer tried to acquire $100,000 worth of stock in the bank but was only able to get half that amount.[13]

Carlos de Zaldo was installed as president of the new institution. Zaldo was a prominent businessman and, as Cuban secretary of state and justice under President Estrada Palma, had signed the US-Cuban reciprocity treaty. The board of directors included Spanish businessman Sabás E. de Alvaréz, produce merchant and Banco Nacional de Cuba director Elias Miro, Leandro Valdés of the merchant bank Valdes Alvarez y Cia., José Ignacio de la Cámara, a businessman and original board member of the Banco Nacional de Cuba, and Federico Zaldo. As with the Banque Nationale de la République d'Haiti, two advisory boards were established, one in Paris, one in New York City. Together, they reviewed the bank's business and approved its loans. Vanderlip appointed John E. Gardin as the City Bank's representative. James H. Post of the National Sugar Refining Company and a member of the firm B. H. Howell and Son also joined the New York committee.[14] James C. Martine, a Cuban who worked in the City Bank's bond department, managed the Havana headquarters. Martine was one of the original contributors to *No. 8*, the City Bank's employee journal, and his essays on Cuban banking and financial conditions in *No. 8* and the *Bulletin* of the American Institute of Bank Clerks provided US bankers with an early introduction to the particularities of banking in Cuba.[15] The City Bank also recruited John H. Durland, a Kansan who had worked for the New York Life Insurance Company and Samuel M. Jarvis's North American Trust Company when they first arrived in Cuba. When the Banco Nacional de Cuba took over the Cuban operations of the North American Trust Company, Durland organized its Matanzas branch.[16]

The Banco de la Habana opened on October 1, 1906.[17] With an authorized capital of $5 million with $2.5 million paid in, it was organized for foreign interests to capitalize on the expanding sugar industry and to compete with what were then the three most prominent commercial banks in the country: the Banco Nacional de Cuba, the Banco Español de la Isla de Cuba, and the Royal Bank of Canada (RBC). Its establishment also paralleled the advent of the second United States intervention in Cuba (1906–9) and the reestablishment of US rule under the governments of William H. Taft and Charles Magoon. For Vanderlip, the US occupation of Cuba offered a business opportunity. He urged US officials to instate the Banco de la Habana as the government's fiscal agent in Cuba. The Havana manager wrote to Magoon that the bank would "fulfill any banking functions" required of the US authorities.[18] The US administration, however, was disinclined to make any changes to the existing arrangements through which government funds were held and disbursed. Vanderlip persisted. He pointed to the "international character of the administration of the new bank," and its plans to open agencies in Cardenas, Matanzas, Sagua, Santiago de Cuba, Cienfuegos, and other cities in Cuba. Furthermore, he argued that the Banco de la Habana "is as much American as it is a Cuban institution . . . and this feature in itself ought to have weight with the deciding authorities in the choice of its fiscal agent." Vanderlip also pointed out that he had received information that the RBC was attempting to bid for the government deposits. Indeed, in October Francis J. Sherman, manager of the RBC's Havana branch, wrote to Taft, offering the bank's services to the US military authorities.[19] "We would feel very much chagrined if they were successful over and above our efforts in this respect," wrote Vanderlip, "and I would therefore ask you to do what is needful to see that the weight of your influence is thrown in our direction."[20]

Taft eventually designated both the Banco de la Habana and the Banco Nacional de Cuba depositories for treasury funds.[21] Yet despite the infusion of capital, the fortunes of the Banco de la Habana during its first years of operation were mixed. Stockholders of the Bank of London and Central and South America reported that the Havana bank had not shown a dividend in its first half year of operation. A year later little had changed.[22] In 1908, contradictory rumors circulated within Havana's business press surrounding the bank's fate. On the one hand, it was reported that Edmund G. Vaughan and the Banco Nacional de Cuba were going to absorb the Banco de la Habana and that Zaldo had been pushed out; on the other hand, it was speculated that Carlos de Zaldo had been authorized by J. P. Morgan to begin negotiations with Vaughan with the intention of the City Bank assuming practical control of the Banco Nacional de Cuba's operations. The press suggested that the talks of mergers and liquation emerged from a realization that there simply was not enough banking business in Cuba to sustain both institutions and warrant the extent of the bank's capitalization.[23] In reality, the City Bank had sent Gardin to Havana with the intention of reducing the bank's capital as a process of, as Vanderlip put it, "the elimination of the French interests," a prospect that Vanderlip saw as "desirable."[24]

By 1909, the desire for the elimination of European financial interests in the Caribbean was not confined to Vanderlip's stake in the Banco de la Habana. Under President William Howard Taft and his secretary of state, Philander Knox, the use of finance and banking was emerging as a potent tool of US diplomacy—a policy of "dollar diplomacy," of purportedly substituting dollars for bullets. According to the policy, private banks, financial advisers and experts, and foreign states worked together in an attempt to bring political stability to the Caribbean region through the organization of nominally national government banks, through the institution of currency reform and the refunding of sovereign debt, and by taking control of customs collection and revenue distribution. In this context, Vanderlip found Taft enthusiastically probusiness and supportive of the City Bank's expansionist desires. "It would be more nearly possible at the present time to obtain some color of government patronage or at least very cordial good will for a South American banking enterprise in the right hands than ever before," Vanderlip wrote to Stillman. "Mr Taft is particularly anxious to see some steps taken toward closer commercial relations."[25] While the City Bank was not a private bank it actively sought to benefit from the policy. Yet the City Bank's participation was limited. Vanderlip's approach was cautious; Stillman's even more so: he rejected the potential participations deemed too risky. Furthermore, the propositions were sometimes defeated locally as national congresses voted against them in the interests of economy and national sovereignty.

The range of proposals considered by the City Bank was vast. Vanderlip refused a proposition from the government of Guatemala and was offered but turned down a contract to refund the Nicaraguan debt.[26] At the suggestion of Knox, the City Bank, alongside Speyer and Co., purchased stock in the Banque Nationale d'Haiti and participated in the consortium led by Kuhn, Loeb and Co. that refunded European loans to the Republic of Liberia, their first venture on the African continent.[27] The City Bank proposed refunding the entire Costa Rican debt, then held in Europe. It wanted to float a loan through which the entire customs duties were pledged to the bank, and, in the case of default, the United States was granted the right to military intervention.[28] However, the Costa Rican government rejected the contract.[29] The City Bank had similar issues two years later during negotiations with Honduras. The City Bank was part of a consortium that included J. P. Morgan and Co., Kuhn, Loeb and Co., and the First National Bank of New York that proposed to reorganize the finances of the government of Honduras. But the contract, which would have contained concessions for the national railway, a government bank, a commercial bank, and control of customs collections, in addition to flotation of a $10 million loan, was rejected by the Honduran national congress.[30]

During this period, Vanderlip also had conversations with both W. R. Grace and Co. and J. P. Morgan and Co. regarding the possibility of jointly establishing a South American bank; at one point they considered former secretary of state Robert Bacon as its head, a plan US president Taft approved. Vanderlip backed out of a syndicate with the Deutsche Bank and Speyer and Co. for what became the Banco Mexicano de Comercio e Industria.[31] Vanderlip also considered purchasing an already-existing international bank outright and absorbing its branches into the City Bank fold. He watched the growth and progress of Thomas Hubbard's International Banking Corporation and had John E. Gardin investigate its condition and reputation with the potential aim of purchasing it. Vanderlip also coveted the Caribbean branch networks developed by the Royal Bank of Canada and the Bank of Nova Scotia.[32] In 1909, Vanderlip considered a proposal from City Bank vice president Joseph H. Talbert, who argued that the City Bank should buy the Bank of Nova Scotia wholesale. The Bank of Nova Scotia was founded in Halifax in 1832 and had developed a modest branch network in the British West Indies, Puerto Rico, and Cuba. Talbert suggested that the City Bank purchase the Bank of Nova Scotia, close its Canadian branches, and move its staff to the Caribbean, providing the City Bank with a ready-made foreign branch network.[33]

Nothing came of Talbert's plan to purchase the Bank of Nova Scotia, or of any of the grand schemes for international expansion Vanderlip considered. Instead, the City Bank's problem of foreign expansion was addressed in a surreptitious and indirect fashion, through a question of domestic regulation and the debate over the legality of the National City Company (NCC). The NCC was a "stock-holding adjunct" (sometimes referred to as a "securities" or "bastard" affiliate) organized by Vanderlip in July 1911.[34] The NCC was modeled after the First Securities Company (FSC), the affiliate of George F. Baker's First National Bank of New York, organized in 1908. Baker and the First National had wanted permission for the bank to engage in the buying and selling of stock in other national banks and other corporations but had been informed by the comptroller that this was illegal under the National Bank Act.[35] To do so, they organized the FSC. Similar to the International Banking Corporation, with its parallel organization of a state bank, the International Bank, with a state charter, FSC was legally a separate entity from the First National Bank. However, its trustees were the First National's president, vice president, and cashier. First National sold stock to the FSC at below market value so that it could engage in the sale and marketing of securities not permitted by the bank itself—commercial and investment functions were effectively combined, as there was little but a legal conceit separating the two entities. The profits the FSC garnered for the First National's directors were reportedly 12 percent annually.[36]

Hundreds of other banks in the country had established securities affiliates since Baker organized the FSC. However, the size of the City Bank

attracted scrutiny from federal bank regulators, as did the fact that immediately following its formation, it had acquired controlling interests in banks
across the country, disregarding the provisions of the National Bank Act and
leapfrogging regulatory hurdles meant to restrict monopoly and concentration in banking.[37] With the initiation of the Pujo Committee investigation
led by attorney Samuel Untermyer, and its inquiries into the question of
concentration and control in banking, the City Bank, and the National City
Company, came under suspicion. An assistant US district attorney paid a
visit to Vanderlip at the suggestion of the solicitor general. He "desired to
have full information in regard to the organization and purposes of the
National City Company." Vanderlip initially obliged. He was convinced of
the legality of the National City Company and wanted to appear magnani-
mous, open, and cooperative. His open-spirited approach to the investigation soon turned sour. Vanderlip bristled at the incursions the attorney
general made into the private records of the bank. He felt that the investigation was led by antibusiness "radicals" who had created the bogeyman of
a "money trust" to score political points. And while the attorney general
felt that the NCC was "accomplishing by indirection" what was expressly
prohibited by the spirit and in the letter of the National Bank Act, Vanderlip
claimed that, given the inadequacy of federal banking regulation, it was the
only way forward.

Wary of the scope of the investigation, Vanderlip mobilized a team to
lobby the offices of the attorney general and the White House. Milton Ailes,
one of his liaisons in Washington, formerly of the Treasury and the director
of Riggs National Bank in Washington, "got all the Treasury officials and
others completely in hand," Vanderlip reported, "so that they are working
with us in connection with the Department. He has relations with the Solicitor General which, I think, will absolutely protect us from any difficulty so
long as we show an amenable spirit."[38] Even so, Vanderlip realized that to
deflect criticism and neutralize the investigation he would "have to sever the
relation that exists between the Bank and the Company in the form of the
beneficial interest stamped on the bank stock," explaining further that "we
shall have to abandon that position and issue the shares of the NCC directly
to the stockholders of the Bank." He transferred both the securities held by
the City Bank–controlled United States Investment Company and the "incidental stock interests" deposited with the bank to the NCC, moved a pool of
accumulated funds not listed on the accounts of the bank to the books of the
security affiliate, and sold off stock in other banks held by the NCC so as to
"[show] a disposition to reduce our holdings."[39] In consultation with bank
lawyer John Sterling and in a work of legal and political subterfuge, Vander-

lip decided to recast the NCC as a foreign banking institution. He planned to develop "very strongly the idea that the real purpose of the NCC is to aid in the extension of our foreign banking, particularly in South America."[40] Writing to Stillman, Vanderlip argued that the promotion of the NCC as an entity whose main purpose was to develop the United States' presence in international banking would deflect attention from its domestic activities, as it would appear to have been organized for purposes that had been suggested by the US State Department:

> I think we can do some things that will amount practically to doing them at the request of the State Department, which will put the Government in an awkward situation to tell us to discontinue. In that way, I believe we can create a situation . . . where we can say what is really the fact, that the taking over of these bank stocks was an incidental and by no means an imperatively important thing in the work of the NCC, that its real purpose is to do the very things that the Government is urging us to do and that we are already moving to minimize the one thing about which there seems to be any objection and are disposed further to minimize.[41]

Vanderlip announced the NCC as a foreign banking concern whose purpose was to facilitate the opening of US foreign trade. "The entrance of the NCC into the South American field," Vanderlip announced to the press, "probably marks an epoch in the history of banking in the western hemisphere. It is the first real effort toward a comprehensive scheme for bringing into closer relationship this country with the countries of South and Central America." The NCC was organized, Vanderlip stated,

> for the purpose of bringing about eventually the extension of American banking facilities to our merchants and others doing business in Mexico and South and Central America. Altogether the country has become largely interested in these countries, and its investments relate very largely to bonds of the state of Sao Paulo, the great coffee-producing state of Brazil; bonds of the Argentine Republic, of the city of Lima, Peru; of Costa Rica, and of Haiti. The company is also interested in the Chinese financial situation, and is one of the participants in the Manchurian loan.[42]

As a statement of intent, Vanderlip recruited W. Morgan Shuster and Henry Vibert Cann to embark on a yearlong fact-finding mission that would examine possibilities for banking, finance, and commerce in South America. Shuster had most recently been the financial adviser to Persia; Cann had a long association with the Bank of Nova Scotia, including as inspector of its West Indian branches.[43] The trip, argued Vanderlip, "will establish in the public mind a *raison d'etre* for the City Bank Company, and that is an admirable thing to do. It will show that in our efforts to extend our foreign banking relations, hampered as we are by the inadequacy of our banking laws, we have had to resort to this method."[44]

Despite the recasting of the NCC as an entity organized to promote international trade and finance, Vanderlip still worried about the impact of the Pujo Committee investigations into the City Bank's organization and operation. In an attempt to gain some assurances regarding the City Bank's status, Vanderlip sent Roger Farnham to have a series of informal conversations with President Taft and his brother, Charles P. Taft. Farnham had just joined the City Bank from the offices of William Nelson Cromwell that March and had quickly become involved in the City Bank's international affairs. He knew the Taft brothers from his work with Panama on the canal concession. Farnham described the content of his meetings in a long memorandum sent to Vanderlip in October 1911. The memorandum summarized his encounters with and opinions of Taft and gave a detailed account of Taft's senses of Untermyer, the attorney general, and the investigation. According to Farnham, Taft expressed his disgust with the character of Untermyer and told Farnham that he "did not propose to play into his hands any further than by law he was absolutely required to do."[45] Farnham noted Taft's "friendly attitude" toward the City Bank and told him that he believed the bank's internal affairs were of no business to the public—"only governments—and only to make sure they were in compliance with the law." Taft told Farnham that he had "no sympathy with the so-called 'Money Trust Investigation'" and actually believed that there was no such thing. He was aghast that the banking community was under investigation and was being "harassed by the inquisitors," but he confessed that he was unable to intervene directly in the affairs of the Department of Justice. That said, Taft told Farnham that the City Bank had no need to worry about the outcomes of Untermyer's prying attempts at getting confidential information from the bank, as Taft would stretch the laws as far as possible to resist the inquiries.

Taft also told Farnham that if he were reelected, he would completely gut his cabinet. He was certain that there would be a new attorney general after March 4, 1913—a fact that the president's brother, Charles P. Taft, reiterated "in even plainer terms." Charles Taft told Farnham that if President Taft were reelected, he would select an entirely new cabinet, and Attorney General Charles W. Wickersham would not be a part of it. "This, he said, he could absolutely assure me of, and, while I must realize that at the present time such an announcement could not be made in any sort of public way by the President or anyone representing him, nevertheless he felt that I should let those whom I represented privately understand that such was to be the case." Furthermore, if Taft were reelected, he would make sure his cabinet was pro-business—at which point Farnham suggested that the "financial interests of the country" should have a say in selecting his cabinet—in particular the attorney general and the secretary of the treasury. "Not to the end of dictating those who should be named for those positions," Farnham qualified, "but in order that he should have the benefit of the judgment, advice, and knowledge of men of affairs." Taft enthusiastically agreed with Farnham. "I am satisfied that should he be re-elected," Farnham wrote, "such a conference between the representatives of the large financial interest and the Presidents would readily be had, in order that he could have such aid in the selection of some of the members of his cabinet." Taft, meanwhile, realized that his chances for reelection were slim and that if bankers and their officials advocated for him, it would probably further hurt his chances for a second term.

When the Money Trust report was released, its general conclusion was that there was in fact concentration in banking: that the interlocking boards of directors of banking institutions and corporations created a dangerous concentration of wealth and money power.[46] However, the commentary on the existence of the NCC was somewhat ambiguous. The investigations largely left the City Bank unscathed, and they were not forced to relinquish any of their holdings. But an opinion by Solicitor General Frederick W. Lehman argued that the organization and operation of the NCC expressly violated both the intentions and the law of the National Bank Act. It threatened to create the kind of monopoly and concentration in money and banking that the National Bank Act was designed, in part, to avoid. President Taft suppressed Lehmann's report. The existing order of things between the National City Bank and the National City Company was preserved.[47] Vanderlip, with the assistance of Roger Farnham and others, had successfully evaded the legal orders attempting to regulate and curtail the activities of the City Bank.

By 1913, the City Bank's international profile remained modest compared to the profiles of its Canadian and European competitors, although it was relatively robust for a federally chartered commercial bank whose ambitions were impeded by regulations. The City Bank had interests in a commercial bank in Cuba, the Banco de la Habana, and a government bank in Haiti, the Banque Nationale de la République d'Haiti, and it was increasingly involved in projects encouraged by the US State Department to refund the national debt and take control of currency regimes and central banks. It was awarded the contract for a short-term 6 percent $1.5 million loan to the Dominican Republic, beating out Samuel M. Jarvis's Banco Nacional de Santo Domingo and subsequently finding itself embroiled in the acrimonious fracas sparked by Jarvis and Frank J. R. Mitchell.[48] It also participated in the J. P. Morgan and Co.–organized syndicate, which offered a similar short-term loan to Cuba.[49]

In 1913, W. Morgan Shuster and H. V. Cann returned to New York City after traveling first to London and then crossing back across the Atlantic and touring South America on the business-finding mission organized by Vanderlip. Nothing concrete came of their journey. Vanderlip thought that the City Bank might secure a forty-year charter from Panama for a government bank that would serve as the state treasury, receiving and paying all governmental transactions while having the unlimited right to issue currency, save a 33 percent gold reserve requirement. Vanderlip saw the Panama bank as the potential gateway to the opening of further City Bank–controlled banks in Central and South America.[50] Yet the Panama bank was never organized, and when Shuster reported back to Vanderlip, he painted a pessimistic picture of the possibility for foreign expansion. Shuster feared that the City Bank and the NCC would not be able to compete with established European bankers, and that American investors would be reluctant to invest in Latin American securities given the high yields of domestic security and bond issues.[51] Within a year, conditions in Europe would change. The City Bank would find the opportunities that Vanderlip had been searching for for almost a decade.

The year 1914 was a watershed in the history of the City Bank. A set of historic events provided Vanderlip with the platform and possibility for the foreign expansion that he and Stillman had long dreamed of, and positioned the bank to assume an international, imperial presence that would allow it to compete with its European and Canadian rivals. Together, the operationalization of the Federal Reserve Act following its signing late in 1913, the opening of the Panama Canal in August 1914, and the onset of war in Europe brought about these new possibilities for the City Bank. It was a convergence of events that one City Banker described as "providential."[52] The European conflict upended the global conditions for banking, finance, commerce, and trade. Shipping lanes were disrupted, severing the markets of Asia and the Americas from Europe, and European agriculture and industry were devastated. The imperial British, French, and German banking houses active in the Caribbean and South America were disabled, depriving Caribbean and Latin American countries of their traditional sources of credit.

They turned to Wall Street for their financing needs and to the United States as a market for their raw materials and agricultural products. The United States was positioned as the sole imperial power in the hemisphere. It underwent a stunning transformation from a net debtor to a net creditor as it rapidly paid off its Civil War debts and repatriated the gold and US government securities held in Europe, reversing a centuries-old trend and raising New York City to global prominence in international finance.[53]

While the opening of the Panama Canal reordered the geography of US trade, cutting down shipping times, the United States was able to take advantage of the financial conditions brought on by the war because of the organization of the Federal Reserve System. The Federal Reserve created an international system of discount, allowing national banking associations to handle foreign "acceptances"—the primary instrument of international trade—of an amount that could extend to the entirety of a given bank's paid-up capital stock and surplus.[54] The permission to use acceptances in foreign trade repatriated commissions previously lost through American use of European banks—a complaint heard as early as the International American Conferences of the 1890s—and promoted the dollar as an international commercial currency.[55] In addition, Section 25 of the Federal Reserve Act permitted national banking associations capitalized at $1 million or more to establish branches outside of the United States with permission from the Reserve Board.[56] A later clause permitted national banking associations to deploy up to 10 percent of their capital and surplus for the purchase of stock in corporations whose primary purpose was the American export trade. Domestic branches were disallowed under the National Bank Act for fear that their expansion could lead to concentration in banking and regional control over financial and money power. In the international context, branches were seen as a necessary support for the foreign trade and commercial empire that Vanderlip and others within the City Bank had long advocated.[57]

Vanderlip was ready to take advantage of the new financial order. He had long been an advocate of regulatory reform, and he had participated in many of the early discussion leading to the establishment of the Federal Reserve, including the secret December 10, 1910, meeting on Georgia's Jekyll Island with J. P. Morgan's Henry P. Davison, Kuhn and Loeb's Paul M. Warburg, First National's Charles D. North, and US Senator Nelson D. Aldrich.[58] Despite the ambivalent returns of the missions by Shuster and Cann to the Caribbean and South America, these trips had provided the City Bank with a set of commercial contacts and business files. Furthermore, as part of his research into foreign trade and banking expansion, Vanderlip had sent out questionnaires to thousands of domestic merchants and bankers inquiring after their specific needs and requirements to engage in foreign commerce.

Vanderlip quickly organized an overseas division in 1914. It was divided into two units: a foreign exchange department run by John E. Gardin, and a foreign trade department run by Herbert R. Eldridge and Stephen H. Voorhees that handled matters of foreign branch expansion. Born in Charleston, Gardin learned the banker's trade in Germany before returning to the United States to work in the foreign exchange department of the First National Bank of Chicago. He developed a reputation writing and lecturing on foreign exchange and, after Vanderlip recruited him in 1904, Gardin expanded the City Bank's foreign department into the largest of any US bank, handling transactions of more than $1 billion annually by 1909.[59] Eldridge was born in Decatur, Illinois, to a wealthy family and worked for years in Texas commercial banks, his expert knowledge on the instrumentalities of foreign trade bringing him to Vanderlip's attention.[60] Voorhees had joined the RBC from the Chase Manhattan Bank in 1899 and had organized the RBC's New York agency. He had traveled extensively in the Caribbean, visiting the RBC's Puerto Rico and Cuba branches, and was the treasurer of William Van Horne's Cuba Railroad, whose accounts were held by the bank.[61] Both the foreign exchange and foreign trade departments were overseen by Samuel McRoberts, a City Bank executive manager and former lawyer from meat-packing concern Armour and Co. who also sat on the board of the Banque Nationale d'Haiti.

The City Bank already owned stock in commercial and government banks in Cuba and Haiti, but in November 1914, it opened its first overseas branch in Buenos Aires, Argentina.[62] Argentina was chosen largely because US Steel Corporation president James A. Farrell had wanted a US bank to help finance his $100 million business in that country. Farrell asked Vanderlip to open a branch in Buenos Aires and offered to help obtain deposits from International Harvester, Armour, and Swift (all of which were selling in Latin America) as well as access to their credit files. The accounts provided the City Bank with an immediate capital base as well as an archive of information that helped it conduct and expand its foreign business. For the Buenos Aires branch, Vanderlip pulled together a team consisting of individuals with prior business and banking experience in the Caribbean. John H. Allen, who had been managing the Banque Nationale de la République d'Haiti in Port-au-Prince; James C. Martine, who had helped established the Banco Nacional de Cuba in 1906; Robert O. Bailey, former secretary of the treasury; and M. D. Carrell, who had worked with the Philippine tariff commission and had been involved in developing trade between the United States and

Puerto Rico. With a staff of ten assistants, they traveled to Argentina on November 2, 1914, and took over a suite of rooms in the stock exchange building on Calle Rivadavia, near the Banco de la Nación.[63]

On November 14 the City Bank opened its doors for business in Buenos Aires. Under Allen's management, the branch was a success. In less than a year it had corralled nearly $4 million in deposits, and Allen proposed opening subbranches at Rosario and Bahía Blanca as well as in Montevideo, Uruguay. Herbert R. Eldridge wrote enthusiastically to Vanderlip about Allen's work, arguing that if the City Bank could keep him, he would need to be elected a vice president and allowed more time in the United States to be with his family.[64] The City Bank's competitors in Argentina were less enthusiastic. Barings Bank, for instance, realized that the war meant their long run of financing in Argentina was coming to an end, and hoped that the republic would decelerate its borrowing. The Barings agents lamented the arrival of the City Bank and despised the methods of Allen. They accused him of being a US trade spy and complained that he was "not a gentleman, simply a common North American bounder-bully, entirely unscrupulous," while chafing at his aggressive business tactics.[65]

On March 17, 1915, the Federal Reserve Board authorized the City Bank to establish a branch at Havana supplemented by subbranches in Santiago de Cuba, Matanzas, Cienfuegos, Guantanamo, Camagüey, Cardenas, Manzanillo, as well as in Kingston, Jamaica, and Santo Domingo, in the Dominican Republic. While the branches in Kingston and Santo Domingo were never organized, the authorizations were nonetheless a statement of intent for the City Bank.[66] Eldridge and Farnham soon journeyed to Cuba to investigate purchasing the Banco de la Habana. Though they argued over the price, quibbling over the quality of some of its assets, they agreed to buy it at par, taking over the Banco de la Habana's new building on Cuba Street in the process.[67] George E. Roberts traveled to Cuba to oversee the transition. A longtime newspaper man from Iowa and a former director of the US Mint, Roberts was brought on as Vanderlip's special assistant; he ended up editing the City Bank's *Monthly Letter* for twenty-five years, growing its circulation to 200,000 copies.[68] Opened on August 20, the Havana branch was dubbed the "West Indian Branch." It was to become the center of a Caribbean network, grouped under an administrative "Caribbean District" whose purview included both the Antillean archipelago itself and the Caribbean ports of Central and South America.[69] Porfirio Franca, a wealthy Cuban who was a founding member of the Vedado Tennis Club, was appointed manager. Like the Buenos Aires branch, the Havana branch turned a quick profit in a matter of months, in part thanks to the liquidation of moribund loans, while quickly garnering new accounts.[70] In April of the following year, a branch was opened in Rio de Janeiro, followed by subbranches in São Paulo, Santos, and Bahia, the latter two cities the centers of the Brazilian coffee and sugar trade, respectively. In August it opened a branch in Montevideo, the center of the Uruguayan hide trade, and in Valparaiso, Chile's main port and a center for nitrates and copper. Branches in Colombia and Venezuela followed, and in the coming years, Vanderlip authorized the opening of branches in Europe.[71]

During these early days of foreign branch expansion, the City Bank also took over the International Banking Corporation (IBC)—an institution long coveted by Vanderlip. IBC founder Thomas H. Hubbard died on May 21, 1915, and the City Bank used the NCC to purchase a controlling stake in the IBC and its parallel, state-chartered institution, the International Bank. The purchase immediately gave the City Bank a ready-formed and staffed system of branches in the Asia-Pacific region. By 1915, the IBC had branches in Bombay, London, Calcutta, Hankow, Manila, Shanghai, Hong Kong, Singapore, Cebu, Tientsin, Kobe, Peking, and Yokohama, as well as in Colón, Panama, and San Francisco.[72] (The City Bank sold the San Francisco bank at profit when it realized it was "receiving deposits there somewhat in contravention of the law," as Vanderlip put it.) Control of the IBC helped the City Bank compete with the Hongkong and Shanghai Banking Corporation and other British imperial banks in Asia. It also provided the bank with a presence on the Isthmus of Panama, where the Washington, DC, Commercial National Bank had just arrived. Vanderlip had long watched Panama, having abandoned plans to establish City Bank branches there on multiple occasions. The City Bank's purchase of the IBC initiated a debate over how best to incorporate it into the fold of the City Bank proper. While there was universal agreement as to the value of the IBC as an institution—despite its history of poor management and middling returns—Vanderlip and the officers of the City Bank considered operating it jointly with European institutions in a cooperative venture, maintaining it as a solely US entity, and folding its branches into the City Bank, effectively eliminating the IBC as an independent unit.[73] While a strategy was slowly worked out, the IBC's management and board of directors became increasingly dominated by members of the City Bank's overseas division. John E. Gardin was elected chairman of the IBC's board, and over the coming years H. T. S. Green, Lawrence M. Jacobs, Guy Cary, Arthur Kavanagh, Samuel McRoberts, and Roger Farnham were all appointed as directors.[74] In 1917, the IBC acquired the business of Puerto

Rican banker Santiago Michelena in the Dominican Republic.[75] Michelena remained in the IBC's management. He was joined by J. L. Manning, formerly treasurer of the insular government in the Philippines.

The foreign branches had a number of functions. They provided all of the financial services of a domestic branch: accepting deposits, issuing letters of credit, handling exchange, and extending credit to individuals and business. They were also the clearinghouses for credit information on local governments and businesses. Branch representatives studied local trade conditions, alerted US manufacturers to potential marketing opportunities, and explained the technical details of regional and local trade and customs protocols.[76] They compiled monthly reports on commercial possibilities and natural resources. They offered up-to-date country profiles outlining current rates of exchange, prices of goods, and the nuances of local business culture, as well as assessments of local political conditions and their effect on business. They sent regular dispatches back to 55 Wall Street where they were compiled and released to the City Bank's correspondent banks, private investors, and the press, and used in the *Monthly Letter*. Within its first year of operation, for example, the Buenos Aires branch produced nearly 400 reports.[77]

These dispatches were part of a broader, comprehensive system of publicity and representation initiated by Vanderlip that included writings on fiscal policy and banking reform, as well as reports on crop movements, consumer demand, manufacturing output, and labor conditions. Under Vanderlip's watch, the City Bank began producing journals, news reports, circulars, monographs, and trade manuals on foreign trade and international commerce while initiating a coordinated pedagogical program that educated US investors and merchants, as well as the bank's own staff, in the protocols and etiquette of international trade and finance.[78] The City Bank's staff magazine, *No. 8*, increasingly carried dispatches from the foreign branches and articles on foreign trade and commerce, and Vanderlip launched *The Americas*, a monthly periodical distributed free to investors and businesspeople, aiming "to create a medium which will be of assistance in bringing the business men of the United States and South America closer together, and to provide an instrument for the interchange of ideas regarding the aims and projects of pan-American commerce."[79] Under Vanderlip, the City Bank also published a pamphlet series on foreign commerce. The first in the series was Oscar Phelps Austin's *Trading with Our Neighbors in the Caribbean*.[80]

Together, these texts attempted to help both businesspeople and the wider American public to conceptualize the United States as part of a global economy, and the Caribbean and Latin America as regions worthy of investment. "In establishing a comprehensive system of branches all through [the Caribbean]," the City Bank's Allen wrote, "the National City Bank has tried to *visualize* the development which is certain to come to this interesting and prodigally rich part of the world."[81] In doing so, the bank responded to what one City Banker described as the United States' "national ignorance," as well as to the behavior and attitudes of US businesspeople overseas. It offered a corrective to US perceptions of the tropics. Well aware that "distance [lends] enchantment," as an editorial in *The Americas* put it, bankers tried to debunk the scurrilous representations of foreign countries that circulated in the United States.[82] They realized they had to counter the representations of the Caribbean and Latin America circulating in travel writing, yellow journalism, and lurid romances that offered up the region as an irreconcilably foreign space, a space marked by backward customs, racial degeneracy, and tendencies toward incessant revolution and decivilizing barbarity.

Yet while serving as a corrective to US misrepresentations of the world, these texts also often reinforced those misrepresentations while reproducing the assumptions concerning race, culture, and difference that formed the basis for many of the City Bank's policies overseas. Certainly, some of these representations evoked a quaint, if exoticized, sense of difference between the United States and the world. But often one sees the unabashedly racist depictions of Africans and Indians. Irving M. Barnard's essay "Five Years in Jungle Land," describing the City Banker's visit to the IBC in Panama, offers a case in point, evoking, as it does, the same set of antiblack images performed through the City Bank Minstrel Show as well as the racist and paternalistic accounts of Haiti by Roger Farnham and John Allen (see chapter 4).[83] At Kingston, Jamaica, Barnard's first port of call after leaving New York, he describes the "little niggers" diving for coins thrown into the ocean for the amusement of the ship's passengers. In Panama he encounters a "tribe" of West Indians who are humble, affable, bewilderingly ignorant, and "quick imitator[s]": after being wished a Merry Christmas, one Caribbean migrant repeats the greeting incessantly but, either mishearing it or, as Barnard thinks, expressing his gratitude to his northern patrons, it comes out as *"American Christmas."* Indeed, Barnard's description of Panama's West Indians echoes both James Morris Morgan's accounts of African Americans in Reconstruction South Carolina and the depictions of blacks in the City Bank Minstrel Show. Black people are fungible for Barnard. The West Indian is conscripted into a racial performance populated by white caricatures of African Americans and in "Five Years in Jungle Land," he acts as the interlocutor in the Panamanian scene of a worldy "coon" show staged for the City Bankers in New York:

> The lingo of the West Indian, supposedly English, is almost incomprehensible to one whose ear has not been trained to it. They frequently misunderstand us Americans. For example, one day at breakfast (which is there the mid-day meal, served about eleven o'clock) the cook served meat, which was not touched, as we happened not to be hungry. I told the cook to take it back and heat it up for dinner. At dinner we had the customary layout, minus meat. When I inquired, he replied, "Meat, sir? I thought you told me to heat it hup, sir!" I affirmed that such was the case, and asked him to pronounce it. "But, sir," he stammered, "I did—I hate it hall hup, sir." I had neglected to take into consideration the bally English "haitch," you know.

The City Bank's overseas branches and Vanderlip's engagement of the machinery of representation were part of the development of a larger financial and commercial infrastructure supporting US foreign investment. Vanderlip recognized that neither representations nor branches alone would bring business to the City Bank. To this end, Vanderlip organized two other, supplementary entities to bring business to the City Bank. First, he energized the National City Company, the controversial securities affiliate he had organized years earlier. In March 1916 Vanderlip recruited a young, energetic bond-salesman named Charles E. Mitchell to run the NCC and authorized the NCC's purchase of N. W. Halsey and Co., the second largest bond house in the country. The purchase immediately gave the City Bank a $100 million bond portfolio.[84]

Vanderlip also organized the American International Corporation (AIC), a holding company whose purpose was to facilitate the movement of US capital and manufactured goods overseas. Drawing on the combined strength of the country's largest financial and manufacturing concerns, the AIC was to serve as a channel to funnel surplus capital into overseas development projects. Within a year of its organization, the AIC had received more than 1,200 propositions for consideration, a majority from South America and the Caribbean. From the AIC's initial projects building waterworks and sewage systems in Uruguay, it financed the construction of utilities and public works projects throughout the world. Subsidiaries, like the China Corporation and the Grace Russian Company, were for the development of railways and canals. The production of rubber, rosin, turpentine, and tea was consolidated through the formation of AIC's companies, including the

United States Rubber Company, the Rosin and Turpentine Export Company, and Carter Macy & Company. Arguably, the AIC's most important contribution to US foreign trade was its almost single-handed revitalization of the US mercantile marine. In partnership with W. R. Grace, the AIC purchased a stake in the Pacific Mail Steamship Company, with lines extending from Baltimore through the Panama Canal and through the Pacific as far west as India. The AIC bought stock in the United Fruit Company, whose vessels traversed routes to the Caribbean and Central America, and purchased the International Mercantile Marine Company, a Morgan-controlled company then in receivership. The AIC also acquired the New York Shipbuilding Corporation and its 160-acre facility at Camden, New Jersey. The purchase made the AIC the world's largest shipbuilding concern. During the war, it garnered guaranteed contracts through the federal government's Emergency Fleet Corporation for 200 ships; after the war it tendered numerous commercial and private contracts.[85] The AIC used the City Bank's branch network to handle its financial transactions, and the bank stood to make a profit from the service fees and exchange commissions on any transaction it handled.[86] For City Bank and AIC directors, AIC was to play as important a role in imperial financing and development as the Hudson's Bay Company and the East India Company.

———————————————————

What appeared as a blur of activity on the part of Vanderlip and the City Bank in New York actually moved at a languid pace on the ground in the Caribbean and Latin America. And what for Vanderlip was meant to be a systematic and rational approach to internationalization was prone to poor judgment, human error, vanity, and the frissons of cultural difference. The result was an often haphazard, improvisatory, and experimental system. The practical, quotidian life of finance capitalism and US imperialism as ordered through the City Bank's foreign branch system often appeared frail and tenuous. Vanderlip appointed a branch bank committee that operated out of an office at 55 Wall Street and consisted of members of the foreign exchange and foreign trade departments, as well as of the IBC and included at various times Stephen H. Voorhees, Roger L. Farnham, John E. Gardin, William S. Kies, as well as Lawrence M. Jacobs and H. T. S. Green of the IBC.[87] They held weekly meetings where they read aloud the incoming correspondence of the branch banks, discussed issues of policy, and authorized return memos. The meetings were consumed with the most mundane matters of policy and management: details of staffing arrangements, salary demands, requests for transfers and vacations, the resolution of personal disputes between foreign staff members, and personal and family matters. They passed judgment on larger loan issues and foreign credits and considered questions of further branch expansion and the takeover of local institutions. In these meetings, for instance, they considered opening a branch at Camagüey in eastern Cuba to serve the Cuban Railway Company and passed judgment on the viability of opening branches of the IBC in Santo Domingo and San Pedro Macorís. They discussed the possibilities of acquiring the Danish Bank of the West Indies after Farnham wrote a report recommending purchase if the United States took over the Danish islands.[88] Farnham also reported on a meeting he had with the State Department concerning the City Bank's acquisition of the Mercantile Bank of the Americas. It was a proposition the committee agreed they were not interested in pursuing.[89]

The problems of foreign branch banking were most pronounced in Cuba, the location of the City Bank's most dramatic growth. The Cuban branches highlighted the difficulties of management and the associated questions of authority exercised over distance. The relations between the home office at 55 Wall Street, the Havana branch headquarters, and the Santiago de Cuba subbranch surfaced in the letters and memos sent from Cuba inquiring about bank policy, seeking advice on branch management, and complaining about staff personalities. There were questions concerning who had the authority to approve the loans and overdrafts of the subbranches, and to what amount.[90] There were grievances about staff and staffing (Gardin rejected the request from D. A. Menocal in Rio de Janeiro for a move to Havana because of his lack of judgment, and Menocal was later sent to Peking to manage a branch of the IBC).[91] There were questions of salary increases.[92] There were attempts to settle conflicts between Havana and Santiago. After numerous letters from Juan B. Roqué of the Havana branch complaining about the conduct of the Santiago branch, the committee wrote to Roqué to tell him to stop interfering with the daily operations of the Santiago branch, and warned the Santiago branch to keep better track of its loans. To the dismay of the committee, Roqué also applied for a $10,000 personal loan from the bank; the committee decided to refuse it.[93] In the correspondence between New York and Havana a practical branch policy slowly congealed out of a set of informal approaches.[94]

Cuba's importance to the City Bank was largely due to the status of the political economy of Cuban sugar in the context of World War I.[95] Cuba officially joined the Allied powers in 1917, but its economic allegiances were clear long before that. An Economic Defense Law passed on October 29, 1914, to protect the economy against the financial instability of the war, demonetized all foreign currencies except that of the United States while establishing a Cuban national currency at par with the US dollar, breaking the government's reliance on the French and Spanish bullion that had become prohibitively expensive as a result of the war.[96] The new law helped rationalize many of Cuba's daily commercial transactions while tying the national currency and the Cuban economy to the US dollar.[97] Sugar and tobacco acceptances were exclusively paid either in the new national currency or in US dollars, and quotations on the Havana Stock and Produce Exchange were made in Cuban instead of Spanish gold. The complicated custom of keeping multiple accounts that had so vexed the early bookkeepers and accountants of the Banco Nacional de Cuba was done away with, and the hundreds of money changers in the streets of Havana were forced out of business.[98]

The war years saw the rapid growth of banking in Cuba.[99] Both Cuban and Spanish institutions expanded their branch networks throughout the country while growing the portfolio of credits to sugar planters. The Banco Nacional de Cuba, now controlled by José "Pote" López Rodríguez, led the way, expanding its branch network throughout the island and converting its New York City agency into a state bank, the Bank of Cuba in New York, with offices at 34 Wall Street.[100] Older banking institutions—including the venerable Banco Español de la Isla de Cuba, merchant banks such as H. Upmann and N. Gelats, and local upstarts like the Banco Internacional de Cuba—extended their domestic branch networks while competing to offer planters loans. North American financial institutions including the Royal Bank of Canada, the Bank of Nova Scotia, and the Standard Bank of Canada also began to play an increasingly important role in Cuba's banking landscape. Between 1914 and 1920 the number of bank branches in Cuba almost doubled, growing from 148 to 294.[101] From 1916 to 1920 deposits in domestic banks increased from $109 million to $325 million; in foreign banks they showed similar growth, expanding from $30.7 million to $88 million.

The City Bank followed suit. The bank built on the connections it had made through the Banco de la Habana and its own increased investments in the Cuban economy. It used the occasion of the opening of the West Indian branch in Havana as an opportunity to seek out accounts from Cuban sugar planters. The bank opened a $2 million line of credit for Manuel Rionda and the Czarnikow-Rionda Company and later invited Rionda to join the board of directors of the bank, an offer he declined.[107] The National City Company issued a $6 million bond for the Cuban-American Sugar Company, controlled by board member Robert Hawley, who was the owner of a number of holdings in the Caribbean republic including the Chaparra Sugar Company, the Chaparra Railroad Company, the San Manuel Sugar Company, the Tinguaro Sugar Company, the Mercedita Sugar Company, the

Cuban Sugar Refining Company, the United Sugar Company, and the Colonial Sugars Company.[103] The City Bank's participation in the Cuban sugar industry peaked in 1917 with the announcement that the entire Cuban sugar crop of three and a quarter million tons, would be funded by a syndicate of US banks and then purchased by the United States Sugar Equalization Board, stabilizing the market while guaranteeing Cuba's economic success. The year was not without conflict, however. US troops landed in Cuba to protect the interests of US sugar properties in the eastern provinces after a short uprising against President Mario García Menocal. A military order designed to stabilize the regional economy during the crisis saw the Santiago de Cuba branches of the City Bank, Royal Bank of Canada, and the Banco Nacional de Cuba briefly suspend operations.[104] The manager of the City Bank's Santiago de Cuba branch later defied an order from insurgent commander Rigoberto Fernández to reopen, informing Fernández that he would have to petition the head office in New York.[105]

The year following the armistice was marked by tumult and change for the City Bank. In March 1918, James Stillman died. With his death, the City Bank lost not only a figure who had shaped its destiny for almost three decades, but a man who represented a living, historical connection to the old merchant world of New York. In July 1919, Frank A. Vanderlip resigned. Vanderlip's resignation came as a sudden surprise to Wall Street as he was well regarded both within and outside the bank. Before Stillman's death, however, conflicts between the two men had been simmering. Vanderlip had sought a greater share of stock in the bank as his influence in its operations increased, but he had been repeatedly rebuffed by Stillman, the largest shareholder, who wanted to retain his control. There were other issues. The City Bank's branches in Russia were nationalized by the Bolshevik government soon after they were opened in 1917. The bank lost all of it deposits, and Vanderlip was held responsible. After touring Europe at the conclusion of the war, Vanderlip quickly wrote and published an assessment of conditions there whose frank allocations of blame and bold prescriptions for reconstruction upset the City Bank directors. He was forced out. James "Jamie" Alexander Stillman, Stillman's son, was appointed bank president following Vanderlip's departure. The elder Stillman's final words to his son were reportedly, "Jamie . . . never, never accept the presidency of the bank. Don't let them make you take it."[106] While Stillman increased the City Bank's capital from $25 million to $40 million, he was a mediocre banker and a weak leader. His short tenure at the City Bank was marked by both personal and political-economic crises.

Even before Vanderlip's resignation, change was afoot in the City Bank's foreign operations. In January 1919, Roger Farnham was removed from the Caribbean District and reassigned to a fledgling district consisting of Africa and Australia.[107] Appointed in Farnham's place was John H. Allen. The vice president in charge of the South American District, Allen had managed the Banque Nationale de la République d'Haiti in Port-au-Prince and opened the City Bank's first foreign branch in Buenos Aires. Allen brought energy and aggression to the City Bank's Caribbean branch organization. His editorials and essays in *The Americas* were enthusiastic statements on the growth of US-Caribbean trade and he matched his rhetoric with policy, supercharging the bank's branch expansion.[108] Allen ordered his subordinates to ramp up the opening of new branches in Cuba while increasing the bank's branch footprint throughout the Caribbean region.

By July 1919, the City Bank had twenty-one branches in the Caribbean District. It added four in Cuba (in Santa Clara, Unión de Reyes, Pinar del Río, and Ciego de Ávila), a second branch in Venezuela in the Caribbean port city of Maracaibo, and a branch in Port of Spain, Trinidad, British West Indies.[109] In Port of Spain, it encountered local resistance from the Canadian Bank of Commerce and the Royal Bank of Canada. They argued that a US bank should not be permitted entry into the colony, as British banks could not operate in New York.[110] By August 1919, six more branches were organized in Cuba, and the IBC added two in Asia.[111] September witnessed more branch openings in Cuba, in Brazil, and in the Dominican Republic, where the IBC opened a new branch. On January 1, 1919, the City Bank had fifteen foreign branches. By December 31, it had forty-seven. The City Bank's twenty-fifth Cuban branch was opened at Nuevitas, in March 1920. By the end of 1920, the City Bank had ninety-five overseas branches, the most branches of an US banking institution and a network rivaled only by the Royal Bank of Canada among North American banks.[112]

The branch expansion under Allen was matched by the City Bank's lending policy. It was ambitious and loose. With competition from other financial institutions, credit was made easily available, and rather than risking losing business, money was offered with little collateral, little inquiry into personal backgrounds, and often on properties that were heavily mortgaged but whose profits depended on the maintenance of the price of sugar. Through the war, sugar markets were stabilized through the regulation of the Sugar Equalization Board. But the board's belated decision to refuse to purchase the Cuban sugar crop late in 1919 exposed the commodity to the mercurial temperaments of the open market.[113] The price of sugar skyrocketed as rumors of scarcity prompted hoarding by consumers and distributors and encouraged the operations of speculators and shysters. Speculators stockpiled sugar in an attempt to influence prices. Their efforts worked. By May 20, 1920, Cuban raw sugar reached 22 ½ cents per pound on the New York Sugar and Coffee Exchange—its highest price in history and a figure far surpassing the 5 or 6 cents most commentators believed was necessary to sustain the Cuban market.[114]

The inflation in values—or what one witness described as a "distortion of values"—unleashed a period of easy money as both local and foreign bankers sought to capture quick profits off the rising prices of sugar and other commodities.[115] In the Cuban countryside, especially in the eastern provinces of Oriente and Camagüey, the upheavals of geography that had begun during the war continued apace. Ancient forests were clear-cut and replaced by fields of sugarcane. Angular, modern *centrales*, or sugar mills, were thrown up against the horizon. A shoddy boomtown of banks, brothels, hotels, and canteens—all filled with black immigrant labor brought in from Jamaica and Haiti by US sugar companies—was cobbled together to support the industry.[116] In Havana there was increased investment in real estate, and increased spending on consumer goods by the Cuban nouveau riche. Sugar had turned Havana into gold. The city expanded east past the remains of the wall that once marked its boundaries into Vedado and across the Almendares River into Miramar, where merchants and financiers built massive suburban estates. Havana's rapid population growth, combined with skyrocketing inflation, made affordable housing scarce. Rolls-Royces, Isotta Fraschinis, and Packards competed for space on the Prado and Malecón with taxicabs, *guaguas*, and electric trams, and Havana's nouveau riche thronged to the casino, the races, the jai-alai frontons, and the pornographic theaters.[117]

But behind the façade of prosperity, another city was becoming visible. The cost of labor and machinery had increased 100 percent, and that of transportation between 30 and 40 percent, contributing to an inflation in prices that was felt in all aspects of life. Housing became all but unaffordable to anyone who could not build a mansion in Vedado or Marianao as property speculation increased alongside speculation in sugar. Frustrated tenants staged rent strikes, and Cuban president Menocal complained of the "outrageous profiteering by landlords," though he claimed he was powerless to do anything about it. The City Bank's staff had to economize; bachelors moved into shared accommodations, and married couples rented apartments together. Streetcar workers went on strike, and stevedores demanded pay raises.[118] Havana was subjected to almost daily bomb attacks by what the press dubbed anarchists and "revolutionary Negroes," while the signs of resentment toward black immigrant labor were becoming visible.[119]

The City Bank had contributed to the inflation of values and the feverish culture of speculation in Cuba. Porfirio Franca and Juan B. Roqué in the Havana branch had authorized loans far in excess of the limits set by the New York committee, advancing credits on properties that could not realize value and with collateral and security that was dubious at best. The City Bank made heavy advances to *colonos*, the small, often highly indebted independent planters tied to the mills through long-term contracts, who were considered risky clients at the best of times, and to the sugar mill owners themselves, who sought to expand their mills in anticipation of the coming harvest at rates and amounts that presumed that the high price of sugar would be sustained indefinitely. The Hershey Company borrowed heavily from the bank, plowing funds into the expansion of its Cuban properties. Cuban estate owner Marcelino García Beltrán borrowed $15 million to refurbish his plantations. Advances were made to Cuban president Menocal for his personal purchase of mills and plantations. Roqué was pushing the bank to authorize a $5 million loan to planter Domingo Leon for the purchase and expansion of sugar properties.[120] Roqué was also agitating to join Leon as a business partner.[121]

Fueled by speculation and enabled by loose lending practices, the price of sugar reached 22 ½ cents per pound on May 22, 1920. Writing in *The Americas*, John H. Allen was characteristically enthusiastic about Cuba. He argued that Cuba could easily double its output of sugar, the only impediment to the expansion of the sugar industry being a shortage of labor.[122] Allen's assessment would soon appear misguided and delusional. By the end of the summer of 1920, the price of sugar had begun a precipitous decline. As sugar dropped from its heights in May, companies like Cuba Cane Sugar and Punta Alegre experienced a steady decline in valuation. Credit became increasingly constricted as worried bankers no longer lent as freely as before. The circulation and movement of goods slowed to a crawl as buyers found they could not afford many of the US and European goods they had ordered during the boom times. Collections lagged, and the port of Havana became congested, partly because of an inefficient lightering system, partly because importers could no longer afford their orders. In September, rumors appeared in the Cuban press that a young businessman had withdrawn all his assets from various banks and placed them in a safe-deposit box. "They say," wrote the *Times of Cuba*, "that he must expect a panic or something."[123]

On October 11, 1920, panic hit. Merchant Pedro Gómez Mena presented a draft, rumored to be over $2 million, to the Banco Internacional de Cuba, one of the "mushroom" banks that had sprouted during the boom years, opening branches across the country.[124] When news got out that the Banco Internacional was unable to redeem Mena's draft, panicked depositors stormed its Havana headquarters in a desperate attempt to withdraw their funds. While the Banco Internacional was forced to suspend payment, the panic spread throughout Havana as confidence in the banking system plummeted. A two-day banking run ensued that was only halted when Cuban president Menocal intervened. After consulting with the banking community and local merchants, Menocal declared a fifty-day moratorium on bank withdrawals. The City Bank declined to take part in the moratorium, continuing the policy of ready money that had secured the bank its reputation during the tenures of both Moses Taylor and James Stillman. It was subject to heavy withdrawals from depositors and was forced to ship almost a million dollars a day from the United States to Cuba to bolster its reserves. By November, $16.1 million had been sent to the Havana branch, but it kept its doors open to its customers.[125]

In the initial days of the crisis, Havana branch manager Porfirio Franca worked alongside his counterparts at the Royal Bank of Canada, the Trust Company of Cuba, the Bank of Nova Scotia, and other institutions to draft a memorandum offering a solution to the banking crisis. They suggested the organization of a clearinghouse for Havana and the issuance of "collateral trust certificates" that would ease the illiquidity of capital and provide planters with a means of short-term financing that could fund the harvest.[126] Their plan was dismissed outright by the State Department. As delegations of Wall Street bankers buzzed through Havana's streets and visited Cuba's sugar properties, US president Woodrow Wilson appointed US lawyer Albert Rathbone as a financial adviser to the Cuban government. Rathbone's appointment prompted the resignation of the finance minister, Leopoldo Cancio. Rathbone spent two weeks in Havana at Cancio's desk and wrote a report saying little that the Cubans did not already know: he recommended that Cuba contract a loan from Wall Street and sell the previous year's sugar crop to inject liquidity into the banking system. Upon his return to the United States, Rathbone promptly billed the Cuban government $50,000 for his service.[127]

The remaining sugar crop was left unsold. Purchasers refused to buy, even with the price hovering around 5 cents per pound. Planters were unable to generate credits from the banks for the coming crop. Menocal petitioned Wall Street for a $50 million dollar loan to shore up the price of sugar and maintain the government, the banking industry, and the Cuban economy. Wall Street refused. While the bankers offered credits to their own interests, they argued that they could not lend financial support to sugar growers, given that American cotton and wheat growers were facing the same depressed prices for their own crops and had been denied relief.[128] Menocal also sent planter and financier José Miguel Tarafa (who had earlier partnered with Roland Conklin on the consolidation of Cuba's railroads) to New York City to confer with City Bank director Robert B. Hawley, also a director of the Cuban-American Sugar Company.[129] Hawley let Menocal know that the City Bank would offer $10 million to Cuban planters, and asked the Cuban government for "some word of expression from you to the Bank commending its action."[130] Menocal was happy to oblige. "I need hardly say that such an attitude on the part of a great financial institution like the City is highly gratifying," Menocal gushed,

> and doubly welcome in the present trying moment, as it will materially help to strengthen confidence in the fundamental stability and future prosperity of Cuba whose economic situation, while temporarily disturbed, is fundamentally sound . . . I shall appreciate it if you would be good enough to convey to the Board of Directors of the National City Bank my personal appreciation of their attitude and to assure them that such disinterested and friendly action will not be soon forgotten.[131]

John H. Allen tempered his earlier assessments of Cuban affairs but remained cautiously optimistic. In *The Americas* he argued that Cuba was experiencing a "normal" situation given the recent excessive financing. For Allen, the only "danger" was the potential exacerbation or aggravation of the situation stemming from an overreaction on the part of the Cubans. He stated that "by reason of the temperament of the [Cuban] people," who, he asserted, were not always open to wise counsel or known for coolheadedness, the situation could be inflamed. He otherwise saw the crisis as a "necessary readjustment," and suggested that although there should be concern about speculation in real estate, sugar, and other commodities, he was "hopeful" about Cuba's future.[132] It was Allen's last essay in *The Americas* and his final public statement on behalf of the City Bank. With the turmoil in Cuba, the directors had seen enough. Allen was forced to resign from the bank at the end of October 1920.[133] Almost immediately after leaving the City Bank, he assumed the position of president of the American Foreign Banking Corporation, which was controlled by the City Bank's emergent rival, the Chase National Bank of the City of New York.[134]

In the wake of Allen's dismissal, the Overseas Division of the bank was reorganized. Roger L. Farnham was recalled to take charge of the Caribbean District, its purview now expanded to include the West Indies, Central America, Australia, and Southern Africa.[135] Farnham promptly traveled by steamer from New York City to Cuba, accompanied by Vere Brown. Brown was a newly appointed City Bank vice president who was recruited from the Canadian Bank of Commerce, where he had worked since 1889, most recently in Winnipeg, Manitoba, as manager of its Western Canadian division. While Farnham toured the City Bank's sugar properties, Brown studied the accounts in the Havana branch and interviewed its staff. Both men came away with a favorable impression of the management of the Cuban operations. The only problem Brown saw was in the difficulties Cuba's commercial houses were experiencing from the overextension of finance; he worried that if the moratorium were lifted, they would fail.[136] But he was as optimistic as Allen. "As far as our interest in the sugar business is concerned," Brown reported, "I can imagine no banking credits to growers and manufactures being on a more satisfactory basis as to security than loans resting on the cane and sugar contracts in use in Cuba. Moreover, the record of the sugar crop reveals a comparative freedom from serious failure—in any case failure of a sugar crop is not as costly to the grower as is failure to a cereal crop." In Brown's assessment, many of the problems of the City Bank in Cuba were down to questions of personality and branch management—both the internal dynamics of the Havana branch, and its relations to the home office at 55 Wall Street and to the country branches. He found that Havana branch manager Porfirio Franca was "laboring under a feeling of injured pride," as his authority had been undermined by Allen, on the one hand, and the submanagers, on the other; and argued that the bank should clean up and rationalize the lines of authority and responsibility. Farnham's impression was also positive. He returned to New York City and immediately worked to authorize a line of credit to Cuban planters.

Farnham was back in Cuba in the spring of 1921. Upon arriving in Havana, he conferred with the staff of the Cuba Street branch and assessed the nature of its loans and the quality of its collateral. He met with General Enoch Crowder, sent to Cuba by President Wilson to oversee the fall 1920 elections. He had an audience in the National Palace with newly elected president Alfredo Zayas. He conferenced with the officials of the Comisión Temporal de Liquidación Bancaria, the Cuban government agency supervising the liquidation of the failed Cuban banks. Farnham gave few words to the press during this visit, but both the banking and the sugar situation appeared dire. Faith and confidence in banking institutions and the financial system had been gutted. Businesses refused to use checks. Currency was suspect. Gold was reappearing as a medium of exchange. The practice of hoarding returned as millions of dollars were withdrawn from banks and placed in safe-deposit boxes, pillowcases, drawers, and mason jars, resulting in millions of dollars being taken out of circulation.[137]

The City Bank, whose investments in the republic were once seen as a beacon of economic modernity, national development, and civilizational progress, was increasingly viewed in Cuba with a bitter opprobrium. Similar to the Banco Español de la Isla de Cuba decades before, it was being recast as a symbol of neocolonialism and a sign of the extinguishment of Cuban sovereignty. As a result of defaults to sugar properties, the deeds to fifty-six sugar mills—one-quarter of the mills in Cuba—were now in the hands of the City Bank. In January 1921, the Havana daily *El Mundo* engaged in what one City Banker later described as "anti-American attacks" on the City Bank, the RBC, the Mercantile Bank of the Americas, and the American Foreign Banking Corporation. The articles in *El Mundo* sparked runs on both the City Bank and the RBC and forced Roger Farnham to join with the RBC's F. R. Beatty in appealing to the US State Department to intervene. J. P. Morgan's Dwight Morrow, in Cuba for loan negotiations with the government, asked General Crowder to talk to *El Mundo*'s editor, Rafael Govin. Govin flatly refused to stop publishing the attacks, allegedly because he felt they were good for circulation.[138] North American banks were defended by some members of the Cuban press; *El Mercurio*, for instance, described *El Mundo*'s attacks as "pernicious libel."[139] But the damage was done. The City Bank took out advertisements in the Cuban press reminding customers that the Cuban branches were backed by the reserves of Wall Street. Even so, attacks made the work of reconstruction difficult. The City Bank was forced to increase its reserves from 25 percent to sometimes upward of 65 percent as a safeguard against panic and contagion, which meant that the amount of capital that could circulate decreased, as did the bank's profits. Along with other foreign institutions, the City Bank threatened to withdraw from the island entirely if the attacks against them did not stop.

Things took a turn for the worse that spring. On April 29, weeks after Farnham's departure, the Banco Nacional de Cuba's José "Pote" Rodríguez hung himself in his Vedado mansion. The suicide of the president and largest stockholder of the Banco Nacional de Cuba spurred a wave of banking failures over the coming year that would leave dozens of Cuban banks with

hundreds of country branches shuttered and untold losses to Cuban depositors.[140] The City Bank was not unaffected by the crisis. Of the $60 millon
loaned to Cuban sugar producers, 80 percent, or $48 million, amounting to
60 percent of the bank's working capital was at risk.[141] A total of $25 million
was wiped off the bank's books. A number of Cuban branches were closed
in an attempt to consolidate their operations. The effects of the collapse in
commodity prices also reverberated throughout the Caribbean region. In
August 1921 the Port of Spain branch was sold and the Colombian branches
were shut down. In Panama, the IBC's branches were subjected to repeated
runs by nervous depositors.[142]

During 1921, Farnham worked to ensure credits were available to the
City Bank's Cuban customers and to the Cuban government, and he returned a number of times to the republic. But his standing in the bank was
faltering. He was at the center of two of the biggest crises the City Bank had
faced in its more than one-hundred-year history: the crisis in Cuba following the dance of millions and the investigation of the bank's activities in
Haiti following the sensational accounts of the US occupation. As Frank A.
Vanderlip's appointee, Farnham represented an old regime within the City
Bank, a regime that for many inside the bank was beginning to look like a
failure. New blood and new ideas were needed. When James A. Stillman resigned the City Bank presidency in 1921 after a brief, scandal-ridden tenure,
Farnham's time with the bank appeared to be nearing an end. Stillman's
replacement, Charles Edwin Mitchell, took the bank in a new direction. He
abandoned many of the practices initiated during the City Bank's first era of
imperial expansion under Frank A. Vanderlip and James Stillman, and he
began gathering a new team of managers and vice presidents. Where Farnham was at one time invaluable to Vanderlip and Stillman, Joseph H. Durrell, a relatively new hire at the bank and at one time Farnham's subordinate,
became Mitchell's right-hand man in the Caribbean. In 1923, Durrell was
promoted to lead the Caribbean district. Farnham, after more than a decade
with the City Bank, resigned.

Farnham's involvement with the Caribbean did not end in 1923. He
remained involved with US business in the Caribbean. He was still president of the Caribbean Construction Company, the Haiti Company, and the
National Railroad of Haiti.[143] In 1920, he had also been appointed as the
receiver of the National Railroad, as the US federal district court initiated
proceedings to protect the railroad's investors and creditors and to oversee
the rehabilitation of its construction. In 1924, a hearing was held in New
York to determine the payments due to those involved in the receivership.
For his work as receiver, Farnham was paid $100,000 with an additional

yearly salary set at $18,000. Sullivan and Cromwell, his old employers who now served as his attorneys, received $80,000. Julius M. Mayer, the justice who had allocated the payments, was gushing in his praise of Farnham. Mayer proclaimed that he could not "fully express in language [his] sense of appreciation" to Farnham for his work as receiver over the past four years. He asserted that "if the amount at the disposal of the Court were larger, [he] should not hesitate to award [Farnham] larger compensation."[144] Others were more critical of Farnham's role in Haiti and less enthusiastic about his lucrative payouts. Farnham, noted one critic, "has been an expensive luxury for the Haitian peasants to support."[145] The same thing could have been said about the City Bank in the Caribbean.

FIVE

American Expansion

Attired in bespoke white linen suits and stiff-brimmed straw boater hats, a stylish crowd of bankers, merchants, planters, journalists, and curious members of the general public had flocked to the main banking room of the Banco Mercantil Americano de Cuba on the afternoon of September 1, 1919.[1] With baroque pleasantries and firm handshakes they offered their congratulations and extended their goodwill on the occasion of the Banco Mercantil's move from its temporary offices just down the street at Amargura 23, where it had been housed since January, to the main floor of the Edifico Barraque, a new, eight-story building on the corner of Amargura and Cuba streets in Havana's commercial district. Guests arrived to find the main banking room done up to mark the occasion. Potted palm trees were placed throughout the room. Bouquets of roses were suspended from the marble columns. Intertwined Cuban and American flags, meant to symbolize the commercial and political intimacy of the two republics, were draped on the walls. A six-piece jazz band brought in from New York City played the latest numbers. A hot luncheon was served buffet style, after which guests were offered desserts, champagne, and Cuban cigars. Fernand J. Oehmichen, the Banco Mercantil's general manager, read a statement that was published in *Bamericuba*, the well-designed monthly journal whose launch coincided with the inauguration of the Havana branch, and that was reprinted in English and Spanish in the financial press of both the United States and Cuba. "Little by little we shall increase our services in the island," Oehmichen declared to his guests. "Little by little our clientele will realize the benefits of our organization, which does not work with the sole idea of accumulating deposits of money. It works under a modern banking policy, the same as that of the great institutions of credit which consider the bank as a distributive center of service to commerce, agriculture, and industry."[2]

Burdened with cliché and laden with the bromides of economic growth, financial modernity, mutuality, and binational cooperation, Oehmichen's bland platitudes were befitting of a middle manager. Yet his comments were also something of an understatement. They downplayed the momentousness of the occasion, for the arrival of the Banco Mercantil Americano de Cuba in Havana in 1919 and the inauguration of its new premises on the ground floor of the Edificio Barraque was just a part of a larger transformation of the landscape of Cuban banking and finance in the aftermath of World War I. For many observers, it was not a transformation that occurred "little by little," to borrow Oehmichen's phrase, but one that came with abrupt and sudden force: seemingly without warning, massive upheavals and wholesale changes reordered the cultures of banking and finance in Cuba, and, simultaneously, the spatial character of Havana.

Indeed, the Edificio Barraque, named after and built by a Cuban firm specializing in corporation law, signified these upheavals and changes. A rude interjection into Havana's Moorish urbanism, the Edificio Barraque appeared unadorned, hulking, austere, almost brutal; it lacked the ornate detailing and neoclassical façades typical of the architecture of an earlier era of Havana's history. In a city where buildings were but two stories tall, at eight stories—and with the added curiosity of an elevator—the Edificio Barraque punctured Havana's low skyline while suggesting that its primary design attribute was its multiplication of ground rent. Even the copywriters of *Bamericuba*, after conceding the difficulty of photographing the Edificio Barraque given the tight perspectives generated by Havana's narrow streets, concluded their profile of the new building by haplessly stating, *Es un rectangulo*—"It is a rectangle."[3] But the tight crossroads of Cuba and Amargura actually served to highlight its difference from the buildings surrounding it while accentuating the architectural distinctions of Cuba's economic history: on one corner stood the baroque mass of the San Francisco convent, constructed in 1627; on another, a late nineteenth-century apartment building, the Hotel Union, its exterior designed in a modest and romantic *bellas artes* style. The Edificio Barraque represented a violent break with both traditions while highlighting the unfolding architectural history and the spatial contradictions and transformations of Havana and Cuba as the republic was increasingly brought into the orbit of US finance capitalism and under the control of Wall Street's imperial banks.[4]

The arrival of the Banco Mercantil Americano de Cuba as the ground-floor tenant of the Edificio Barraque was both a sign and symptom of these economic and cultural changes in Cuba, and across the Caribbean. Chartered in Connecticut in 1919, the Banco Mercantil de Cuba was a subsidiary

of the Mercantile Bank of the Americas (MBA). The MBA had been organized four years earlier by a powerful Wall Street consortium that included
private bankers J. & W. Seligman and Co., Brown Brothers and Co., and the
Guaranty Trust Company, an institution controlled by J. P. Morgan and Co.
These institutions also drew on the capital resources of a half dozen federally chartered national banking associations across the United States who,
together, created an imperial banking institution whose purpose was to displace European banking and finance in the Americas. The MBA represented
the fulfillment of the desires and dreams of the US statesmen and bankers
of two decades earlier who wished to create a US-based international commercial bank—a Pan-American or American international institution—that
could dominate the financing of the commerce of the Americas. Those early
plans had largely been stillborn. The International Banking Corporation
proved to be the only surviving venture from that era, though its success was
circumscribed by questions of personnel, scale, the regulatory constraints of
the American banking system, and the indifference of global credit conditions. The Mercantile Bank of the Americas arrived in a different era. By the
time it was chartered, World War I had drastically reordered global credit
flows, and the United States had emerged as the world's greatest creditor.
The Federal Reserve System, operationalized in 1914, provided the legal
machinery to facilitate the foreign expansion of American banking and
the financing of international trade. The branch bank network of the City
Bank was rapidly expanding as it recast itself as an imperial institution. Wall
Street's turn on the stage of global finance appeared imminent.

The MBA was a radical and unprecedented experiment in the history of
US banking. It represented a new managerial and organizational structure
for imperial accumulation—one distinguished by concentration, carteliza-
tion, coordination, and collusion. It was the product of an emergent US
imperial legal regime and emerged within a new context of regulation and
empire. Paralleling the City Bank's foreign expansion under James Stillman
and Frank A. Vanderlip, the history of the MBA offers another account of the
ways in which imperial bankers navigated plural legal regimes and uneven
regulatory geographies in the context of the changing financial conditions of
World War I and the postwar era. Yet the rise and fall of the Banco Mercantil
Americano de Cuba, and its off-Wall Street parent, the MBA, also demon-
strates the ambiguous history of Wall Street in Cuba, and in the Caribbean
region more generally. It suggests something of the paradoxical fortunes and
doubtful fates of the internationalization of US banking and the expansion
of US imperialism in the early twentieth century. The story of the MBA is not
about the inevitable hegemony of the United States in the Caribbean, but

about its staggered incursion; it is not a tale of invincibility and triumph, but one of vulnerability and failure. Its time at the pinnacle of imperial banking and finance in the Caribbean was short, and almost as quickly as the cigar smoke had drifted away, the jazz band had packed up, and the well-wishers and businesspeople had drifted into the enveloping warmth of Havana's September dusk, the Banco Mercantil Americano de Cuba abandoned its premises on the main floor of the Edifico Barraque, its offices were sold, and its history was relegated to the lost archives of banking and empire.

The MBA's origins were in the mercantile world of the nineteenth-century Atlantic and the blood-washed annals of capitalism and slavery. The two institutions behind the MBA—the private banking houses of Brown Brothers and Co. and J. & W. Seligman and Co.—were part of a small group of international concerns based in New York that had transitioned from merchant to merchant bank to investment bank, while maintaining a business organization largely based on close-knit family ties.[5] Founded in 1818, Brown Brothers grew out of the Baltimore business of Irish linen merchant Alexander Brown.[6] In 1800, Brown had closed a successful auctioneers business in Ireland and traveled to the United States, where he established a linen warehouse in Baltimore. His four sons (William, George, John, and James) continued the Brown family business, exporting cotton, tobacco, and other commodities to Britain and importing linen. The firm secured a practical monopoly of the linen trade in Baltimore. It established agencies in Charleston, Savannah, New Orleans, and Mobile and began functioning as a merchant bank: lending money to slave owners, trading in bills of exchange, issuing commercial credits, and financing all aspects of the commerce in cotton as that commodity moved from Southern plantations to Lancashire mills via the port cities of the United States and through Liverpool. The Brown banking business was founded in Philadelphia in 1812 as an outgrowth of the mercantile business and soon outgrew it. Brown's sons organized Brown and Company (later, Brown, Shipley & Co.) in Liverpool in 1813, and Brown Brothers and Co. in New York City in 1825. The New York affiliate was organized when the firm recognized that the opening of the Erie Canal would divert commercial traffic through the port of New York. Brown Brothers was opened by James Brown in a building at 191 Pearl Street before moving to a long-term home at 59 Wall Street at Hanover. In 1836 the dry goods business of the firm was liquidated, and the firm focused its energies on international banking, emerging as an important agency for the marketing of Union bonds during the Civil War.

J. & W. Seligman and Co. was founded by Joseph Seligman, a university-educated currency trader from Baiersdorf, Bavaria, who arrived in New York City during the Panic of 1837. He worked for a year as an account manager for a firm in Mauch Chauk, Pennsylvania, before embarking on his own as a peddler provisioning goods throughout the South. He settled first in Mobile, Alabama and, joined by his brothers, soon expanded the business to other southern cities and then to San Francisco, where they did a brisk and lucrative trade during the gold rush years. Like Brown Brothers, Seligman's commercial business began to bleed into financial services. The Seligmans opened the banking house J. & W. Seligman and Co. in New York City in 1848, and in 1862 organized a network of international affiliates whose organizational model was inspired by the networks of August Belmont and the Rothschild family. Seligman Brothers was organized in London, Seligman Frères in Paris, and Seligman & Stettheimer in Frankfurt—all were family owned and operated. While branches in New Orleans and San Francisco followed, the European affiliates would become independent concerns by 1897.[7] During the Civil War, the Seligmans contracted as sutlers for the federal government and began marketing US government securities in Europe. In 1863, they introduced US government bonds to German investors.[8]

By the first decade of the twentieth century, both Brown Brothers and Seligman had emerged as among the most important investment banking houses in New York City, with Seligman housed at 1 William Street, and Brown Brothers at 59 Wall Street. Seligman, in particular, became tied to some of the largest and most notorious industrial projects of the age, pairing with both Jay Gould and Cornelius Vanderbilt on their railway schemes and helping to underwrite the Standard Oil syndicate. Seligman also participated in the financing of the Panama Canal, a project the firm had been interested in since the late 1880s, when, alongside J. P. Morgan and Co. and Winslow, Lanier & Co., it was a member of the US committee of the Panama Canal Company when it was still under French control. While they had resigned from the committee before the company collapsed, wiping out the savings of thousands of French workers and peasants, they received some $400,000 in fees.[9] By the second decade of the twentieth century Seligman began working on another Caribbean project in conjunction with Brown Brothers. In what marked a shift in operations for both institutions, but was entirely in line with the trend of finance and politics at the time, Seligman and Brown Brothers became embroiled in the politics of dollar diplomacy in Nicaragua through their ownership and control of the Banco Nacional de Nicaragua (BNN) and the refunding of Nicaragua's sovereign debt.

Their interests in Nicaragua had relatively innocuous origins but quickly

spiraled into a clotted mess of international diplomacy and military intervention.[10] In 1910, Brown Brothers was approached by English businessman Samuel Segar. Segar was looking to retire and wanted to liquidate
much of his stock portfolio. The portfolio included shares in the firm of
George D. Emery and Co., a Boston-based company involved in the hard-
wood business. Emery and Co. held real estate in Massachusetts and had
extensive timber rights in Nicaragua—some of which were embedded in a
1909 protocol between the United States and Nicaragua. The protocol was
established when Nicaraguan president José Santos Zelaya revoked Emery's
right to a lucrative timber concession on the grounds it violated the Nicaraguan constitution. In response, the firm argued that the cancellation of
the concession was a violation of the law and an infringement on the company's right. It filed a claim against the Nicaraguan government for future
income lost. The dispute was settled through international arbitration, with
the company's assets transferred to Nicaragua, and Emery awarded a settlement of $600,000, although the payment was suspended and folded into
the protocol.

That Brown Brothers approached J. & W. Seligman and Co. and together they
formed a syndicate to take over the Massachusetts properties and the Nicaraguan protocol while selling the timber rights to a New York company.
They retained corporate lawyer Severo Mallet-Prevost to handle the negotiations. Born in Mexico, Mallet-Prevost had extensive experience in the
Caribbean and Latin America. He had served as a commissioner handling
the Venezuela-British Guiana boundary dispute, had emerged as one of the
foremost experts on international law, and had offered legal advice on regional bond issues, railroad projects, and sugar plantations.[11] Mallet-Prevost
traveled to Washington to investigate the history of the protocol in the State
Department records and, while there, learned that the US government was
searching for a US bank through which a loan could be negotiated for the
government of Nicaragua as part of a broad plan to reorganize and "rehabilitate" the finances of Nicaragua along the lines of what had been worked
out in the Dominican Republic. Mallet-Prevost brought this information
to the attention of Brown Brothers, and on February 2, 1911, James Brown,
the grandson of the Brown Brothers patriarch Alexander Brown, wrote to
Secretary Knox expressing interest.[12]

That summer, the United States and Nicaragua signed the Knox-Castrillo
Convention, authorizing the provision of a $15 million loan to reestablish
the credit of the Central American republic via a refunding of the public
debt, the paying off of outstanding claims against the country, and the stabi-
lization of finances through the controlled collection of customs. Although

the State Department approved the Brown Brothers and Seligman bid for the loan, and the convention was approved by the Nicaraguan Congress it was blocked by the US Senate.[13] As a result, the State Department decided to turn to short-term financing of a lesser amount, bundling a small loan with a number of attached agreements for the establishment of a fiscal agency for the control of customs, a banking concession, and a concession for the construction of a railway from the Atlantic coast. Once the agreement was signed, the bankers hired Charles A. Conant and Francis C. Harrison to investigate conditions in Nicaragua. Conant had already worked on fiscal and monetary reform in Mexico, China, and the Philippines. Harrison had recently served as head commissioner of the paper currency of British India. Paid $10,000 each from the Nicaraguan treasury, they traveled to Nicaragua and stayed for almost five months. They found that conditions in Nicaragua were worse than expected, as government issues of currency had increased the cost of retirement. Nonetheless, they advocated retiring the depreciated paper currency that had been in use since 1893 and adapting a gold coin, the córdoba, at par with the dollar. They also proposed the organization of a government bank, and the flotation of a $10 million loan secured through a lien on customs receipts.[14]

On January 4, 1912, James Brown and J. & W. Seligman's Frederick Strauss incorporated the National Bank of Nicaragua, Inc., in Connecticut.[15] (Frederick Strauss was one of two brothers, the other being Albert, who were non-family partners of Seligman. They joined the firm in 1866 and became partners in 1901.[16]) Capitalized at $5 million, the new institution was granted a ninety-nine-year concession, given exclusive rights to act as the fiscal agency and depository of the Nicaraguan government, and tasked with stabilizing the Nicaraguan currency by organizing and operating the new monetary system though a US dollar loan. It had the right to both issue bank notes and other monetary instruments and act as a commercial bank. Brown Brothers and Seligman had a 51 percent stake in the new institution; the Nicaraguan government held the other 49 percent. In New York City, where the authority over the National Bank of Nicaragua rested, a room was set up in Brown Brothers' offices with a secretary, stenographer, and clerk to serve it.

W. Bundy Cole was installed as manager of the bank in Managua. Born in England, Cole's experience in the Caribbean and Latin America dated to the 1880s. He worked as an auditor for the Guatemalan Northern Railroad and as an accountant for the Banco Internacional de Guatemala before joining Samuel Jarvis's North American Trust Company, and later the Banco Nacional de Cuba, in their Santiago de Cuba and Matanzas branches.[17] Cole helped organize branches of the International Banking Corporation in

Mexico City, Panama, and Colón before briefly serving as president of the Vera Cruz Banking Company.[18] He then joined the National Bank of Nicaragua. Cole despised Caribbean and Latin American people. "I have no use for any of them," he wrote in a memorandum on the BNN.[19] He believed that their African and Indian populations were racially inferior to whites and incapable of self-rule. "I do not think any Indian or any negro is capable of self-government," Cole stated. "And they are all Indians in Mexico, and they are all Indians in Nicaragua," he continued. "If we go on the principle of calling an Indian an Indian, the same as we do in calling a nigger a nigger—that is, where a man has one drop of Indian blood in his veins—in my opinion he is an Indian." When he eventually returned to the United States to take up the management of a taxi company in New York City, he said he did it "in order to quit Latin America, I hope, forever."[20] Cole's comments were not strictly personal opinions; the racist claims of his speech were part of the policy of Brown Brothers and Seligman in their management of the National Bank of Nicaragua and their decision making on fiscal matters.

Cole was embroiled in Nicaragua's internal political affairs almost from the moment of his arrival. Two weeks after he reached Managua, an attempt to overthrow the Adolfo Díaz government in a coup was launched by Díaz's former secretary of war, Luis Mena. Attempts by the US minister to diffuse the sitation failed, and sections of the railroad properties owned by the BNN fell into the hands of the insurrectionists, hindering the railway's ability to operate. The manager of the railroad lodged a protest within the Nicaraguan government, and Cole sent a private cable to James Brown at his Park Avenue residence in New York, asking for support and protection. Brown promptly replied that he was advised by the State Department that everything possible was being done to protect the Brown Brothers and Seligman interests, and vessels were on their way.[21] Forty-eight hours later, the US Marines arrived, ordered to protect US life and property—in particular, the interests of Brown Brothers and Seligman. The marines took over Managua, and half their number used the BNN as temporary quarters. Mena was soon captured and imprisoned, and at the end of August 1912, President Taft authorized a full-scale military invasion of Nicaragua, sending US Marines to ensure the protection of US interests and to maintain the republic's political stability.

For the bankers, the continuing presence of US Marines in Nicaragua provided the ideal conditions for conducting business. They doubted Nicaraguans were capable of self-government, and they believed that stability could only be ensured through the continued US military presence, the threat of force, and the strong arm of US paternalism. Cole was certain that without the marines, the Díaz government would be forced to flee, and the country would fall into revolution. "I think the present Government would last until the last coach of marines left Managua station," Cole stated. "I think President Díaz would be on that last coach."[22] Both James Brown and Albert Strauss were convinced that the presence of the marines offered a moralizing force in a country that, to them, was marked by immorality and depravity; Strauss deemed it "an economical expenditure of force." They also believed that the Nicaraguans cared little if the United States occupied their country, and had little interest in national questions per se. While Strauss admitted he had never visited Nicaragua, he argued "that there not such a thing as public opinion in the sense that we know it in this country. The peon is a laborer and is satisfied if he makes a living."[23]

The presence of US Marines in Nicaragua strengthened Brown Brothers and Seligman's positions in the country. They were able to use the threat of withdrawal against the Díaz regime, and Díaz, who was politically and financially vulnerable, had little choice but to acquiesce to their demands if he wanted to remain in power. Díaz was personally insolvent and had to beg the Banco Nacional for his salary and expenses. His government was not much better off. Cole withheld the salaries of government officials, agreeing to release funds only if the government agreed to cede control of the National Railway to the bankers. "There is no money," Cole stated in response to a request for funds from the Nicaraguan ministers, "nor will there be any, nor will the bankers advance another dollar unless the assembly approves this contract."[24] Desperate for an infusion of cash, in the fall of 1913, the Nicaraguans appealed to the State Department to authorize the creation of another bank that could serve as an alternative to the BNN. They spoke favorably of a tentative agreement drawn up with Samuel M. Jarvis, of the Banco Nacional de Cuba and the Banco Nacional de Santo Domingo, for an additional loan and the organization of a new financial institution. While the Jarvis plan appeared to be a ruse to support his endeavors in the Dominican Republic, it died when Brown Brothers and Seligman stepped in with further financing, tightening their control of the Nicaraguan economy.[25] By 1914, three short years after Mallet-Prevost had first approached James Brown, Nicaragua had become a mere item in the accounting ledgers of Wall Street. Seligman partner Frederick Strauss was appointed as president of the National Railroad of Nicaragua, the only line in the country. James Brown of Brown Brothers remained president of the Banco Nacional de Nicaragua, the republic's most important commercial bank and its de facto government bank. Brown's signature on the Nicaraguan córdoba—like that of the City Bank's Roger Farnham on the Haitian gourde—became both a sign of authority, and the marker of the compromised independence of a country that would come to be known as "The Republic of Brown Brothers."[26]

The National Bank of Nicaragua was the first foreign venture of Brown Brothers and Seligman. It was not to be their last. Indeed, the onset of war in Europe on July 28, 1914, sparked a remarkable expansion of Brown Brothers and Seligman in the international field as they sought to create a US imperial bank that could take advantage of the new, unsettled conditions of global trade and finance. For James Brown the war was marked by possibility. Brown was among the more cosmopolitan figures in US banking and business. He had been educated at preparatory schools in Europe before he was graduated from Columbia University in 1883. When he joined the family firm he first worked in Europe and in England. He was fluent in Spanish, had an international vision of financial conditions, and, after becoming a partner in the firm in 1901, continued to work on international issues.[27] The organization of the BNN was largely the result of his vision, and he now contemplated organizing a "pan-American" banking institution.[28] In May 1915, Brown and Seligman's Albert Strauss attended the Pan-American Financial Conference in Washington, DC, where they represented both the National Bank of Nicaragua and the republic itself. Organized by the Pan-American Union, the conference brought together businesspeople and bankers to discuss the possibility of expanding the trade and finance of the hemisphere. Brown and Strauss were joined by other bankers, including Albert H. Wiggin and A. Barton Hepburn of the Chase National Bank, J. P. Morgan and Co.'s Henry P. Davison and Willard D. Straight, Frank A. Vanderlip of the National City Bank, Jacob H. Schiff of Kuhn, Loeb and Co., and Benjamin Strong, the first governor of the Federal Reserve. Among the conference resolutions was an affirmation of the importance of "the granting by United States bankers and businessmen of ample credits to Latin America and the prompt vision of the necessary organization and facilities for this purpose."[29] James Brown realized the moment had come.

In August 1915, Brown's Pan-American banking house was born. That month, he launched an institution called the Mercantile Bank of the Americas, Ltd., Like the National Bank of Nicaragua, it was chartered in Connecticut and capitalized at $5,000,000. Brown was installed as president of the new institution while the directorate was filled by Albert Strauss, William S. Cox, Thatcher M. Brown, Jason Neilson, and Frederick Strauss, all of whom were directors in either Brown Brothers or Seligman. Alfred Meyer was appointed general manager of the New York parent at 20 Exchange Place. Meyer would be joined in 1918 by Frank J. R. Mitchell, who had been the president of Samuel M. Jarvis's ill-fated Banco Nacional de Santo Domingo.[30] Before the Mercantile Bank of the Americas commenced operations, it underwent a massive shift in its organization and management. In the spring of 1916, the bank's directors issued an additional 6,000 shares, valued at $100 each. All of the shares were purchased by the Guaranty Trust Company, and the trust company added directors, including Charles H. Sabin, president of the company, and Albert Breton and Eugene W. Stetson, to the MBA board. The purchase gave the Guaranty Trust Company a controlling stake in the MBA while giving the MBA the authority and financial clout of the most powerful financial institution in the United States: J. P. Morgan and Co.

Morgan and Co., like Brown Brothers and Seligman, dated back to the nineteenth century. The original firm was founded by Baltimore merchant George Peabody. Peabody moved to London and became active trading commodities, offering financial services to US importer-exporters and promoting US securities. His firm was almost wiped out in the Panic of 1857, only rescued by the Bank of England, and eventually taken over by another US merchant, Junius Morgan. Morgan's son, John Pierpont, partnered in 1871 with Anthony Drexel to create Morgan and Co. Drexel provided the capital, and Morgan offerered the connections. After the Civil War, the firm raised millions of dollars in the securities markets for the federal government and the railroads.[31] With Anthony Drexel's death in 1895, the company became J. P. Morgan and Company, retaining ties with Drexel and Company in Philadelphia, the Morgan, Harjes & Company of Paris, and J. S. Morgan & Company in London. Morgan served as a conduit for European capital into the United States. While its role in securities issues was initially subordinate to European banking houses, as it grew more powerful, it was increasingly the senior partner in issues. At the same time, the firm began looking at financing beyond the state, becoming involved in the financing of foreign governments and overseas industrial projects.[32]

In 1909, Morgan acquired the Guaranty Trust Company (GTC), purchasing it from the estate of railroad magnate E. H. Harriman, who had acquired a controlling interest from the Mutual Life Insurance Company. Morgan quickly enlarged the GTC. It acquired the Morton Trust Company and the Fifth Avenue Trust Company in 1909 (and, later, in 1912, the Standard Trust Company), creating the largest trust company in the United States.[33] With the acquisition, the GTC became the fiscal agent for the Dominican government (the Morton Trust Company had served as agent since 1906).[34] The GTC's history in the republic was dubious; the commissions it charged on the handling of Dominican funds were found to be illegal, and it was forced to return $228,000 to the Dominican treasury in 1923.[35]

The GTC also acted as the fiscal agent for the Morgan loan to Honduras.[36] In 1911, a loan was proposed to place the government on sound financial footing by retiring a debt of $26 million, bloated to $128 million with accrued interest, that had accumulated since the end of the nineteenth century. The debt crippled the Honduran government and appeared to the State Department as a potential threat to the stability of the region. A group of bankers—Morgan; Kuhn, Loeb; the City Bank; and the First National Bank—proposed settling claims by European countries by refunding the entire debt for $10 million, raising the funds through a 5 percent bond sold at 88. The customs receipts were set aside for interest payments and internal improvements, and the syndicate received a claim to the railway and a concession to establish a commercial bank acting as fiscal agent, depositor, and the national mint. With their purchase of a majority holding in the MBA, Morgan, alongside Brown Brothers and Seligman, was poised for one of the most spectacular foreign expansions in the history of Wall Street. It was an expansion enabled by the law.

The legal organization of the MBA allowed it to subvent domestic regulations meant to restrict concentration and monopoly in banking as a means of supporting the development of an infrastructure for the US export business. At the same time, its organization enabled the smoothing over of the complex and plural legal geography of international trade and finance. The MBA's structure paralleled a model that had been in place for almost two decades: that of both the International Banking Corporation with its double charter and split organization (the Connecticut-chartered International Banking Corporation and the New York State–licensed International Bank), as well as that of the City Bank's National City Company and other securities affiliates. Following this, the MBA first obtained a charter in Connecticut and then petitioned for a license to operate an agency in New York City under supervision of the New York banking superintendent, though, as a foreign banking institution, it was not allowed domestic deposits.[37]

The development of the MBA was also made possible with the signing of the Federal Reserve Act in December 1913 and its operationalization the following year. Section 25 allowed national banking associations capitalized at $1 million or more to own and operate foreign branches, but few banks took advantage of the provision.[38] The City Bank quickly established a branch network, beginning with the opening of the Buenos Aires, Argentina, branch in the fall of 1914. Boston's First National Bank followed the City Bank into Buenos Aires. Washington's Commercial National Bank opened branches in Panama City and Colón.[39] Some institutions were reluctant to establish branch banks overseas. The Irving National Bank, for instance, while actively engaged in foreign trade, argued against encroaching on territory where local banks were already present.[40] Instead, the Irving Bank preferred working with already established institutions. It cited its correspondent relationships with London's Barclays and Co. and Paris's Irving Cox & Company. Bankers also expressed concern that resentment could arise because foreign banks were not permitted to set up branches in the United States. They argued for reciprocity and encouraged opening the domestic market to foreign banks.

Section 25 was amended on September 7, 1916, to further encourage the development of US foreign banking. The amendment authorized national banking associations to invest in the stock of state-chartered corporations engaged in foreign banking, as long as the corporations agreed to supervision by the Federal Reserve Board.[41] The amendment allowed the kind of collusion and cooperation of domestic banking institutions for the purposes of international trade financing that was not permitted within the United States itself. Rival banks that would have been competing with each other within the boundaries of the United States banded together in a national effort to strengthen the US presence overseas. Such cooperation allowed them to take advantage of the vulnerable position of European banks during the war, while preparing Wall Street for the anticipated revival of European banks after the conclusion of the war. Soon after the GTC acquired a controlling share of the MBA, other institutions joined, increasing its capitalization and strengthening its directorship. The consortium backing the MBA soon stretched beyond Wall Street to the regional centers of US capital and commerce. Additional participants in the MBA included the National Shawmut Bank of Boston, the Anglo & London Paris National Bank of San Francisco, the Hibernia Bank and Trust Company of New Orleans, the Central Union Trust Company of New York, and the Continental and Commercial National Bank of Chicago.[42] The MBA handled the foreign business of its shareholder institutions (as well as that of a number of nonaffiliated institutions) through the overseas agencies and correspondents.[43]

The organizers of the MBA quickly decided that the best way to establish a commercial bank for hemispheric trade was not through the establishment of overseas branches directly controlled by the parent—a policy encouraged by the Federal Reserve and taken up by the City Bank. Indeed, the only actual branches organized by the MBA were in the United States and Europe—in New Orleans, San Francisco, Paris, Madrid, Barcelona, and Hamburg—and their purpose was to provide support to the MBA's affiliated banks. In London the MBA operated through the branch of the GTC and Brown, Shipley & Co., an affiliate of Brown Brothers.[44] Instead of branches, the MBA developed two strategies for overseas organization. First, it aimed to organize, control, and operate regional government banks that would manage fiscal affairs, currency issue, customs collection, and taxation. The MBA built on the financial infrastructure developed, on the one hand, by US and European merchants who had sought foreign banking concessions in the nineteenth century to support local agricultural exports, and on the other, through the establishment of the kinds of nominally national central banks that were privileged during the era of dollar diplomacy. Second, the MBA organized a group of affiliated local commercial banks, chartered in their home jurisdiction, that had a semi-independent relationship to their New York parent. These commercial banks were managed by both US and local representatives, but their directorship and ownership remained with the MBA.[45] They were authorized to open and manage their own sub-branches, but they used the MBA to clear their European and US business.[46] Although partially capitalized by the Wall Street parent, these affiliated banking houses drew on both the social networks and capital resources of local merchants and planters.[47]

The expansion of the MBA was stunning. Its growth eclipsed that of the International Banking Corporation a decade before and rivaled the City Bank's development of a foreign branch network. Taking over already-established merchant banks and banks of issue in Nicaragua, Honduras, Costa Rica, and Guatemala, in an instant, the MBA became the most powerful financial institution in the Central American region. The BNN, the bank of issue organized by Brown Brothers and Seligman in 1911, was the first institution brought into the fold of the MBA. It took a 51 percent share of the BNN's stock, an amount previously held by Brown Brothers and Seligman, while the remainder was held by the Nicaraguan government, a government beholden to both its Wall Street financiers and the forces of US military occupation.[48]

The takeover of institutions in British Honduras, Costa Rica, and Guatemala followed. In Honduras, where the GTC was already operating as J. P. Morgan's fiscal agent, the MBA acquired a controlling interest in the Banco Atlántida. Based in La Ceiba on the north coast, the Banco Atlántida was founded in February 9, 1913, by the New Orleans banana planter Vaccaro Brothers and Co., the predecessor of the Standard Fruit Company.[49] The Banco Atlántida had been granted a fifty-year contract as a bank of emission and credit and assumed a central role in Honduras alongside the Vaccarro operations in financing the harvest and export of bananas even as the Vaccarro Brothers assumed a predominant position in the region's distilling, shipping, and railroads. With branches in Tegucigalpa, San Pedro Sula, Puerto Cortés, Tela, and Amapala, the Banco Atlántida was one of the most powerful financial institutions in the country. Competition in Honduras came from the Bank of British Honduras.[50] Incorporated in 1902 by Mobile, Alabama capitalists financing Belizean hide and mahogany exports, it was taken over by the Royal Bank of Canada in 1912.[51]

In Costa Rica, the MBA acquired shares of the Banco Mercantil de Costa Rica. Headquartered at San José, the Banco Mercantil de Costa Rica had been established by the firm of Rojas y Fernandes, and opened in 1908.[52] In Guatemala, the MBA gained control over the Banco de Guatemala. The Banco de Guatemala, established in 1895 and partly controlled through the German-American merchant Adolph Stahl and Schwartz and Co., along with its agencies at Antigua, Cobán, Coatepeque, Escuintla, Jutiapa, Mazatenango, Pochuta, Quetzaltenango, Retalhuleu, Salama, and Zacapa.[53] Through the bank, Stahl had lent freely to his friend Guatemalan dictator Manuel Estrada Cabrera, offering him short-term loans whose interest hovered around 20 percent and whose amortization the state revenue privileged and whose proceeds often went to goods sold by Stahl himself.[54] Stahl and the Banco de Guatemala helped to bankrupt the country while angering foreign bondholders. A director of the Anglo & London Paris National Bank of San Francisco, Stahl joined the directors of the MBA and became an important influence in its Cuban affiliate, the Banco Mercantil Americano de Cuba.

In addition to the purchase of governmental banks, the MBA also organized a series of commercial banks, each independently capitalized by both the parent bank and the stockholders in the MBA. The Banco Mercantil Americano de Peru was the first commercial bank organized by the MBA. It was chartered in September 1916 under the incorporation laws of Hartford, Connecticut, and looked to finance the export of Peruvian cotton, sugar, wool, hides, and skins. Its headquarters were in Lima, its offices there under the stewardship of Ferdinand J. Oehmichen, who would later run the Havana branch of the Banco Mercantil Americano de Cuba. The MBA opened branches in the cities of Arequipa, Chiclayo, Callao, and Trujillo, while forming a local board of directors, supplemented by Brown, Strauss, Breton, and Neilson.[55] The following year, the Banco Mercantil Americano de Caracas was organized in Venezuela, with branches in Caracas, La Guayvra, Maracaibo, Puerto Cabello, and Valencia. The American Mercantile Bank of Brazil was organized for that country, with branches in

Pará and Pernambuco, the centers of the coffee and sugar trade, respectively. With the organization of the Banco Mercantil Americano de Colombia, the MBA was the first US financial institution to establish itself in Colombia. It opened with branches in Bogotá, Barranquilla, Cartagena, Medellín, Cali, Girardot, Manizales, Honda, Armenia, Bucaramanga, and Cúcuta. The MBA opened the Banco Mercantil Americano de Cuba with branches in Havana and Ciego de Ávila to take advantage of the financing of Cuba's increasingly lucrative sugar industry.[56] It entered Argentina in 1920 after forming the Banco Mercantil y Agricola de Buenos Aires jointly with a group of US and Argentine business interests.[57] The MBA also had agencies in Panama, Bolivia, Ecuador, El Salvador, Paraguay, China, Japan, the Philippines, the Canary Islands, England, Belgium, and Russia.[58] It also organized a trading company, the Mercantile Overseas Corporation (Compañía Mercantil de Ultramar), for buying and marketing Latin American commodities in the United States.[59]

In Cuba, the MBA's expansion occurred with an unmatched urgency and aggression. In 1919 the MBA's executive committee met in a special session in its offices at 44 Pine Street in New York City to discuss the establishment of a bank there. They believed that postwar conditions had created a strategic window to commence the financing of Cuban sugar and advance loans on future shipments. Eventually they would move to other areas of industrial and agricultural financing in the republic. The officers of the MBA authorized the registration of the bank, approved a search for new headquarters, and gave it a mandate to immediately begin making loans against warehoused sugar.[60] The organization of the Cuban bank followed the pattern of other commercial banks within the MBA's portfolio. Named the Banco Mercantil Americano de Cuba (BMAC), it was chartered in Connecticut, but also licensed under Cuban laws. It took up temporary quarters in Havana on Havana and Amargura streets until it was moved to the ground floor of the Edificio Barraque in September 1919 (as noted earlier in this chapter). Fernand Oehmichen, recruited from the MBA's Lima, Peru, institution, was installed as manager, as was J. Ashton Heap, at one time a US foreign consul in Mexico.[61] The MBA was the BMAC's largest stockholder, holding 80 percent of its stock, while Brown Brothers and Seligman both had significant holdings.[62] Charles H. Sabin of the GTC was elected president of the BMAC, and the GTC's Albert Breton was elected vice president. Frederick Strauss of Seligman and Thatcher M. Brown of Brown Brothers, along with Alfred Meyer, Jason A. Neilson, and Walter M. Van Deusen, all of the MBA, served

Table 5.1 Financial interests in the Mercantile Bank of the Americas and in the Banco Mercantil Americano de Cuba, May 3, 1921

	MBA (%)	BMAC (%)
Guaranty Trust Co.	41.2218	52.9774
Brown Brothers	10.6945	8.5556
Adolph Stahl	10.4628	8.3703
Shawmut Corp. of Boston	7.0653	5.6522
Anglo & London Paris National Bank	6.6468	5.3174
J. & W. Seligman & Co.	6.1476	4.9181
Columbia Trust Co.	3.9519	3.1615
Continental & Commercial Securities Co.	3.7367	2.9894
Hibernia Bank & Trust Co.	3.5334	2.8267
Czarnikow-Rionda Co.	4.4840	3.5872
Guardian Savings & Trust Co.	2.0552	1.6442
	100.00	100.00

Source: Minutes of a Special Meeting of the Directors of the Banco Mercantil Americano de Cuba, held on the 9th day of June, 1919, at 44 Pine Street, Borough of Manhattan, City of New York, at 11:00 o'clock in the forenoon, Financial, Mercantile Bank of the Americas, Record Group II, Series 10a-c, Manuel Rionda y Polledo, Subject Files, 1911–1943, Box 7, Braga Brothers Collection, University of Florida, Gainesville.

as directors.[63] In time, the consortium providing the financial backing for the BMAC grew to include most of the institutions in the MBA (see table 5.1).[64]

The BMAC's directors were heavily involved in the sugar industry. Manuel Rionda and Miguel Arango of the recently formed Cuba Cane Sugar Corporation, the tenant directly above the BMAC in the Edificio Barraque, joined the board, and Cuba Cane contributed to the BMAC's capitalization.[65] Cuba Cane also provided the BMAC with much of its business. The brainchild of Cuban American sugar magnate Manuel Rionda, Cuba Cane was organized in 1915. Rionda sought to capitalize on the wartime conditions of Cuban sugar production by consolidating the integration of the processing and distribution of sugar to create economies of scale. Rionda had watched the work of the Punta Alegre Sugar Company, which had engaged in a mammoth operation in eastern Cuba to clear land for cane. But Rionda was impatient. He did not want to wait for the cycle of the fifteen-month growing season to end before he turned a profit, and he realized that the war could be over before the cane was available for harvest. Instead of following the model of Punta Alegre, Rionda sought to buy up smaller, independently owned plantations around Havana and the neighbouring province of Matanzas, updating their machinery, and consolidating them into a conglomerate that could integrate the cultivation, refining, and distribution of Cuban raws, in the process reducing the cost of production through economies of scale.[66] Rionda contacted Albert Strauss of Seligman with a proposal for the new company. He stressed to Strauss that even with sugar at its lowest price on the market—2 cents per pound—the company would earn "at least 1 ½ times the dividends on the preferred stock." For the coming year, 1915, Rionda estimated that earnings would not be less than $15 per share of common stock, based on an estimated price of $3 ¼ per share.[67]

J. & W. Seligman served as syndicate manager for Cuba Cane, and the GTC served as the depositor for the issue. (The GTC had also offered a line of credit to Czarnikow-Rionda of up to $1 million security on warehoused Cuban sugar in 1914. In return, the bank received a commission of three-eighths of 1 percent on the cash drawn. With the GTC's money Rionda aimed to finance Cuban planters.[68]) Albert Strauss, working with Alfred Jaretzki of Sullivan & Cromwell, set about organizing a syndicate that could float the $50 milllion company in New York.[69] The House of Morgan itself purchased a one-third interest in the initial stock $50 million issue, with the first call for funds slated for December 31, 1915.[70] By February 3, 1916, all the common shares held by the syndicate had been disposed of.[71] By March the principal had been refunded to the syndicate participants and on March 23, 1916, shareholders received notice of their first distribution of the profits. Within two years of operation, the Cuba Cane Sugar Corporation had cleared $19 million in profit on the back of the purchase of seventeen sugar mills, combining 500,000 acres of land with 500 miles of railroad track, 400 locomotives, and 2,500 cane cars.[72]

Much of the business of the BMAC came through the ties the GTC and Seligman had to the Cuba Cane Corporation, especially through the financing of the *colonos* that provided sugarcane for the corporation. The Ciego de Ávila branch of the BMAC was organized for precisely this purpose.[73] The *colono* system had emerged as means to rectify the problem of labor after emancipation and grew up at the same time as the new, modern, rational, quasi-industrial "central system" of the late nineteenth century. A small planter contracted to a certain parcel of land, the *colono* delivered raw sugarcane to the mill owner, the *hacendado*—in this case, Cuba Cane. Leland Hamilton Jenks described the *colono-hacendado* relationship as a "tributary" one and pointed out that the mill owner typically made advances to the *colono* secured by future crops, and so all the risk of production fell on the *colono*.[74] Working with both Cuba Cane and Czarnikow-Rionda, the BMAC began making advances to Cuban *colonos*. While the sugar company brought in the clients, the bank provided the capital; under their arrangement, two-thirds of the financing would come from the bank, and they would divide the 6 percent interest payment plus commissions. The company agreed to hold warehouse receipts for sugar in trust while the *colonos* were contracted to liquidate the advances at the end of the crop with either cash or receipts on warehoused sugar.[75] By May 1919, the BMAC held local personal and corporate accounts amounting to $829,826.60,[76] and by the end of August, it had made loans and advances to the amount of almost $10 million to Cuban *colonos*, ranging from $5,000 to Domingo Casal in Matanzas to $80,000 to Julian Garrau Atorrasagati, with most credits between $20,000 and $40,000.[77]

As we saw in the previous chapter, the sugar financing during these years was increasingly reckless. Banks made credits easily available, and planters took advantage; planters demanded increasingly aggressive terms of finance, and bankers obliged. In October 1919, José Ignacio Lezama approached Havana branch manager Fernand Oehmichen and the BMAC with a proposition.[78] Lezama was a Spanish planter who controlled the Luis, San Cayetano, Triunvirato, and Limones *centrales*. An original customer of the bank, Lezama had deposited almost $40,000 with it and had already endorsed loans to *colonos*, but he sought to expand the BMAC's involvement in his affairs.[79] In a long conversation with Oehmichen he explained that he wanted to consolidate his business interests and shelter them in a single financial institution. He claimed that his outstanding debts totaled approximately $8 million, all of which was "fully secured," and that once the present sugar crop was sold, he would have more secured through a first mortgage on all of his properties, whose value, Lezama suggested, was conservatively estimated at $26,265,000.

Oehmichen was enthralled with the prospects of the financing. He immediately wrote to his superiors in New York City suggesting that they could easily gain control of Lezama's business if he were authorized to grant the $9 million credit. "Lezama assures me that his titles are all clear, having been examined by attorneys of the Royal Bank of Canada, Trust Company of Cuba, Banco Nacional de Cuba, Chase National Bank, all of which have granted him large accommodations," Oehmichen wrote. He asserted that if market prices remained the same, the sale of Lezama's warehoused sugar would net them almost $150,000 in commissions. His worry was the length of time of the arrangement in Lezama's proposition: Lezama asked for three to four year terms on the credit—even as he assured Oehmichen that his return on the coming crop would easily liquidate his indebtedness, leaving quite a handsome surplus. "I consider this business desirable and it would be a tremendous advertisement for us if we got control of it," Oehmichen wrote to the MBA directors. "General opinion is that Lezama is a shrewd business man and has made considerable progress. Faith is given to his statements as to value of his property."[80] He asked the MBA if he should offer the credits to Lezama while warning them that there was a certain urgency to it being settled, as "a large steamship company" was waiting to offer Lezama a similar deal.

Walter M. Van Deusen, manager of the New York office of the MBA, forwarded Oehmichen's memo to Manuel Rionda. Van Deusen wanted to know the quality of the securities and the character of Lezama. Rionda strongly disagreed with Oehmichen's assessment of both the man and his money. "I do not share Mr. Oehmichen's idea that the value of the properties, stated at $26,250,000.00, is extra conservative," Rionda replied. "On the contrary, I consider it extra excessive." He wrote that he was against such a large transaction, even if they could extend the credit, claiming that an advance of $9 million would be "excessive." Rionda also questioned Lezama's reputation and character. "In addition to all this," he concluded, "the moral standards should be looked into."[81]

Oehmichen reluctantly refused the credit to Lezama based on the advice of his superiors. For the MBA, it was fortuitous that Rionda questioned Lezama's "moral standards." A year later, Lezama's business was exposed as almost entirely fraudulent. Lezama declared bankruptcy in May 1921 and fled the country, leaving behind $7,758,197.24 in debts, largely to the Banco Nacional de Cuba.[82] In the wake of his bankruptcy and disappearance it was revealed that Lezama had borrowed heavily from the Banco Nacional to finance his purchases, not only leveraging his assets to extend his credit, but engaging in full-scale forgery of acceptance documentation, allegedly forging signatures on promissory notes he presented to the Banco Nacional, the Royal Bank of Canada, and other institutions. He was described as a "damn thief" and accused of falsifying warehouse receipts and colluding with the managers of the American Foreign Banking Corporation in a mammoth campaign of fraud and graft.[83] However, Lezama's request was typical of the era. Extra excessive sugar financing, to borrow Rionda's phrase, was the order of the day, and during the dance of millions, values were stretched and distorted, speculation was rampant, and dizzying sums of money were made, seemingly overnight.[84]

For some within the MBA, portents of trouble within the Cuban economy were appearing by the end of the summer of 1920. In *The Compass*, the MBA's house organ, the relentlessly optimistic and upbeat editorials on Cuban economic conditions increasingly included dire assessments of a slump in commodity prices, comments on a return to bartering, the abandonment of the banking system, and the withdrawal of savings as individuals questioned the solvency of the banks.[85] Credit became increasingly constricted as bankers no longer lent as freely as before, and the circulation and movement of goods slowed to a crawl as buyers found they could not afford many of the US and European goods ordered during the dance of millions. Unsold goods piled up on wharves and were left to rot as debts were left uncollected, importers abandoned orders they could no longer afford, and Havana's nouveau riche curtailed their spending. For the directors of the MBA, the first signs of a problem were in rice, not sugar. During the July 22, 1920, meeting of the directors of the BMAC, they discussed the worrying phenomen "arising from a combination on the part of Cuban mechants to repudiate purchases of rice in view of the decline in price, especially with reference to the bank's possible loss in this connection."[86]

On September 1, 1920, Manuel Rionda wrote to W. A. Merchant of the Banco Nacional de Cuba. He was blunt in his assessment of Cuban conditions but offered a glimmer of optimism. "The sugar situation is very bad," he wrote. "Personally I believe that we have seen the worst." Later in the month, Rionda wrote Merchant again, stating, "The market remains the same. I think if we are able to keep the market around these figures for another thirty days, the worst will be over but in order to do that it is necessary that Cuba should not be offering sugars. During the past few days I notice a little more desire to sell."[87] In September *The Compass* offered a tentative picture of the circumstances, noting the increased scarcity and tightening of money, but attributing it to "the usual effect on long time credits," and the difficulties local merchants were having filling their outstanding orders, though attributing this to the "lack of proper shipping facilities." It noted that the cost of living remained high, but believed it "reasonable to suppose" that although a shortage of housing remained a problem, "the peak had been reached." It also noted that while there were no new labor troubles in Cuba, convict labor had been conscripted to move the freight at Havana's wharves.[88]

When the crisis hit the Banco Internacional de Cuba on October 11, *The Compass* was circumspect about the run, calling it "unwarranted" and stating that it was caused by

> alarmist articles published in certain local newspapers which predicted Cuba's bankruptcy on account of the drop in the price of sugar. The great majority of the withdrawals from the banks were from small savings accounts on the part of timid depositors who had paid too much attention to these erroneous reports. One bank was obliged to temporarily suspend payments at nine o'clock Saturday morning, on the presentation, and subsequent protest, of a check in

excess of the stock of ready cash. The remainder of the institutions continued payment until the regular closing hour, meeting all obligatons as presented, and putting additional pay windows in service for the accommodation of the public.[89]

Even so, like the City Bank and the Royal Bank of Canada, on October 12, the MBA shipped $500,000 from the United States to the BMAC to shore up its reserves. Subsequent shipments followed on October 16, 18, 21, 25, and 30, amounting to $2,915,000.[90] The infusions of cash allowed the BMAC to keep its doors open during the moratorium while it attempted to maintain the confidence and trust of its depositors and clients. At the same time, officials of the BMAC joined with other members of the Cuban banking community, both local and foreign, to try to hammer out a solution to the crisis. Their proposal, to issue short-term certificates of indebtedness to planters to allow them to finance the coming harvest, was immediately shot down by the US State Department.[91]

In the middle of November, Brown Brothers, the GTC, and Seligman organized a $12 million acceptance credit to help the MBA finance the planters it had under contract. Subscribers to the credit were reassured that the BMAC's "existing loans are amply margined, and that its capital and surplus are unimpaired."[92] While some in Cuba placed the blame for the disorder squarely on the BMAC—singling out the actions and irresponsible loaning policies of MBA general manager Alfred Meyer and assistant manager Walter Van Deusen—the bank was in deep crisis.[93] In the spring of 1921, the BMAC had $21 million in loans outstanding to sugar planters and merchants, most of which were secured by hypothecated or warehoused sugar. But the collapse in the price of sugar had severely devalued the collateral, and it soon became apparent that the debtors would be unable to pay off their loans as they became due. It was expected that many of the debtors would take years to pay off their debts, and assumed that others would be forced into bankruptcy. The situation was compounded by the fact that the *colonos* indebted to the BMAC did not have access to other sources of credit once the Cuban banking sector had collapsed, throwing the financing of the coming grinding season into chaos. As a result, the *colonos* were forced to pledge the coming crop to the bank for additional credits, securing it through mortgages on their properties.[94]

With plans for the organization of a clearinghouse association in the works, there were fears on the part of the BMAC officers that they would be excluded from participation because of the bank's outstanding loans and that they would not be able to present a "satisfactory statement for admission." At the same time, the officers realized that the collapse of the Cuban banks presented them with an opportunity: if they could remove the sugar loans from the bank's books, it could enter the clearinghouse association, and assume a prominent role in Cuba's financial landscape. To do so, the directors decided to liquidate the sugar loans to another corporation, the Foreign Bond and Share Corporation (FBSC). Founded in 1919, as an investment house, the FBSC was owned by interests that were shareholders in both the MBA and the BMAC. The stock of the FBSC was taken over entirely by the stockholders of the BMAC in the same ratio as their stock in the bank. The FBSC purchased $17 million of the outstanding debt to Cuban sugar planters, mills, and merchants from the BMAC, plus $3 million of additional notes while taking over the contracts and assuming all liabilities.[95] However, as the season advanced, the yield would be low, and the price of sugar continued to decline; the value of the sugar produced was only $6 million instead of the anticipated $8 million. The financial plan was "deranged," as the corporation was $4 million short based on estimates against the 1921–22 crop.

While the Cuban affiliate was flailing, the MBA was also in trouble. It had $45 million in obligations maturing between June 1, 1921, and the end of the year, and its officers recognized that their failure to meet the obligation could precipitate a broader crisis within the US banking community. In May, they initiated an attempt to shore up the MBA through an infusion of capital. The MBA raised $20 million from its stockholders through the sale of additional stocks and notes and formed a banking syndicate to extend a further $35 million in credits to the bank. Seventeen New York City banks joined the syndicate, including Bankers Trust Company, the City Bank, the National Bank of Commerce, and J. P. Morgan and Co.[96] By August, more than half of the $35 million pledged by the seventeen banks had been advanced, but it did not cover all of the MBA's liabilities. Additional credits were required. J. P. Morgan organized a second syndicate, this time headed by Gates W. McGarrah of the Mechanics and Metals National Bank and Morgan partner Edward R. Stettinius. According to Stettinius, a further infusion of cash into the MBA from the new syndicate "eliminated" "further cause for anxiety" concerning the bank.[97] Stettinius also instituted a plan that absolved the directors of the GTC of personal liability should the MBA fail. He advised the syndicate partners to organize a new company, called the Imports Advancement Corporation, that bought the GTC's claims and obligations against the MBA, thus relieving itself of the MBA's obligations to the tune of $16 million. Participants recovered about $11,200,000 of the $16 million they had put into the syndicate, represented by participation certificates, but nothing on their stock or other obligations held.[98] Senior partners in the syndicate were able to recover 70 percent of the money they advanced to the MBA and its subsidiaries. Subordinate creditors and stockholders received nothing.

By the fall of 1921, it was acknowledged that the MBA was a lost cause. J. P. Morgan stepped in and began to supervise a slow dismantling of its branch network and its international affiliates. In September 1921, at a meeting at J. P. Morgan's office, the bankers decided to close the BMAC. They soon announced that they would consider offers for its branches as well as the branches of the MBA's affiliate organizations. The following month, the City Bank purchased the MBA's Cuban branches and transferred its assets and balances to the City Bank's Havana branch.[99] Around the world, MBA staff were laid off. The bank's Paris, Barcelona, and Madrid branches were shut down.[100] It sold its Argentine affiliate, the Banco Mercantil y Agricola de Buenos Aires, to the First National Bank of Boston.[101]

Circulated to shareholders on January 19, 1922, the MBA's annual report for 1921 painted a despondent picture of the institution. "We hand you herewith a statement dealing with the operations of this corporation for the year 1921," the directors wrote. "We regret that the unprecedented decline in the price of sugar, and the complications which that decline has caused in Cuba and Cuban business do not enable us to make a more encouraging report."[102] By August 1922, to expedite the MBA's liquidation while salvaging some of its capital, J. P. Morgan and Co. partner Stettinius organized a new institution, the Bank of Central and South America (BCSA), with the main purpose of taking over the branches and affiliates of the MBA in order to remove the MBA from the accounting ledgers of its parent institutions. The other banks in the syndicate behind the BCSA included the Corn Exchange Bank, the Mechanics and Metals National Bank, the Columbia Trust Company, Hard & Rand, W. R. Grace, and the International General Electric Company, as well as the three original organizers of the MBA, the GTC, Brown Brothers, and J. & W. Seligman. The GTC owned 40 percent of the stock in the new institution.[103] Of the institutions behind the financing of the BCSA, the Mechanics and Metals National Bank was among the most significant. It had been founded in New York City in 1810, and by the 1920s had absorbed a number of smaller banking houses and trust companies while expanding its branch footprint in Manhattan.[104] Robert F. Loree was elected the BCSA president, and its directors included James Brown and Albert Strauss, alongside representatives of J. P. Morgan and the new institutions.

The dismantling of the MBA was as rapid as its initial expansion. The

BCSA swiftly moved to take over the remaining affiliated institutions of the MBA in Colombia, Venezuela, Peru, Ecuador, and Costa Rica, mopping up its network of illiquid and insolvent branches and banks.[105] In Nicaragua, the site of the earliest experiment in foreign branch operation by Brown Brothers and Seligman, the circumstances surrounding the takeover of the BNN were as contested as its formation almost a decade before. In 1924, the BCSA absorbed the MBA's 51 percent stake in the BNN. A month later, the Nicaraguan government bought out the BCSA shares for $300,000 and, at the same time, took over the trading company, the Compañía Mercantil de Ultramar.[106] The news of the sale provoked a crisis of confidence in the bank in some quarters. Wealthy depositors rushed to withdraw their funds. They worried that nationalization and Nicaraguan control would encourage unsound banking practices and lending policies based on patronage and the issuance of "political loans." Holders of the Nicaraguan debt feared that nationalization would destablilize the economy, leading to the depreciation of the córdoba. There were also concerns that the withdrawal of the New York bankers from the directorate meant the end of auditing and inspection according to the standards of the Federal Reserve. The value of shares in the BNN plummeted.

In response to the concerns, Nicaraguan president Bartolomé Martinez allegedly "begged" the US directors to remain "as a friendly service to the Nicaraguan people," and pledged to adhere to the inspection regimes of the Federal Reserve. To quell the anxieties of depositors and bondholders, the bankers agreed to maintain friendly relations between the BNN and the BCSA, and by proxy, with Brown Brothers, Seligman, the Guaranty Trust Company, and J. P. Morgan and Co. Robert F. Loree of the BCSA and the Guaranty Trust Company was appointed president of the BNN. Meetings of the BNN's board were held in New York City. Management of the Managua headquarters remained under the control of Wall Street: the directors demanded that authority to make managerial appointments remain in their hands while dictating that the manager would report directly to New York, not to the Nicaraguan government.[107] During the transaction, not only did the bankers manage to maintain control of an institution that was supposed to be nationalized, but they did so at great profit. When Brown Brothers and Seligman first bought the shares, it paid $153,000; it was sold back to the Nicaraguan government for $300,000. The deal for the bank was criticized in both the United States and Nicaragua. However, Louis S. Rosenthal insisted the benefit redounded to the Nicaraguans. Appointed in 1924, Rosenthal was the new manager of the BNN.[108] A former journalist and civil engineer who had joined the BNN as assistant manager of the Managua branch in

1919, Rosenthal remained with the BNN until 1929, when he joined the Chase National Bank in Havana. In the meantime, Rosenthal asserted that in the sale of the BNN, no allowance had been made for good will in the sale price and he claimed that the actual realizable value of the BNN was at least $610,000.

For the rest of the 1920s, the BNN remained a contested symbol of Nicaragua's sovereignty and a target for both political aspirants attempting to seize power from the prevailing government and for anti-imperialist insurgents seeking the removal of US influence from the country. In 1926, the Bluefields branch of the BNN was broken into, and 161,642.06 in unissued córdobas were stolen. The branch was temporarily closed, though Rosenthal pledged to stand by all of its obligations, and both Rosenthal and Robert F. Loree sent protests to the US State Department.[109] Like Bundy Cole before him, Rosenthal was in the thick of such conflicts and, through his position as both manager of the bank and receiver general of the Nicaraguan government, actively intervened in Nicaragua's internal affairs. And like Cole, Brown, and Strauss before him, Rosenthal insisted that economic conditions in Nicaragua could only be improved if political conditions were stabilized, and he pushed for a $12 million loan that could support the financing of a Nicaraguan national guard to maintain order in the country.[110] Negotiations for the loan floundered because of differences between Wall Street and the State Department. Yet even without the additional financing, BNN was a lucrative piece of business for Wall Street because of its dominance in Nicaragua's commercial and financial life; but its stranglehold on the economic life of the country was also a motivating force behind the coming years of peasant insurgency against US imperial rule in Nicaragua, led by Augusto Sandino.[111]

The official losses to the investors in the Mercantile Bank of the Americas were placed at $20 million. Privately, the figure was estimated to be $80 million.[112] The actual figure is less important than the fact of failure. The rapid rise of the MBA represented the headstrong ambitions of Wall Street as it attempted to assert itself within the foreign financial markets from which it had long been excluded. Yet to some degree, such ambition was fired by an arrogance that represented both a misreading of the global market and the difficult, oftentimes unfortunate, decisions concerning foreign branch management, and, thus, represented the ambivalent fortunes of US imperial banking. While short-term profits were realized, a long-term vision was never secured.

The Royal Bank of Canada (RBC) most benefited from the collapse of the MBA and its failed attempts at imperial banking. Although the RBC was rumored to have lost $25 million in Cuba because of the collapse of the price of sugar, it used the crisis as an opportunity to strengthen its position in Cuba and throughout the Caribbean and Latin America. In Cuba, the RBC took advantage of what bank president Herbert S. Holt referred to as the "elimination of weak local banks."[113] Its Cuban deposits almost doubled overnight as depositors withdrew funds from the failing local banks, and by the middle of the 1920s, the RBC held close to half of Cuba's deposits and sixty branches across the island.[114] The RBC absorbed the assets of the Trust Company of Cuba and acquired the banking business of the Cuban merchant Pedro Gómez Mena. It also took over a number of eastern Cuba sugar mills that had defaulted on their mortgages, acquiring the Central Tacajo, Central Bagauanos, and Central Oriente, and formed a holding company for their operations.[115] Elsewhere in the region, the RBC took over many of the old MBA institutions now controlled by the BCSA.[116] In 1925, the RBC purchased the remaining BCSA affiliates in Peru, Colombia, Venezuela, and Costa Rica, including seventeen branches.[117] The purchase added to a Caribbean network with nodes in the Bahamas, Barbados, Jamaica, Grenada, Costa Rica, Antigua, Dominica, St. Kitts, Nevis, Montserrat, Tobago, and Haiti.[118] In the coming years, as the memory of the MBA faded, the RBC, the City Bank, and a relative upstart in the international field, the Chase National Bank of the City of New York, came to dominate the banking and finance of the Caribbean.

SIX

Imperial Government

On the corner of Compostela and O'Reilly streets within the narrow, askew grid of old Havana stood the new Cuban headquarters of the National City Bank of New York. Replacing the bank's premises at 76 Cuba Street, where it had been housed since the Banco de la Habana was converted into the City Bank's "West Indian Branch" in 1915, the new building was constructed on the site of the late seventeenth-century Santa Catalina de Sena convent. While some lamented the loss of the convent and saw in its demolition the relentless razing of Havana's architectural heritage, the new City Bank building consciously evoked Cuba's Spanish colonial history. It was a high-ceilinged, two-story structure, designed in a style described as Spanish Renaissance. Thick columns of Botticino marble and tall windows grated with hammered Spanish iron guarded its façade, while its floors were lined with French tiles, its woodwork was of Cuban mahogany, and its heavy exterior walls were constructed of mottled coralline *jaimanitas* and *capellania dura* drawn from local quarries.[1] Yet the City Bank's ersatz historicism masked a building that was robustly modern, and indelibly American. It was a grand monument to the financial might of the City Bank in Cuba and to the ascendance of US imperial power in the Caribbean and Latin America. Indeed, where the floorboards of the Santa Catalina convent had held relics of Saint Lucida and Saint Celestine, and its walls were buttressed by investments in the kingdom of heaven made by Spanish merchants, planters, and slave traders, the two-story steel vaults and the 2,100 safe-deposit boxes of the new City Bank contained the amassments of earthly speculation: the deeds, mortgages, bonds, securities, and species of the economies of sugar and tobacco and the tribute of the twenty-one City Bank branches spread out across Cuba whose fealty was not to God, but to 55 Wall Street.[2]

The new bank was opened to the public on May 17, 1925 (see figs. 6.1, 6.2).

That evening, 8,000 people passed through its doors. They were ushered into the cool confines of the large main banking room and were served champagne, cigars, sandwiches, and sweets. They toasted the progress of Cuba, marveled at the new building, and paid tribute to the City Bank. The Most Reverend Manuel Luis, archbishop of the Havana Archdiocese, having already blessed the building earlier that morning, gave a brief sermon on the importance of institutions of credit to the building of wealth in the Cuban republic. City Bank president Charles E. Mitchell, who had flown in from Key West with a cohort of City Bankers for the occasion, spoke of the United States' favorable view of Cuba's development and progress since gaining its independence from Spain. Mitchell then introduced Wall Street's patron saint in Cuba, Cuban president-elect General Gerardo Machado y Morales.[3] In his remarks to the City Bank congregation, Machado pledged to maintain Cuba's political stability to ensure the functioning of business and economic growth. He offered assurances that Cuba's days of revolution and political upheaval were behind it and promised to ensure an orderly and democratic transition at the end of his term. He committed himself to a program of fiscal responsibility while vowing that the republic would assume no further debt.[4] And he lauded the work of the City Bank in Cuba, reserving a special note of praise for an individual he described as "a very dear friend," Joseph H. Durrell.[5]

Durrell sat between Machado and Mitchell. He did not give a speech that evening—or the evening after, when he hosted a private banquet for Machado, Mitchell, and 350 of the City Bank's employees and officers in the rooftop garden of Havana's Sevilla-Biltmore Hotel. But he basked in the adulation and praise and beamed at the throngs of business rivals and well-wishers.[6] And rightly so, for the City Bank's new Havana headquarters were a product of Durrell's vision. Durrell had commissioned the building. He had worked closely with the New York architectural firm Walker & Gillette in choosing the Santa Catalina site. He had contributed to the development of its design and architecture. Perhaps most importantly, he had overseen the construction of the financial edifice in Cuba on which the bank was built. First hired as superintendent of the City Bank's Cuban branches in 1918, in 1922 Durrell was placed in charge of the City Bank's entire Cuban operations. As such, he was tasked with rescuing the reputation and recovering the returns of a bank that had nearly collapsed under the weight of investments in Cuban sugar during the sharp financial crisis following the postwar sugar boom. On the wreckage of the Cuban banking scene, struggling against the depressed price of sugar on world markets, Durrell brought the City Bank in Cuba back to respectability and profitability. The new building

6.1. Charles E. Mitchell and the archbishop of Havana at the opening of the National City Bank in Havana, Cuba, 1923. *Joseph H. Durrell Diaries*. Used with permission.

6.2. Opening of the main branch of National City Bank of New York, Compostela and O'Reilly, Havana, Cuba, 1923. *Joseph H. Durrell Diaries*. Used with permission.

at Compostela and O'Reilly was the material rendering of Durrell's success. But the returns on his efforts also redounded to him personally and professionally: as the decade progressed, not only did the City Bank's Caribbean and South American District come under Durrell's charge, but he was appointed vice president of the Overseas Division, presiding over a portfolio that included the City Bank's network of ninety branches in twenty-four countries, the International Banking Corporation, and the Banque Nationale de la République d'Haiti.[7]

Despite his labors, Durrell barely registers within the historiography of the City Bank and the internationalization of Wall Street.[8] Instead, he dwells in the shadow of his boss, bank president Charles E. Mitchell. While Mitchell has become a legendary figure in the City Bank's history, Durrell is hardly known. He appears as but an incidental historical presence lost among the City Bank's undifferentiated masses of managers and vice presidents. In some respects, Durrell and Mitchell are a study in contrasts. Mitchell was fetishized within the financial columns of his day. Square jawed and straight talking, providing a hypermasculine counterpoint to the gnomic James Stillman and the professorial Frank A. Vanderlip, Mitchell was described as a "he-man,"[9] a "human power plant" who was "in constant physical trim."[10]

Journalists recounted how every day Mitchell strode the three miles from his midtown home to his 55 Wall Street offices with his breathless associates hanging off him. Charismatic, white, and relentlessly optimistic, "Sunshine Charley," as Mitchell was dubbed, is remembered in two opposing though equally outsized fashions: either as a financial visionary, a prophet of deregulation who valiantly tried to soften the effects of the credit stringency of the late 1920s by personally intervening in the economy through a massive injection of liquidity in an attempt to shore up capital markets; or as a reckless, gun-slinging cowboy who broke the hard and fast rules of sound banking by demolishing the legal barrier separating the City Bank's commercial and investment banking functions and almost single-handedly pushed the United States to financial apocalypse.

Durrell, on the other hand, was a banker's banker. He was known as "Jack" to his friends, and his training came through employment at the counters and behind the banking cages of the small country banks serving the farmers and rural settlers of Iowa and the Oklahoma Territory and in the rural branches of the legendary Banco Nacional de Cuba. While not averse to publicity and self-promotion, he had nowhere near Mitchell's public profile. Despite being a prolific writer, compiling over the course of his life a remarkable multivolume biographical document that stretches to hundreds of pages, Durrell did not emerge within City Bank lore and literature.[11] Where Mitchell was brash, Durrell was conservative. Where Mitchell promoted the radical expansion of commercial banking, Durrell held on to old-fashioned principles of sound banking. Although deeply loyal to Mitchell, Durrell viewed with skepticism the collapse of commercial and investment banking, the reckless lending, and the unchecked speculation of the later years of the 1920s. He had warned his superiors about the excesses of the dance of millions and anticipated the financial troubles that hit Cuba in October 1920; nearly a decade later he saw the writing on the wall of the investment boom of the 1920s, dubbing the period "the dance of billions." Durrell was cautious but not risk-averse, entrepreneurial but not reckless, and his Methodism curtailed any tendency toward high-stakes gambling, but he was cocksure, confident, and cunning, and quick to seize an opportunity for profit. At the same time, Durrell bucked the effete and gentlemanly conventions of the international financial elite and, in some ways more than Mitchell, embraced the roguish, Rooseveltian self-fashioning of the frontier banker; he loved boxing, baseball, aviation, and hunting, and his career was punctuated by a scarcely believable number of adventures and near escapes: he was a regular witness to Caribbean revolutions, was forced to hike by foot from Alaska, received at least one threat of assassination, and, using the debased vernacular of the time, colored his stories with jarring depictions of his encounters with "niggers," "wops," "coons," and Jews.

Together, Durrell and Mitchell shaped the City Bank's internationalization during the 1920s. Mitchell encouraged a sea change in conceptions of finance, promoting the idea of the middle-class citizen as an investor, diversifying the retail activities of the City Bank, and through the National City Company engaging in the broadest marketing of corporate and foreign bonds the United States had ever seen. Domestically, the City Bank moved away from its traditional corporate clientele to middle-class and wealthy investors; internationally, it moved away from the direct investment in and, by extension, direct ownership of sugar mills and other assets toward a policy of financing both sovereign debt and corporate bonds. Durrell pushed a new retail strategy for the bank in Cuba and in the City Bank's Caribbean District more broadly. This strategy was based on the elegantly simple financial instruments of thrift and savings. Although the practices of thrift and savings had been preached by US business in Cuba since the arrival of Samuel M. Jarvis and the North American Trust Company in Cuba in 1898, they received a new impetus under Durrell and became part of the coordinated and concerted policy for the entire Caribbean and, later, the entire Overseas Division.

Both thrift and savings were a response to the financial crisis of the early 1920s, both were curtailed by that of the early 1930s, and both operated through notions of economy and self-discipline that were to be applied to the nation-state, on the one hand, and to the individual citizen, on the other.[12] Both demanded a form of self-government even as they eroded sovereignty. Furthermore, the ideas of economy and self-discipline emerged from and were shaped by the turn-of-the-century discourses in the United States around race, gender, and political economy that governed notions of US imperial expansion and Caribbean development more broadly. It is through such discourses that a figure such as Mitchell was publicly elevated to a sort of paragon of masculinity, the hypertrophic representation of the white race—and, by extension, the human embodiment of the financial genius, the genius of racial capitalism, embedded in the City Bank and in Wall Street. At the same time, if Mitchell's celebrated manliness stood in for the glorified identity of the City Bank, and the United States, such manliness only made sense against its feminized and emasculated others—in this case the purportedly infantile, developmentally retarded Cuban. Mitchell himself stated as much during the opening of the new City Bank headquarters in Havana in 1925. "The United States," Mitchell remarked, "has been viewing Cuba as an infant who needed guidance, who needed sympathy, who must be encouraged; we have awaited the coming of the manhood of Cuba." For

Mitchell, by the mid-1920s this manhood had arrived. "Cuba was no longer an infant . . . she had achieved the age of manhood," Mitchell continued, "and . . . she was represented by a real man."[13]

Mitchell's "real man" was Durrell's old friend Gerardo Machado. The Cuban independence leader, businessman, and Liberal Party politico would become central to the fate of the City Bank in Cuba, as he was for all North American financial institutions. During a tour of the United States before his May 1925 inauguration, Machado let the US business and banking community know that he was their ally. On April 29, 1925, weeks prior to the opening of the new City Bank building at Compostela and O'Reilly in old Havana, Machado was given a private luncheon hosted by Mitchell at 55 Wall Street. Mitchell presented Machado with a gold cigarette case engraved with a dedication and Machado's initials. Machado spoke of the work he was willing to do on behalf of the bank's success in Cuba. "I wish to say that my administration will offer full guarantees to all business and enterprise which are worthy of the protection of the Government," Machado told the gathering of City Bankers assembled in the building's main banking hall, "and that there is no reason to fear that any disorder will occur, because I shall have sufficient material force to stamp it out and because I shall have besides, the support of public opinion."[14]

Two weeks later during the opening of the City Bank in Havana, Machado reiterated his claims. "The Government of Cuba is in duty bound to lend protection to financial institutions," he stated, "as the well-founded reputation of a powerful institution like The National City Bank of New York cannot be destroyed."[15] Machado made good on his promise. His repression of protests by labor, students, and intellectuals became the necessary conditions for Wall Street's expansion in Cuba during the 1920s, and as his rule descended from democracy into dictatorship, his grasp on power was as much dependent on foreign loans as domestic force; US bankers willingly turned a blind eye to the horrors of his regime as long as amortization payments were made according to schedule. Indeed, if *thrift* was the watchword of the City Bank, *terror* was Machado's, and in a perverse fashion, the spectacular violence of the Machado regime became the counterpoint to the banality of empire and the everyday practices of finance capital deployed by Durrell and the City Bank in Cuba.

Joseph H. Durrell was born in 1879 near Pilot Mound in Boone County, Iowa, but grew up in nearby Dayton, where his father, having previously tried his hand at farming and hawking insurance policies, published the

Dayton Review.[16] Durrell's first job was with the *Review*. He spent his summers at the journal, learning to fold papers and set type and developed writing and journalistic skills that would serve him for the rest of his life. After completing high school he was hired by Dayton's First National Bank. Durrell started with the bank on January 2, 1896, and over the next few years received a hands-on education in country banking. He began by doing odd jobs and custodial work around the Dayton institution, called on to be janitor, fireman, and office boy; he swept floors and dusted furniture, kept books and served customers, worked as a messenger and a loan clerk, and as a mail teller, receiving teller, and paying teller. He worked without pay for the first six months and then was granted a monthly salary of $10.[17] The owners of the bank, the father and son team of J. C. and John T. Cheney, saw Durrell's promise as a banker, and he was promoted to bookkeeper and from bookkeeper to cashier.[18] Durrell fondly remembered the Cheneys and attributed his own beliefs as a banker to their influence and training: they were conservative with credits, cautious with expansion, and scrupulous in their appraisals of collateral and character.

However, it was also at the First National Bank that Durrell received the first taste of culture that would both shape his career and plague the putatively rational organizational and institutional arrangements of American banking: the culture of competiveness, pettiness, professional rivalry, favoritism, and factionalism that was the festering condition of expansion. While Durrell would thrive in such conditions—driven, as he was, by ambition and a burning competitiveness—they would not only have consequences for his own professional ambitions but also shape the financial organization of US imperialism in the Caribbean. Durrell's introduction to this culture began in 1901 when a rumor reached him that he was going to be demoted so that a friend of the manager of the Fort Dodge National Bank could take his place. Rather than waiting for events to transpire, Durrell preemptively resigned from the bank, boarded a southbound train to the Oklahoma Territory, and found employment as the cashier of the Farmers State Bank at Ames in the Cimarron River valley. Durrell soon came into conflict with his new employers over their credit policy and over salary increases and came to see his employers as both incompetent bankers and crooks. Within three years, he sold his interests in the bank, reaping a large profit, and with help from the Cheneys, took over the capital stock of the American State Bank in Enid, Oklahoma. He brought in John Cheney as president and Charles M. Lewis as cashier. Business went well until the county treasurer demanded an exorbitant personal bond for a sum held on deposit. Unable to satisfy the bond, Durrell sold his interests in the bank and decided to abandon the business.

Durrell was unsure of his next move. He was married with his first child on the way, unemployed, and stuck in the middle of the Oklahoma Territory with a small savings from his investments and stock sales. He encountered friends who had just returned from Cuba who spoke in glowing terms about the republic and its economic possibilities. Intrigued, Durrell set out on an exploratory trip, sailing from New Orleans at the end of May 1905 and reaching Havana in June, near the end of the administration of President Tomás Estrada Palma, independent Cuba's first president. For Durrell, after the country towns of Iowa and Oklahoma, Havana was a vision of cosmopolitanism and urbanity. He was struck by the Malecón, Havana's ambling seaside breakwater restored during the US administration, and the wide boulevards of the Prado thronged with strolling Habaneros. His travels in the countryside, however, revealed another Cuba. Beyond Havana, the effects of the war were still visible; sugar mills and plantations lay in ruins, cane fields were uncultivated and overgrown, and it was clear that the republic's productive capacity was nowhere near to being restored. For Durrell, as for many Americans, the tattered and broken landscape was one of promise and possibility. With the same settler ambitions and accumulative pulsion that had encouraged him to seek employment in the Oklahoma Territory, he brought his wife and infant son permanently to Cuba that October, where they were joined by the family of Charles M. Lewis. After an unsuccessful stint farming with Lewis on a property near Paso Real de San Diego, Durrell and Lewis both obtained positions at the Isle of Pines Bank at Nueva Gerona, a US institution serving the American colonists seeking their fortune in Cuba's citrus craze.[19] During their time in Nueva Gerona, they also invested in a brick-manufacturing scheme on a thirty-three-acre farm east of Havana in Arroyo Arenas; it failed spectacularly, swallowing up much of their savings. There, Durrell and Lewis wandered the battlefields of the 1906 Battle of Wajay and the unsuccessful uprising against the government led by Cuban independence war hero Quintín Bandera (and, as Durrell put it, "an army of perhaps thirty-five niggers").[20] The revolt was suppressed, and Bandera was killed by the rural guards, and his mutilated body was placed on display in Havana's morgue. Soon thereafter, protests against Estrada Palma's electioneering prompted the second US intervention, the installation of Charles Magoon, and an occupation that lasted almost four years. Durrell meanwhile quit the Isle of Pines Bank and moved his family back to Havana, having secured a position at the Banco Nacional de Cuba.

By the time Durrell joined the Banco Nacional de Cuba (BNC) it was the most powerful financial institution in Cuba. Largely unopposed and entirely unregulated, it had a branch network that covered the country, a near monopoly on government deposits, and a predominant role in the financing of sugar. That fall, the BNC had abandoned its original residence on Cuba Street and moved into a new, neoclassical building at the corner of Cuba and Obispo. But despite the outward signs of the BNC's success, Durrell soon became frustrated with its organization. It was, as he put it, "indifferently managed, and practically insolvent." The BNC was run by a cohort of Americans, Cubans, and Latin Americans, most of whom were patronage appointments of bank founders Samuel Jarvis and Roland Conklin and their underlings, and decisions regarding promotions and pay were based on favoritism, flattery, and sycophancy. Durrell viewed Edmund and William Vaughan as incompetents. He described them as "bluffs pure and simple," who, along with most of the other officers in the bank, knew little about banking. The cashier, a Venezuelan named Hermán Olavarria, "would not assume the slightest responsibility and was afraid of his shadow." Of A. A. Brown, the chief of the accounting department under whom Durrell worked, Durrell stated, "They had spoiled a perfectly good Yankee potato-peddler to make a rotten accountant." The only individual Durrell trusted in the bank was William A. Merchant, a former agent for Dun & Bradstreet in the West Indies. Merchant became Durrell's ally and advocate over his years with the BNC—even though many individuals in the American colony in Cuba viewed Merchant with suspicion.[21]

Durrell began as a bookkeeper with the BNC in 1907 and briefly managed its branches in Cienfuegos and Camagüey. When promised salary increases did not materialize he was forced to take on extra ledgers in the evenings to supplement his income. Durrell's frustration at working with the Vaughans and their cohort was such that when the opportunity arose in 1909 to become branch inspector, he gladly took it, as it meant that he would spend most of his days away from Havana. Yet traveling throughout the country only confirmed his views concerning the mismanagement of the bank. He realized the BNC's country branches were not making a profit. Although they held some $14 million in deposits, they operated at a loss. The branches did not channel capital back to the main branch in Havana; each one was run as "a little republic" with no adherence to the internal standards of the institution as a whole and with little concern for the authority of the Havana branch. But Durrell saw their potential and, with the blessing of Merchant, purged the branches of incompetent staff, developed a system of promotion based on merit, shunting the "days of influence" to the past, and secured new quarters and erected new buildings.[22]

The external growth of the BNC only served to exacerbate its internal tensions. The jockeying for power and influence by its principals increased. The

Vaughan brothers tried to push Merchant out, offering Durrell a promotion in exchange for his fealty. Durrell, loyal to his friend, refused the promotion and informed Merchant of the Vaughans' scheme. Merchant, however, had already moved against the brothers. He had allied himself with José "Pote" Rodríguez, who had quietly been purchasing the BNC stock floating on the open market and had reached the point where he had enough shares to make himself the majority shareholder. When the Vaughans tried to push out Merchant, Rodríguez threatened to start a rival institution if the Vaughans did not cede management to Merchant. Reluctantly, the Vaughans left the bank. Over the next few years Durrell worked in relative peace. He continued to build the BNC's branch network, was promoted to general auditor in 1914, and in 1915 liquidated the New York agency and organized and launched the National Bank of Cuba in New York under a state charter to handle its New York accounts. Soon, however, he found working under Rodríguez as difficult as working under the Vaughans: Rodríguez was a vain, temperamental, and corrupt figure who ran the bank as a vanity project. When Rodríguez took a million-dollar overdraft on his own account with the BNC and used it to buy up its remaining stock, Durrell had seen enough. He confronted Rodríguez on his actions. To placate him, Rodríguez offered him a well-paying position as vice presidency. Disgusted, Durrell refused the promotion and decided to leave the bank. Only his old ally Merchant convinced him to refrain from tendering his resignation until he found other employment.

It was an opportune moment to leave the BNC. By 1918, the deposits in the BNC's country branches totaled $115 million with profits annually averaging $3 million, some 80 percent of its total profits. The bank's success was due as much to the increased circulation of capital in Cuba following World War I and the influx of foreign investment in the sugar industry as to Durrell's own dogged efforts. By 1918 the banking landscape in Cuba had undergone rapid changes. The sleepy years immediately after 1898 when the BNC was dominant had long given way to a new era of banking competition fueled by the influx of North American capital into Cuba that accompanied World War I. Local institutions like the ancient Banco Español de la Isla de Cuba were expanding their operations, while new banks like the Banco Internacional de Cuba aggressively entered the field, rapidly opening branches and adopting an easy and generous policy of credits. North American financing corporations were also discovering Cuba as they realized the lucrative possibilities of wartime sugar financing. The Guaranty Trust Company and Brown Brothers quickly organized the Mercantile Bank of the Americas, whose Cuban affiliate, the Banco Mercantil Americano de Cuba, made a well-publicized arrival in the republic. The Chase Manhattan Bank joined with a slate of other institutions to form the American Foreign Banking Corporation with branches throughout the Caribbean and Latin America, although Cuba again was its focus. US commercial banks operating under a federal charter, including the First National Bank of Boston and the National City Bank of New York, also sought to expand their operations on the island.

Durrell was courted by both the First National Bank and the City Bank. The Boston house had recently opened up its first foreign branch, in Buenos Aires, Argentina, and was looking for men to staff its proposed branch in Havana.[23] The City Bank had had a presence in Cuba since the organization of the Banco de la Habana in 1907, an institution converted into a proper branch of the bank in 1915, but its growth had been modest, and its profits negligible. City Bank vice president Roger L. Farnham, in charge of the Caribbean District, corresponded with Durrell concerning the means and possibilities of expanding their business. In their discussions, Durrell suggested to Farnham that both the difficulties of the Banco Español and the ongoing internal turmoil of the BNC offered the City Bank a promising opportunity in Cuba; he suggested that the City Bank could take over the BNC.[24] Durrell traveled to the United States from Cuba in the spring of 1918, to meet with representatives of both institutions. He was offered a position as vice president with the First National, but after meeting with Frank A. Vanderlip and his assistant, George E. Roberts (whom Durrell knew from Iowa, where Roberts had owned a newspaper that had a friendly rivalry with the *Dayton Review*), in New York City, he agreed to join the City Bank.[25] Durrell resigned from the BNC late that summer and commenced his work for the City Bank that fall.[26]

Durrell was appointed as superintendent of the City Bank's Cuban branches. He was to work under Roger L. Farnham and alongside the City Bank's Havana manager, a Cuban socialite by the name of Porfirio Franca, whom Durrell described, with typical acerbity, as a BNC "cast-off." Authority for the City Bank's Cuban operations was split between Durrell and Franca, although the lines determining who did what—and who ranked whom—were not, as Durrell soon found out, exceedingly clear. Durrell was tasked with organizing a chain of country branches in Cienfuegos, Cardenas, Matanzas, Sagua la Grande, and Camagüey—five or six branches in the coming year, with additional branches opened until the City Bank had approximately twenty branches operating in Cuba.[27]

Despite his years of experience with the BNC, Durrell found the work difficult. He encountered strong resistance to the establishment of foreign branch banks among Cuban merchants and planters. There was often little interest or support for the expansion of a foreign financial institution on Cuba soil, largely because of the belief that foreign banks did little for the economy of the country. Durrell heard complaints that foreign banks were only interested in generating profits for their head office, that profits would flow to New York not Havana, and that they did little to increase the circulation of capital within the country, as their deposits drew on local sources while their profits were repatriated abroad instead of being reinvested in the country. A similar discussion of national sovereignty and economic independence had generated resentment toward the Banco Español de la Isla de Cuba during the era of Spanish colonialism and at the beginning of the US occupation.

Despite such resistance, Durrell believed that the expansion of the City Bank in Cuba made economic sense for both the bank and the republic, and he was not swayed by arguments concerning national sovereignty and independence, especially as he viewed the Cuban banks as being unable to provide the credit demanded by Cuban agriculture. Local banks like the BNC were "overloaned"—they had already extended their available reserves to their clients—and, thus, were unable to assist with or meet the credit demanded by the coming sugar harvest. In the gap between local ability and local demand, Durrell saw a potentially lucrative opportunity for the City Bank. Durrell also asserted that the criticism of Wall Street was factually wrong; he pointed out that the Cuban branch of the City Bank had already overdrawn $6 million from its Wall Street parent. Durrell calculated that if the City Bank announced its willingness to lend a total of around $20 million to planters "during the first six months of the coming year" it would enable the bank to best its rivals and secure Cuba's best accounts.[28] Conditions on the ground encouraged Durrell, with Farnham's blessing, to accelerate the City Bank's plan for the opening of new branches. They believed that they could have twelve branches in operation by July 1, 1919. Durrell believed that the City Bank was poised to become the "leading financial institution" in Cuba.[29]

The year 1919 began with promise. Early in the new year Durrell opened three new branches and was given the authorization to secure new buildings for the branches in Manzanillo and Guantanamo.[30] But the new year also brought word of a shake-up at 55 Wall Street. Durrell learned that Roger Farnham had been removed from City Bank's Caribbean District and replaced by John H. Allen.[31] Durrell had met Allen on previous occasions. There was a mutual dislike. Dislike soon blossomed into open antipathy, as

Durrell thought Allen a poor banker, and Allen sided with Porfirio Franca, the Cuban manager of the Havana branch, on matters of Cuban business.[32] Durrell also chafed at Allen's directives. Allen had made a four-day visit to Cuba early in the year and upon his return to New York promptly overturned Farnham's policy on branch expansion.[33] Allen discarded Farnham's relatively measured approach—and even Durrell's relatively ambitious extensions—and ordered Durrell to accelerate the opening of new branches in Cuba. He wanted twenty-three new country branches in Cuba operating within the coming year, joining an ambitious Caribbean-wide expansion that saw new City Bank branches opened in Port of Spain, Trinidad, and Venezuela's Caribbean port city of Maracaibo.[34] Durrell found Allen's proposal "ridiculous." He saw it as overambitious, dangerous, and marked by a misreading of the needs and possibilities of the Cuban context, even with the increased demand for Cuban sugar. But Durrell followed orders. By the end of 1919, in addition to reorganizing the branch in Santiago de Cuba, Durrell had organized twenty-two new City Bank branches in Cuba.[35] In the process, he brought in a remarkable slate of new business: 6,000 new depositors, an aggregation of $8 million in deposits, and loans of $13 million. Durrell expected that new branches would cover losses and the cost of installation. He believed that it would emerge on a paying basis by the end of the coming year and would generate profits exceeding $500,000.[36]

Despite his apparent successes, Durrell began to feel as if he was not getting the credit he deserved for his work under Allen's regime. Durrell had little respect for Franca as a person or as a banker, and the tensions between the two men were exacerbated by an administrative structure within the Cuban side of the organization that permitted a modicum of ambiguity regarding authority. Durrell asserted that he was more than willing to work with Franca but that Franca wanted a title without the labor associated with it; Franca wanted to be garlanded with authority without assuming any responsibility and tried to undermine Durrell's standing with many of the employees. Durrell found the newer employees brought in by Franca and Allen were incompetent. The Cuban managers knew nothing of banking, while the American accountants were "a bunch of school boys with neither experience [in Cuban banking] nor a knowledge of Spanish."[37] Durrell critiqued in withering form the character and personalities of the staff hired by and loyal to Franca. Juan B. Roqué, the foreign exchange manager and a Roger Farnham promotion, was "a trouble-maker and business-loser."[38] Rafael Brito was "not, and never has been, an accountant, and as for his organizing a big office and managing a large staff he is hopeless." J. H. Mazaurieta was "average" as a clerk but horrible as a person; his morals were abhorrent and an embarrassment to the bank: at one point he had seduced one of the secretaries in the Havana office, made her his mistress, and absconded with her to New York City, abandoning his wife and three children in Havana. Mazaurieta only returned to Cuba once Franca promised him a promotion. Frustrated by Allen's management style and increasingly at odds with Franca in the Havana branch, Durrell broke the chain of command and wrote directly to James A. Stillman, president of the bank since 1919, and the senior officers in New York. Durrell was summoned to 55 Wall Street, where Stillman and the officers of the bank proposed an assignment that would have Durrell leave Cuba. Durrell was ordered to Mexico to investigate the possibilities of the country for branch expansion. It was not the resolution that he had hoped for. He considered resigning from the bank but believed that besides Allen, Stillman and the officers were keen to retain him, and felt that his work in Cuba was not yet finished. Durrell reluctantly accepted their proposal and began making plans for his passage to Mexico.[39]

Durrell's time in Mexico was brief. He made the two-day passage from Havana to Vera Cruz in mid-January 1920 and, the morning after his arrival, boarded a heavily armored train that took him through the mountains to Mexico City. Allen had given Durrell strict orders: Durrell was to send dispatches to 55 Wall Street on Mexico's economic and political situation and its business and financial landscape and begin to compile credit information on, and secure accounts from, local businesses. But he was not to use or display the City Bank's name in any fashion, and he was not to move toward opening a branch until he was given the signal from New York.[40] For Durrell, it seemed like an elaborate make-work scheme to keep him away from Havana. Nevertheless, he found lodging at the University Club, opened an office in his own name above the Mercantile Banking Company, and began his explorations. He traveled throughout Mexico, visiting the larger cities and inspecting mining operations and smelters. He was impressed with the commercial possibilities of the country, as he was with Mexico City itself—except for the beggars and the lack of street life at night—but he worried that the Mexican currency was unstable, the country's credit system nonexistent, and its banking and financial infrastructure weak. Durrell secured a number of accounts for the City Bank while compiling a substantial dossier of credit information from local business. He also made the acquaintance of President José Venustiano Carranza, the Secretary of the Treasury Don Luis Cabrera, and Carranza's political opponents, Generals Álvaro Obregón and Pablo González.

Durrell was unconvinced by Mexico's political climate and worried that its political instability would impede the City Bank's ability to do business in the country. John H. Allen was convinced that President Carranza was a figure similar to former president Porfirio Díaz, an individual with a strong, dictatorial grip on the country who could bring the sort of political stability demanded by foreign capital. Durrell was less certain of Carranza. He doubted how long Carranza could hold onto power and realized that many towns were already under the control of anti-Carranza forces. Furthermore, the country seemed afflicted by lawlessness and social upheaval, both encouraged by a weak state. Soon after Durrell arrived in Mexico, a planned trip to a paper mill at the foot of the Popocatépetl volcano was called off when it was learned that the Zapatistas had plans to kidnap Durrell's traveling party. In Mexico City itself, a number of US expatriates who were Durrell's friends and acquaintances were stabbed, robbed, or executed while he was there. Meanwhile, the military attaché to the US legation had been kidnapped from a train and held for ransom. Durrell came to the conclusion that the economic situation in Mexico was such that business would be in danger due to political instability.[41] He anticipated that Carranza would be in office for no longer than a year, "probably less."[42]

Durrell's instincts were correct. At the end of April 1920, González and Obregón moved against Carranza. Carranza moved the seat of government from Mexico City to Vera Cruz. Durrell joined Carranza's caravan as it evacuated the city—a convoy of twenty-three trains carrying 3,000 civilians, 5,000 soldiers, and 40 million pesos in gold from the treasury. The train moved slowly, and Carranza's guard engaged fire with rebel troops along the way. Three days into a journey broken up by dynamited train tracks and running gun battles that left a growing tally of dead on both sides, Durrell secured a pass to carry on ahead in a Packard commandeered by the government through a series of backroom deals. But Durrell was forced to go with a character he called "Nigger Ellis," "a colored promotor [sic] of unsavory reputation" and "the latter's near white secretary." And the secretary of the treasury asked him to smuggle out of the country $2 million in drafts, $200,000 in American currency, and $300,000 worth of diamonds. Durrell declined, although Ellis and his companion gladly agreed to do it. According to Durrell, Ellis closed the deal claiming he would happily slit a man's throat for $50, let alone the bounty proffered by the secretary. Together, they somehow found their way to Vera Cruz, arriving on May 17. Durrell found passage on a Spanish steamer to Cuba, arriving back in Havana on May 20. Days later, he learned of Carranza's execution.[43]

Although Durrell was in Mexico for less than six months, the Cuba he returned to—at the peak of the dance of millions—was scarcely recognizable.

"Everyone was a millionaire, real or fancied," Durrell recalled, "and wild-cat speculation was the order of the day. The merchants were ordering four times as many goods as they could possibly dispose of. Real estate was booming. The banks were extending credit recklessly and I learned that our Bank had joined the mad scramble."[44] During Durrell's absence, the City Bank had abandoned its measured policy of branch expansion and dispensed with its conservative policy of issuing credits. From his conversations with Juan F. Rivera, a Puerto Rican with whom he had worked at both the City Bank and the BNC (where he had served as the secretary to Edmund G. Vaughan), Durrell learned that Porfirio Franca and Juan B. Roqué were caught up in the speculative madness and had participated in what he later described as a "wild orgy of loaning."[45] "To me, who had been living out of that atmosphere," wrote Durrell, "and in a country where there was no such thing as credit and with fifteen years of Cuban banking behind me, it was clear that the bubble must burst soon."

Recognizing the economy was unsustainable, Durrell settled his business in Cuba, selling a farm near Pinar del Río, disposing of a number of lots he held in Havana, and shipping his furniture to New York.[46] Durrell wrote to John H. Allen, warning him of the potential dangers inherent in the City Bank's overexposure to sugar.[47] Allen did not acknowledge his letter. When they encountered each other that summer in New York, Allen dismissed Durrell's warning, telling him "that times had changed and world conditions with them," and making it clear that Durrell's advice on Cuba was unwanted.[48] Although his previous complaints had led to his temporary exile in Mexico, Durrell again decided to break with the City Bank's chain of command. He went over Allen's head and outlined his views of the Cuban situation to bank officers John H. Fulton and Charles V. Rich. After listening to his warnings, they placed him on a committee responsible for supervision of the bank's loans by the Foreign Division. Durrell was assigned the South American loans, of which he knew little, but against Allen's wishes, Durrell took over the Cuban loans from a young assistant cashier who admitted he had no knowledge of Cuban conditions. Reviewing the Cuban accounts, Durrell "discovered they were even more of a mess than I had anticipated, and well knew that once the crash came, which I was certain was near, we would be faced in Cuba with a dangerous situation." He urged the loan committee to restrain from making more advances to Cuba while trying to settle what was outstanding. Porfirio Franca, meanwhile, had been promoted by Allen from Havana branch manager to the City Bank's general manager of Cuba branches, taking over the portfolio once held by Durrell.[49] Soon after the appointment, Durrell wrote a memorandum requested by the City Bank comptroller, James Addison, heavily critical of Franca and his appointments, saying that he was "not a business-getter" and that his suspicious and tactless character choked the possibility of generating confidence, goodwill, and loyalty among his staff.[50]

On September 16, 1920, an explosion interrupted the work of Durrell and the loan committee. The building at 55 Wall Street was rocked by the blast, its windows shattering from the explosion's concussive force.[51] Durrell quickly climbed out on the ledge of the City Bank building and, looking east down Wall Street, saw scenes of carnage: the street between J. P. Morgan and Co. and the US Assay Office was littered with bodies and smoking debris. Durrell ran from the building to the 34 Wall Street offices of the Bank of Cuba in New York, the BNC affiliate he had organized in 1914. Its offices were severely damaged, and two clerks were injured, but he found his old friend J. T. Monahan unhurt.[52] Durrell later learned that a horse-drawn carriage, loaded with lead window sashes and packed with dynamite, had been detonated in front of the J. P. Morgan office. Morgan was in Europe at the time, but 34 others—mainly messengers, porters, and clerks—died in the explosion, and 200 were injured. Suspicion immediately fell on anarchists, who were largely Eastern European immigrants to the United States, and had claimed responsibility for other attacks throughout the country, and who, for the press and the attorney general, where the obvious perpetrators of any attack on the financial heart of the United States. No one was ever charged with the bombing.

Less than a month later another explosion rocked Wall Street, this time from Cuba. The collapse of sugar prices led to a run on the Banco Internacional de Cuba on October 11, 1920, which quickly spread to other banks. Durrell's fears were realized. The sugar boom was over. The Cuban economy teetered on the verge of collapse. The City Bank, along with other North American banks, found themselves holding a portfolio of bad loans contracted to planters, *colonos*, and merchants who were now all underwater. John H. Allen was forced to resign, and Roger L. Farnham was recalled to take charge of the Caribbean District.[53] The rest of Latin America was divided between Joseph T. Cosby and William G. Brady. Cosby was assigned Great Britain, France, Switzerland, Italy, Spain, Portugal, Mexico, Uruguay, Argentine, Chile, Bolivia, and Peru. Brady took over Brazil, Paraguay, the Guianas, Venezuela, Colombia, and Ecuador. Later known as the "Iron Duke," Brady was a tough, hardworking, abrasive, no-nonsense Brooklynite who had come to the City Bank's Foreign Department from the Bankers Trust Company around 1915 and had been promoted to assistant cashier in 1916.[54]

Farnham promptly left for Cuba to investigate matters, accompanied by

Vere Brown. Durrell had cordial relations with Farnham. Durrell's animosity toward Brown, on the other hand, was visceral. It is unclear what interactions the two men had had in the past, but Durrell described Brown as "arrogant and a misfit" whose brusque style alienated the other officers.[55] After a month away, Farnham and Brown reported back with an enthusiastic and glowing assessment of the bank's loans on sugar properties and an endorsement of Porfirio Franca and his people. A second trip to Cuba in January returned the same results.

Durrell was astounded. He was convinced that Porfirio Franca had charmed Farnham and Brown while somehow managing to cover up the actual state of the City Bank's Cuban positions. In response, Durrell stepped up his campaign of highlighting the irregularities in the City Bank's lending practices in Cuba and the sour nature of its Cuban loans. He took his complaints directly to one of the officers, Charles V. Rich, who had previously been a sympathetic audience. Rich was furious about Durrell's charges. But he heard him out and responded by commissioning Brady to investigate Cuban conditions. Brady returned from Cuba a few weeks later, and his report was, as Durrell put it, a "corker." It boded well for Durrell's position in the bank. Durrell was appointed an assistant vice president. Porfirio Franca was forced out, and became the president of the floundering BNC, replacing Durrell's old ally William A. Merchant.[56] All of the New York officers in Cuba were recalled. Durrell was sent to Cuba, "delegated the thankless task of taking over the Cuban wreck on the ground."[57]

Durrell's days in the wilderness were over. He returned to Cuba on February 1, 1921, and spent a few days in Havana before traveling to the City Bank's country branches. He was shaken by what he saw. "It was a sickly, sorry, disheartening mess," he recalled. "An incompetent and disorganized personnel, a rotten lot of loans that required instant attention, and scarcely a first-class man on hand to take hold with me was the situation I faced."[58] The destruction wrought by the policies of Franca and Allen was horrific. As a result of defaults, the deeds to fifty-six mills—one-quarter of the mills in Cuba—were now in the hands of the City Bank. Of the $60 million loaned to Cuban sugar producers, $48 million was at risk—amounting to 60 percent of the bank's working capital.[59] The work was grueling, "cruelly hard." "We worked like demons through that hot summer to salvage the wreckage," wrote Durrell. "The branches were overstaffed with salaries cutting in to profits," and most of the employees were "incompetent and worse." The bank was roiled by instability, as Durrell kept firing and hiring employees, attempting to purge the bank's staff of the crew assembled by Franca, and recruiting former colleagues from his time with the BNC. He had to fire

196 / Chapter Six

"everyone down to the porters" at one branch. The country branches were physically dilapidated, broken down, depleted, operating at a loss. Durrell also soon realized that the officers in charge of the district were of little use and had little authority. Farnham's standing in the bank was waning, and Brady, though supportive of Durrell's decisions, knew little of the Cuban situation.

Compounding Durrell's difficulties, Cuba's general economic climate was one of insecurity and uncertainty. The price of sugar remained depressed, hindering the possibility of a market. Banking runs were frequent, often spurred by hostile reporting in the Cuban press on the solvency of financial institutions. And the banking crisis had shaken Cuban confidence in the banking system and unleashed a groundswell of mistrust and antipathy toward foreign banks and the foreign corporations that had, practically overnight, taken a predominant place in the Cuban sugar industry. Perhaps the most damaging aspect of the crisis for the City Bank was psychological: the crisis had eliminated trust in banks, confidence was eroded, goodwill erased, and all the work that the US bankers thought they had done teaching Cubans about "American" banking methods, self-government, and fiscal responsibility, and breaking the "Spanish" practices of thinking about money, finance, and markets that they had seen since their arrival in 1898, was wiped out in a matter of months. While both Havana and Cuba's rural districts were littered with boarded-up, closed, and empty bank buildings, the architectural remains of a lost age of wealth and speculation, those banks still standing found all of their safe-deposit boxes were being rented, as people abandoned checks and interest-bearing accounts and hoarded currency and species.[60] It was estimated that between $100 million and $150 million had been withdrawn from circulation, buried in the ground or hidden in people's homes.[61] When Durrell's old boss at the BNC, José López Rodríguez, committed suicide the entire system collapsed.

It was too much for Durrell. He resented having to clean up a mess made by the errors of others against his protests, and he saw little reward in the job. He had lost faith in both the City Bank and Cuba. In June he decided to abandon the project and quit. Upheavals at 55 Wall Street persuaded him to stay.

Durrell was not alone in his frustration with the condition of the City Bank in Cuba. In New York City, the City Bank directors were spooked by the impact of the Cuban crisis on the solvency and standing of their institution and had lost faith in the bank's president, James A. Stillman, who was forced to resign. Of Stillman, his close friend, Durrell wrote he was "always the play-boy." "Though intelligent he never liked to work, and having plenty of means he was not forced to labor," wrote Durrell, sympathetically. "He loved life including the ladies and several of the latter reciprocated his affection and generosity by attempted, and too often successful blackmail."[62] In Stillman's stead, the board of directors appointed Charles E. Mitchell as president of the bank and the National City Company, and Eric P. Swenson as the chairman of the board of directors.[63] It was clear, however, that Mitchell was in charge of the future of the bank, and Swenson was to play a secondary role.[64]

Mitchell was born in Chelsea, Massachusetts, on October 6, 1877, to an affluent family with colonial roots. His father had made his fortune as a wholesale merchant and as a partner of the Boston firm Mitchell, Dexter, and Co. and served as Chelsea's mayor for a number of years.[65] After graduating from Amherst College in 1899, Mitchell went to work for the Western Electric Company in Chicago, rising to assistant manager by 1905. He then moved to New York and entered the world of finance, serving as assistant to financier Oakleigh Thorne of the Trust Company of America. The Trust Company of the America had gone on a tear of mergers early in the century, absorbing in the process Jarvis and Conklin's North American Trust Company, and with it, their accountant, Frank W. Black, a figure who would remain a business associate of Mitchell's for many years to come. By 1907, however, the Trust Company of America was in crisis. The panic saw its Wall Street offices besieged, and it would have joined the Knickerbocker Trust Company in suspension and liquidation if it had not been for the intervention of J. P. Morgan and James Stillman, the former bullying his confreres into ponying up the capital to save the teetering institution. As Thorne's assistant, Mitchell was witness to both the panic and the efforts to save it. It remains unclear what lessons he learned from the experience.

Mitchell established his own investment banking firm, Charles E. Mitchell and Co., in 1911. Its success brought Mitchell to the attention of Vanderlip, and in March 1916, Vanderlip hired Mitchell to run the National City Company (NCC). At the time, the NCC was dormant; its function as the bank's holding company for its international operations had declined with the development of the branch network following the organization of the Federal Reserve System and the bank's purchase of the International Banking Corporation. Mitchell revived the NCC. Under Mitchell, the NCC absorbed the bank's bond department (a modestly successful affair since its organization by Vanderlip) and purchased outright N. W. Halsey and Co., the second largest bond retailer in the United States. Through the purchase, the NCC immediately had a $100 million business retailing and marketing domestic railroad, utilities, and municipality bonds. The NCC increased its capital stock from $10 million to $25 million,[66] and its staff rapidly expanded: it had 364 employees in 1916, 571 in 1917, 928 in 1918, and almost 1,300 by 1919.[67] The volume of its business burst from its suite of offices at 55 Wall Street and took over its own building, across the street, at 50 Wall Street. The NCC opened an uptown sales office at Fifth Avenue and Forty-Third Street and expanded into more than fifty cities throughout the United States and Canada, opening regional subsidiaries like the National City Company of California alongside overseas offices in England, Switzerland, Denmark, and Japan, while maintaining hundreds of agents, staff, and correspondents.[68] By 1923, the City Bank's bond department was the most active in the country, marketing $1 billion in securities annually.[69]

Mitchell's appointment brought energy, charisma, and personality to the City Bank. It also marked a sea change in the City Bank's managerial and organizational strategy, as he broke with many of the systems and practices from the previous decade that Frank A. Vanderlip had cultivated (and James A. Stillman had inherited). The system of rotating executive managers was eliminated, and authority and power were concentrated in the office of the president—what the *Wall Street Journal* decribed as the restoration of "one-man power"[70]—with a smaller number of managers directly responsible to Mitchell.[71] The policy of academic schooling was abandoned in favor of a return to on-the-ground training. In response to the changing financial and banking landscape in the United States in the 1920s, he promoted institutional consolidation through mergers, domestic branch banking expansion, and the development of the retail and bond-selling apparatus of the bank. Mitchell's appointment represented both a crisis in the history of the internationalization of Wall Street and US finance capital and a sign of its failure: what soon became apparent to Mitchell was that the policy of foreign branch expansion under Vanderlip was a disaster. He was tasked to find another way.

Durrell was energized by Mitchell's arrival. Mitchell's appointment renewed his faith in the City Bank and rejuvenated belief in his own career within it. Durrell was summoned to New York City for a conference with Mitchell and Swenson in June. During the meeting he "fell under the hypnotic spell of the new president," and, like the directors, swooned over Mitchell.[72] Mitchell convinced Durrell not to quit. He encouraged him to continue in Cuba, and bumped up his salary to $24,000 per year.[73] But Durrell, being Durrell, also played it straight and offered him a blunt assessment of the City Bank's position in Cuba. He told Mitchell that Vere Brown was a "total loss" and should be let go, and that Brady should replace Farnham as the head of the division. He told the directors that the bank's sugar business, the site of so many of the bank's negative entanglements and complications, should be separated from the daily ledgers and operations of the bank proper. Durrell also proposed that Mitchell, Swenson, and the other directors should come to Cuba to see firsthand the bank's Cuban investments and operations.

Vere Brown was let go that fall. Durrell returned to Cuba in the middle of October 1921. The following February Mitchell and Swenson headed a party to Cuba that included Percy A. Rockefeller, Guy Cary, directors Lee Olwell, Roger Farnham, and William G. Brady, Colonel E. A. Deeds, Gordon S. Rentschler, and George W. Houston—the latter three figures, businesspeople interested in the City Bank's sugar properties.[74] They flew from Key West to Havana in a record seventy minutes on the Aeromarine's "aircruiser," appropriately named the Ponce de León.[75] They began their two-week trip with a call on President Zayas in the presidential palace and then toured the country via special trains provided by American-owned Cuba Railway and United Railways, visiting the City Bank's country branches and the sugar properties and mills deeded to the bank. Mitchell gave impromptu speeches from the train platform and, at the end of his tour, addressed a group of 200 businesspeople during a luncheon at Havana's private Midday Club, perched atop the Royal Bank of Canada building.[76] Mitchell was at his magnetic best during the trip, and he did well projecting the strength of the City Bank and its energetic commitment to Cuba during the dark days of crisis and financial stringency. The visit receiving glowing coverage in both the Cuban and US press and appeared a striking success for the bank (fig. 6.3).[77]

It was not so for Durrell, however. For Durrell, the group's visit to Cuba was a disaster, filled with insecurity, anxiety, and an acute sense of humiliation. The luncheon at the Midday Club was only organized after the Chamber of Commerce canceled its engagement for Mitchell, and Durrell was forced to scramble to put together an event at the last minute. Ever thin-skinned but ambitious, Durrell felt that Mitchell ignored him during the trip; he felt that he and Brady were "non-grata"—a fact he later attributed to Farnham's "working his hammer overtime on Mr. Brady and myself for six months." Yet when Mitchell returned to New York, he wrote a letter to Durrell marked by its stolid charm and easy flattery. Mitchell lauded Durrell's work in Cuba. He marveled at Durrell's knowledge of the country and his ease and intimacy with the Cuban people. Mitchell suggested that the branch network should be reduced, especially as its functioning was hampered by the inadequacy of transportation and the inconvenience of traveling within the island, but

6.3. Visit of the Directors of the National City Bank of New York to Cuba, 1922. *Left to right:* Percy Rockefeller, William G. Brady, Roger L. Farnham, E. P. Swenson, Guy Cary, Charles E. Mitchell, Joseph H. Durrell, Lee Olwell, F. Rodriguez. *Joseph H. Durrell Diaries.* Used with permission.

that the bank would do better if it was granted a measure of administrative stability, a permanent executive in Cuba who could act as a liaison with Cuban businesspeople while reporting to 55 Wall Street. Durrell proposed a position of resident vice president, and nominated himself to hold it.[78] On April 11, 1922, Mitchell cabled Durrell notifying him that the board of directors had elected him a vice president of the City Bank.[79] "I had, of course, been aiming at the goal and had dreamed that some day this promotion would come," Durrell later wrote, "but I had not dared to expect it so soon."

An indirect and darkly fortuitous consequence of the banking crisis in Cuba, Joseph Durrell's promotion to vice president served as a vindication for his methods as a banker and a reward for his perseverance, ambition, and guile. By the time of his promotion, all of his "ill-wishers"—all his rivals in the bank—"each of whom had gone out of his way to make life miserable for me, were out and I was in," he later wrote with barely concealed satisfaction. John H. Allen, Vere Brown, and Porfirio Franca were all forced out of the City Bank, and Durrell was able to cull and dismiss the staff they had brought with them.[80] At the same time that Durrell was promoted, Roger L. Farnham resigned.[81] With Allen, Brown, Franca, and Farnham disposed of, and with practically a direct line of communication with Mitchell, Durrell now had the authority, leeway, and head office support to craft and reorganize the Cuban operations of the City Bank according to his vision. He had become the single most important individual of the expansion of the City Bank in Cuba. He was on the verge of becoming the single most important individual for the expansion of the bank in the Caribbean region.

Durrell spent the spring of 1922 investigating the conditions of the Cuban branches. He visited every branch on the island a number of times, occasionally accompanied by Brady, and subjected them to a rigorous inspection. He uncovered accounting irregularities, evidence of dishonesty and graft, and everywhere, what he described as a lack of efficiency. Reversing Allen's policy of exuberant overexpansion, Durrell, with Mitchell's concordance, scaled back the bank's operations in Cuba while streamlining its organization by culling and reducing the staff.[82] Over the course of the year Durrell closed two of the City Bank's twenty-five branches in Cuba, replaced managers at nineteen branches, and reduced the countrywide staff by 117 people, shaving $175,000 off the payroll in the process. He sought out a "a better type of American" than had been appointed by Allen and Franca, believing the bank could increase productivity from a small workforce made up of more competent staff, and he organized a local inspection force tasked with frequent random audits of the branches to make sure they conformed to head-office standards and practices.

At the same time, Mitchell followed Durrell's advice regarding the sugar business. Mitchell formed a holding company, the General Sugar Company, in March 1922.[83] The General Sugar Company took over control of the properties that had fallen into the City Bank's lap as a result of defaults and bad debts. Through the company, the City Bank organized a series of subsidiary companies that came to occupy a central place in the Cuban (and the Dominican) sugar industry. Despite public proclamations by both Mitchell and Durrell in the wake of the crisis that the City Bank had no intention of holding onto Cuban sugar properties, the bank's position in the industry was actually consolidated and secured. The companies held by the General Sugar Company included the Camaguey Sugar Company, which controlled the Camagüey, Estrella, and Pilar *centrales*, the latter two the former property of Cuban planter Domingo Leon; the Vertientes Sugar Company, owner of the Agramonte and Vertientes mills; the Cuban Dominican Sugar Company, with a dozen mills in both Cuba and the Dominican Republic and which held 90 percent of the stock of the Ceballos Sugar Company; and the West

India Sugar Corporation. All told, through the General Sugar Company, the City Bank held in Cuba almost a million acres of land, hundreds of miles of railroad, and a dozen mills—responsible for a quarter of Cuban production. Financing for the subsidiaries occurred through bond issues of the NCC. The NCC retailed them to a banking group that included the City Bank, J. P. Morgan and Co., and other Wall Street houses, who then sold them in turn to their corporate and individual clients.[84]

Durrell's recovery efforts paid off, if slowly. Even against the continued nervousness and suspicion on the part of many Cubans toward the banking industry and financial institutions, deposits increased by more than $6.5 million within a year. The City Bank's current account totals came close to the peak figures of the boom years. Concentrating its efforts on the Havana branch, it emerged as the largest financial institution in Cuba, its clearings outstripping rival banks in the city and its current balances, at $16.5 million, greater than the total of the BNC at its peak. The City Bank was able to secure collateral and proper documentation for many of the still-outstanding dubious loans contracted by Franca and his cohort while creating credit files on Cuban merchants and businesspeople.[85] Profits slowly returned, though the bank was hindered by the abnormally high reserves it was forced to maintain to protect against bank runs, and by the fact that it was not generating interest on many of its outstanding loans. While in 1921, the bank had failed to cover its operating expenses in Cuba, profits in 1922 were just over $10,000, and in the first half of 1923, $200,000.[86]

Durrell believed the bank could see returns of more than $900,000 in 1924, but neither he nor Mitchell was satisfied with the profits. Durrell worried that the Cuban operations were in danger of becoming a "piker" district, and he blamed the state of business on the damage done by the management of Franca and Allen, the skittish nature of Cubans regarding banking, and the quality of the buildings the City Bank occupied in Cuba. The buildings housing the country branches were in poor condition, rundown and in disrepair, while the Havana branch, at 76 Cuba Street, was "sadly outgrown." Even though they had expanded the building by adding another story, it was still too small. Its location was also less than desirable: a streetcar rattled by on a regular basis just inches from the building's main entrance. For the country branches, Durrell saw an opportunity presented by the suspension of the BNC and the shuttering of its branches. The BNC buildings were being held by the Comisión Temporal de Liquidación as it worked through and settled the claims against the defaulted and suspended banks. Offering to purchase them from the Comisión, Durrell received the BNC's buildings in Cardenas, Manzanillo, Matanzas, Pinar del Río, Sagua la Grande, Santa Clara, and Santiago de Cuba—many of which Durrell had originally opened—as well as the Banco Mercantil Americano de Cuba's branch building at Caibarién.[87] At the same time, Durrell began searching for a lot for a new building in Havana. He considered the premises of the Trust Company of Cuba, as well as a lot on Habana Street fronting Obispo and O'Reilly, though both locations were too small. He also considered the lot of the Santa Catalina convent on Compostela and O'Reilly, believing that he could negotiate a cash-and-swap deal for the property. When Mitchell and the directors returned to Cuba in February 1923, for a second visit, Durrell petitioned them for a new building but was rebuffed because of the poor showing of the bank.[88]

Durrell did not get his building, but the trip paid dividends in other ways. In July 1923, he received another promotion. On Mitchell's recommendation Durrell's district was expanded to encompass not only Cuba, but also Puerto Rico, Mexico, and Central America. The City Bank had had branches in San Juan and Ponce since 1918, though they lagged far behind the Royal Bank of Canada and other banks in deposits and profits.[89] Mexico still did not have a branch of the City Bank, since the International Banking Corporation had shut its office in 1917, and, for the present time at least, conditions there were as unfavorable for the bank as when Durrell had visited in 1920. Meanwhile, the Central American republics presented themselves as a new field for the bank. For Durrell, the appointment meant that for the first time since 1905—for the first time in almost twenty years—he would be based in the United States. Although the next few years would be spent traveling throughout the district on inspection tours, he would have a desk at 55 Wall Street, and he could live with his family at the home he purchased in Scarborough-on-Hudson near Frank Vanderlip's residence. On the eve of Durrell's departure from Havana, his Cuban staff gave him an emotional going-away party at the Plaza Hotel.[90] But over the next few years, Durrell found that he was never that far away from Cuba or the Caribbean.

If for Durrell the effects of the banking crisis in Cuba were personal and professional, for the Republic of Cuba they were resolutely political. El crac served as another interruption in the fraught history of Cuban independence in the early twentieth century while offering a stern test of the republic's sovereignty. With Cuba's autonomy already compromised by the paternalistic strictures of the Platt Amendment and the Economic Defense Law of 1914, the events of the early 1920s served to further bind Cuba politically and economically to the United States.

While US bankers were pushing fiscal reform on the Cuban government they were simultaneously undermining the ability of the Cuban state to manage its own fiscal affairs. Durrell and the City Bank were instrumental here, as his actions to expand the City Bank's operations on the island undermined Cuba's sovereignty by replacing the functions of the state with those of private capital. With the collapse of the BNC, which, despite being a privately owned institution, had become the de facto central bank of the Cuban republic, the City Bank stepped in as the Cuban government depository and in 1923 received the contract for the monthly disbursement of $2.5 million in government salaries. The contract was received through the kind of nepotism—among Cubans—that Durrell despised and J. P. Morgan and Co. frowned upon. An old friend of Durrell's, Manuel Despaigne, was appointed secretary of the treasury by General Crowder. Durrell used the connection to secure the contract, advancing the Cuban government the sum based solely on his word. While the City Bank promised to reduce or eliminate the "abusive" and "extortionate" discounts previously involved in the payment of state employees, much was made of the nature of the contract. The bank asked for no collateral or security on the part of the government; instead, based on trust and Despaigne's good word, the contract was sealed with a handshake, in the old Spanish way.[91] Durrell and the City Bank also participated in the organization of the Havana Clearing House Association, which was formed by the largest private banks in the country as a means of expediting the cumbersome and inefficient procedures of interbank transactions.[92]

The statutes of the Clearing House Association advocated the establishment of banking regulations in Cuba, and most observers agreed that the crisis of 1920–21 was exacerbated by the fact that Cuba had neither banking laws nor a proper government bank.[93] Yet while the Cuban Congress passed legislation proposing the establishment of both, the actions of Wall Street and the US government worked to undermine the development of such laws and a government bank as the US Federal Reserve System was extended over Cuba. Already on September 29, 1921, the City Bank had been appointed a correspondent of the Federal Reserve Bank of New York in Cuba, though this was mainly a publicity move to ensure and bolster the strength of the banks in the volatile days immediately following the panic in the fall of 1920 and the subsequent imposition of the banking moratorium.[94] But on September 1, 1923, the City Bank's role as an agency was discontinued as both the Boston and Atlanta banks of the Federal Reserve opened in Havana.[95] There was a flurry of protest from Durrell and Mitchell regarding the appointments. When they learned that the First National Bank of Boston was going to host the Boston Reserve Bank, they complained to the directors that it was an "unthinkable injustice" to the City Bank that it was not considered, and that it gave the Boston institution a "wholly unjustifiable prestige" in Havana.[96] The matter was eventually resolved when the Atlanta branch was housed in the City Bank, and the Boston branch in the First National. The split locations also marked the division of labor of the two Federal Reserve banks in Cuba: Boston was assigned banking operations; Atlanta handled the issuing of US currency, largely because of the proximity of its Jacksonville branch to Cuba and the ease and cost of remitting currency from Florida instead of New York or Boston. As with the Clearing House Association, the Federal Reserve in Cuba protected the interests of its member banks but did little for those bankers, businesses, merchants, and planters who were outside of the system.[97] It did not regulate or inject credit into the Cuban economy except according to the needs of its North American member banks, and its monetary policy was not based on the needs of Cuban industry or agriculture, but North American banking.

The City Bank's assumption of some of the governmental functions of the Cuban state led, if indirectly, to Durrell's securing permission from 55 Wall Street to move forward on securing new premises for the bank in Havana. While Durrell had been repeatedly rebuffed by the directors at 55 Wall Street in his attempts to secure a new building, when the date of the first pay period for the Cuban government came around, Durrell stumbled on a plan. That day, knowing that the bank's foyer would be crowded with employees coming to cash their checks, he hired a photographer. The photographer snapped shots of the employees crammed into the bank. He sent the photographs to the directors in New York. The directors immediately authorized him to begin negotiations on a new lot. Durrell had his building. He quickly moved to secure the site of the Santa Catalina convent, a building constructed in 1688 at Compostela and O'Reilly in old Havana, had the building demolished (after the remains of the monks were interred in the Colón cemetery), and worked with Walker & Gillette to design a new building. Despite its architectural detailing referencing Cuba's Spanish colonial history, the new building was a robust reminder of the role the City Bank was playing in Cuba's neocolonial present. Durrell also secured an option with Purdy and Henderson on the adjoining lot, and together, they built an eight-story steel and concrete office tower. Durrell sold his shares in the building soon after it was completed, reaping a substantial personal profit from the sale.[98] The building, called the Edificio "La Metropolitana," or Metropolitana Building, leased space to many of the most important firms doing business in Cuba. Twenty-five million dollars in cash and securities were moved from the old building to the new by armored trucks of the Havana Terminal Railroad watched by police on horseback. The archbishop blessed the building and every department, and Charles E. Mitchell and Cuba's president-elect, Gerardo Machado y Morales, gave speeches. "When Mr. Mitchell returns to New York I wish him to remember that he is held in great esteem in Cuba," proclaimed Machado, "and that banking institutions will receive due attention and protection from my government."[99]

For Durrell, the opening of the new Havana branch coincided with the enlargement of his terrain in the Caribbean—as well as a new approach to banking in the Caribbean. In 1925, Mitchell asked him to take over the City Bank's operations in the Dominican Republic and Panama. In Santo Domingo, the bank had absorbed the operations of the International Banking Corporation (IBC), in the process taking over the IBC's contract with the Dominican government as the designated depository of government funds, even though the US military occupation had ended in 1924.[100] The IBC also had a chain of branches—in Barahona, La Vega, Puerto Plata, San Francisco de Macorís, San Pedro de Macorís, and Santiago de los Caballeros, as well as the capital, Santo Domingo City. In Panama, the bank had branches at Colón and Panama City and was heavily involved in toll transactions for canal traffic as well as doing a general banking business.[101]

In the meantime, as Durrell's district expanded, the nature of the business of the bank was being transformed. Mitchell was leading an attempt to rebrand and reposition the City Bank and build its business through bond retailing as well as the targeting of middle-class savers and investors, and, increasingly, through mergers and acquisitions. By 1923, the City Bank's bond department was the most active in the United States, dealing in $1 billion annually. Mitchell claimed the bank did $20 billion in securities business, averaging about $2 billion in sales per year until the crash.[102] As the City Bank's investment portfolio expanded, so too did the profile of its investors. In part, Mitchell and other bankers attributed the success of the bank's bond sales to the impact of World War I on the popular understanding of ideas of thrift and economy. The US government had initiated an extensive education, publicity, and advertising campaign to conscript people into the war effort through the Liberty and Victory Loans. The purchase of the loans turned hoarded cash into capital activated by the life-giving breath of patriotism through the purchase of bonds issued by the federal government and marketed through the nation's financial institutions. "These great Liberty loan drives developed a great understanding among the people as to what thrift and investment mean," wrote Mitchell. "The business that developed therefrom is small in volume, but what we are finding is that the number of orders, the number of people served, is constantly increasing."[103] The notion of thrift was nothing new to US workers. Thrift had had celebrated proponents such as Benjamin Franklin, and for years, savings associations for workers and laborers had proved popular throughout the country.[104] However, in the context of the Liberty Loans, thrift was translated from an individual concern into a collective duty—one tied to national defense and the financing of total war. The success of the Liberty Loan campaigns alerted bankers to the fact that such martial intensity and fiscal discipline could be mobilized for peacetime profitability and accumulation. "[The bond] promotes the projects of peace and national life," the NCC wrote in the publication *Bonds & Bankers*, "as the Liberty Bonds served the country in time of war."[105] After the war, thrift was given new modes of organization and application and became a critical part of the expansion of finance capital and empire.

As important as this education in the ways of savings and thrift was a shift in both public perceptions of banking and finance and bankers' perceptions of themselves. Under Mitchell, the NCC tried to eliminate the social and cultural stigma attached to bond retailing. According to Mitchell, it was "almost unethical" for bankers to actively seek out retail business. He argued that there was a mysterious and solemn aura that shrouded investment banking based on the pretense of a distinction between the elegant, discreet, and gentlemanly world of high finance and the brash and vulgar huckster-ism of the barker, the salesman, and the bond retailer. Mitchell sought to change that. "We thought that if we could tear from the investment banking business the veil of mystery and false dignity that surrounded it," he wrote in 1919, "if we could keep thrift and investment ideas constantly before them so that they might obtain a better idea of what a large part these actors might play in their success; if we could spread through a big organization the gospel of economic independence to be achieved by saving and investing, we could build up a large volume of business and at the same time accomplish something very desirable for the national welfare."[106]

Mitchell wanted to overturn common wisdom concerning banking practice. Where he saw a retail potential in banking, it was generally held that bankers, in order to maintain their good name and public confidence, should maintain conservative and sound banking practices, avoiding stock speculation, leaving trust management to the trust companies, and bond retailing to the bond retailers.[107] Nonetheless, Mitchell both expanded the financial business of the bank and engaged in a sort of investor populism, what he described as a "theory of getting closer to the people." In some cases, this was quite literal: the NCC made sure its offices were in accessible, street-level locations.[108] It also embarked on an advertising campaign that dispensed with the "staid and unappealing" promotional materials used by bankers and bond houses up to that point. It expanded its research department and trained its sales force to become more aggressively entrepreneurial in their approach to securities management. It kept an eye out for underperforming companies potentially needing refinancing. It sent out a monthly list of bond offerings, hired a stable of financial experts who advised customers on the creation of portfolios and constantly monitored overseas political, financial, and industrial conditions.[109] It encouraged what was termed "high pressure salesmanship" to hawk securities to ambivalent and often unaware investors.[110]

Mitchell was leading a cultural transformation in the apprehension and engagement of the public with money and banking. Early in the 1920s he created an "Automatic Savings Plan" for bank employees through which small amounts were deducted from their monthly salaries and deposited into an interest-bearing Investment Fund through which they created special savings funds for Christmas and vacations.[111] *No. 8*, the City Bank employee journal, increasingly ran articles encouraging employees to save and offering practical advice on budgeting and learning the "budget habit," as well as more detailed rationales, written by bank officers, on the nature and importance of savings.[112] The bank began observing Thrift Week, held in January to coincide with the January 17 birthday of Benjamin Franklin—a figure identified by the City Bank as "the father of thrift" and "the great apostle of savings"—and made Franklin's folksy capitalist vision a staple of its marketing.[113] The success of Mitchell's work, alongside that of other New York bankers at the time, in creating not only a market for bonds but a *culture* of investing in the United States can perhaps be seen in the fact that, by the end of the 1920s, the bond market and foreign investment would become water cooler talk for an increasing number of Americans. Investing was almost a national pastime. Americans kept a constant eye on the stock market ticker, and places like Bolivia and the Dominican Republic that were once seen as exotic came to seem as familiar as the names of domestic corporations such as Radio, General Motors, and American Can.

In 1922, the City Bank embarked on a publicity and marketing campaign targeting the public at large as part of its strategy for expansion; it was aimed at the middle- and working-class individuals whose banking needs were provided by mutual aid and building societies, and government and postal savings banks. The bank opened a branch at Forty-Second Street and Madison in New York City.[114] This branch was designated the Compound Interest

Department (CID), and its clientele were not corporations and wealthy individuals—City Bank's regular customers—but average "men, women, and children." The branch was "equipped for persons of small means." An account could be opened with a deposit as small as a single dollar, though it took a minimum $5 balance to generate the 3 percent compound interest offered by the bank.[115] The City Bank held its first CID contest from March 24 to May 5, 1923. It was, noted *No. 8*, "probably the biggest cooperative undertaking ever proposed by a banking organization."[116] The contest had the same martial intensity of the Liberty Loan campaigns. The entire bank's staff in New York, that is, 3,000 individual "Go-Getters" drawn from all segments of the City Bank "family"—the National City Company, the International Banking Corporation, the National City Realty Corporation, the National City Safe Deposit Company, and, of course, the City Bank itself—were mobilized in an incredible collective effort to get new customers and deposits. A carefully orchestrated program of internal publicity was organized to motivate the bank's staff while encouraging participation and competition. The contest was a stunning success: almost 50,000 new depositors with deposits, aggregated from amounts ranging between $5 and $1,000, amounting to more than $3 million. A total of 45,226 new depositors opened accounts with the branch. New deposits totaled $3,259,335.04. When the City Bank repeated the contest three years later it had similar results: more than 50,000 new accounts were opened containing more than $8 million. *No. 8* noted it was as if the entire population of Atlantic City, or two-thirds of Nevada, opened accounts with the City Bank.[117]

These efforts were soon brought to the Caribbean. With the success of the CID campaigns in New York City, Durrell and Mitchell saw the possibilities of growth through savings in the Caribbean and initiated, in 1923, a CID contest in Cuba and Puerto Rico modeled on the example of New York City and the Forty-Second Street branch. Mitchell and Durrell hoped that between 12,000 and 15,000 new depositors could be enticed to open new accounts. It was a figure that both Mitchell and Durrell believed was overly ambitious.[118] There were only 630 staff members in Cuba and Puerto Rico, in comparison to the 3,000 plus in New York, and the islands had neither the population density nor the per capita wealth of the city. The Caribbean contests proved to be an even greater success than they imagined. By October 30, 1925, one month into the contest, the Cuban and Puerto Rican branches had already obtained 11,502 new accounts with total initial deposits of $1,159,497.37. When the campaign closed on December 18, 1926, almost every branch exceeded the campaign quotas, and total deposits were 50 percent higher than anticipated[119] More than 30,000 new accounts were opened, twice what Durrell had expected, with deposits of $4,304,407.05, more than a hundred thousand dollars more than the New York drive had gained. The success of the Cuban and Puerto Rican contest prompted the City Bank to expand its geographic reach. In 1928, it organized a "World-Wide Contest" pitting the Caribbean District against South America. The contest brought in 74,082 new accounts with a total of $10,226,884 in deposits. The Caribbean beat out South America, with every branch exceeding its quota in deposits.

Among the accounts opened by the staff of the City Bank in Cuba was one for Gerardo Machado. It had been secured by Durrell's secretary, Miss A. M. Klender, who had managed to obtain an audience with the president and was able to convince him to open accounts for himself, and for his wife and daughter.[120] This approach became a critical strategy for the bank's staff in expanding their operations in the Caribbean: the corralling of "group" accounts through which informal social and familial ties were canvassed to create great clusters of depositors. The City Bank asked its Caribbean staff to turn to friends, acquaintances, and family members to build the bank's presence in the region. "Group" accounts—clusters of new depositors known to each other and to the staff member who signed them up—were critical to the campaign.[121] "Every town on the Island was canvassed and in some cases re-canvassed" in the search for new accounts. As a result, "accounts representing every town and village in Porto Rico were obtained, and thousands of new friends were made for the bank." Two janitors, one from the San Juan branch, the other from the Caguas branch, secured 156 accounts between them. One staff member brought in fifty-two accounts, out of a possible seventy-five, from a San Juan department store. Accounts were obtained from a local sugar company.[122] In Cuba, staff members used genealogical records to secure accounts by plotting family histories:

> Many of the contestants penetrated on horse back to the farm districts of Pinar del Rio to bring accounts to the Lonja branch located in the importing provision district of Havana. High pressure salesmanship and oratory were used in tobacco factories, where the official "readers" eulogized the National City organization and urged workers to open savings accounts. In one day we received reports from contestants who returned from out of the way places within a radius of one hundred miles, where they had obtained accounts from people working in cement factories, tobacco fields, coffee plantations, sugar cane colonies, cattle ranches, copper and iron miens, workers on Cuba's new central highway, stevedore and dock laborers and in more accessible places every type of prospect possible. By that time there was not a person in Cuba

who did not know that a world-wide savings contest was being carried to a successful climax.[123]

Through the CID contests, Durrell, Mitchell, and the City Bank had found an effective, self-governing means of expanding the bank's capital—and extending modern imperialism.

Despite the success of the CID campaigns and the efforts by the City Bank to build deposits in Cuba, the City Bank's status there was contested, and the enthusiasm portrayed in the pages of *No. 8* was belied by a growing animosity toward the bank in Cuba and a resistance, often through inchoate, infrapolitical forms, to the governmental regimes of savings and the modes of US imperialism that they signified.[124] Since the crisis of 1920–21, the Cuban press had often taken a cool stance toward Wall Street and North American banks. As the Banco Nacional de Cuba went into liquidation— and as agencies of the Atlanta and Boston Federal Reserve banks established themselves in Havana—newspapers including *El Mundo, El Comercio, Diario de la Marina, El Triunfo,* and *El Correo Español* all published editorials criticizing the presence of the US reserve bank in Cuba while attacking foreign banking, foreign ownership of mills and land, and the circulation of foreign currencies.[125] There was a sense that not only were US bankers and businesspeople leading a campaign against the organization of a Cuban central bank, but that they were waging a war against it.[126] "Cuidado con la banca de Wall Street," wrote one editorialist: *beware of the Wall Street banks.* The writer pointed to the role of Wall Street in the financial affairs of Haiti, the Dominican Republic, Costa Rica, Nicaragua, Panama, and Puerto Rico as cautionary tales of the nexus of foreign-owned banks, military power, and regional sovereignty.[127] Editorials argued that without proper banking laws and without a central bank, Cuba would become a "Finca de Wall Street" (a Wall Street estate)[128] or "una colonia de plantación" (a colony of a plantation).[129] Cuba, they argued, needed a bank modeled after the central banks of the United States, France, England, and Spain.[130]

The press attacks against the City Bank increased at the end of 1924. *El Universal* ran a series of articles asserting that the City Bank was on the verge of bankruptcy. With the continued fall of the price of sugar, *El Universal* claimed that the bank was faced with a catastrophic shortage of money.[131] The journal asserted that the bank was unwilling to pay obligations contracted by its subsidiary, the General Sugar Company, which were due to planters, merchants, and businesspeople who had provided services to it.

The articles prompted another spate of withdrawals, costing the bank about $5 million in deposits, 50 percent of which came from the Havana branch.[132] Durrell was certain that the money would soon return to the bank, but he had little sympathy for the Cuban press. He saw the newspaper stories as a form of blackmail and extortion and claimed the editors had demanded a $100,000 payment in order to stop their publication. Others within the City Bank were more sympathetic to the Cubans. Lee Olwell, Charles Mitchell's assistant and the individual in charge of the City Bank's press and publicity, developed a compassionate view of the Cuban press and their reasons for attacking the bank. In January 1925 Olwell had an extended meeting with Rafael Govin, the publisher of *El Universal*, in New York City. Govin told him that he was sympathetic to the bank, but not to the City Bank's General Sugar Company, or any of the other US corporations that had emerged in Cuba. For Govin, it was an issue of Cuban sovereignty: by taking over ownership and control of Cuba's sugar production, these corporations had become certain targets. Their behavior was poor, and their treatment of Cubans was shoddy. From a personal perspective, Govin told Olwell that the Cuba Cane Company had appropriated a piece of property for its plantations that had been in the Govin family for generations.[133]

"I am of the opinion that the National City Bank has got to pay in one way or another for some of the d—fool things that have been done by some American corporations in their dealings with Cubans," Olwell wrote to Durrell following his meeting with Govin. He wrote that whether or not what Govin said was true it was the perception that was important. Yet, if it were true, an American company "deliberately antagonizing" Govin and other Cubans was shortsighted policy. "I have no doubt you yourself are cognizant of cases where other American controlled corporations have shown an equal lack of business judgment." He continued:

> The National City Bank is something tangible. It is something for a newspaper to point at and shout about. People in Havana and other cities see its buildings and if they want to throw a rock, they have something to throw it at. The big American companies are something intangible as far as the people of the cities are concerned. They are not doing business directly with the people in the way we are and can ride through attacks of one kind or another without injury to themselves and without paying much attention to them. We are a shining light and they can make us wince, for they can say things about us that not only annoy us but actually hurt our business.
>
> I have a feeling that the National City Bank in Cuba is standing right now at the threshold of what may be the beginning of a long and unpleasant fight.

The earmarks are evident in the clippings you have sent me that forces are already at work to again try to start a movement to have Cuba develop its own banking structure. Throughout the Island there is, in my judgment, a certain amount of slumbering and a certain amount of active enmity, the result of the natural business activities as well as the unfortunate way in which no doubt certain American and foreign interests have proceeded with their relationships on the Island and I very much fear the National City Bank is going to be from time to time, the Maypole around which the dance will be held.[134]

Despite the protests and the enmity, the City Bank and other foreign banks in Cuba had a powerful ally in the Cuban government: President Gerardo Machado. Among the last of the generation of Cuban independence fighters to run for public office, Machado was elected by a broad swath of liberals and progressives, partly because of public dissatisfaction with incumbent president Zayas, and partly because of Machado's progressive "Platform of Regeneration," with its mandate to rebuild the country by strengthening its sovereignty, expanding education, diversifying its economy, and forswearing the assumption of further debt. Despite the populist overtures, Machado was a businessman at heart. He owned a number of Cuban businesses: the Santa Marta sugar *central*, a construction company, a paint factory, the newspapers *El País* and *Excelsior*, a shoe company, a contracting business, and a market. He also held investments in several other local enterprises, including a soap factory and a brewery.[135] Machado recognized that his own desires for power were tied to the whims of American capital. His presidential campaign was financed with $500,000 from the American and Foreign Power Company, which controlled the foreign holdings of General Electric's subsidiary for Latin America, the Electric Bond and Share Company.

During his visits to the United States in the months before he assumed power, Machado repeatedly gave assurances to US businesspeople and bankers that their interests would be protected and that prolonged labor disruptions would not be tolerated. He asserted that the role of government in Cuba was to defend foreign capital. In April 1925, Machado addressed an audience at a banquet at the Bankers Club in New York attended by Durrell and sponsored by Earl D. Babst of the American Sugar Refining Company. Machado spoke of the importance of business to the Cuban economy and pledged that his government would provide "an absolute guarantee" for businesses operating in the country, especially against attacks from and disruptions by labor.[136] A month later, at the inauguration of the City Bank in Havana, he further addressed the question of press attacks on foreign banks operating in the country. "There are times, when such institutions are attacked by the newspapers," Machado stated, "but the President of the Republic will be on the alert in order to punish severely those who are responsible for the attacks. I wish to be very closely connected with these institutions so that in such an event I may unhesitatingly be able to say that the credit of the institution involved is sound, and should it be lost, the Republic of Cuba will also suffer the loss of such credit."[137]

Machado took the oath of office on May 20, 1925, and quickly demonstrated his commitments to North American capital. He arrested members of the Cuban Communist Party, used force against strikers, dissolved unions, and suppressed radical publications, all with the support of the US State Department.[138] In June 1925, he embarked on an ambitious public works program that would radically increase the public debt of the Cuban republic (see chapter 7). In April 1926, he defended the banks against another round of newspapers attacks.[139] A number of newspapers published reports of a rumor that the Cuban government was about to institute another banking moratorium to block the withdrawal of funds to protect insolvent banks. Panic followed. Merchants began withdrawing deposits from the Royal Bank of Canada's Havana branch on Thursday, April 19, and depositors clamoring to withdraw their savings sparked a subsequent panic. Thousands of small depositors besieged the bank, and the panic spread to the country branches of the RBC and the City Bank. By Saturday afternoon, hysteria was at a peak.[140]

Machado quickly intervened. He arrived at the RBC branch in Havana, strode through the lobby directly to the receiving teller, and, with great ostentation, pomp, and purpose, counted out and deposited $100,000 US in the Canadian institution.[141] He then turned to the nervous and fretful crowd that had gathered in front of the bank: the run, he said, was stupid, the rumors unfounded, and the strength of the RBC was demonstrated by the fact that he kept his personal fortune there. If necessary, the RBC could rely on $40 million from the Cuban treasury to back its deposits.[142] While this was happening, Carlos Miguel de Céspedes, the Cuban minister of public works (and an individual who had only recently obtained a $500,000 loan from the City Bank), arrived at the Banco del Comercio and repeated Machado's actions.[143] Machado attributed the rumors of insolvency to former employees of the RBC who told a reporter at *El Imparcial* that the bank was in trouble. He promised that the "secret judicial police" were searching for them.

Afraid of the dangerous possibilities of contagion generated by the run, the foreign banking community quickly mobilized behind the scenes. The

Havana branch of the City Bank used its newly installed wire system, with its direct line from Cuba to 55 Wall Street, to request a transfer of funds through the Federal Reserve System to shore up its deposits.[144] The Federal Reserve branch in Atlanta sent $35 million from Jacksonville to Key West, loaded it on a postal cutter, and rushed it to Havana where a portion of the currency was loaded onto a special train that took it out to the City Bank and the Royal Bank branches in the country.[145] An additional $45 million was expected early in the week. It was rumored that the demand for funds in Cuba was causing a crisis of liquidity in New York and a sell-off on the New York Stock Exchange. And even with the City Bank's new wire, it was said that if a Sunday had not intervened, the contagion would have been worse. All told, the City Bank claimed that its net losses from its twenty-five branches on the island came to $2,936,000, of which $700,000 was a normal commercial transfer of funds to New York, and $1,380,000 represented withdrawals by local banks, leaving actual withdrawals on the part of the public at only $856,000.[146] The Boston Reserve Bank withdrew from Cuba a few months later, frustrated by the instability of the Cuban banking system.

An editorial in the City Bank's *Monthly Letter* of May 1926 reassured its readers that "there has been at no time cause for nervousness" during the April panic in Cuba.[147] It claimed that while sugar was selling below the cost of production, as loans on sugar were made based on low valuation, banking on the island was not affected, the panics were far different from those in 1920, 1921, and 1922, and the sugar industry was not facing anything approaching a crisis.[148] But by the next year, the economic and financial situation had changed drastically. "The general economical situation in Cuba is worse to-day than at any time since the declaration of the moratorium in 1920," Durrell wrote to Mitchell on July 5, 1927.[149] Durrell evoked a dire portrait of Cuba's economy. Business had slowed to a crawl. Collections were languid, and Havana's harbor, usually crowded with steamers and sugar tramps bringing goods from Europe and the United States, was empty of vessels. Businesses were failing throughout Havana, and storefronts and offices stood vacant. The Cuban government was only able to keep up the appearance of prosperity through the construction projects associated with the public works projects funded by loans contracted by the Chase National Bank. In Havana, the building of the Capitolio and other projects projected the image of good times, but in the countryside, the construction of the Central Highway, a centerpiece of the public works program, had slowed down. Local contractors in Matanzas and Santa Clara had run out of money. Elsewhere the Warren Brothers, who were awarded the bulk of the contracts, refused to begin construction as they knew their funds would quickly be exhausted. Machado, according to Durrell, declared that only the gamblers and bums were idle in Cuba, but the fact was that there was massive unemployment, and the number of unemployed was growing with the release of state employees from the government payroll, while in some parts of Cuba, people were facing starvation.

Machado's hold on both economic and political power was also becoming increasingly tenuous. Early in 1927, Machado had sounded out the US State Department, looking for an endorsement to extend his term of office. When he visited the United States in April, President Coolidge gave him the tacit approval that he sought.[150] During the same trip, he was feted by Wall Street and the US business community. Mitchell and Durrell hosted him for a one-hour banquet at 55 Wall Street, and 700 businesspeople heard him speak at the Hotel Astor.[151] "The wealth of foreigners in Cuba must and will be protected," Machado stated during his talk. "Capital in Cuba will be defended as it is in the United States."[152] This was precisely what they wanted to hear. Machado left New York having secured a $9 million loan from J. P. Morgan, with Morgan partner Thomas Lamont proclaiming of Machado, "We do not care by what means, but we would like to see such a good administrator remain in power."[153]

For many in Cuba, Lamont's words signified the birth of the Machado dictatorship. In Havana, copies of the newspaper *Diario de la Marina* were seized by the government after they published a manifesto written by Carlos Mendieta's opposition Unión Nacionalista denouncing Lamont for his statements in support of the indefinite extension of Machado's term in office.[154] Yet for the most part, Machado's suppression of the press was such that no one was speaking out against what was quickly becoming a tyrannical regime.[155] Durrell wryly noted that such suppression was a boon to the City Bank, as the newspapers were no longer willing to print incendiary stories on the solvency of the bank. Still, the City Bank was not unaffected by the economy of Cuba. Durrell expected a falloff in deposits in the coming dead season, and he noted that the Havana Clearing House figures (the only statistical barometer of business available) between the first five months of 1925—when the new building was built—to the same period in 1927 had indicated a drop from $1.049 billion to $851 million. The City Bank, however, was the least affected by the falloff in interbank clearances. The Royal Bank, which had sixty-five Cuban branches compared to the City Bank's twenty-five, saw a much greater share of the fall in deposits. Furthermore, the fact that the price of sugar never recovered from the heights of 1920—indeed, never approached the 1920 heights—meant that the City Bank's attempts to consolidate its sugar properties were unsuccessful. The General Sugar Company, the holding company formed by the City Bank in 1922, turned a profit in the years when sugar hit 5 cents a pound, but after tens of millions of dollars of investment in the modernization of machinery and the expansion of sugar properties,[156] Mitchell and the directors decided to write the General Sugar Company, the holding company for Cuban and Dominican sugar properties they had created after the crisis of 1920-21, off the books of the bank. When attempts to unload their mills proved unsuccessful, the NCC absorbed the sugar company's stock through a $25 million stock issue, and cleared its outstanding loans to its sugar mills, allowing the City Bank proper to remove the unprofitable properties from its ledgers.[157]

A year later the state of the Cuban economy had worsened. "I am now more than ever convinced that Cuba is facing the most difficult economic situation in her history," Durrell wrote to Mitchell.[158] The tourist season gave the appearance of prosperity in Havana: the racetrack and the casino were filled with gamblers, and the hotels and bars around the Parque Centrale and the Prado were making a brisk profit. But away from central Havana, in the suburbs and the countryside, Durrell described "a sad story," as his branch managers reported that business and trade conditions were simply worse than the previous year. At the same time, as the economy worsened, and Machado's dictatorship consolidated power through force, repression, and the arbitrary application of the rule of law, Machado began to turn on the North American financial institutions that he had previously pledged to support.

Machado began what Durrell described as a "tax persecution" campaign that threatened to further disrupt and demoralize the Cuban economy. "Dozens of tax collectors swarmed though the Island wringing the last possible dollar from a bankrupt commerce," wrote Durrell. "Few were exempt. Commercial houses, sugar companies, and financial concerns were all levied additional taxes." The Atlanta Federal Reserve was hit with a $70,000 assessment that was only dropped when Durrell pleaded with Ambassador Orestes Ferrara, who contacted Machado directly, insisting the assessment would mean the loss of the agency in Cuba. Late in 1927, the City Bank received its own tax bill from the Cuban government. Durrell protested to the chief attorney and spokesman for the government, Don Claudio Mendoza, and was granted an extension to pay as well as being assured that an official demand would not be made until the banks had had a chance to talk with the president and the minister of finance. But on February 20, 1928, the

demand was renewed. Machado had instructed the minister to cancel tax assessed on interest paid to head offices for the fiscal years between 1922 and
1925, but insisted on payment for 1926, 1927, and in the future. For the City
Bank, this meant its assessment was reduced by $56,600, down to a total of
$393,000. The Royal Bank was notified that it owed $900,000. Other banks
were charged lesser amounts. Only the Chase Bank, which maintained an
open line of credit with the Cuban government and kept Machado's son-in-
law on the payroll, avoided an assessment. "Summed up," Durrell wrote,
"we have been forced at the point of a gun to pay certain taxes that we do
not owe, and to advance the Government our prospective taxes for the years
1928 and 1929."[159]

Elsewhere in the Caribbean, the fortunes of Durrell and the City Bank were
mixed. In Panama, Durrell was disgusted by the state of the bank and displeased at its position. "We have run a poor second to the Chase National
Bank," Durrell wrote to Mitchell concerning Panama. For Durrell, the bank's
status was surprising. He could not understand how, given the fact that the
City Bank had once had a near monopoly on banking in the Caribbean since
1904, when James Morris Morgan opened the first branch of the IBC on the
isthmus, the bank could be in such a bad shape. It was a "burning shame,"
Durrell wrote, that the City Bank's dominance had been slowly eroded, first,
by the Commercial National Bank, then by the American Foreign Banking
Corporation—a "rottenly mismanaged institution"—and now by the Chase
Bank. How the City Bank permitted the Chase Bank "to even exist locally"
was beyond Durrell: "That it was allowed to take a commanding lead at both
ends of the Canal Zone is almost beyond comprehension."[160] Although the
IBC had handled the majority of the tolls "at a reasonable profit" from the
opening of the canal in 1914, by the time the City Bank took over the IBC
branches in 1926, their share of toll charges had dropped to 48 percent.
This figure was further reduced to 26 percent when the Chase Bank cut its
rates on toll traffic and its president Albert H. Wiggin offered to carry the
accounts of the International Mercantile Marine at no charge, even though
it meant a loss to the bank. The Chase Bank also offered retail customers
a competitive 4 percent interest rate on current deposits, and as a result, it
was able to quickly claim 50 percent of deposits in Panama and in the Canal
Zone.[161] It also secured a monopoly of the business of the US Army and Navy
in Panama.

As in Cuba, Durrell believed that the growth of the City Bank in Panama
was handicapped by its quarters. In Panama City, the bank occupied a build-

ing that had been secured by the IBC years before. Its location was poor and with a lobby barely six feet wide the bank's customers were rammed together, upsetting the color bars prevailing in the republic. Writing to Mitchell, Durrell noted that the bank's lobby was "usually congested with Jamaicans and East Indians, which has resulted in our being known locally as 'the Nigger Bank.'"[162] Durrell commissioned a new building that was due to be opened late in the summer of 1928. Designed by Purdy and Henderson, its architecture replicated that of the City Bank's recently constructed branch at Canal and Broadway in New York City. It marked a turn in the design of the bank: the European neoclassicism of 55 Wall Street was replaced by Egyptian-styled buildings that drew their inspiration from the Ramses II era. While such design was becoming the standard for the City Bank's branches globally, in Panama the new branch, like the Compostela and O'Reilly branch in Havana, marked a transition in the architecture and spatiality of the city, as it was built near the demolished colonial ramparts of the old city.[163] And while the bank played a progressive role in hiring Panamanian women as clerks, Durrell also made sure that the design of the bank was done "with the idea of segregating the spades and the ragheads." By doing so, Durrell was sure that the City Bank would "secure the lion's share of the white business" in Panama.[164]

Staffing was also an issue in Panama. For Durrell, the staff the City Bank inherited from the IBC was less than desirable. One employee had been worked so hard by the bank he had had a nervous breakdown. Another was a "lemon" who "flivvered"—and was a failure at banking. Another had his professional prospects destroyed by marital problems. To remedy the staffing situation, Durrell recruited J. H. Drumm from the IBC's branches in the Dominican Republic. Drumm had sixteen years of banking experience behind him, having worked with the First National Bank of Boston and the Commercial National Bank of Washington, DC, before joining the IBC. Durrell described him as a "two-fisted go-getter" and was impressed with the work he had performed in organizing four new branches of the IBC in the Dominican Republic. Furthermore, Drumm had been poorly treated by George S. Schaeffer, the local manager of the Chase Bank—and a person whom Durrell described as a "particularly obnoxious individual"—when they had worked together at the Commercial National Bank. Durrell thought he could exploit the animosity by fostering the rivalry between the two men to the City Bank's benefit: "He welcomed the opportunity to pay off old scores and is already making Schaeffer's life miserable," Durrell wrote to Mitchell.[165] Drumm had already made inroads with members of the Panamanian business community, who were beginning to bring their business to the City Bank, and he had also made good with Panamanian president Florencio Arosemena, and was even granted a seat to immediate right of the president at a dinner. Durrell hoped that Drumm's inroads with Arosemena would secure a loan for Panama through the NCC. Drumm was successful in his efforts, beating bids from two other bankers. The NCC lent Panama $12 million.[166]

In Haiti the City Bank enjoyed a secure and lucrative position. With the US occupation ongoing, Haiti was politically and economically stable, and the City Bank had none of the worries about internal and external political interference that had plagued the operation of the Banque Nationale de la République d'Haiti after its initial chartering in 1880. The early Cacos insurgencies against the military occupation had been successfully (and brutally) gutted, while the squall of negative publicity had subsided. The United States had established a tightly integrated system of rule with a client-president, Louis Borno, a onetime critic of US intervention, as its titular head. Hosted by Mitchell and the directors at 55 Wall Street in 1926, Borno's trips to the United States were marked by protests from Haitian exiles, and humiliation and slights from US dignitaries.[167] Economically, Haiti was going through a period of relative prosperity, thought it did little to aid the backbone of the country, the Haitian peasantry. The military occupation did little to expand Haiti's agricultural or industrial productivity, but the high price of coffee on world markets through the 1920s, as well as the increased efficiency of the collection of customs and tax revenue, ensured that the neocolonial Haitian state was doing well.[168]

This translated into a lucrative business for the City Bank through the BNRH. Through the NCC, the City Bank had gained complete control of the Haitian bank in 1922. In 1925, the bank had formed a Connecticut-chartered holding company, the Bank of Haiti, to purchase the stock of the BNRH for the City Bank while installing the City Bank's executives, including Charles Mitchell, as its directors.[169] The BNRH was the occupied republic's central bank as well as its most important commercial concern. It handled the amortization payments of the NCC–held sovereign debt and acted as the government depository, taking in all the revenue from customs receipts and other sources. The BNRH did so without paying the government interest, and what interest was generated by the government funds remained with the City Bank. Balances were held in New York and used by the City Bank in its commercial loans, generating interest income.[170] "Today," noted the US financial adviser W. W. Cumberland, "the little Republic of Haiti is lending money in Wall Street, instead of begging it."[171] Revenue also came to the bank from the profits it made on the "slave trade" in blacks between

Jamaica and Haiti and Cuba and the Dominican Republic, where the emigration of cane workers brought profits from a head tax.[172]

By 1929, the imperial frontiers for the City Bank seemed endless. Domestically, under Mitchell, the bank was embarking on a spate of mergers and acquisitions and expanding its loan portfolio.[173] Internationally, its branch expansion continued apace with new branches planned for Mexico, Colombia, El Salvador, Honduras, Guatemala, and Nicaragua. In August 1929 Durrell took a well-deserved summer break and departed on a six-week hunting trip in Alaska with James A. Stillman. At the time of their departure, the bank stock was at historic highs, buoyed, in part, by the stock-ownership scheme that Mitchell had initiated a few years earlier, enabling employees to invest in stock of the bank. At the same time, Mitchell wrote to all the directors, asking, "If the destinies of The National City Bank were completely in your hands, what major step or steps (if any) would you take now or in the immediate future to extend or broaden the sphere of service or increase the usefulness to the public of this institution?"[174] Durrell's wrote his response, titled "If I Were King," days before his departure for Alaska. He outlined an ambitious plan for increasing the bank's deposits, expanding the branch footprint in greater New York, and continuing its overseas expansion.[175]

Returning to Anchorage after having been cut off from communication with the world for sixty days, Durrell and Stillman were "were shocked to learn the extent of the market boom that had occurred during our absence." By the time they traveled down the Pacific coast to Seattle, the City Bank stock was selling at $590. Reaching New York City soon after, they found the stock price had remained the same but was rumored to go even higher—with some saying its ceiling was $1,000 per share. Durrell was told by many in the bank that he should cash out his holdings, but refrained from doing so out of his loyalty to Mitchell and, when the stock began to slide—eventually reaching a low of $17—out of Mitchell's faith in the bank. When the October crash came, while many who held the City Bank's stock were wiped out—Durrell's secretary, A. M. Klender, who had solicited accounts from Machado, was ruined—Durrell's conservative approach to investing meant he was barely exposed.[176] But as in 1920–21, he benefited, if indirectly, from the crisis. In November 1929, Mitchell proposed that Durrell's portfolio expand again and asked him to helm the entire Overseas Division. Durrell took over the division in 1930—just as it was heading toward crisis.

SEVEN

Odious Debt

The Cuban outpost of the Chase National Bank of the City of New York was housed in a four-story building at Aguiar 86 between Obispo and O'Reilly in the cluttered grid of Havana's old city. Opened in January 1925, the branch displayed the throwback colonial style and the ornamental eclecticism of Havana's affluent merchant classes. Neoclassical motifs, second-story Doric columns, and terracotta acanthus friezes marked its façade in indiscriminate fashion. But the bank was solid and spacious. Built of stone and containing wide doors and high ceilings, it was designed with an understated and pre-possessed stateliness that exuded confidence, assurance, and stability, even as the economic foundations on which it was built were fragile, tenuous, and uncertain.[1] Indeed, while in January 1925, the United States was about to embark on what Alfred H. Wiggin, the president of the Chase Bank since 1911, would later recall as "the wildest orgy of speculation that the present generation remembers," the sugar-dependent Cuban economy had never fully recovered from the hangover that followed the dance of millions.[2] The price of sugar had remained depressed since peaking in May 1920 and demand for Cuban raws had fallen on the world market as European beet sugar production recovered after the First World War. Crippled by foreign debt and undermined by reduced revenues, the Cuban government was perennially starved of funds. Inflation was high. Unemployment was rampant. The republic was in a state of political unrest and agitation, and for many Cubans, financial institutions like the City Bank, the Royal Bank of Canada (RBC), and the Mercantile Bank of the Americas (MBA) were viewed as the root cause of their economic problems.[3] Antibanking sentiments were simmering within the country, and a nascent nationalism was stirred by what appeared as the wholesale transfer of Cuba's sugar mills and plantations, of the very lifeblood of Cuba's wealth and prosperity, to foreign interests—and by the decimation of the local banking sector and the emergence of a few powerful foreign banks. It was, it seemed, an inopportune time for the Chase Bank to expand into Cuba.

The Chase Bank came late to Cuba and initially avoided the anger and frustration increasingly directed at the City Bank and the RBC. By the 1930s this would change. More than any other foreign institution, the Chase Bank came to symbolize the graft, fraud, and profiteering of the shadowed and speculative practices of US imperial banking in the early twentieth-century Caribbean. Soon after establishing its branch at Aguiar 86, the Chase Bank began an aggressive campaign to court Cuban president Gerardo Machado with the hopes of securing the loan contracts for an ambitious public works project whose ostensible aim was to relieve unemployment and rejuvenate the stagnant Cuban economy but whose cost became a heavy burden to the Cuban people. What began as a $10 million financing contract covering a new capital building, a central highway connecting Havana to the provinces, and an extension of the Malecón, Havana's waterfront esplanade, ballooned into an $80 million debacle for a half-built highway and a spectacular but unpractical capital building. As government employees went unpaid and Cuba's working classes faced starvation, interest payments drained the republic's coffers, and the proceeds of the loans allegedly went into the pockets of Machado and his allies. The Chase loans became emblematic of the reckless excesses and speculative financial binging of the twenties, and the bank itself was seen as underwriting the violence and repression of the Machado regime.

While the Chase Bank's Cuban loans were made during an era of radical expansion and diversification, the crisis of sovereignty and finance capital in Cuba precipitated by the loans was determined by the contingencies of law.[4] The history of the conflict between Cuba and the Chase Bank—between country and creditor—was enacted through a contest over the legal and regulatory frameworks governing questions of debt, credit, investment, and accumulation—and the attempts to negotiate, avoid, and in some cases change the legal field in which this conflict was situated. This legal field was shaped by three contentious elements. First, the legality of the operations of the Chase Bank's securities affiliate, the Chase Securities Corporation, according to both US federal banking law and the legality of the modes of publicity and representation through which it marketed Cuban bonds to American investors. Second, the legality of the Chase Bank's Cuban loans according to the strictures of the Platt Amendment and its paternalist restraints on Cuba's ability and authority to contract debt. Third, the legality—and morality—of the debts themselves, based on the constitutional legitimacy of

the Machado government. By the end of the 1920s this legitimacy was challenged by a broad sector of Cuban society, leading to Machado's overthrow
in 1933. After Machado was forced from power, his successors stood up to
the onerous burden of debt and refused to make further interest payments
on the Chase loans. Citing the doctrine of "odious debt," they claimed that
the Chase loans to Cuba were knowingly made to an illegitimate and tyrannical government and thus were not the responsibility of the Cuban people.
The argument was a repudiation of the methods of dark finance that the
Chase Bank had employed in the Caribbean, and it helped to bring such
methods into the light.

Founded in 1877 by banker and entrepreneur John Thompson, the Chase
National Bank of the City of New York took took its name from Salmon P.
Chase, Abraham Lincoln's secretary of the treasury and the organizer of the
national banking system. In its early years, the Chase Bank was a domestic
wholesale bank. It serviced corporations and other banking institutions in
both New York City and the US Northwest and counted railroad magnate
James J. Hill among its early depositors and directors. By 1896, the Chase
Bank's $5 million in deposits consisted of accounts from 165 national
banks, 409 state banks and bankers, and 242 individuals.[5] By 1900, its deposits had shot up to $43 million, 70 percent of that figure coming from
other banks.[6] When Albert H. Wiggin joined the Chase Bank as a vice president and director in 1904, it was still a traditional commercial bank. Its
operations were largely domestic, and its policies were shaped by a succession of august and conservative executives, including Henry W. Cannon and
Alzono Barton Hepburn. Elected president of the Chase Bank on January 11,
1911, Wiggin broke with the older guard of Chase bankers and sparked a
radical transformation in the bank's culture, organization, and activities.

Wiggin's family connections paved a road to prominence within the
merchant-banking circles of late nineteenth-century Boston and opened
doors into the rarefied social worlds of high finance in early twentieth-
century New York. The son of a Unitarian minister, he was born in Med-
field, Massachusetts, in 1868 and went to high school in Boston, where he
spent his summer vacations running errands and doing office work for local
banks.[7] Following school, Wiggin worked for J. B. Moors & Co. Moors was
a Devonshire Street merchant bank with correspondents throughout the
United States. It served as the US representative of European banking houses
including Morton, Rose & Co. and Layard Bros. & Co. of London and Crédit
Lyonnais of Paris.[8] At Moors, Wiggin was introduced to the rudiments of

foreign exchange, but he was also tasked with more prosaic duties, including taking care of the Moors's farm.

Wiggin left Moors after eighteen months to work as a runner at the National Commonwealth Bank, where his uncle and namesake was the president. He was promoted after twelve months to a position as a book-keeper. In 1891 he became assistant national bank examiner of the Boston District, and three years later was appointed assistant cashier of the Third National Bank and vice president of the Eliot National Bank.[9] In 1899, Richard Delafield offered Wiggin the position of president of the National Park Bank of New York. Founded in 1856 and so named because of its location in a prominent and visible position across from City Hall Park, the National Park Bank was a commercial bank that had pioneered the development of a mercantile credit department and was one of the earliest US institutions with a sterling desk.[10] Wiggin accepted the offer, moved to New York, and while working for the National Park Bank developed a reputation as one of the best credit-men in the country—and one of its nicest bankers. Wiggin's easygoing and genial nature caused him to be known as "the banker with a million friends."[11]

The National Park Bank had an august and wealthy directorship made up of financiers and industrialists including John Jacob Astor, August Belmont, Cornelius Vanderbilt, Stuyvesant Fish, and Isaac Guggenheim. Wiggin joined the board after the death of banker Edward Poor. The appointment signified not only Wiggin's increasing personal wealth, but also the prestige and renown he was gaining as a banker among the older generation of Wall Street sages. The esteem of the old-school leaders for Wiggin was shared by the youth set then emerging. Indeed, when Henry Pomeroy Davidson, then of the First National Bank, later of J. P. Morgan, organized the Bankers Trust Company in 1903, Wiggin was among the first to join. The Bankers Trust Company served the accumulated wealth of a powerful cabal of bankers: the largest private and commercial banks on Wall Street that handled the fiduciary business of the national and state banks of the country.[12] Wiggin also became a director of the Guaranty Trust Company, Astor Trust Company, Lawyers Title Insurance and Trust Company, and the Union Exchange Bank while associating with the Mutual Bank and Harlem's Mount Morris Bank.[13]

Wiggin remained with the National Park Bank for five years, but his ambition, success, and popularity led him to the Chase Bank, first as a vice president and director, then, in 1911, as president. Over the next decade, Wiggin liberated the Chase Bank from the straitjacket of commercial banking, often pushing beyond the legal constraints imposed on a federally chartered national banking association. He diversified and expanded its activities by creating an energetic investment unit in the Chase Securities Corporation, and he built an institutional machinery for the bank's international expansion, initially through the American Foreign Banking Corporation (AFBC). Both the securities corporation and the banking corporation were organized at about the same time. But the former was relatively inactive in its early years and only became the center of the Chase's financial activities after 1925. In the meantime, the AFBC joined the US rush into foreign commerce during and after World War I, and suffered a fate similar to its direct rival, the Mercantile Bank of the Americas. Like the MBA, the AFBC's history was short, sharp, and plagued by corruption and speculation.

The AFBC was chartered on July 9, 1917, under section 25 (1) of the Federal Reserve Act, the amendment authorizing national banking associations capitalized at $1 million or more to organize corporations for the purposes of foreign trade (fig. 7.1).[14] The same amendment had authorized the creation of the MBA, and like the MBA, the AFBC was organized to create a vehicle that could pool US capital resources to take advantage of the changing conditions of global trade and finance during and after World War I. In terms of organization and structure, the two institutions paralleled each other. Just as the MBA was led by a small, dominant group of financiers and supported by a number of secondary interests, at the head of the AFBC was the Chase Bank, and beneath it were more than a dozen other institutions.[15] The Chase Bank was was joined by other national banking associations in the United States.[16] The AFBC did not create the network of affiliated foreign institutions that the MBA used for its expansion, relying instead on the organization of foreign branches. The AFBC's international presence was not as comprehensive as the MBA's, but its expansion was equally as reckless.

The AFBC began operations on November 1, 1917, eight months after the United States entered the war. Its business quickly grew. It moved offices twice in the search for expanded space, before settling in 1920 on a leased five-story building at 53 Broadway.[17] The AFBC's enlarged presence off Wall Street signified its rapid growth overseas, especially in the Caribbean.[18] It established branches in Manila, Harbin, and Brussels, but the Caribbean and, to a lesser extent, Latin America, were the focus of its activities. Its first international branch was opened on January 17, 1918, on Roux Street in Port-au-Prince, Haiti. Further Haitian branches were organized at Saint-Marc and Cap-Haïtien.[19] On February 25, it opened a branch in Havana and a month later in Panama City, Panama, and Cristóbal in the Canal Zone.

7.1. Advertisement for the American Foreign Banking Corporation. *The Blue Book of Haiti* (New York: Klebold Press, 1920). Archive.org.

Branches in Rio de Janeiro, Brazil, and Cali, Colombia, followed later in the year, and in the Dominican Republic in 1919.

In New York City, the Chase Bank under Wiggin was garnering a reputation as an ambitious upstart challenging the dominance of the City Bank. This rivalry continued in the Caribbean as the AFBC competed with the

City Bank's branch networks for commercial deposits and business loans. In Haiti, for instance, the AFBC attempted to challenge the dominance of the Banque Nationale de la République d'Haiti (BNRH) in Haiti's commercial and financial affairs. By 1918, the BNRH's management was controlled from 55 Wall Street, and it occupied a privileged position within the State Department and with the authorities of the US military occupation. When it appeared the BNRH would be granted a monopoly on the import and export of species according to a new treaty between Haiti and the United States, the AFBC joined the RBC in protest.[20] The AFBC signed onto a letter sent to the State Department opposing the treaty, and it successfully lobbied for a favorable modification of the treaty's terms. The arrival of the AFBC in Panama placed it in direct competition with the City Bank's International Banking Corporation.[21] The AFBC purchased the Cristóbal and Panama City branches of the Commercial National Bank of Washington, DC, and immediately challenged the IBC for the transshipment accounts. In the Dominican Republic, the AFBC purchased the assets and goodwill, such as it was, of the Banco Nacional de Santo Domingo (BNSD), organized by Samuel M. Jarvis. However, by the time of the AFBC's purchase of the Banco Nacional, Jarvis had died and his son-in-law, F. J. R. Mitchell, had gone to work for the Mercantile Bank of the Americas in New York as an assistant manager. Henry C. Niese, one of the BNSD's founders, joined the AFBC at its Buenos Aires branch in 1920.[22] The AFBC's purchase of the BNSD gave the AFBC a ready-made banking network with branches in Santo Domingo City, San Francisco de Macorís, Santiago de los Cabelleros, San Pedro de Macorís, La Vega, Sanchez, and Puerto Plata.[23] As with the BNSD before it, in the Dominican Republic the AFBC was in competition with both the City Bank interests, through the International Banking Corporation, and the Royal Bank of Canada, an institution whose role financing sugar in the republic was growing rapidly.

The Havana branch of the AFBC opened at 21 O'Reilly Street on January 2, 1919, but the Chase Bank's ties to Cuba began much earlier.[24] Since 1915, Chase president Wiggin had been a director of the American Sugar Refining Company, and the bank had commercial accounts with sugar brokers Czarnikow Rionda, Cuban-German merchant-bankers H. Upmann and Co., and other businesses involved in US-Cuban trade.[25] The Chase Securities Corporation joined a group of banking houses including J. P. Morgan and Co., the City Bank, the Guaranty Trust Company, the RBC, and the Banco Nacional de Cuba to create the Cuban Sugar Syndicate, a financial company designed to provide credits to Cuban planters.[26] With the organization of the AFBC the Chase Bank's ties to Cuban sugar were strengthened. Many prominent sugar brokers joined the AFBC's directorate including Boston capitalists E. V. R. Thayer, Hayden Harris, and E. F. Atkins. Thayer was a Chase Bank executive from 1917 and a blue-blooded descendant of Boston financiers. He had long been involved in sugar financing through the Merchants National Bank of Boston—as had Harris, through the investment firm Hayden, Stone, of which Harris was a partner.[27] The Atkins family had been in the Cuban sugar trade since the mid-nineteenth century, while Edward F. Atkins was behind the organization in 1915 of the Punta Alegre Sugar Company, a consortium of sugar companies that was aggressively buying land and building plantations in eastern Cuba.[28] Punta Alegre was financed in part via Thayer's Merchants National Bank of Boston and Harris's Hayden, Stone Co.[29] The Havana branch of the AFBC funded the plantations within the purview of Punta Alegre and served as a conduit for US financing of Cuba mills including the Fidencia and Romano plantations in Santa Clara Province, Central Union in Matanzas, and San German in Oriente.[30]

The Havana branch quickly became the most active of the AFBC's foreign branches. Its total assets leaped from $2.6 million in June 1919 to more than $6 million in June 1920.[31] As with other institutions in Cuba during the postwar period, the AFBC and its staff were caught up in the speculative delirium of the dance of millions. Overeagerness to lend money and the easy availability of credit were combined with poor management and the abandonment of fiscal conservatism and sound banking practices. The City Bank's Joseph H. Durrell later described the AFBC as a "rottenly mismanaged institution."[32] The AFBC's handling of an acceptance credit to the Havana sugar factors L. R. Muñoz and Co. affirmed Durrell's statement. It also provides an an example of the inner history of the AFBC's financing operations and the associated problems of corruption and mismanagement that characterized this moment in imperial banking.

In early October 1920, just weeks before the banking crisis in Cuba, the New York offices of the AFBC solicited participation from its member banks in a $2.65 million credit to Muñoz for the coming sugar harvest. The collateral securing the loan consisted of contracts to deliver 305,000 bags of sugar, worth an estimated $8 million, due for importation into the United States before the acceptance came to maturity. The AFBC described the business as "in the first class" and offered it with an interest rate of 9 percent.[33] Fifteen banks from across the United States, all but two of them member banks in the AFBC, agreed to participate in the syndicate through amounts ranging from $100,000 to $250,000.[34] One of the institutions, the National Commerce Bank of St. Louis (NCBSL), was offered a participation of $250,000 for ninety days with an option for one renewal. NCBSL vice president E. J.

Mudd wrote to the AFBC asking for details regarding the collateral. Maurice M. Manasse, assistant manager of the AFBC's Havana branch, assured Mudd that the Havana branch held the proper agreements signed by Muñoz, as well as collateral worth more than $10 million, reserved in proportion to member participation.[35] By December, after the NCBSL had inquired as to whether the acceptance would be paid at maturity, J. Laughlin, Jr., of the AFBC, replied that a ninety-day renewal had been given and asked that the NCBSL accept the revised conditions as of January 4.[36]

Before signing the new agreement, the NCBSL inquired as to whether or not the AFBC had in its possession signed acceptance agreements covering the payment of these drafts at maturity. It also wanted to know the makeup and value of the collateral securing the obligation. The NCBSL received a reply January 10 with a list of collateral that included contracts with refineries for 305,000 bags of sugar, first mortgage bonds on Colonia "San Cayetano," Havana and Company, Central "Altmira," and Central "Limones," as well as promissory notes amounting to $100,000 from various Cuban sugar merchants and refiners. At the end of the ninety-day renewal, on March 12, the NCBSL received a wire from the AFBC in New York stating that while the Havana branch had informed the AFBC that Muñoz and Co. would pay almost one-half of the outstanding credit, the AFBC was also extending and renewing the remaining balance. On March 23, the NCBSL received a telegram from the AFBC stating that the sugar expected to liquidate the credit had not yet been marketed, although the Havana branch was doing everything possible to protect the interests of the syndicate. The AFBC also suggested that the best course of action would be to extend the credit for another thirty days. The NCBSL reluctantly accepted the renewal but expressed surprise that the AFBC's Havana branch was both financing an import credit *and* marketing processed sugar. The NCBSL complained that the information it was receiving concerning the credit and the activities of the Havana branch was "vague and indefinite."[37]

By May 1921, definite information concerning the credit was still not forthcoming. The NCBSL directors were becoming increasingly irritated by the state of affairs of the Muñoz credit and its handling by the AFBC. The director's discomfort was compounded when AFBC directors Gerhard Dahl and Charles G. Farrell (the former a director of the Chase Bank and a partner in Hayden, Stone; the latter the president of the National Newark & Essex Banking Company) traveled to St. Louis to present a statement of the situation to the executive committee of the bank.[38] Dahl and Farrell expressed shock at the Muñoz syndicate's turn of affairs and explained the nature and the extent of the indebtedness of Muñoz to the AFBC. They suggested that if the AFBC could liquidate $15 million of acceptances—of which the Chase Bank was willing to carry the $4.5 million owed it while lending another $1 million if necessary—the AFBC could be kept afloat. But the NCBSL directors also assigned two officers, L. S. Mitchell and E. J. Mudd, to investigate the situation and sent the legal counsel of the NCBSL to New York to discuss the legality of the purchase of their acceptance with the Chase Bank's legal department.[39]

Mitchell and Mudd presented their findings on the AFBC and the Muñoz syndicate to the NCBSL president, John G. Lonsdale, and the board of directors of the bank on May 6, 1921. Through their investigations, they learned that the AFBC's handling of the Muñoz credit was messy, unprofessional, and risky. "The situation with respect to this whole matter is remarkable," Mitchell and Mudd wrote. "It seems strangely corroborative of the old saw that facts are stranger than fiction."[40] Mitchell and Mudd discovered that the 305,000 bags of pledged sugar did not exist. What sugar there was was still cane growing in the field, uncut and unprocessed. The proceeds from the sale of only 2,170 bags of sugar had been distributed to the committee, a small amount considering that by May they were far along in the grinding season. While they were given assurances that they would get money from the coming crop, and in some cases on the real properties, the properties themselves were heavily mortgaged. Bonds of Central "Altamira" were not held by the bank; in their place was a verbal promise by an attorney to deliver them once they had been executed. Those of Havana and Company had not been inscribed, and its property was currently at auction. The bonds for Central "Limones" had been pledged as collateral to the RBC and had several mortgages attached to them. Proceeds from the promissory notes from H. Upmann and M. Llerandi had gone to the Peoples State Bank of Detroit and the Bank of Pittsburgh, N.A., instead of being distributed pro rata to the syndicate as they should have been. The receipts for warehoused sugar that had been delivered to the AFBC's Havana branch had been returned to Muñoz and Co. and turned over to planters and refiners as a way of generating liquidity to finance current grinding and processing operations.

These actions were justified by the AFBC's managers, who claimed that it was necessary to do so or "else the wheels would have stopped, resulting in total loss of the remainder of the crop."[41] But Mudd and Mitchell observed that as the price of sugar had fallen to such a low level, such actions were probably inadvisable. Furthermore, it appeared that the delivery of the receipts had amounted to the relinquishing of their collateral. "Their redelivery to Muñoz and Company," they wrote, "resulted in nothing more nor less than an open book credit without security."[42] Mudd and Mitchell discovered that the Havana offices of the AFBC contained letters in which Muñoz acknowledged receipt from the AFBC of warehouse receipts for a total of 380,906 bags of sugar, with promises to deliver "NY exchange" totaling $4,759,329.02 between February 20 and March 20, 1921. But the bank in fact never had possession of these receipts.[43] Mudd and Mitchell also questioned the judgment and motives of Frank W. Black, the manager of the Havana branch, in his handling of the credit on the ground in Cuba. Black, they pointed out, was given permission by New York to extend to Muñoz up to $3 million in credit. When this credit limit had been reached, he grossly extended it without receiving permission from New York. When the obligations were presented at the AFBC head offices, Black was merely given a slap on the wrist and told not to do it again. He did anyway. Mitchell and Mudd surmised that the New York office must have known and condoned Black's actions, since, after granting the initial $3 million credit it approved its explosion into a $9.2 million liability due to the stockholding banks of the AFBC, as well as an additional $2 million advanced by the bank to Muñoz.[44]

Despite their findings, and despite resistance from members of the board of directors, Mitchell and Mudd recommended supporting the AFBC in relieving the NCBSL of the Muñoz liabilities. They argued that it was necessary to do so in part to ensure the continued operation of the AFBC, and in part to protect the Chase Bank. While the share of the NCBSL's participation in the syndicate amounted to a quarter of a million dollars—which Mitchell and Mudd determined the AFBC was liable for because of what they sympathetically referred to as "misrepresentations . . . unintentionally made"[45]—the AFBC's total obligations to the Chase Bank amounted to $13,360,000. Although Mitchell and Mudd did not say so explicitly, the failure of the AFBC would have devastating consequences for the Chase Bank and its losses in Cuba from the Muñoz credits alone would have rivaled the $25 million in total losses incurred by the City Bank and the Royal Bank of Canada in Cuba during the same period.[46] The NCBSL was unwilling to let the Chase Bank suffer such a fate. It pointed to both the friendly relations and goodwill that historically existed between the two institutions. Lonsdale, the NCBSL's president, expressed his confidence in both Wiggin and his counterpart in the AFBC, John H. Allen, the former manager of the Banque Nationale de la République d'Haiti and former vice president of the National City Bank.[47] Mitchell and Mudd were assured by Allen that Black, the Havana manager, did not act out of malice but out of incompetence and fear. They were told that Black's actions occurred as a result of being intimidated by Muñoz, and that Allen was "disposed not to impute dishonest motives to Mr. Black and does not believe that Black profited personally by any of the transactions, but believes that he was too weak a man to cope with Muñoz."[48] Furthermore, they were assured that those responsible in the Havana branch had been removed from their positions.[49] Mitchell and Mudd were reluctant to see the actions of the Havana branch, or, for that matter, the New York headquarters, as anything more than a few occasions of lazy accounting and innocent misrepresentation. They noted that while "circumstances of slipshod methods are numerous," in only one case did they discover "actual falsification."[50]

Mitchell and Mudd concluded their report by pointing to its limitations. "Our investigation was necessarily confined to Muñoz credits," they wrote.

> In the course of it, there were sundry references to general conditions in Cuba and their effect on the branch at Havana, but little or nothing was said to us about any of the other branches of the American Foreign Banking Corporation. This report is intended to cover the Muñoz situation alone and that only to the extent which we were able to obtain from the New York office of the American Foreign Banking Corporation.[51]

They did not look into the underlying causes of the financial crisis in Cuba, nor did they consider the activities of the AFBC beyond their own narrow interests. If they had, they probably would have been shocked by what they found. They would have learned that not only were "general conditions" a factor in the liquidation of the Muñoz credits, but many of the major players within the AFBC and behind Muñoz—in New York and Havana—were suspected of graft and corruption. Lezama, the Cuban planter and speculator, had declared bankruptcy in May 1921. He had $7,758,197.24 in debts, largely to the Banco Nacional de Cuba.[52] In the wake of his bankruptcy and disappearance it was revealed that Lezama had borrowed heavily from the Banco Nacional to finance his purchases, not only leveraging his assets to extend his credit, but engaging in full-scale forgery of checks and acceptance documentation. After the banking collapse, he was charged with forgery, allegedly falsifying signatures on promissory notes he presented to the Banco Nacional, the Royal Bank of Canada, and other institutions, and when his business, worth some $24 million collapsed, he fled the country.

Similarly, while the AFBC's president John H. Allen defended Havana branch manager Frank W. Black and suggested that Black did not personally profit from the AFBC dealings, others suspected that not only did Black know of Lezama's racket, but that he reaped its ill-gotten rewards: pocketing $100,000 for every $300,000 mulcted by Lezama.[53] The allegations against Black were never substantiated. However, as we saw in chapter 1, Black's career was pockmarked with allegations of graft and fraud. He was arrested for embezzling while working with the American National Bank of Kansas. He was the bookkeeper with the Jarvis-Conklin Mortgage Trust Company immediately before its acrimonious liquidation in 1893. He worked as an auditor for the North American Trust Company in Santiago de Cuba and Havana during its early, scandal-ridden years. When the Trust Company of America absorbed the North American Trust Company and the City Trust Company, Black stayed on as an auditor, remaining until 1912. Black then joined future City Bank president Charles E. Mitchell and Francis L. Hilton, a future president of the Bank of the Manhattan Company, in forming C. E. Mitchell and Co., a bond and investment business. While Black left Mitchell's investment house to work for the foreign department of the Equitable Trust Company and later the AFBC, he served as Mitchell's accountant, preparing his taxes over the next decade. Black later admitted to falsifying Mitchell's returns when Mitchell was under investigation for tax evasion.[54]

Black was not the only corrupt figure within the AFBC. John H. Allen's role in the AFBC debacle is unclear, but he arrived at the institution with a blemished record as a banker, dating back to his history with the City Bank. Not only was Allen Roger Farnham's accomplice in the incidents surrounding the Banque Nationale de la République d'Haiti that led to the US occupation of Haiti, but his arrogant and unreceptive management style led to the reckless overexpansion of the City Bank's Cuban branches and the assumption of many bad debts. The reputations of Edward F. Atkins and Eugene V. Thayer were also clouded by controversy. It was rumored that Atkins and the Guaranty Trust Company's Charles Sabin competed to see who could "lend the most money on the least security."[55] Thayer was reportedly loaning money to friends and colleagues and accepting valueless property as security. When confronted about his actions, Thayer dismissed the concerns, claiming that he was doing things the Cuban way. He was forced out.[56] Another employee, J. M. Syne of the AFBC's Havana branch, was arrested on May 27 along with members of L. R. Muñoz and Co. on charges related to the Lezama case.[57]

By 1921, a mere five years after its incorporation, the AFBC began closing its branches and agencies, liquidating its business, and transferring its assets to other institutions. The Port-au-Prince branch, the first opened, was the first closed. The Royal Bank of Canada purchased its assets.[58] Unable to dislodge the City Bank from its position of preeminence in the Dominican Republic, the AFBC's branches were also closed in 1921, as were those in Honduras and Belgium. The Buenos Aires branch was taken over by the First National Bank of Boston.[59] Although the AFBC was not formally dissolved until 1929, it was no longer functioning by the end of 1924, as the outstanding liabilities of the AFBC's New York City, Havana, Panama, and Cristóbal branches were purchased by the Chase Bank for approximately $11 million.[60]

Early in 1925—the year that "Dark Finance," the short story mocking African American financial illiteracy appeared in *The Chase*—the Chase Bank initiated another attempt at overseas expansion, using the AFBC's Cuban and Panama branches as a platform.[61] The Chase Bank never realized the kind of extensive foreign branch networks of either the City Bank or the Royal Bank of Canada. Instead, the Chase Bank built on the remnants of the AFBC operations in Panama and Cuba (and, in 1933, added a single branch in San Juan, Puerto Rico).[62] In Panama, the Chase Bank continued to provide the financial services demanded by the US military presence on the isthmus as it took the $1,395,298.27 in US government deposits the AFBC held in Panama City and the $85,242.86 in Cristóbal.[63] The Chase Bank also continued to finance the maritime traffic through the canal by providing transshipment financial services.[64] It muscled the International Banking Corporation out of the toll business and saw its share of the toll fees leap from 52 to 74 percent within three years, largely because Albert H. Wiggin personally intervened with the Mercantile Marine and offered to hold its accounts at no cost.[65] At the same time, the Chase Bank's share of deposits in Panama and the Canal Zone grew to 50 percent as it offered retail customers a competitive 4 percent interest rate on current deposits, while providing financial services to local merchants and exporters of sugar and bananas.[66]

The Chase Bank rapidly emerged as a dominant presence in Panama. In Cuba it lagged behind its more established Wall Street brethren. Speyer and Co. and J. P. Morgan and Co. had a lock on the funding of the republic's sovereign debt. The City Bank and the RBC were the most powerful commercial and retail banks in Cuba. The executives of Morgan, the City Bank, and the RBC occupied privileged places as hosts when Gerardo Machado embarked on a tour of the United States in April 1925 as Cuba's president-elect. Machado and his entourage had private dinners with the City Bank's Joseph H. Durrell and J. P. Morgan and Co.'s Dwight W. Morrow, who also presided over a dinner for Machado at the Hotel Astor. City Bank president Charles E. Mitchell hosted a luncheon for Machado at 55 Wall Street and presented him with an engraved gold cigarette case. F. T. Walker, head of the New York agency of the Royal Bank of Canada, organized a similar event in Machado's honor at the Bankers Club. By way of contrast, the Chase Bank's

Albert H. Wiggin was but one of more than a dozen people on the dinner committee for the event at the Hotel Astor organized by Morgan's Dwight W. Morrow, while Chase officials such as vice president Robert I. Barr sat in near anonymity among the close to 100 businesspeople and financiers in the ballroom who had come to hear Machado speak.[67]

The Chase Bank sought to reverse this sorry state of affairs after it opened its Havana branch at Aguiar 86, moving into a building in old Havana commissioned, constructed, and first occupied by the failed Banco de la Libertad, an institution formed during World War I by the Pedrosas, a family of Cuban merchants.[68] The bank moved quickly to its expand its footprint in the Cuban sugar industry. It attempted to make a $4 million cash bid for the notes of the Compañía Nacional de Azúcares de Cuba, S.A, an institution whose stock was held by the Banco Nacional de Cuba. It purchased a portion of the debt of Nombre de Dios, a small plantation in Guines, near Havana. It played an increasingly important role in the management of Punta Alegre.[69]

However, the Chase Bank's incursion into the sugar industry became a secondary activity to its primary focus: the financing of Cuba's sovereign debt. And like the black characters of "Dark Finance," the miscomprehensions and refusals of debt would lead to conflict and violence between debtor and creditor. The Havana branch of the Chase Bank became an important hub for networking with Cuban officials and businesspeople, but it was not through the bank itself that the labor of lending occurred, but through the bank's securitiy affiliate, the Chase Securities Corporation (CSC). The CSC was chartered in New York State in 1917, the same year that AFBC received its charter. Wiggin had decided the bank needed what he called a "companion organization" modeled after the securities affiliates of the First National Bank and the City Bank.[70] As in those cases, the directors of the CSC sought to generate greater profits from the inactive capital that its commercial business had generated during its decades of tremendous growth. "We thought that a securities company could make money for the same stockholders," Wiggin recalled, "that they could share in underwritings, in wholesalings, that would not come to the bank, or could not come to the bank."[71]

Wiggin created the CSC in consultation with Rushmore, Bisbee and Stern, the Chase Bank's legal representatives. As in the case of the First National Securities Corporation and the National City Company, through the CSC the Chase Bank skirted the legal prohibitions preventing national banking associations from owning stock in other national banking associations or dealing in bond issues and securities. The separation between the two entities was achieved through a measure of legal parsing. A thin membrane of lawyering separated the two institutions but allowed the bank to preserve the identity of interests that stockholders held in both entities. Stockholders were bound to relinquish their ownership in both of the companies if they attempted to sell their interest in one. The capital for the securities affiliate, initially $2.5 million, came in the form of a dividend from the stock of the bank, and stockholders of the Chase Bank were given an equal amount of stock in the securities affiliate. In the early years of the latter, stockholders received two different stocks, one for the bank, another for the securities affiliate, but in later years, apparently because of matters of economy, stockholders were issued what was described as a "two-faced certificate":[72] on one side of the certificate was printed the stockholders agreement with the bank, and on the other side was printed the agreement with the affiliate. This physical connection only added to the ambiguous separation between the two entities and generated a confusion that was admitted by the bank itself. An article on the CSC in the May 1923 issue of *The Chase* began with the question, "Chase Securities Corporation and The Chase National Bank— what relation do they have to one another? . . . How many of us have not floundered miserably when asked this very question?" While noting the two different legal authorities governing the two institutions (the bank was regulated by the federal government; the securities affiliate by the state of New York), *The Chase* lamely concluded by suggesting that the two were part of the same family—but not related.[73]

The CSC did not make the high-profile arrival of the National City Company (see chapter 4). Its activities were barely publicized during the first decade of its life. Its name did not appear on advertisements offering new securities, even if CSC originated them, and it generally sold wholesale issues to other banks and dealers.[74] The CSC had a relatively modest participation in securities issues, and its most significant and well-publicized action was, not through the flotation of debt, but through the purchase on October 29, 1919, of a controlling interest in another financial institution, the Metropolitan Bank.[75] The Metropolitan Bank had been created by the Metropolitan Life Insurance Company through the purchase of the Maiden Lane Bank in 1905, and the Shoe and Leather Bank, originally organized in 1852, in 1906.[76] (The Metropolitan Bank took over the Hamilton Trust Company in 1921.[77]) The CSC bought 51 percent of the stock from the insurance company at $350 a share. At first, the Chase Bank ran the Metropolitan Bank as a separate entity, keeping its management in place. Wiggin eventually converted it into the Metpotan Corporation. Its New York State charter was maintained, and, in the second half of the 1920s it was used as a vehicle to buy and sell stock of the Chase Bank as a means of manipulating its price and value. It was a practice that would come to define the Chase Bank—and that would contribute to Wiggin's downfall.

At the same time, during this period the CSC worked in concert with the Chase Bank in Cuba to secure the contracts for loans to the government of President Machado. In June 1925, the Machado government passed a public works law mandating an ambitious program to undertake massive construction projects across the island in an attempt to both create and improve public utilities, improve the internal transportation and communication infrastructure of Cuba, and relieve unemployment. The program included the creation of a modern central highway linking Havana to the provinces, the paving of local roads and streets in the underdeveloped towns and hamlets of the provinces, the dredging of ports and the construction of wharves and seawalls, the building of tubercular sanitariums and hospitals, the establishment of normal and reform schools, the construction of government buildings in Havana, and the provision of adequate sewerage.[78] For Machado, the announcement of the program fulfilled one election promise while betraying another. He had promised to redress the widespread problem of unemployment in the country. He had also forsworn any activity that would increase Cuba's public debt. Keeping the first promise meant breaking the second.

Within six months of opening its branch on O'Reilly, the Chase Bank began investigating the possibility of purchasing Cuba's floating debt through the CSC. On June 15, 1925, CSC vice president Robert L. Clarkson spoke to Henry Catlin regarding the possibiliy of taking over the debt. Catlin was an American lawyer and speculator affiliated with the General Electric Company. He had accompanied Machado on his US tour, and Machado later appointed him vice president of one of his electric companies. Catlin was also hired the same month as an adviser to the Havana branch of the Chase Bank, and he appeared to try to take advantage of the bank's naïveté and ignorance of Cuba's internal affairs to better secure his own financial interests.[79] Catlin urged the Chase Bank to create a syndicate that could purchase the outstanding coupons for Cuba's current foreign debt, arguing that the bank could quickly turn a profit on them. Stating that he wanted a 25 percent interest in the syndicate, he told the officials of the bank that he had already formed a corporation for the purchase of which he had a majority of the common stock. He also warned the bank that if it did not move quickly, the notes would soon be purchased by other businesses; a syndicate headed by Speyer and Co., he told Chase officials, had already been formed to do exactly that. Catlin also claimed his offer to the Chase Bank could have gone elsewhere. He told them that while he was close to the City Bank's Charles

Mitchell, he "prefer[red] to play with the Chase crowd," mainly because of his very high regard for Wiggin.[80]

Nothing came of Catlin's entreaties. But when news of the public works program was announced, the Chase Bank scrambled to find the means to finance it. In January 1926, the bank organized a syndicate headed by the CSC and complemented by Blair and Co., New York construction contractors James C. Stewart Co., Inc., and Guy Currier, a wealthy Boston lawyer who was counsel for Bethlehem Steel and Cuban railroad magnate Colonel José N. Tarafa, whose interests were partly financed by Roland R. Conklin.[81] Together, they sought to offer a $70 million credit to the Cuban government for the public works program. But the syndicate moved slowly. Currier pressed the group to action in February, pointing out that they were currently paying the engineers of James C. Stewart Co. for preliminary work on the highway. By April, the Chase Bank and Blair had decided to withdraw from the syndicate.[82] Despite its collapse, rumors concerning the syndicate and the proposed loans caused a stir among the Cuban public, who were surprised and shocked to learn that the government would be taking on more debt. In response, Machado released a statement that attempted to reassure and quell the anxieties. Stating his desire to break with the policies of previous regimes, he reaffirmed that he would not negotiate any new foreign loans during his presidency, no matter the economic situation of the country.[83]

The rumors persisted. By March they had reached the ears of General Enoch Crowder, US ambassador to Cuba since 1920.[84] Having heard that the CSC and Blair and Co. were trying to negotiate a $100 million loan with the Cuban government, an agitated Crowder sought out the Chase Bank's George Graves while Graves was enjoying an afternoon at the Havana Jockey Club. Crowder chastised Graves for considering the loan, pointing out that the country was already $98 million in debt and that the "financial and economic condition of the country was in such a deplorable state" that it made no sense for the republic to incur further indebtedness. Furthermore, Crowder pointed out that if the plan was consummated, he—Crowder— would be forced to lodge a protest with the US State Department. A loan of this sort, Crowder stated, violated article 2 of the Platt Amendment with its provisions constraining the republic's ability to assume sovereign debt. Graves and the bank were indifferent to Crowder's appeals. They viewed the Platt Amendment as a mere impediment to business. They also suspected that Crowder's agitation was partly due to his loyalty to J. P. Morgan and Co., which had negotiated Cuba's previous loans under Crowder's watch. They decided to keep Crowder unaware of their plans and were determined to find a way to provide the financing regardless of the legal obstacles. "It is clear that the bank should preserve cordial relations with the US Ambassador," Graves wrote to Tinker, "but while not telling him anything that would damage our interests in Cuba, to be careful not to make any statements which he might easily learn were contrary to facts."[85] The Jockey Club incident signaled the beginning of a legal crisis over the loans that would return to haunt the bank in the 1930s.

In the summer of 1926, the CSC sent Charles F. Batchelder and A. M. Williams of Rushmore, Bisbee and Stern to try to hammer out an arrangement with the Cuban secretary of the treasury that would allow the bank to avoid the legal impediments imposed by the Cuban constitution. The CSC's lawyers suggested returning to the plan floated by Catlin the previous summer: the organization of a corporation that was a separate entity from the Cuban government through which the financing would take place and which could exist outside of the prohibitive legal confines of the Platt Amendment. The CSC was facing competition; the Cuban press was reporting that Gordon A. Rentschler, Joseph H. Durrell, and Juan F. Rivera of the City Bank were holding conferences with Céspedes, the minister of public works, over the organization of a similar institution. Under the "institute plan," as the Catlin scheme was called, the Cuban government would authorize the creation of an independent corporation that could issue securities and collect revenue from the public works fund but, by existing outside of the normal revenue streams of the republic, would not be beholden to the Platt Amendment, or to the Cuban people.[86] "You are familiar with the President's statement that he would not make any foreign loan," Batchelder wrote to Edward E. Tinker. "I agree that the Institute idea is the most practical and will enable him to save his face, but there is this difficulty in connection with this situation at this time."[87] However, Batchelder also concluded that it would be difficult for the Cuban president to pass the required legislation, and the institute idea was soon abandoned.

In November 1926 the Cuban government solicited bids for the $10 million public works financing. A total of six proposals were received. The Chase National Bank, in conjunction with Blair and Co., were the successful bidders. On February 19, 1927, they entered into a contract with the Cuban government to finance payments of up to $10 million for the first phase of the program: the construction of an arterial highway linking the provinces to Havana.[88] The contract was convoluted in form. It cast the financing as "credit operation" and, by doing so, violated the spirit, if not the text, of the Platt Amendment and its prohibitions on contracting new debts and financing the debts through the "ordinary revenues of the republic."[89] During the period July 1, 1927, to June 30, 1930, the Chase Bank would purchase from the contractors building the highway what were termed "deferred payment work certificates." These certificates were issued by the Cuban government to the contractors for highway construction actually completed, up to $10 million. The contractors would redeem the certificates for payment from the Chase Bank. The bank would then present the claims to the Cuban government, which would redeem the certificates in gold at the bank in New York City on a semiannual basis. In addition to the 6 percent interest payments, the bank received "as compensation for its commitment and services" four payments of $100,000 each due upon the "execution and delivery of the agreement" and on the first day of July for each of the three years of the agreement. All notarial charges and taxes were also to be assumed by the Cuban government. The only restriction was that to fund the program the government could not "issue any certificate of indebtedness"—that is, it could not take out loans, nor could the cost of the projects exceed the normal revenues of the republic in a given year. To get around these restrictions, the government proposed paying for the public works program through the creation of a "Special Fund for Public Works" that existed outside of the regular balance sheets. The special fund was created from 90 percent of the revenues, estimated at $18 million per year, generated from a new tax on land transportation, gasoline, sales and gross receipts, luxury items, imported goods, nonnecessary items, the exportation of currency, rental income, and fancy items. These taxes were to be of a temporary nature and were to expire on June 30, 1930, at which time it was contemplated all of the construction work would be completed.

The Chase Bank was not satisfied with the $10 million credits. They were eager to secure more contracts for what they saw as an incredibly lucrative enterprise. To do so, they turned to Machado's son-in-law, José Emilio Obregón, attempting to use him as an intermediary between the Cuban government and the bank. Married to Elvira Machado, Obregón lived in the presidential palace. He had previously worked as a branch manager for the Royal Bank of Canada and was well known within both Havana and New York banking circles.[90] He and Elvira Macado honeymooned in the United States after their June 1926 wedding in Havana, an affair attended by 4,000 guests. While in the United States, Obregón called on the White House and dined with both Albert Wiggin and Robert I. Barr of the Chase Bank and the City Bank's Joseph H. Durrell.[91] On April 1, 1927, Obregón was hired as "new business man" for the Chase Bank's Havana branch. He was responsible for obtaining new accounts for the bank and was given a salary of $12,000. It quickly grew to $19,000 plus a 10 percent bonus. After several months, Obregón was made joint manager of the Havana branch with William Ignatius Quealy, a position he held until April 13, 1931.

Despite whatever prior experience Obregón had, officials in the bank recognized that as a banker, his skills were of a limited nature. "As we know," Chase Bank vice president James Bruce wrote to his colleague, Joseph Rovensky, "from any business standpoint he is perfectly useless. He has neither any ability for banking nor has the slightest ability in negotiation, which was something which we thought it might be possible to build him up to."[92] They found that "Joe" was best deployed to entertain customers when they came through Havana during the winter season. James Stewart, the contractor who had previously worked with the Chase Bank, described Obregón as a handsome and charming fellow who was good at procuring prostitutes.[93] Officials of the bank also heard from Cubans that Obregón had "very little standing with the President." Obregón was derisively described as a "paper charge" for the bank, yet it was recognized that, given the state of the economy, it was better that the bank paid his salary rather than the president.[94] But Obregón was not completely useless in business. Through him, the Havana branch of the Chase Bank secured the services of Guillermo Hernández Cartaya, formerly Cuban secretary of the treasury and an important adviser to Machado concerning financial matters. Cartaya had prepared the documents in connection with the $10 million credit, and the bank kept him on a $57,000 retainer to provide legal advice with financial "propositions."[95] Moreover, Obregón alerted bank officials of Machado's desire to increase the funding for the public works program so as to expedite work on both the central highway and the congressional palace in Havana.[96]

While both projects required an additional $5 million each, for both Machado and the Chase Bank, the question remained concerning how additional funding could be procured without creating additional public indebtedness. At the same time, the Chase Bank learned that it was in danger of losing out on the additional loan to its competitors. Two different syndicates, one led by the City Bank, the other by Dillon, Read and Co., had prepared similar propositions for $20 million in additional financing, with the possibility of an extension between $32 million and $35 million, without changing the existing law.[97] According to their plans, the financing would occur through a junior lien on the taxes funding the already existing $10 million credit arrangement in place with the Chase Bank. Officials of the bank realized that the only way to continue the financing was by breaking the terms of the initial public works contract by making the new financing a direct obligation of the Cuban government. They would violate the terms of the Platt Amendment in the process, potentially incurring the anger of the

State Department. They also felt that their partners would not be willing to risk the financing without guarantees and protection of their interests from the Cuban government. In a memo to Albert Wiggin, the CSC's Halstead G. Freeman outlined the problem:

> Our understanding is that the Cuban government does not consider that financing of this character comes within the scope of the Platt amendment. On the other hand, we understand that the Washington authorities probably consider the amendment, liberally construed, applies to financial obligations of this nature. Our judgment is that, without a change in the law, we would not feel justified in taking the risk involved for so large an amount, but we would like to talk to you further about it before definitely making this recommendation to our partners.[98]

Heading a syndicate composed of the CSC, Blair and Co., the Equitable Trust Company, and the Continental National Bank and Trust Company, the Chase Bank submitted a proposal to the Cuban government on May 12, 1928. The Chase Bank was successful in its bid and entered into a supplemental agreement with the Cuban government on June 22, 1928.[99] Jose Obregón reportedly received a $500,000 kickback for his services in obtaining the contract. The new agreement expanded the Chase Bank's original $10 million credit and transformed it into a revolving $60 million credit. When the bank amassed work certificates amounting to $10 million, the certificates would be presented to the secretary of the treasury and converted into public works 5 ½ serial certificates, which were then sold to the public. Once these were converted into serial certificates, the Cuban government was able to extend its credit by issuing additional work certificates.[100] Both serial and work certificates were to be secured via a first lien on 90 percent of the revenues generated from the public works taxes. The original commission schedule was preserved, but a supplemental agreement added an additional 1 percent charge on the $50 million of serial certificates. Additionally, once the work certificates were converted into serial certificates, the bank was authorized to receive 1.8 percent of the principal amount of the work certificates up to $50 million. The amount loaned to the bank within the new contract was capped at $50 million, making a total of $60 million available for financing payments to the contractors.[101]

The Chase Bank's new plan involved what Halsted G. Freeman of the Chase Securities Corporation described as "a slight change in the law."[102] On July 24, 1928, the Public Works Law was amended, and the temporary taxes imposed to pay for the program became semipermanent. They were to remain for twenty years, retroactively starting from July 15, 1925, or until the works program was paid for. The change gave the bank a preferential lien on all the revenues of the republic. And if the 1927 loan of $10 million relied on an open-ended interpretation of the Platt Amendment, the current loan involved the outright rejection of it.

What had started as an initial $10 million credit in 1925 had, in three years, swollen to $60 million. And while the interest payments on the loan were originally drawn from a set of taxes outside of the normal revenues of the Cuban republic, they increasingly burdened the Cuban people, who, by the end of the decade, were already suffering from the country's economic malaise. Indeed, for Cubans, the final years of the 1920s were marked by an intensifying crisis that was both political and economic. Politically, the democratically elected Machado government had become an unconstitutional regime. Machado reneged on his promises to hold elections at the end of his term and in November 1928, extended his term of office for an additional six years, gaining assent for the extension by bribing those parliamentarians whom he did not threaten. Resistance to the regime was galvanized by Machado's actions. The ABC, an underground leftist organization made up of intellectuals and students, emerged at this moment, while trade unions, Communists, and anarchists became increasingly vocal opponents of the Machado regime and its ties to Wall Street, US imperialism, and "yanquilandia."[103] Dissent was met with increasingly violent repression. Newspapers were censored, and the "Porras," a gang of henchmen and henchwomen, intimidated, tortured, and murdered Machado's political opponents. Economically, the price of sugar remained depressed, and the harvest was scaled back. Unemployment was rampant, and the payment of salaries for workers and public servants was increasingly delayed. Throughout Cuba, starvation gripped the populace.

For the Chase Bank, the concern with Cuba was not the constitutionality of the Machado regime nor the republic's worsening economic or political conditions. The concern was to protect the holders of Cuba's debt, to ensure the amortization payments on the loans were remitted on time, and to find additional opportunities to profit from further loans to the Cuban government, regardless of the nature of economic and political conditions. To wit, on December 11, 1928, Chase Bank vice president Robert I. Barr opened up a revolving, renewable $100 million credit line with the bank.[104] And even as the bank saw the crisis unfolding in Cuba, it escalated its funding of the Cuban government, entering into a new financing agreement worth $80 million.

In May 1929, both the Chase Bank and the Cuban government realized that tax revenues would be insufficient to meet the government's obligations of interest on the maturities that were soon coming due on the previous debts. The Cuban government would be unable to carry on with the public work projects while meeting its regular budget and paying the serial certificates as they reached maturity. To overcome the deficit, the government would have to transfer $9 million per year from the approximately $18 million collected per year under the Public Works Law.[105] On October 24, 1929, the government appealed to the Chase Bank, asking it to stop issuing further deferred payment work certificates—to stop the short-term debt obligations that were being generated through the revolving public works credit—and to restructure the debt as a long-term issue. Over the next few months, the Chase Bank's Robert I. Barr and Henry Catlin conferred on the restructuring, with Barr traveling to Cuba to investigate the sale of the public works' debt in the short-term bond market as a way of protecting the Chase Bank's positions. Early in 1930, the Chase Bank and the Cuban government had settled on a plan for a long-term debt restructuring. Against the backdrop of the growing global economic crisis, it appeared an act of fiscal insanity.

On February 26, 1930, the Chase Bank and its associates entered into a third financing agreement with the Machado government. This agreement surpassed the others in both size and temporal scope, and where the previous agreements had pushed against the principles of the Platt Amendment, the new credit dispensed with it altogether. It provided for the government authorization of $80 million worth of 5 ½ gold bonds, dated January 1, 1930, and due, fifteen years later, in 1945. Of the $80 million worth of bonds authorized, the Chase Bank was to purchase from the government $40 million at 95 (or $37.6 million) and interest. These bonds were then sold by the Chase Bank to the public at 96 ($38.4 million) and interest, the Chase Bank immediately pocketing the one-point spread, or $800,000, as a profit. The remaining $40 million worth of bonds was to be held by the government as collateral for a credit of $20 million from the Chase Bank, and the Chase Bank would, at the same time, sell for cash at par to the Cuban government the $40 million worth of serial certificates and deferred payment works certificates that it was then holding.

In short, while the Cuban government was responsible for the repayment of $80 million in bonds, it only received an advance of $20 million. Even with the new financing in place, Machado complained there was not enough money to continue the construction and pleaded with the bank to take up the option on the $40 million bonds, which were expiring on August 5, 1930, or to make another advance of $20 million. The bank, however, hesitated. It was learning that much of the money was being squandered. Very little of it was actually going to fund the construction of the public works; Machado and his inner circle were rumored to be pocketing substantial amounts. The Chase Bank wanted the government to clean up its financial affairs and balance its budget before it considered making further loans. To move forward, it wanted complete autonomy and control of the Cuban budget. In a memo to Wiggin, James Bruce stated that he thought the bank should not "make any advance of any sort to the Government unless we are entirely in control of their future financial program."[106] Bruce apparently wanted the bank to adhere to the models of fiscal control that had been imposed on the Caribbean and Central America earlier in the decade while trampling on the Platt Amendment's paternalistic hold on Cuban finances. There is no evidence to suggest that Wiggin felt otherwise.

Criticism of the Chase loans increased as Machado's repression escalated and the Cuban economy worsened. Cuban exiles attempted to use the anti-banking sentiment in the United States, growing after the October 1929 stock market crash, and the burgeoning disgust with Wall Street to turn public opinion against the Machado regime—and the Chase Bank—and to persuade the State Department to intervene in Cuban affairs. Opponents of Machado appealed for US intervention under the banner of the Platt Amendment, arguing that both Machado and the bank were violating its terms. Criticisms of the Chase Bank were also raised on moral grounds— which had as much to do with the ethics of the credit operations as they did with their legality. In the pamphlet *Cuba's Finances*, for instance, Octavio Seigle, a newspaperman and cofounder of Cuba's Unión Nacionalista, provided a brief history of the bank loans while raising moral and political questions concerning the ties of the Chase Bank to the Machado regime and the ethics of US support of Machado.

Self-published by Seigle in 1930, *Cuban Finances* was a four-page monograph of which 10,000 copies were printed, with the majority of them sent to banks and brokerage firms in the United States.[107] Seigle pointed to the fact that thousands of Cubans were starving while Machado had assassinated hundreds of people, deported thousands more, and muzzled the press. "Can American business men commit themselves to uphold such conditions?" Seigle asked. "Is it either patriotic, or even businesslike to entrust

American money to such lawless and ungrateful an administration?" Seigle brought up the fact that Machado's son-in-law, Joe Obregón, had gone from being a majordomo of the presidential palace on a $200-a-month salary to being the manager of the Chase's Havana branch and the Havana clearing-house, where he reportedly received a $500,000 kickback for negotiating the 1928 credit. Moreover, while the phrase was not used explicitly, Seigle was perhaps the first writer to argue that the Chase loans to Cuba were an example of "odious debt"—debt contracted by an illegal, illicit, and odious regime. He argued that the Machado regime was illegal and had been since May 20, 1929, when a constitutional government in Cuba had ceased to exist. "Thereafter all contracts and legislative acts, as well as governmental decrees, are null and void," Seigle wrote, "vitiated by a fundamentally illegal regime. Any contract entered into with such regime is bound to create future trouble." Seigle continued:

> The Chase Bank has actually given the Machado dictatorship a two years' lease on life. It has permitted the wholesale murder and exploitation which has characterized the Machado despotism. Any and all money advances to the present Cuban dictatorship of General Machado by American bankers, can only be viewed by the Cuban people as an act inimical to their sovereignty, despotically usurped by the prevailing regime.

Similar criticisms of the Chase Bank loans were being made in Cuba itself. In 1931, the Havana paper *El Mundo*, the same journal that had at-tacked the City Bank and the RBC only a few years earlier, ran a series of articles decrying the mismanagement and waste of the Chase loans while criticizing the Cuban government's myopic approach to a problem of debt that would burden the republic for years to come. *El Mundo* pointed out that after amassing five years' worth of debt, the country had little to show for it, as the public works projects were largely a failure. They wrote of the "serious errors of its famous five years" and criticized the "government financiers of the epoch" who sought "formulas expedient for obtaining money to con-tinue the triumphal march of those works, and the expenses thereof." *El Mundo* continued:

> Therefore, in five years a debt has been rolled up which reaches double the indebtness of the Republic's twenty-three previous years. And all the country has on this date is four beautiful parks or squares, a valuable Capitol, a few meters more of promenade along the water, an unfinished Central Highway, and several additional works of minor importance to the economic, moral

and spritiual progress of the Cuban people, who are subjected to heavy tribute which must be increased, during long years of their existence, because
of the excessive and unexplainable costs of that reconstructive work of the
Government.[108]

By the early 1930s, neither Machado nor the bank could ignore the
mounting problems associated with the Chase loans and the Cuban debt.
For Machado, the problem of debt was a problem of holding onto personal
power. For the Chase Bank, the problem was one of supporting a regime
that could protect its investments and maintain its schedule of payments. A
November 1932 meeting at the presidential palace with Machado and officials of the bank highlighted the situation. During the meeting, the Chase
Bank's Timothy M. Findlay and José Lopez Fernandez outlined a new plan
proposed by Louis S. Rosenthal (a vice president who had been recruited
from the Banco Nacional de Nicaragua) to restructure the existing loans
and the Cuban budget. Machado, Findlay later noted, was "very much displeased" with the plan.[109] He could barely muster a response to the bankers'
proposals and told them they should send him a written memorandum
outlining their suggestions. Realizing Machado was in a disturbed state, they
asked him for his opinions on the proposals. They wanted to speak to him
not as businesspeople but as friends, and they tried to soften his mood with
a sympathetic appeal.

Machado told them that he could not accept the new plan, "and he would
not accept it under any conditions." Machado said he was surprised by it. He
felt as if Shepard Morgan and Louis S. Rosenthal had made commitments to
him that they were now reneging on. He noted that he did not understand
why the Chase Bank "did not feel a moral obligation to him and to the
government and also the investors who had purchased securities sponsored
by the Chase." Machado claimed he was making "superhuman efforts" to
fulfill his "obligations" to the bank. He admitted that he was "holding everything down with an iron hand, starving government employees" and facing
a groundswell of opposition from both his traditional political opponents
and his followers and allies in his own government, who all advised him
to "immediately suspend payment on the foreign obligations and devote
the entire government income to local needs."[110] Machado asserted he was
preparing to balance the Cuban budget through a previously agreed-upon
reduction of expenses amounting to $6 million. One million dollars of this
figure would be taken from the army appropriation.

Machado claimed that he had gone to great lengths to convince the generals that the diversion of funds was necessary to maintain the debt pay-

ments and to keep the creditworthiness of the republic beyond reproach, as well as to maintain the standing of both the nation and himself with the Chase Bank. Machado also told the bank officials that he had assured the Cuban cabinet that because of his standing with the bank, the bank was willing to give him an additional $4 million to help with the budget. Writing to Rosenthal about the meeting, Findlay stated that for Machado "to be forced to admit publicly that he is unable to obtain what he promised leaves him in a frightfully embarrassing situation." Machado's situation was a desperate one, according to Findlay, and he was willing to use the threat of default to force the bank's hand. He told Findlay that if the Chase Bank could not give him the $4 million requested "there was nothing to do but go into a complete and total default and that he had no objection to doing so immediately."[111] Machado planned to halt the regular deposit of revenues from the taxes allocated for the public works fund, justifying his actions through an interpretation of the loan agreements that focused on the voluntary nature of the deposits on the part of the Cuban government. For the Chase Bank, default was not an option. The issue for the bank was not merely economic—it could withstand the missed payments—but political: default would draw attention to the nature and methods through which their financing had occurred.[112] The bank buckled. It made a strategic calculation of risk and acceded to Machado's request. In response to Machado's pleas the Chase Bank agreed to advance a total of $3,106,250, and an additional loan of the same amount, based on the Cuban government putting up $5 million in serial certificates maturing on December 31st. More than $3 million of this was used for the payment of interest on the previous loans. Meanwhile, the Cuban people bore the cost of the loans through a new set of additional taxes on rice and sugar.

By 1932, the Chase Bank's difficulties in Cuba appeared as a broader symptom of the larger problems of the structure, organization, and methods of the bank. Certainly, under Albert H. Wiggin, the growth of the Chase Bank was spectacular. When he first joined the Chase Bank it was capitalized at $1 million, its surplus was $1 million, and its deposits were $54 million. When he was made president, its capital was $5 million, its surplus was $5 million, and its deposits were $100 million. By 1927, the Chase Bank passed the billion-dollar mark in total resources.[113] Two years later, when the Chase Bank merged with the Equitable Trust Company—at the time, the greatest bank merger in history—it was said that the combined resources of the two institutions were equal to one-third of the earth's gold supply.[114] The growth was spectacular but illusory. Much of the bank's capital was fictitious and the figures were inflated through the overextension and leveraging of its capital stock, speculation of investor funds by the Securities Corporation, and a convoluted shell-game through which Wiggin bought and sold bank stock through dummy corporations to inflate the bank's valuation. Wiggin had encouraged bank staff to take out loans to buy the bank stock, further inflating demand and price, while using bank funds to buy stock for his family.

Over time, Wiggin came to physically embody the growth of the Chase Bank. By the early 1930s, the grotesque excesses of the era hung off his frame. Commentators described a man of dropped chin, generous jowls, and substantial girth. Once known as "the banker with a million friends" and "the most popular banker in Wall Street," Wiggin became a pariah in the banking world as the revelations of his management of the Chase Bank came to light.[115] Increasingly withdrawn, impatient, brooding, taciturn—even surly—shuttered behind a phalanx of lower executives, he sat at his desk in a fourth-floor corner office that looked out across the Sub-Treasury building toward the Equitable Trust Company, and whose dark mahogany paneling, with its somber, brooding pallor, set the mood for his final days with the bank.[116]

Late in 1932, Wiggin was forced out of his position as president by the board of directors, largely as a means of salvaging the bank's reputation in the context of the public's growing disgust toward Wall Street. Winthrop W. Aldrich was appointed president of the Chase Bank in Wiggin's place. Aldrich was a well-connected lawyer who had never worked in a bank, although he was respected within the banking community and had presided over the merger of the Equitable Trust Company and the Chase Bank. He was hired to bring stability to the institution and to salvage public confidence in what had grown to be the largest financial institution in the country. For Aldrich, it would prove a difficult task. He only began to get a sense of the inner problems of the bank after his appointment, and he was soon forced to handle the Cuban situation and answer for the Chase Bank's funding of Machado.

Machado was overthrown in a military coup on August 12, 1933, less than a year after Wiggin was deposed from the Chase. He fled to Nassau, allegedly carrying $2 million in cash, and met with an official of the RBC.[117] He then sought political asylum in Canada, but was only permitted to stay in Montreal long enough to work out his financial affairs, also with the RBC.[118] Meanwhile, in Cuba on September 10, 1933, Ramon Grau San Martín was appointed president after three short-lived provisional presidencies. His government was carried by the anger against Machado and the radical, anti-imperial energies pulsating through Cuba at this time. In an October 1933 radio address widely reprinted in the US press, Grau called bankers "enemies" of the Cuban people and charged that "certain financial interests" were conspiring to destroying his government. "You know these American interests," he proclaimed. "They have also brought havoc to their own fellows, and your depression has been their masterpiece. . . . We can no longer tolerate puppet governments born of monopolies and concessions, converting Cuba into a sweatshop for a privileged few."[119]

Grau backed his rhetoric with action. On December 31, 1933, the Cuban government withheld interest payments on a portion of their debts to the Chase Bank, defaulting on $366,750.59 on a principal amount of $12,336,380. Grau asserted he was not repudiating the debt, but merely questioning its legality. "The legality of the issues was not open to question," Aldrich asserted in response. The Chase Bank immediately protested Grau's decision, and Aldrich warned that default would damage the creditworthiness of the Cuban Republic.[120] The Cuban government ignored his warning. A January 15, 1934, decree suspended payments to the Chase Bank and ordered the restitution of a portion of the amount already paid to the Chase Bank.

Although Grau was overthrown early in 1934, ending a period known in Cuba as "the Hundred Days," provisional president Carlos Mendieta continued Grau's policies. Mendieta ordered an investigation into the legality and morality of the Chase Bank's debts and the advisability of the Cuban government's repayment.[121] At the heart of the inquiry was the question of whether the Machado government was legitimate and legal; this fact would determine whether the loans themselves were legally contracted and whether or not they could legally be annulled or repudiated. The inquiry turned to the history of sovereign defaults and repudiations as precedents, examining the refusal of the United States to honor Confederate indebtedness and the Soviet rejection of the foreign debt contracted by the czar. It also recounted the electoral history of the Machado regime, questioning whether or not Machado "obtained the plausible investiture" required to give his government legitimacy. Their conclusions mirrored those of Octavio Seigle in *Cuba's Finances*: they argued that since May 20, 1929, when Machado reneged on promised elections and extended his term, his government had lost its constitutional legitimacy and had become an illegal dictatorship. The Machado government constituted an illegal regime. The Chase Bank loans had been contracted illegally. There was no legal reason for the Cuban government to honor its obligations to the Chase Bank.

Aldrich and the Chase Bank were furious at the findings. Aldrich sent a formal protest to the Cuban government on June 29, 1934, complaining of the investigation's "numerous perversions of truth and the injustices of its conclusion," and warned that the Cuban government's decision would "irreparably injure the credit of the Republic and vastly delay or even prevent the economic reconstruction of Cuba." Aldrich asserted that the legal arguments for repudation as outlined in the report were "unsound" and he insisted on the "validity" of the public works obligations.[122] The Chase Bank published a 500-page rebuttal to the Cuban government report that provided what amounted to a line-by-line refutation of the claims of the commission, arguing that the Chase Bank knew little of Cuba's political conditions and defending the bank's lending policies as both moral and legal. The Chase Bank insisted on the continuation of payments.

Aldrich and the Chase Bank won their battle with the Cuban government over the questions of debt and default. The Cuban courts decided to uphold the Chase Bank loans, claiming that they were both legal and constitutional. By then, the outstanding arrears amounted to $14,432,391 on a principal of $60,000,000.[123] The courts did not comment on the moral question of the loan, however, and for some time, many people in both the United States and Cuba sided with the government against the bank, especially as revelations of what one investor described as "the Wiggin method of doing business" came to light during the US Senate investigations into banking and stock market manipulations led by Ferdinand Pecora.[124] An investigation with the Foreign Policy Association concluded, "the Chase Bank did not use sound business judgement in entering into these financial arrangements [with Cuba]." It suggested that the bank had "employed methods of securing . . . business which overstepped the bounds of sound banking policy and banking ethics."[125] Even Aldrich, as belligerent as he was concerning the Machado debts, was forced to concede that the methods of the bank during the Wiggin years were unsound and unethical. In a move that came as a surprise to the Wall Street community but that Aldrich justified as a return to sound banking principles after the madness of the 1920s, Aldrich severed the commercial and investment wings of the Chase Bank, and dissolved the Chase Securities Corporation.[126] One of the legal entities supporting the imperial infrastructure of the Chase Bank was now gone. But the burden of the Chase debts on the Cuban people remained.

Racial Capitalism

In the final, feral days of the 1920s, both the Chase Manhattan Bank of the City of New York and the National City Bank of New York broke ground on new buildings in lower Manhattan. The Chase Bank building, at 18 Pine Street, was a severe and modern fourteen-story structure whose style was alternately described as Egyptianized and Gothicized Renaissance. Its heavy massed forms were set back from the street and anchored by a three-story vault encased in steel and reinforced concrete and embedded in Manhattan's bedrock.[1] Just steps away, at 20 Exchange Place, the City Bank erected a fifty-four-story tower of white Rockwood Alabama stone (a stone said to turn whiter over time), with fourteen massive carved stone heads representing the giants of finance—seven scowling, seven smirking—staring down on the streets below from the eighteenth story.[2] The new building broke with the neoclassicist stylings of the City Bank at 55 Wall Street. Instead of an architecture of façades and veils coyly masking the City Bank's emerging imperial history, the new building offered a raw display of modern financial power through a striking evocation of capitalism and empire.

The buildings were of a style that was dubbed "bull market architecture"[3]—an architecture engineered through the calculation of ground rent and the maximization of profit—but their Bessemer steel frames were also encrusted and bejeweled with the ornamental excesses, the opulent waste, and the extravagant ostentation of the 1920s. The towers contained columns and tiles of limestone, marble, and granite drawn from southern quarries, paneling and cabinetry of mahogany and teak harvested from the West Indies and East Asia, finishing of burnished nickel, silver, and bronze from the mines of Ontario and Mexico, and the most advanced and extensive telephone lines and switches, elaborate air purification systems, high-speed elevators, and high-security vaults (see fig. C.1). Both buildings were vainglorious

C.1. Irving Underhill, City Bank Farmers Trust Company Bldg., William & Beaver Sts., New York, 1931. Library of Congress Prints and Photographs Division, Washington, DC.

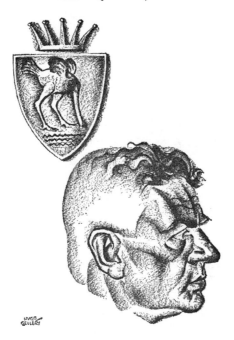

C.2. Drawing of Charles E. Mitchell by
Hugo Gellert. From *The Mirrors of Wall Street,
Illustrations by Hugo Gellert* (New York: G. P.
Putnam's Sons, 1933). Used with permission
Mary Ryan Gallery, New York/Hugo Gellert
Estate.

monuments to the egos of their leaders: 18 Pine Street to the Chase Bank's
Albert H. Wiggin, the rotund, jocular, jovial, and corrupt New England cad;
20 Exchange Place to the City Bank's square-jawed, fast-talking Charles E.
Mitchell (fig. C.2), a figure who, more than any financier of the era, dragged
the identity of the banker from its ethereal and purportedly gentlemanly
registers down to that of a barker, a promoter, a salesman.[4]

By the early 1930s, the financial edifices supporting the Chase Bank and
the City Bank crumbled, and both Wiggin and Mitchell were dethroned and
unceremoniously pitched from their vaunted perches at the heights of the
US economy. Soon after both buildings were completed, the bull market
staggered. The repercussions of the panic of October 1929 spread throughout the US economy, triggering a wave of bankruptcies and bank failures
across the country. The crisis unleashed a public hostility against banking
and the deities and wizards of high finance in whom so many US citizens
had placed their faith—and their savings—and, in the coming years, as the

US economy lurched toward depression, the disgust and anger toward Wall Street exploded.

In the Caribbean, the banking collapse and the economic crisis ignited the simmering anti-imperial antipathy circulating in the region for decades. The years of military intervention and occupation, of financial strangulation and banker control, were finally coming to a head. The crisis unleashed a current of nationalism targeting the United States and Wall Street. Anti-imperialism found its voice in a war song against banking, finance capitalism, and corporate authority—against the punitive regimes of debt, the monopoly presence of foreign financial institutions, the suffocation of nationhood and independence.[5] Calls for the return of Haitian sovereignty redounded by the late 1920s and the early 1930s, often with an attack on the US "money-dogs" who ran the Banque Nationale de la République d'Haiti and were behind the US occupation. In Cuba, there were increasing attacks on Wall Street interests—on the City Bank and the Chase Bank, but also on the Royal Bank of Canada. In Puerto Rico a militant nationalist movement saw in the foreign control of banking and sugar a symptom of the exploitative regimes of colonialism, and the perils of economic dependence and servitude. In the Dominican Republic, independent sentiment congealed in a toxic cocktail of xenophobia, economic sovereignty, and an emergent fascism.

The crisis of finance capitalism in the United States was a crisis of racial capitalism in the Caribbean. Across the region critiques and indictments of the prevailing racial order accompanied nationalist resistance to foreign banking and corporate monopoly. Calls for sovereignty and invocations of anti-imperialism often drew on figures of blackness—of Africa in the Caribbean—to critique the political economy of white colonialism. These evocations of blackness were ambivalent and often contradictory, however. On the one hand, they were marked by an embrace of blackness and of African-ness as an aesthetic and ethnological alternative to white capitalism: in the embrace of a Caribbean cultural difference rooted in the Caribbean peasantries mocked and murdered by Americans, of the black primitive as a life-giving alternative to the deadly regimes of white financial modernity, of black political-economic independence as a means of repelling the dangerous follies of dark finance. Often progressive in its intentions, it was paternal in its manifestations. On the other hand, the critique of imperialism, banking, and finance capitalism also emerged as an *attack* on black bodies. Blackness, African-ness, became the sign and figure of racial capitalism's challenge to Caribbean sovereignty. The Jamaican and Haitian workers—the *jornaleros* and *braceros*—who were brought to Cuba and the Dominican Republic to work on US-controlled sugar plantations became the physical representation of a finance capital that had eroded local sovereignty by undermining local labor. Jamaicans and Haitians were accused of having brought disease into Cuba, and they were rendered as cancers or parasites destroying the national body. They were subject to a grisly torrent of racial violence — anti-immigrant legal regimes, deportations, lynchings, massacres — sanctioned in the name of economic sovereignty, national integrity, and anti-imperial policy. The nationalism of the 1930s led to changes in imperial law and regulation — from the repeal of the treaty between the United States and Haiti to the abrogation of the Platt Amendment to the severing of the bond between commercial and investment banking. It also forced the reordering of racial capitalism and its reconstitution within a new neocolonial register.

In his annual report to shareholders of the Chase Bank, bank president Winthrop Aldrich wrote that 1933 "stands alone as the most critical year in American banking history."[6] The City Bank's Joseph H. Durrell was more explicit and more cynical. "My memories of the year 1933," Durrell later wrote, "correspond to those of an exaggerated nightmare."[7] By the early thirties, the depression had taken firm hold of the US economy and the financial system was on the verge of collapse. Federal Reserve policy had done little to mitigate the crisis, and Charles E. Mitchell, perhaps recalling his time in the offices of J. P. Morgan during the dark days of the panic of 1907, tried to intervene directly. He provided an injection of the City Bank's cash to the pinched and constricted economy as a desperate means to increase liquidity. His efforts proved but a temporary balm.[8]

In February 1933, Mitchell was called to testify before the Senate Committee on Banking and Currency regarding the financial methods of the City Bank and the National City Company in the stock market. There had been prior investigations into the activities of bankers before 1933, most significantly the 1931–32 investigations into the sale of foreign bonds that brought representatives of Wall Street's biggest banking houses to Washington and concluded with statements of protests by the governments of Cuba, Haiti, Chile, Colombia, and Peru. Investigators during these hearings had no access to bank records and bank executives, coached by their legal teams, evaded questions or gave flat, unrevealing responses. The 1933 hearings were different. Fernand Pecora, an energetic and sharp former assistant district attorney from New York, was appointed in January 1933. Pecora's questioning of bank executives was caustic, fearless, and withering. Pecora was also strengthened by the power of subpoena and was given access to bank records. He spent a weekend in the New York offices of Shearman and Sterling reading the City Bank's voluminous minute books.[9] Under Pecora's ruthless and incessant inquiry, and backed by the archived records of Wall Street, the testimony of the City Bank's Charles Mitchell, the Chase Bank's Alfred Wiggin, and other bankers showed them to be arrogant, self-absorbed, and greedy. They appeared self-satisfied, with an aura of infallibility, placing themselves above the law and beyond the reach of states and citizens.[10]

Durrell was disgusted by the Pecora investigations. He found them misguided and wrongheaded. "A stupid Congress plentifully sprayed the flame with gasoline," he complained, "in the form of a Senatorial investigation of the large solvent New York banks." Durrell chafed at the Pecora Commission and the intrusions into the City Bank's affairs by Pecora's agents, describing the "flock of investigators" as "largely of low-class Jewish nationality and headed by a Wop attorney" who "invaded" the offices of Wall Street and "clothed with Senatorial authority, rifled their desks and files, and hauled the officials before the Inquisition." The City Bank was the first "victim" of the Pecora Commission, and Mitchell and a dozen officers were "ordered to Washington," and "for days on end they were grilled and every possible effort made to show that our senior organization was composed of a bunch of rascals."[11]

Part of Durrell's frustration was with Pecora's investigations into his own division, into the City Bank's international operations, especially in the Caribbean and Latin America. Already, during the 1931–32 hearings, the activities of the City Bank in Haiti and Panama were questioned. In the case of Panama, it was alleged that City Bank vice president George E. Roberts—Durrell's old acquaintance from his Iowa days—had willfully deleted "practically every critical comment"[12] in a City Bank report on the finances and economy of Panama written to support a National City Company loan.[13] Roberts coolly denied the accusation, and the matter was dropped.[14] Pecora's team of investigators revealed that similar practices of deception and misrepresentation were rampant in the NCC. They were critical to the methods of marketing and "high-pressure salesmanship" through which bonds were sold to the public. Pecora unearthed an archive of letters and loan agreements that mapped out the City Bank's attempts at financing Cuban sugar after the dance of millions through the failed efforts of the General Sugar Company; he revealed the ways in which the company and its debt were disappeared through an accounting sleight of hand—removed from the ledgers of the bank and burdening its investors with worthless bonds.[15] The claims that the Havana newspaper *El Mundo* had made about the City Bank and its sugar corporation in the 1920s were proven correct.

Pecora's investigations into loans to Peru were especially damaging for the City Bank. Peru had been incorporated into the Caribbean District in 1927, and Durrell had traveled there to investigate conditions in support of a potential National City Company loan to the country worth $25 million. Durrell's report "described the political and economical conditions of that country in none too flattering terms," arguing that the dominant indigenous population would never create the kind of laboring tax base to justify the National City Company credits. The initial report, written by Durrell, caused his name to be "dragged into the picture."[16] Pecora revealed that the National City Company had doctored and edited Durrell's original report when it was packaged for the loan's prospectus in order to convince investors to purchase Peruvian bonds. It was an illegal and immoral practice, but one that had been increasingly used by the NCC during the late twenties to induce the public to invest; it was seen as an example of the kind of venal and unscrupulous salesmanship marking the reign of Mitchell.

The financing of the General Sugar Company and the history of the Peru loan brought the spotlight onto the National City Company and its organization and operation. Pecora returned to the records of Samuel Untermyer's investigation into a "Money Trust" in the 1910s, to the investigation that had so riled the City Bank's Frank A. Vanderlip. In response to Untermyer's investigation, Vanderlip recast the National City Company as a foreign financial organization, using the bank's efforts at internationalization to circumvent the National Bank Act. During Untermyer's investigation, a critical piece of evidence against the City Bank and the NCC had been suppressed: the minority report written by Solicitor General Lehman during the 1912 Pujo Committee hearings, arguing that the organization of the National City Company expressly violated both the spirit and the text of the National Bank Act and threatened to create the kind of monopoly and concentration in money and banking that the Act was designed, in part, to avoid.[17] The discovery of Lehman's opinion would prove a damning piece of evidence against the legality and use of securities affiliates.

Mitchell resigned from the City Bank on February 27, 1933. In Durrell's eyes, Mitchell was "pilloried and crucified" during the hearings, and he made the decision to step down not out of an admission of guilt, but from a desire to save the bank's public image.[18] James H. Perkins was elected chairman of the board, and Gordon Rentschler was elected bank president. Perkins was formerly the president of the City Bank–controlled Farmers Loan and Trust Company. Rentschler was an industrialist who was associated with the City Bank's General Sugar Co. and was involved in Cuban sugar. Although Mitchell was not held criminally liable for his activities with the City Bank, he was later indicted for tax fraud. His long-term accountant, Frank W. Black—the former employee of the Jarvis-Conklin Mortgage Trust Company, the North American Trust Company, and the American Foreign Banking Corporation—had allegedly falsified his taxes for years.

For Durrell, the attacks on Mitchell were politically motivated. He believed that Mitchell's indictment was a direct order from President Roosevelt. Durrell was convinced Roosevelt had a "hatred of banks and bankers, especially the New York variety." Durrell claimed he had been told by political representatives of Colombia, Cuba, and Panama that Roosevelt personally encouraged them to default on their loans. He also believed that Roosevelt was part of a Jewish conspiracy targeting certain banking houses. "A Jewish judge presided at the trial and a Jewish attorney prosecuted him," Durrell later stated in regard to Mitchell's tax case. "Anticipating a Jewish jury might be selected, a Jewish attorney, the famous Max Steurer was engaged to defend [Mitchell]." Mitchell was eventually acquitted.[19]

Officials of the Chase Bank didn't fare any better than Mitchell and the City Bank during the Pecora hearings. The Chase Bank's Albert H. Wiggin came out of retirement to read a prepared statement on his activities as the bank's president.[20] The statement highlighted his role in the expansion of the bank and its great growth in profits under his watch. He appeared pompous, out of touch, and unaware of the level of anger that the public had toward him and his institution. Wiggin revealed that upon his retirement, he had authorized the board to give him a $100,000-a-year pension for life—a fact that left observers incredulous, given that his actions had caused Americans throughout the country to lose their life savings, and the unemployment rate to skyrocket as the global depression continued.

On October 19, 1933, the Chase Bank's Winthrop Aldrich interrupted the testimony of Wiggin and read into the record a journal published the day before. The article claimed a letter had surfaced regarding the flotation of loans for the Machado government. The letter decried the "millions of dollars . . . squandered in waste, riotous costs, and graft in the construction of the two projects," and claimed that Wall Street had sought to suppress information from an inquiry into the loans, as it would generate "anti-American feeling" in Cuba and could lead to "anti-American riots and attacks on American Banks." "Not a dollar was paid to President Machado or any other office or employee of the Cuban Government or anyone else, directly or indirectly, by way of commission or gratuity," Aldrich told the Senate Committee on Banking and Currency. He stated that there was no point to an investigation based on "distorted or false statements" about the bank and denied that the bank's officials "sought in any way to suppress any facts concerning this financing or any other of the activities in Cuba."[21] Aldrich's pleas were of no avail. The Pecora Commission, previously focused on the domestic activities of the Chase Securities Corporation, switched to focus on its Cuban loans. Pecora began a line of inquiry that took the veil off the forms of dark finance through which the bank was operating in Cuba, and the history of its financing of Cuba's sovereign debt slowly came to light. His investigations also supported the Cuban government's case for repudiation of the Chase loans.

While Aldrich had dissolved the Chase Securities Corporation, the signing of the Glass-Steagall Act in 1933 removed the possibility of voluntary action on the part of the bank: securities affiliates—bastard affiliates—were deemed illegal. The combination of commercial and investment banking by national banking associations was outlawed. The National City Company, the vehicle that Frank A. Vanderlip had organized to expand the City Bank's retail activities and to give it a platform for overseas expansion, the institution that enabled Charles E. Mitchell's entrance into the City Bank, the organization that had carried the bank's expansion into a world of speculation and financing in the 1920s, was no more.[22]

Despite the resignations of Wiggin and Mitchell, the banking and financial system remained unstable, and the public had little confidence in Wall Street. In the days after Mitchell's resignation in February 1933, the City Bank branches in New York City were subjected to a brief bank run. Things soon worsened. On March 4, Durrell received word that New York governor Herbert H. Lehman was about to declare a bank holiday, temporarily closing every bank in New York State. Durrell was concerned about how the moratorium might affect his foreign branches, all of which did much of their business through New York. "In all the years I had been handling foreign branches," he recalled, "the one big question always in my mind was what might happen to our branches abroad if some great national calamity occurred here in the States. The question was satisfactorily answered during that day and the following three weeks."[23] Already, in 1930, when he had taken over the foreign branches, Durrell's assessment of global economic conditions was dire. A flurry of bank runs on Cuba's few surviving local banks, including the Banco del Comercio in Havana and the Banco Agrícola de Güines, in October 1930 seemed to prove him correct.[24] Durrell assumed the depression would be "a long-drawn-out affair," and began to act accordingly.[25] He initiated a liquidation policy in the branches, calling in outstanding loans and developing a reserve of ready cash, repeating the conservative policies that had marked the City Bank since its origins in the nineteenth century under Moses Taylor. All of the foreign branches carried large cash reserves, and, operating on a hunch, Durrell increased the reserves of the London and Paris branches in the weeks before Roosevelt's moratorium. The only exceptions were the City Bank's branches in Cuba, the Dominican Republic, Puerto Rico, and Panama. All were on the dollar and Durrell believed they could rely on the Federal Reserve agency at Havana if they required additional resources.

Across the City Bank's global network, the panic began the moment news of the moratorium reached the branches. The branches in Asia and Europe were the first to learn of the bank holiday, as they were still open for business when it was announced. Bank runs began almost immediately. In the Caribbean, within thirty minutes of the opening of the branches, the managers were calling 55 Wall Street, desperate for additional reserves as depositors rushed to withdraw funds. Durrell hoped the Federal Reserve would intervene. It did nothing. Unlike in the 1920s, when the Federal Reserve rushed additional currency from New Orleans to shore up the City Bank and other institutions, this time the Fed sat idle, refusing to provide the funds. By 10 a.m., the Havana branch was filled with a frantic crowd of customers. The managers estimated their reserves would not last the hour. Durrell urged them to hang on, telling them to pay in nickels if necessary, while promising to find the necessary cash. Durrell called Eugene R. Black, governor of the Atlanta Federal Reserve bank and an old friend, for help. Black ordered the Havana agency of the Federal Reserve to exchange its dollars for the City Bank's gold. Durrell credited $1.8 million in gold to the reserve bank, and the Havana branch had the money it needed to get through the day.

At the same time, Durrell sent a million dollars to Puerto Rico and a half million to Panama in anticipation of problems in the branches in both locations. With the cooperation of William G. Brady, who by then was the City Bank's vice president of the Manhattan District, he gathered what he described as the "loose" currency in the City Bank's vault and sent an additional million dollars to San Juan on a chartered plane. He reserved the currency space on the next three flights from Miami to Havana and sent $6 million via the Atlantic Coast Line. It made the trip in a drawing room accompanied by a bank manager and armed guards. Durrell then called Cuban president Gerardo Machado, at the time, in the waning months of his rule, and convinced him to declare a bank holiday in Cuba beginning the coming Tuesday. Through a herculean effort, Durrell and the Caribbean branches had gotten through Saturday. On Sunday, Durrell learned that Roosevelt was about to declare a *national* bank moratorium. He feared that the efforts the City Bank had just been through would have to be repeated on Monday—though on a much greater scale.

Durrell and the City Bank's Caribbean branches survived the moratorium partly because, as Durrell acknowledged, rival banks lent their support
and resources. But politically and economically, the Caribbean was tense
through the 1930s. The status of the City Bank in the Caribbean was increasingly fraught, as was that of all North American banking houses in
the region. Cuba and Puerto Rico, in particular, were volatile. In Cuba, terror was met with violence as the struggle against the Machado regime increased and his repression escalated. Bankers and banking houses became
the subject of intimidation, threats, and violence by nationalists and anti-
imperialists. These actions were a far cry from the protests against foreign
banks in Cuba in the 1920s. What were once critical editorials decrying the
methods of bankers now became death threats. Bank runs were replaced by
bomb attacks. Durrell received a death threat from the ABC. The ABC also
sent letters to Timothy M. Findlay and José Lopez Fernandez, managers of
the Chase Bank in Havana, prompting a Havana police chief to offer them
licenses to carry revolvers.[26] Early in the morning of September 1, 1931, the
Royal Bank of Canada branch, on La Linea Street in the wealthy Havana suburb of Vedado, was almost leveled when a bomb was detonated inside it. Its
mahogany doors were pulverized. The masonry of the building was ripped
away. Parts of the stone exterior were reduced to dust. Large holes were torn
in the ceiling and front entrance by heavy iron slugs packed into the device.
The furniture and interior fixtures was destroyed. Damage was estimated at
several thousands of dollars.[27] Bomb attacks in Havana during this period
became normal. During one night in Havana in 1933, Durrell and his wife
counted more than 200 explosions.

Machado's overthrow in 1933 removed the most important guardian
of the security of foreign banking institutions in Cuba. Bankers lost a figure that had defended them from attacks while expanding their interests
for almost a decade. Early in his reign, Machado had pledged to protect
North American banking interests and had repeatedly intervened on their
behalf at any sign of trouble or panic. With Machado gone, the banks were
increasingly targeted, the most significant attack coming from the Cuban
government through its default on the Chase Bank interest payments and its
attempts to repudiate the debt. But attacks against banks also occurred on
the ground, throughout the island, and by all sectors of Cuban society. A day
after Machado was removed from power the Royal Bank–financed Palmira
Sugar Company in Cienfuegos was occupied by 500 men armed with shot-
guns and truncheons. They were joined by workers from nearby Centrale
Portugalete, a mill the Royal Bank had taken over during the wave of foreclo-
sures in the early 1920s. The protestors presented the managers, appointees

of the bank, with a list of demands for better wages and working conditions. They camped out for several days before dispersing. In 1934, peasants from the district of Realengo 18 stoned the Santiago de Cuba branch as part of a protest against the forcible eviction of 5,000 families from land wanted by the Royal Bank–financed La Compañía Azucarera Maisí. The company enlisted Cuban government forces for the eviction, but they were met by a well-organized peasant resistance who fought under the banner of "land or blood" for the "Republic of Realengo." They eventually reached a compromise with the Cuban government and the planters, though not before inflicting $30,000 in damage on the Royal Bank's Santiago de Cuba branch.[28] Within the bank itself, employees were radicalized by the times. The clerks and tellers formed an association demanding wage increases and the unionization of all employees while seeking to amalgamate with the Cuban Federation of Labor.[29]

Both Puerto Rico and Haiti also became the locations of antibank protests, with the City Bank in particular a target. The City Bank had been in Puerto Rico since it had opened a branch in San Juan in April 1918, following with another in Ponce.[30] In 1929, they moved to purchase the American Colonial Bank, an institution founded in 1899 to take advantage of the possibilities of colonial financing.[31] With six branches and more than $13 million in assets, the Colonial Bank was the largest banking institution on the island. The takeover generated a flurry of protest from local stockholders, who controlled about 20 percent of the Colonial Bank stock. They feared the City Bank would limit local access to funds and complained that the sale price of stock was too low.[32] The sale was approved despite the protests. The City Bank reassured its Puerto Rican customers that it would retain the Colonial Bank's employees and maintain its local lending policies, while increasing the volume of capital in local circulation.[33]

Puerto Rico was heating up during this period. The question of finance capital, banking control, and national sovereignty was growing into an issue much bigger than the complaints of the colonial business classes. In a 1930 manifesto, Puerto Rican Nationalist Party leader Pedro Albizu Campos described the City Bank as a *pulpo*, an octopus, and attacked it and the other foreign banks on the island for their role in Puerto Rico's colonial administration. "Además, las economías de nuestro pueblo depositadas en los bancos van a la disposición de un poder extranjero," Albizu Campos wrote. "Están en poder del National City Bank, del Royal Bank y del Banco Nova Escotia, que refaccionan a interés enemigos del país."[34] A year later, Puerto Rican nationalists reprised the attacks on foreign banks in Cuba that had occurred in the 1920s. They circulated handbills claiming that the island's banks were insolvent, prompting minor bank runs.[35] The City Bank's Havana branch rushed $70,000 by a charted Pan-American Airways plane to the San Juan branch while readying an additional $1.5 million if needed.[36]

Early in 1933, Puerto Rico's banks were subjected to heavy withdrawals, and the City Bank sent multiple shipments of currency to stabilize their reserves.[37] In March 1933, the insular authorities in Puerto Rico followed the lead of Roosevelt in issuing a banking moratorium. The governor sought emergency powers that would allow him to temporarily suspend requirements to pay wages in legal tender, while at the same time giving authority to bankers to issue scrip or certificates in lieu of cash. Albizu Campos was critical of the moratorium in Puerto Rico. He argued that it, alongside the financial crisis in general, would be used by North American financial interests for further intervention into and control of the Puerto Rican economy. For Albizu Campos, the moratorium was a method through which an American financial oligarchy would extend its control over Puerto Rico indefinitely. "El pánico financiero resulta para aquel infeliz pueblo norteamericano una ruina," he wrote in a Nationalist Party communiqué, "pero es uno de los métodos eficaces con que cuenta la oligarquía bancaria yanqui para mantenerse en el poder por tiempo indefinido."[38] By 1933, the City Bank was acting as Puerto Rico's de facto central bank. As in Cuba and Haiti, the City Bank served as the depository of government funds while hampering the development of a truly national institution. In an echo of the critiques of both the Banco Nacional de Cuba and the BNRH years before, Albizu Campos argued that despite the "national" in its name, it was a private corporation legally authorized by the US Congress, whose business was exclusively that of New York City.[39]

Albizu Campos's linking of the banking crisis to the extension of colonial banking and finance in Puerto Rico was astute. Within months of the moratorium, the City Bank reduced the interest rates on the insular government's demand deposits, slashing the rate in half from 2 to 1 percent. It sliced interest rates on savings deposits by half a percentage point, from 3 to 2.5 percent.[40] The City Bank also attempted to further ensconce itself with the Puerto Rican sugar industry. It moved to purchase the United Puerto Rico Sugar Co., then in receivership, for $3.5 million. The price was seen as "absurdly low" and "grossly inadequate," especially given the scale of the company's properties: five factories spread over 31,000 acres, with 155 miles of railroad. Its book value was estimated at $16 million. At the time of the purchase, 6,000 workers were striking at the company, and it was feared that if the company shut down, it would lead to the unemployment of 15,000 people.[41]

Albizu Campos addressed workers at the United Puerto Rico Sugar Co. and led strikes at the Puerto Rico Railway and Light and Power Company and other foreign corporations. In 1936, he was arrested, accused of being behind the assassination of a US colonial official, and charged with sedition. He was convicted by a jury that included Frederick J. Todd, the head of the City Bank's collection department, and Henry Shoemaker, an officer of the Chase National Bank, the latter institution having arrived on the island in 1933.[42] Puerto Ricans working under Todd in the City Bank gave sworn statements alleging that Todd had made negative, biased comments about Albizu Campos and the other nationalists before the trial. Albizu Campos, Todd had declared, should be "burned alive."[43] Todd denied the accusations. In the aftermath of the trial he and the Chase Bank's Shoemaker applied for gun permits to defend themselves against death threats.[44] Years later, Todd took charge of the City Bank's Cuban branches and was appointed a vice president.[45] The City Bank fired the Puerto Rican employees. Albizu Campos spent the better part of the next eleven years in the Atlanta penitentiary.

In Haiti, protests against the City Bank were folded into the generalized insurgency against the US occupation. They began late in October 1929, with student demonstrations at L'École Centrale d'Agriculture in Damien over the withdrawal of state funding for educational bursaries. The Damien protests quickly spread to other schools, leading to a general strike that by December consumed the country and all of its classes.[46] On December 6, a detachment of US Marines shot into a crowd of protestors at Aux Cayes, killing ten and wounding more than twenty. The killings generated an international outcry and prompted a renewed scrutiny of the US occupation. In response, President Hoover sent a commission to Haiti to analyze the conditions of the occupation and to find a way to expedite the withdrawal of marines. When the commissioners arrived in Haiti they were met with well-organized and vocal demonstrations. The streets of Port-au-Prince were thronged with Haitians holding banners and flags calling for elections, denouncing US-installed president Louis Borno, and demanding an end to the occupation. When the commissioners traveled from Port-au-Prince to Cap-Haïtien, they encountered similar scenes. Crowds of Haitian women lined the streets, singing anti-American songs and waving paper flags "darkened with black paper bars to indicate a state of mourning for lost liberties." Disgust with the occupation was uniform across the country. The commissioners were perplexed by the criticism of the occupation. They were "disappointed at the evidence [they] received of the lack of appreciation on the part of the educated and cultured Haitians of the services rendered them by the Occupation and their own Government. Out of many dozen witnesses only one or two made favorable mention of the achievements of their administration."[47]

Hoover recommended free elections and a gradual military withdrawal, but he hedged on the question of relinquishing financial control of the Banque Nationale de la République d'Haiti and transferring the country's monetary sovereignty to the Haitian state. He argued that the interests of investors in Haitian bonds must be considered in any decision, while noting that "investors have supplied capital desired by Haiti and that securities have been issued to them on the faith and credit of the provisions of that treaty and the American financial control which it provided during the life of the bonds."[48] Yet there were growing calls for the nationalization of the Banque Nationale both inside and outside Haiti. The criticism of the City Bank's role in the financial control of the island was also increasing, as the charges that James Weldon Johnson had aired in *The Nation* in 1920 were reprised. Haitian nationalists denounced the City Bank control of Haitian finances in speeches and pamphlets.[49] In 1932, Haitian attorney Georges N. Léger testified during the US Senate hearings on foreign loans on the City Bank's role in the the US occupation and the history of Haiti's debt. The Haitian people, he stated in conclusion, "will not stand for financial and political control of their country until 1953 just to satisfy a group of New York bankers."[50]

The City Bank did not respond to Léger's statement. Instead, US Secretary of State Henry L. Stimpson dismissed Léger's claims in a lengthy rebuttal to the committee, concluding that many of Léger's statements were simply "not correct."[51] But criticism of the City Bank was growing in the United States, especially among African Americans. There had been support for the US occupation in its early years, but after the revelations in Johnson's *Nation* articles, which were widely reprinted in the black press, criticism of the City Bank and the US Marines in Haiti mounted.[52] By 1932, Walter White of the National Association for the Advancement of Colored People could write to the chairman of the Senate committee investigating foreign loans of "the wishes of 12,000,000 American Negroes and many fair-minded whites who are opposed to the throttling of Haiti by financial interests." White urged the committee to investigate the City Bank loans to Haiti and forwarded two NAACP memoranda as evidence.[53] In the same year, writing of a visit to Haiti in the NAACP's *Crisis*, Langston Hughes used the bank as a way to talk about the larger problem of Haitian sovereignty. Hughes offered a critical rejoinder to the BNRH's William H. Williams's comments on the racial lines of power—and the "push of the whiteman" in the bank—from two decades earlier. In Haiti, wrote Hughes, "you will discover that the Banque d'Haiti, with its Negro cashiers and tellers, is really under the control of the National City Bank of New York."[54]

The US occupation of Haiti officially ended on August 1, 1934, with the withdrawal of the US Marines. The nationalization of the BNRH took longer.[55] For the City Bank, the end of the occupation meant the removal of the guarantor of their operations in Haiti. The BNRH remained profitable for the City Bank, but by the early 1930s it was beginning to rethink its position in Haiti. In 1933 the bank had approached the Haitian government and proposed selling it the BNRH. For City Bank chairman James H. Perkins, the proposal was partly a gesture meant to silence the critics in *The Nation* and the *New Republic* and remove the bank from the shadow of negative publicity that had surrounded its activities in the republic. Yet although Perkins was willing to sell the BNRH, he was not interested in ceding control of Haitian finances.[56] Furthermore, while President Roosevelt, who had visited Haiti in 1933, wanted to see Haiti gain control of the bank, like Hoover before him, he was concerned about how nationalization might be viewed by the holders of Haiti's debt. Nonethelesss, negotiations began between the City Bank and the Haitian government over the sale of the BNRH. An initial contract was signed on May 12, 1934, but it was not met with approval by Haitian legislators. On March 27, 1935, an agreement was reached, and in July the BNRH was officially sold to the Haitian government. The purchase price was $550,000.[57] Once an agreement on the terms of succession and sale were reached in 1935, terms of the sale of the BNRH by the City Bank to the government of Haiti were worked out within the coming years. The sale and reorganization of the BNRH merely served to retrench the City Bank's position in the republic in neocolonial fashion. The US financial adviser Sidney de la Rue commented on the sale in one of his last official reports:

The terms of the contract of sale were carefully designed to maintain the bank in a strong position. The bank keeps as its correspondent abroad the National City Bank of New York and its many branches. It is the policy to continue doing its foreign business through that bank as in the past when the Banque Nationale de la Republique d'Haiti was an affiliate of that institution. The personnel and executive staff trained during the years when the Banque Nationale de la Republique d'Haiti was administered by the National City Bank of New York has been retained.[58]

De la Rue's anger at the transition led him to impose a series of punitive taxes and charges on the BNRH during its final day. But he was correct in his assessment.[59] The transfer of the BNRH was gradual, its planned

date of completion being September 13, 1941.[60] The City Bank continued
to have a say in electing the BNRH's officials and board members. The City
Bank's executives were no longer the BNRH's president. The position was bequeathed to William H. Williams, the white man who had been appointed
manager of the BNRH in 1915 in the lead-up to the US occupation. Williams
remained with the BNRH until 1947, at which point he retired, bestowed by
the Haitian government with the National Order of "Honneur et mérite" in
recognition of services rendered to the Republic.[61]

As the City Bank was settling its accounts in Haiti, it was doing the same
in the Dominican Republic. In the Dominican Republic, the City Bank's
branches became a casualty of Dominican president Rafael Trujillo's quest for
economic autonomy and fiscal sovereignty. Trujillo sought to have the control of the Dominican customs removed from the United States, he wanted
to settle the Dominican foreign debt, and he looked to establish a national
reserve bank. A plan for a bank drawn up by the US State Department was
"unsatisfactory," Trujillo told the City Bank's Harry Henneman, "as it would
be neither 'Dominican' nor 'national,' as the control of its board of directors was in the hand of foreigners." In response, the State Department suggested the City Bank might be willing to sell its Dominican branches to the
government to be used as the foundation for a national bank. However, the
City Bank wanted to hold onto the Dominican branches as they were profitable. It proposed the formation of a board of directors composed largely
of individuals representing US interests. Trujillo was against the idea. "The
Dominicans did not propose to buy the branches of the National City Bank
merely to have the Bank run them," Trujillo told Henneman.[62] By 1941, a
compromise was reached. Collection of Dominican customs revenue was
transferred from the US government to the City Bank, and the Santo Domingo branch remained as a depositor. At the same time, the Dominican
government purchased the City Bank branches and used them to establish
a commercial and government bank, the Banco de Reservas de la República
Dominicana.[63] Trujillo used the transfer to label himself "Restorer of the
Financial Independence of the Republic." The City Bank's Joseph Durrell,
who had known Trujillo since he was an army officer and admired him despite his vanity, surmised the new bank was a critical source for the increase
of the dictator's wealth.[64]

The financial crisis of the 1930s was also a crisis of racial capitalism that
rattled the old racial orders in the Caribbean. It destabilized the racial hierarchies that had justified the expansion of finance capitalism while shaping

the terms through which finance capitalism operated. Implicit in the calls for the nationalization or indigenization of state banking, or in the cries to default on sovereign debt, was a refusal to be governed through the implicitly hierarchal—and implicitly racialized—international orders that had subordinated countries like Haiti, Cuba, and the Dominican Republic to the United States. The assertion of sovereignty was not only a claim for economic independence; it was a rejection of the governing tropes of racial paternalism. The rejection of finance capitalism and imperial banking was a rejection of white supremacy and the obliteration of the circular logic associating whites with wealth and wealth with whites.[65] The desire to break the hold and allure of the City Bank and the Chase Bank meant a challenge to the divine laws of racial capitalism. This rejection often occurred on an intimate, micropolitical level; as we have seen, it was through the representatives of Wall Street, through the interpersonal encounters between rogue bankers and Caribbean people, that racial hierarchies were reproduced and operationalized. And it was through the preternatural assumptions of white superiority that the first ledgers of US finance capital and imperial banking in the Caribbean were written—be it by the North American Trust Company's Samuel Jarvis, the International Banking Corporation's James Morris Morgan, the Bank of Nicaragua's Bundy Cole, or the City Bank's Roger Farnham, John H. Allen, or William H. Williams.

As black, as African, Caribbean people did not sit as equals at the table of the white imperial great powers. Bankers made that clear. John H. Allen wrote of the veneration that he and others among the white BNRH staff received from Haitians. He claimed that during a service at Port-au-Prince's cathedral the bankers were ushered to seats next to Haiti's archbishop and far away from the "two thousand energetic perspiring negroes" among whom, to his dismay, he was forced to sit during a prior event.[66] Durrell mocked the formal pretensions of "all the black-and-tan dignitaries of the Republic."[67] Williams, alongside a BNRH staff member named Armand Tellier, sneered at the elite in their "glad rags" and made fun of the ceremony and pomp of the Haitian elite. A dispatch in *No. 8* stated that Williams and Tellier were "considering ordering canes to carry to the office as a means of impressing on their less fortunate fellows the lofty station they have attained in the eyes of the diplomatic circles of Haiti."[68] Tellier was a skilled performer. Described in *No. 8* as "our old minstrel," he was a popular and recurring figure on the stage of the City Bank Minstrel Show at 55 Wall Street.[69]

If for Williams, the "push" of the white man had defined the working relations of the BNRH at the beginning of the century, increasingly black men and black women in Haiti and throughout the Caribbean were pushing

back. It was a pushback that sought control of Caribbean states and economies, but also one that attempted to reimagine Caribbean bodies outside of
the regimes of racial capitalism through which black people were rendered,
as Roger Farnham and others suggested, as machines, animals, or slaves.
Implicit here was an effort to critique the registers of profit making and accumulation through which the Caribbean labor that produced products—
especially sugar—were obscured, shrouded, and hidden in the commodity
form itself. The radical journalist Carleton Beals captured this process in *The
Crime of Cuba*, his account of US finance capital—of the Chase Bank and the
City Bank—and the Machado dictatorship. Early in *The Crime of Cuba*, in his
discussion of the racialized political economy of sugar, Beals evokes Marx's
description of the commodity as a "social hieroglyphic" whose meaning
is only revealed through exegetical means. "For most Americans, Cuba is
but the hieroglyphic of a ticker," Beals writes: "Amer. Sugar 26 5/8 / Cub.
Amer. Sugar 17 1/7 / Cub. Am. Pfd. 18 1/5." He goes further, unpacking, or
deciphering, the meaning of sugar as the story of the capture of black labor
power. "But for me," Beals writes, "all this inner mystery is forever imprisoned in each cube of white sugar I drop into my morning coffee. Black Cuba
and black sweat and black song and dance, crystallized into a snow cube,
held in silver prongs."[70]

Often such critiques occurred under the guises of the Communist Party
and the Comintern, especially through their efforts to build a global movement of radical black labor. The literature and propaganda of black Communists at this time linked racial, or what was called "national," oppression
of black workers to finance capital and imperialism. The pages of the *Negro
Worker*, for instance, contained denunciations of the City Bank's involvement in Haiti alongside accounts of black labor exploitation and colonial
oppression across the African diaspora.[71] The *Negro Worker* was published
under the auspices of the International Trade Union's Committee of Negro
Workers, a subbranch of the Red International Labour Union and an ap-
pendage of the Comintern tasked with mobilizing black labor in worldwide
class struggle against global capitalism. The *Negro Worker*'s one-time editor
George Padmore also catalogued global conditions of black exploitation
in his *Life and Struggles of Negro Toilers*, published in 1931. Padmore was a
young black Trinidadian functionary for the Communist Party's Negro wing
and a prolific writer who edited the *Negro Worker* for a number of years. *Life
and Struggles* presents a sweeping comparative accounting of the conditions
suffered by black people in Africa and the African diaspora and includes attacks on early twentieth-century US expansionism overseas and, with it, the
transformation of Haiti and the Dominican Republic, and Liberia and Abys-

sinia, into colonies of American finance capital.[72] Padmore assails the City
Bank's imposition of debt on the Dominican Republic and the transformation of Haiti into "an American slave colony" during the US occupation. He
lambasts the "Black Ivory Trade"—the conscription of Haitian workers to
the Cuban plantations of the General Sugar Company and the United Fruit
Company. He argues that Haitians were brought to the country "in the same
ways as chattel slaves of former days." Haitians were underpaid, indebted to
their contractors, and housed in segregated and unsanitary barracoons.[73] In
Padmore's writing, finance capitalism was racial capitalism.

Similar critiques were also implicit in Jacques Roumain's novel *Masters of
the Dew*. Roumain was the founder of the Haitian Communist Party. He was
jailed during the waning days of the US occupation. *Masters of the Dew* centers on a Haitian *bracero* who returns to his country from Cuba and attempts
to rebuild Haiti through collective labor and a call for black autonomy. For
Roumaine, the collective pull of the *coumbite* replaces the coercive push of
the *corvée*. At the same time, US banking and corporate interests became the
subject of a radical, anti-imperialist Caribbean literature—a literature that
can be viewed as a counterpoint to the rhetoric of the City Bank, and the
attempts by Wall Street to "visualize" the Caribbean, to borrow John H. Allen's term, for the purposes of exploitation and accumulation. Cuban poet
Nicolás Guillén's *West Indies, Ltd.*, for instance, satirically attacks the corporate transformation of the Caribbean into "the grotesque headquarters of
companies and trusts."[74] In Nicaragua novelist's Hernán Robleto's *Los estrangulados*, the US-controlled Banco Nacional de Nicaragua and the Mercantile
Bank of the Americas' Compañía Mercantil de Ultramar feature as dominant
and domineering institutions undermining the economic independence of
the Nicaraguan elite through its loaning practices.[75] Langston Hughes wrote
of the role of the City Bank not only in Haiti but also in Cuba. He evokes
the transitions from mercantilism to imperialism and colonialism to neocolonialism in Cuba's history and offers a glum assessment of the ability of
"the Little Fort of San Lazaro," standing sentinel at the entrance to Havana's
harbor, facing the Caribbean Sea and the United States, to repel the pillaging
of finance capitalism. "But now," writes Hughes, "Against a pirate called /
THE NATIONAL CITY BANK / What can you do alone?"[76]

Pushback against racial capitalism did not occur only under the auspices
of the Communist Party. Caribbean intellectuals also turned inward to seek
out an autochthonous, anti-imperial critique. This phenomenon was perhaps most pronounced in Haiti. For the Haitian elite, the utter humiliation
of the US occupation forced them to rethink their identities. Their long-
standing identifications with France and European Enlightenment thought

and culture proved an absurdity in the face of the brutal racism of the US occupation. Many among them realized they were suffering from what Jean Price-Mars called a "collective bovaryism"—a deluded and misrecognized sense of self. The Haitian elite slowly realized that Europe was not their home. Africa was. Price-Mars's *Ainsi parle l'oncle*, an ethnological exploration of the culture and folklore of the Haitian peasantry and its African origins, published in Port-au-Prince in 1927, helped spur the development of insurgent literary and national cultures in the Caribbean and throughout the African diaspora.[77]

In Cuba, this turn to blackness as an alternative to racial capitalism took on multiple and contradictory forms. In the early 1920s, writers like Jesús Masdeu, in *La raza trieste*, depicted the black workers on the Cuban *centrales* in sentimental, romantic, and often paternal tones. The racial paternalism began to slip away in *La danza de los millones*, Venezuelan expatriate Rafael Antonio Cisneros's experimental novel with its efforts at narrating the effects of the banking crisis of 1920–21 on his black characters.[78] In *La zafra*, a collection of *poemas de combate*, "combat poems," Cuba's Agustín Acosta recounted the effects of the sugar boom and bust on the country, linking finance capital to racial capitalism, and sugar to blackness, money, and the poison of US empire. Acosta made this explicit in the poem "La danza de los millones." It evokes the incursion of the instruments and techniques of American finance capital into the Cuban economy, portraying it as a turbulent sea threatening to capsize the ship of Cuba's sovereignty:

> Eran mares de oro. Los billetes de banco
> Cubrían la avaricia de los cheques en blanco.
> Eran mares de cifras, de Letras, de dinero . . .
> (Y nadie recordó que el mar es traicionero.)[79]

Acosta warned of "Wall Street, con sus banqueros usurarios" ("Wall Street, with its usurious bankers").[80] In the novel *¡Écue-Yamba-Ó!* written by a young Alejo Carpentier while in Machado's prison in 1927, blackness was rendered as the soul of Cuban culture, and an African alterity became the terms of a critique of imperialism and white finance. "El bongo," Carpentier wrote, "Antídoto de Wall Street!"[81]

The nature of this blackness was contingent. In some cases, blackness itself was cast as a threat to Caribbean sovereignty—especially in Cuba and the Dominican Republic. In Cuba, the fear of blackness had circulated since the beginning of the nineteenth century, the revolts against slavery in Saint-Domingue, and the birth of the Haitian republic in 1804. It emerged in brutal from in the 1912 massacre of black veterans of the war of independence, when black Cubans were killed in Havana's downtown Parque Central and lynched on the streets of the nouveau riche suburb of Vedado. Some US dispatches on the massacre reported rumors that blacks were committing "crimes against white women." They wrote that thousands of Haitians (in some accounts joined by Dominicans and Jamaicans) had "surreptitiously entered the [Oriente] and [were] . . . inflaming the Cuban negroes by citing the example of the Haitians in exterminating the whites in their country," and urging the establishment of a "black republic" in the eastern end of Cuba.[82] Just a year before, the United Fruit Company had begun importing Haitian and Jamaican workers for their sugar plantations.[83] The practice would continue over the next decade, with the City Bank, with its investments in both Cuba and Haiti, profiting on both sides. The "slave trade" of Haitian laborers to Cuba and the Dominican Republic provided a cool source of revenue and a pool of cheap labor for US plantations.[84] It also served to make Haitian and Jamaican workers the symbols of US imperialism, white finance capitalism, and an antinational racial capitalism.[85]

In 1919, the Banco Mercantil Americano de Cuba's *Bamericuba* reprinted a Spanish-language article from Havana's press questioning the desirability of Haitian and Jamaican immigration to Cuba. It argued that for questions of both ethnicity and sanitation, it would be better for the health of the Cuban republic to bring in Chinese and Puerto Rican workers on limited contracts.[86] These questions of race and labor, and behind them questions of economy and sovereignty, would recur over the twenties. The critique of foreign domination by finance occurred through an attack on the presence of the black labor brought in by foreign capital. Violence against Haitians and Jamaicans was rampant in Cuba, and there were calls to remove them from the country in the name of economy, of nationalism, and of what Spanish writer Luis Arquistan described as Cuba's great racial tragedy: its "africanization."[87] Ramiro Guerra y Sánchez summarized the growing sentiment against black immigrant labor in a 1927 article in *Diario de la Marina*, a journal that was also a progressive venue for Afro-Cuban culture: "No más impórtacion de braceros."[88]

In the 1930s the radical organization ABC saw the fight against imperialism in Cuba as a fight against both foreign banks and foreign workers. The ABC, they wrote in a manifesto, is "opposed to the importation of Haitians and Jamaicans."[89] In 1933, the Cuban congress passed laws authorizing the deportation of black immigrant laborers.[90] Over 8,000 Haitians were deported from Cuba between November 1933 and July 1934. In 1937 alone, 25,000 workers were deported. That year also represents perhaps the worst moment in the early twentieth-century history of antiblackness in the Caribbean. Between October 2 and 8, 1937, approximately 30,000 Haitians were massacred at the Haitian-Dominican border under orders of Trujillo. A year earlier, both J. E. Wheeler, manager of the City Bank in Santo Domingo, and T. J. McConnell, his counterpart at the Royal Bank of Canada, published fawning statements praising Trujillo in a commemorative volume.[91] When Trujillo wanted to silence a US senator attempting to investigate the massacres, he bought the senator off by opening an account for him at the City Bank in New York. Trujillo then transferred $25,000 from his personal City Bank account to the senator.[92]

For Wall Street, the crises of the 1930s forced a rethinking of the organization of finance capital and the project of internationalization in a new era of governance, regulation, and sovereignty. The City Bank and the Chase Bank would spend the next decades struggling to return to the heady days of unregulated expansion and unbounded freedom that characterized the early twentieth-century history of imperial banking.[93] For the Caribbean, the crises of the 1930s represented something different. Those years foreshadowed a later history of intervention and exploitation, of debt and repression—of bankers and empire. It was an era from which the region has never recovered.[94]

ACKNOWLEDGMENTS

Any history of banking is invariably an accounting of debt. *Bankers and Empire* is no different. Yet unlike debts to bankers, those incurred during my research and writing are neither burdensome nor odious. They are numerous, however, and it is impossible for me to offer a complete ledger of the individuals and institutions that have lent time and resources and offered trust and confidence over the many years it took to complete this book. My only hope is the end project can begin to settle accounts.

The assistance, energy, and vision of the librarians, archivists, and curators of repositories in the Caribbean, North America, and Europe were critical to the research; my sincere thanks to the staff of the brick-and-mortar institutions named in the notes as well as to a number of digital projects, including ProQuest's Historical Newspapers; the Brooklyn Public Library's *Brooklyn Daily Eagle*; the Library of Congress's *Chronicling America*; the Federal Reserve Bank of St. Louis's Federal Reserve Archival System for Economic Research (fraser.stlouisfed.org); the Digital Library of the Caribbean (dloc.com); the Internet Archive (archive.org); HathiTrust Digital Library (hathitrust.org); and Tom Tryniski and Old Fulton NY Postcards (fultonhistory.org). Financial support came from the College of Social Sciences, University of California, Los Angeles; the College of Arts and Sciences, University at Buffalo, State University of New York; the College of Arts and Science, Vanderbilt University; the Graduate School of Arts and Science and the Center for Latin American and Caribbean Studies, New York University; the Department of History and the Center for Comparative Studies in Race and Ethnicity, Stanford University; and the Center for Latin American Studies, University of Florida, Gainesville. Funding for the index was provided by the Departments of History and African American Studies and the Social Sciences Dean's Faculty Opportunity Fund at UCLA.

Bankers and Empire would not have been possible without access to the private papers of Joseph H. Durrell—and without the generosity and enthusiastic support of the Durrell family. Many thanks to Connie Sheehy and Jim Durrell, Durrell's grandchildren, and his son, Joseph H. Durrell, Jr. Regretfully, both Jim and Joseph, Jr., passed away before I completed the manuscript. While Durrell was very much a product of his times, he was a better man and a better banker than many of the scoundrels of his generation. I only hope that I have been fair to an individual who deeply loved his family and was committed, in his own way, to the Caribbean people. Catherine C. Legrande shared the Royal Bank of Canada's H. H. Hesler's manuscript on banking in Cuba. Mary A. Renda provided detailed critiques at exactly the right time. Phil and Mary Jarvis of Winfield, Kansas, enthusiastically shared information and literature on the history of Cowley County. Timothy Mennel of the University of Chicago Press has been a patient and good-humored advocate while Rachel Kelly, Kelly Finefrock-Creed, and Marian Rogers made a remarkable effort to get this book to bed. Extracts from chapters 3 and 4 of *Bankers and Empire* appeared in different form in my essay "The National City Bank of New York and Haiti, 1909–1922," *Radical History Review* 113 (2013), and are used with acknowledgment to Duke University Press.

Ideas in and iterations of *Bankers and Empire* were floated over the years at a number of conferences and workshops. For invitations, feedback, and criticism many thanks to Vincent Brown, Zoe Brown, N. D. B. Connolly, Sam Ehrman, Glen Ford, Humberto García Muñiz, Kaiama L. Glover, Rebecca Gómez-Betancourt, Josh Guild, Sean Hanretta, Karen Ho, Kelly Baker Josephs, Kari Polyani Levitt, Lisa Lowe, Kris Manjapra, Katherine McKittrick, Stephen Mihm, Bethany Moreton, Susie J. Pak, Melina Pappademos, Ed Perkins, Guy Pierre, Lara Putnam, Inés Roldán de Montaud, Thomas Schwartz, Faith Smith, Nomi Stolzenberg, Christopher Taylor, Christy Thornton, Alejandro Velasco, and Richard White.

The remarkable moment of the American Studies Program at New York University along with the broader academic communities around Washington Square provided a welcoming intellectual home. Thanks to Vivek Bald, Lauren Benton, Kamau Brathwaite, Allysa Burke, J. Michael Dash, Ana Maria Dopico, Lisa Duggan, Ada Ferrer, the late Juan Flores, Michael A. Gómez, Philip Brian Harper, Madala Hilaire, Tanya Huelett, Alondra Nelson, Mary Poovey, Andrew Ross, Ted Sammons, Sukdev Sandhu, Catherine Stimpson, Frances Peace Sullivan, Ngũgĩ wa Thiong'o, Thuy Linh Tu, Adam John Waterman, and George Yudice. Also at NYU, the autonomous Black Marxism Reading Group provided a relentlessly critical space. Thanks especially to

Ifeona Fulani, Forrest Hylton, Carmelo LaRose, Natasha Lightfoot, Seth A. Markle, Njoroge Njoroge, Sobukwe Odinga, Hillina Seife, and Christopher J. Winks.

New friends and colleagues in the Departments of African American Studies and History at UCLA have become immediate sources of support and engagement. My thanks to Steve Aron, Eric Avila, Scot Brown, Sarah Haley, Cheryl Harris, Robert A. Hill, Ghislaine Lydon, David Myers, Melvin Rogers, Peter Stacey, and especially Verna Abe, Tricia Park, Astrud Reed, and Eboni Shaw. During my brief sojourn at the Department of African American Studies at Buffalo I benefited from the hospitality and humor of Keith Griffler, Jim Pappas, Deborah Pierce-Tate, and Lillian Williams. In Nashville, thanks to Tristan Buckner, Bill Caferro, Colin Dayan, Dennis Dickerson, James and Sherry Epstein, Mona Fredericks, Gary Gerstle, Sarah Igo, Peter Lake, Liz Lunbeck, Moses Ochonu, Allison Schacter, Tongia Smith, Sandy Solomon, Ben Tran, Heidi Welch, Edward Wright-Rios, and the experience enhancer, Phillis h. Rambsy. Students and former students, including Rosalee Averin, Destin Jenkins, Javier Muñoz, and Petal Samuel, provided timely interventions. Many thanks to Enrique Salvador Rivera for assistance with the translations.

Early teachers, past mentors, and old friends have left an imprint on the politics and poetics of *Bankers and Empire* in ways they may never know. Thanks to Patrick Andrade, Dara Culhane, Andrea Fatona, Clifton Joseph, Hanif Abdul Karim, R. M. Lacovia, Manjui Leung, Kyo Maclear, Roy Miki, Faybienne Miranda, Melinda Mollineaux, David George Morgan and BBUNO, Rudy and Shirley Murray, Lyndon Philip, Beverly Pitman, Amandeep Singh, Kaoru Carr Suzuki, Rinaldo Walcott, and Victor Wong. Many thanks also to Artspeak Gallery, Third World Alliance, Roots of Resistance, and both the *Gleaner* and *The Bullet is the Word* of the Vancouver Community College's Langara campus. The Maeba-Hawkes clan—Mieko, Kimiko, John, Miki, and Dan Gillis—are always close to my heart and soul. In Los Angeles, the Republic of Bronson has proven a welcome refuge from academia. Many thanks to all of the families on the block but especially those of Danny and Miriam Bravo and of Sarah McNeil and Sonia Camacho. A special mention to Miguel and Maria Bravo. Always up to get down, Otis Noble III, Safiya Umoja Noble, and Nico Noble quickly became family.

Peter Stebbings has been willing to talk since Trimble Hill. David Austin and Aaron Kamugisha have become rare interlocutors of the Caribbean world. Shohana Raven Guy always comes through with the right advice. Alexandra Vasquez understands that the unities are submarine. Celso Thomas

Castilho has been with me in the trenches of football and parenting. Maboula Soumaroho, Keisa Campbell, and Karen Williams remain stalwart sistren.

I've been lucky enough to have had exceptional advisers who have become great friends and colleagues. Walter Johnson understood this project from its very beginning and has been an unflagging supporter. Robin D. G. Kelley's generosity, energy, and profound commitment to the Black Radical Tradition remain a standard to which we all hope to attain. It is always a pleasure to break bread in the brilliant, ethical, and joyful company of Jennifer Morgan and Herman Bennett. Richard J. M. Blackett was always willing to discuss Padmore when I should have been thinking of banking. Cheryl Blackett always kept the door to her home open.

Michael Ramsey Hudson, my one brother, taught me the power of word and sound. Much love. My parents, Newell Hudson, Anna Hudson, and Wayne Chase, have been constant sources of support and sustenance. Ms. Anne Eliza Hudson remains a constant presence. The Pierre and Celestin families, especially Mrs. Lisette Pierre and the late Reverend Delanot Pierre, have welcomed me as one of their own. A massive thank-you to my incredible boys for providing the radical hope inspiring this book. Toussaint Pierre-Vargas makes being a stepdad easy. My old friend Claude Christophe Pierre-Hudson constantly reminds me of the small joys of living.

Finally, Jemima Pierre—my comrade, my co-conspirator, my collaborator—has suffered through the writing of *Bankers and Empire* more than anyone, and more than anyone, she understands and shares the urgency behind its writing. Jemima, I'm grateful for your passion and impatience, for your burning love and righteous anger, for your willingness to raise a family and eagerness to make a world. You are Black star in dark times.

NOTES

1. James Stillman to Elizabeth Pamela Goodrich, December 11, 1908, reprinted in Anna Robeson Burr, *Portrait of a Banker: James Stillman, 1850–1918* (New York: Duffield & Company, 1927), 249; John K. Winkler, *The First Billion: The Stillmans and the National City Bank* (New York: Vanguard Press, 1934), 184; Frank Vanderlip with Boyden Sparkes, *From Farm Boy to Financier* (New York: D. Appleton-Century, 1935), 104.

2. Ezekiel Porter Belden, *New-York: Past, Present, and Future* (New York: G. P. Putnam, 1849), 63; Talbot Hamlin, *Greek Revival Architecture in America* (London: Oxford University Press, 1944), 152–53.

3. The purchase was not uncontroversial. It was alleged Stillman made a deal with Secretary of the Treasury Lyman Gage wherein the bank would take possession of the building, paying the government $3,265,000 while receiving rent from the government until the bank moved in, and avoiding the payment of property taxes. See Harold van B. Cleveland and Thomas F. Huertas, *Citibank: 1812–1870* (Cambridge, MA: Harvard University Press, 1985), 353n1. Lyman Gage defends his role in the transaction in his memoirs: Lyman J. Gage, *Memoirs of Lyman J. Gage* (New York: House of Field, 1937) 129–36.

4. "Rounding Out Fifty Years of Service," *No. 8*, 16.6 (June 1922): 12. The journal *No. 8*'s name references the City Bank's position in the New York Clearing House Association.

5. The preceding descriptions of 55 Wall Street come from "The New Building of the National City Bank," *No. 8*, 3.2 (November 1907): n.p.; "The National City Bank Moves into Its New Building," *No. 8*, 4.4 (December 1908): n.p.; Montgomery Schuyler, "The Old New York Custom House and the New City Bank," *Architectural Record* 24.6 (December 1908): 441–43; "Some Recent Photographs of the Bank," *No. 8*, 8.1 (January 1913): 12–16; *The National City Bank of New York: A Short Sketch of the Bank with a Description of the Building* (New York: The National City Bank of New York, 1914); "'No. 55': Romance of Wall Street," *No. 8*, 16.12 (December 1921): 1–3; and Ada Louise Huxtable, *The Architecture of New York* (Garden City, NY: Anchor Books, 1964), 70.

6. *New York American*, December 24, 1908; "Moving Millions," *No. 8*, 4.5 (January 1909): n.p.

7. Gail Fenske and Deryck Holdsworth, "Corporate Identity and the New York Office Building: 1895–1915," in *The Landscape of Modernity: Essays on New York City, 1900–*

1940, ed. David Ward and Olivier Zunz (New York: Russell Sage Foundation, 1992), 129–59; Lois Severini, *The Architecture of Finance: Early Wall Street* (Ann Arbor, MI: UMI Research Press, 1983).

8. *New York Times*, April 5, 1908.

9. Vanderlip, *From Farm Boy to Financier*, 185.

10. Schuyler, "The Old New York Custom House," 441–43.

11. Lewis Mumford, *Sticks and Stones: A Study of American Architecture and Civilization* (New York: Norton, 1924), 123–51, 133.

12. On the relationship between architecture and finance I have drawn on David S. Landes, *Bankers and Pashas: International Finance and Economic Imperialism in Egypt* (Cambridge, MA: Harvard University Press, 1958), 1–3; John Strauss, "Transparency: The Highest Stage of Bank Architecture," *Wedge* 7/8 (Winter/Spring 1985): 110–17; Hans Magnus Enzensberger, *Zig Zag: The Politics of Culture and Vice Versa* (New York: The New Press, 1997), 147–85; David Harvey, *The Condition of Postmodernity: An Enquiry into the Origins of Cultural Change* (Cambridge, MA: Blackwell, 1989), 66–98; and Llilian Llanes, *1898–1921: La transformación de la Habana a través de la arquitectura* (Havana: Letras Cubanas, 1993).

13. My sense of a racial-historicist narrative within architecture draws from Susan Buck-Morss, *The Dialectics of Seeing: Walter Benjamin and the Arcades Project* (Cambridge, MA: MIT Press, 1991), 26; Albert Boime, *The Art of Exclusion: Representing Blacks in the Nineteenth Century* (London: Thames and Hudson, 1990), 9–10; David Theo Goldberg, *The Racial State* (New York: Wiley, 2002), 26–56.

14. Charles A. Conant, "The Financial Future of the United States," *Proceedings of the Annual Convention of the American Bankers Association* 26 (1900): 142.

15. Oscar P. Austin, *Trading with Our Neighbors in the Caribbean*, Foreign Commerce Series, no. 1 (New York: National City Bank of New York, 1920), 8.

16. See, for instance, Clyde William Phelps, *The Foreign Expansion of American Banks: American Branch Banking Abroad* (New York: The Ronald Press, 1927), 85–104; Jeffrey A. Frieden, *Banking on the World: The Politics of American International Finance* (New York: Harper & Row, 1987), 15–25; Barbara Stallings, *Banker to the Third World: U.S. Portfolio Investment in Latin America, 1900–1986* (Berkeley: University of California Press, 1987), 60–66; Vincent P. Carosso and Richard Sylla, "US Banks in International Finance," in *International Banking, 1870–1914*, ed. Rondo Cameron and Valeri Bovykin (New York: Oxford University Press, 1992), 48–71.

17. For an overview of nineteenth-century US investment banking, see Vincent P. Carosso, "American Private Banks in International Banking and Industrial Finance, 1870–1914," *Business and Economic History*, second series, 14 (1985): 19–26.

18. For a comprehensive overview of the history of dollar diplomacy, see Emily S. Rosenberg, *Financial Missionaries to the World: The Politics and Culture of Dollar Diplomacy, 1900–1930* (Cambridge, MA: Harvard University Press, 1999); Scott Nearing and Joseph Freeman, *Dollar Diplomacy: A Study in American Imperialism* (New York: Viking Press, 1925).

19. See Richard S. Grossman, *Unsettled Account: The Evolution of Banking in the Industrial World since 1800* (Princeton, NJ: Princeton University Press, 2010), 1–16.

20. G. A. Penn et al., *The Law and Practice of International Banking* (London: Sweet & Maxwell, 1987), 1. On sovereignty and law, I am indebted to Siba N'Zatioula Grovogui, *Sovereigns, Quasi Sovereigns, and Africans: Race and Self-Determination in International Law* (Minneapolis: University of Minnesota Press, 1996); and Antony Anghie, *Im-*

perialism, Sovereignty, and the Making of International Law (Cambridge: Cambridge University Press, 2007).

21. On the history of the national banking system, see Bray Hammond, *Sovereignty and an Empty Purse* (Princeton, NJ: Princeton University Press, 1970). On the problems of the dual system, see Richard Dale, *The Regulation of International Banking* (Englewood Cliffs, NJ: Prentice-Hall, 1984), 1–20.

22. E. E. Agger, "The Federal Reserve System," *Political Science Quarterly* 29.2 (June 1914): 265–81; *National Banking under the Federal Reserve System* (New York: The National City Bank of New York, 1921).

23. J. Lawrence Broz, *The International Origins of the Federal Reserve System* (Ithaca, NY: Cornell University Press, 1997), passim.

24. My thinking on legal pluralism is derived from Lauren Benton, *Law and Colonial Cultures: Legal Regimes in World History: 1400–1900* (Cambridge: Cambridge University Press, 2002), 1–79; Boaventura de Sousa Santos, *Toward a New Common Sense* (London: Butterworths, 2002), 89–98; Dieter Martiny, "Traditional Private and Commercial Law Rules under the Pressure of Global Transactions: The Role for an International Order," in *Rules and Networks: The Legal Culture of Global Business Transactions*, ed. Richard P. Appelbaum (Oxford: Hart, 2001), 123–55; and Yvez Dezalay and Bryant G. Garth, *Dealing in Virtue: International Commercial Arbitration and the Construction of a Transnational Legal Order* (Chicago: University of Chicago Press, 1996), 15–17.

25. I have borrowed the notion of "gentlemanly" bankers from P. J. Cain and Anthony G. Hopkins, *British Imperialism: 1688-2000* (New York: Routledge, 2001); and Susie J. Pak, *Gentleman Bankers: The World of J. P. Morgan* (Cambridge, MA: Harvard University Press, 2013).

26. The term "racial capitalism" comes from Cedric Robinson, *Black Marxism: The Making of the Black Radical Tradition* (Chapel Hill: University of North Carolina Press, 2000), 2–3, 9–28. My thinking about the concept also derives from Frantz Fanon, *The Wretched of the Earth*, trans. Constance Farrington (New York: Grove Press, 1963), 35–106; and Butch Lee and Red Rover, *Night-Vision: Illuminating War and Class on the Neo-Colonial Terrain* (New York: Vagabond Press, 1993), passim.

27. Charles Mills, *Blackness Visible: Essays on Philosophy and Race* (Ithaca, NY: Cornell University Press, 1998), 97–118.

28. "Annual Minstrel Show," *No. 8*, 9.4 (April 1914): 27; "The Minstrels as Seen by Bill," *No. 8*, 5.12 (December 1910): 16; "City Bank Club's Annual Minstrel Show Won Unmeasured Approval of 2,000 Who Saw It," *No. 8*, 14.3 (March 1919): 8.

29. "The Minstrel Men," *No. 8*, 7.1 (January 1912): 16; Ann Douglass, *Terrible Honesty: Mongrel Manhattan in the 1920s* (New York: Noonday Press 1995), 75–77.

30. "A Commerce Night: Commerce Minstrels Delight Huge Throng—Big Show a Great Success—Some Sidelights," *Commerce Comments* 4.3 (May 1920): 1, 18; "The Second Annual Dinner of the Guaranty Club," *Guaranty News* 1.2 (February 1913): 15. The minstrel performances of the American Institute of Bank Clerks are noted in various issues of *Bankers' Magazine* between 1902 and 1920.

31. "Annual Theatrical Entertainment," *Guaranty News* 9.11 (January 1921): 362–66; "Guaranty Council No. 107, Twentieth Century Orient, O.M.F: Grand Ceremonial Initiation," *Guaranty News* 4.9 (November 1915): 125–27, 129. Also see "A Night at the Guaranty Club," *Guaranty News* 6.10 (December 1917): 10; "The Second Annual Dinner of the Guaranty Club," *Guaranty News* 1.2 (February 1913): 15.

32. Examples of the City Bank's anti-Semitic and anti-Asian cartoons are found throughout *No. 8*: "Untitled," *No. 8*, 7.12, (December 1912): 26; "Retrospection of the Mas-
querade Ball," *No. 8*, 15.5 (May 1920): 31. For examples of sinophobia, see "A Chinese
Boy's Application for Position in a Shanghai Firm," *The Chase* 5.1 (June–July 1925):
14; "The American Bank in China," *Bulletin of the American Institute of Bank Clerks*
1.21 (April 1, 1902): 15; and "Wall Street Notes: Chinese Exchange—Opened Strong
and Active," *No. 8*, 7.4 (April 1912): 15; and "An American Bank in the Far East," *Bulletin of the American Institute of Bank Clerks* 2.9 (October 1, 1902): 24. For additional
stories, jokes, and anecdotes, see "Tight Money," *No. 8*, 3.2 (November, 1907): n.p.;
"Banking in Jawgy," *No. 8*, 7.12 (December 1912): 25; "Untitled," *No. 8*, 8.1 (January
1913): 18; "Untitled," *No. 8*, 8.3 (March 1913): 29; "Untitled," *No. 8*, 14.3 (March
1919): 38; "Untitled," *No. 8*, 16.11 (November 1921): 23; Jack Nelson, "The Offering," *No. 8*, 18.2 (February 1923): n.p.; "Gloom Chase," *No. 8*, 22.4 (April 1927): 18.
33. "Dark Finance," *The Chase* 8.4 (July 1925): 151.
34. John H. Allen, "An Inside View of Revolutions in Haiti," *Current History* 32 (May
1930): 325–29.
35. John H. Allen, "American Co-Operation Assures a Better Era for Haiti," *The Americas*
6.8 (May 1920): 6, 8.

CHAPTER ONE

1. Samuel Miller Jarvis to General Wager Swayne, August 10, 1898, William Rufus
Shafter Papers, M0072, Dept. of Special Collections, Stanford University Libraries.
2. *Chicago Daily Tribune*, August 31, 1898, 7; *Brooklyn Daily Eagle*, September 15, 1898;
S. M. Jarvis, "Banking Problems in Cuba," *Chicago Banker* 1.3 (March 15, 1899):
291–93.
3. "North American Trust Company," *United States Investor*, August 13, 1898, 1149; *New
York Times*, August 15, 1898.
4. *Chicago Daily Tribune*, August 31, 1898; *Burlington Weekly Free Press*, May 15, 1899.
5. J. Sakai, *Settlers: The Mythology of the White Proletariat* (Chicago: Morningstar, 1989).
6. Conference with Charles M. Lewis, Cuban Representative, Fire Insurance Company,
Hartford, CT, February 10, 1926, Leland Hamilton Jenks Collection on the Cuban
Sugar Industry, 1925–1934, Special Collections, Princeton University.
7. The following biographical information is taken from "Samuel M. Jarvis," *New-York
Tribune*, November 29, 1911; Theodore S. Case, ed., *History of Kansas City, Missouri,
with Illustrations and Biographical Sketches of Some of Its Prominent Men and Pioneers*
(Syracuse, NY: D. Mason 1888), 548; *Leslie's History of the Greater New York* (New York:
Arkell Publishing, 1898), 2: 572–73.
8. S. M. Jarvis, "Valedictory," *Cedar Vale Blade*, December 21, 1877.
9. The biographical information on Conklin is taken from Case, *History of Kansas City*,
464–65; "Roland Ray Conklin," in *New York State's Prominent and Progressive Men: An
Encyclopaedia of Contemporaneous Biography*, comp. Mitchell Charles Harrison (New
York: New York Tribune, 1900), 68–70; Roland Ray Conklin, "Practical College
Spirit," *Alumni Quarterly and Fortnightly Notes*, July 15, 1917, 387–94; "Sagamores of
the Illini, IV: Roland Ray Conklin, '80," *Alumni Quarterly of the University of Illinois* 8.4
(October 1914): 272–75.
10. A. Theodore Brown, *Frontier Community: Kansas City to 1870* (Columbia: University
of Missouri Press, 1963), 197–229.
11. S. Ferdinand Howe, *The Commerce of Kansas City in 1886, with a General Review of Its
Business Progress* (Kansas City, MO: S. Ferdinand Howe, 1886), 51–52.

12. *The Jarvis-Conklin Mortgage Trust Company, Kansas City, MO* (Kansas City: The Jarvis-Conklin Mortgage Trust Company, 1886), New-York Historical Society Museum & Library, New York; *File of Proceedings in the Matter of Jarvis Conklin Mortgage Trust Company, in the High Court of Justice, Companies Winding Up, Petition, No. 00231 of 1894*, National Archives, Kew, UK.

13. The following description is drawn from Testimony of Roland R. Conklin, May 16, 1896, Benjamin M. Fowler, J. G. Zachary, Elizabeth Garnett, and Henry P. Morgan, Complainants, against the Jarvis-Conklin Mortgage Trust Company, Defendant, United States Circuit Court, Southern District of New York, National Archives and Records Administration, New York.

14. Sherry Lamb Schirmer, *A City Divided: The Racial Landscape of Kansas City, 1900–1960* (Columbia: University of Missouri Press, 2002), 15.

15. Larry McFarlane, "British Investment in Midwestern Farm Mortgages and Land, 1875–1900: A Comparison of Iowa and Kansas," *Agricultural History* 48.1 (January 1974): 197; Yorkshire Inv. & American Mortg. Co., Limited, v. Fowler et al. (Circuit Court of Appeals, Second Circuit, January 22, 1897), *Federal Reporter* 78 (1897): 56–62.

16. *A Description of the Location, Works, and Business of the Bear Lake and River Water Works and Irrigation Co.* (Kansas City, 1889), 13–16.

17. "The Methods of Messrs. Jarvis and Conklin," *Investors' Review* 4 (December 1894): 346.

18. Alfred Freyer, *The Great Loan Land* (Manchester: Brook and Crystal, 1887). On such promotional tracts in general, see Robert G. Athearn, *Westward the Briton* (New York: Charles Scribner's Sons, 1953).

19. Roy M. Robbins, *Our Landed Heritage: The Public Domain, 1776–1936* (Princeton, NJ: Princeton University Press, 1942), 217–98.

20. H. Peers Brewer, "Eastern Money and Western Mortgages in the 1870s," *Business History Review* 50.3 (Autumn 1976): 346–80; and Kenneth A. Snowden, "The Evolution of Interregional Mortgage Lending Channels, 1870–1940: The Life Insurance-Mortgage Company Connection," in *Coordination and Information: Historical Perspectives on the Organization of Enterprise*, ed. Naomi R. Lamoureaux and David M. C. Roff (Washington, DC: NBER, 1995), 209–55. For a detailed description of the land mortgage business, see Allan G. Bogue, *Money at Interest: The Farm Mortgage on the Middle Border* (New York: Russell & Russell, 1968); W. Turrentine Jackson, *The Enterprising Scot: Investors in the American West after 1873* (Edinburgh: Edinburgh University Press, 1968); and William Gerald Kerr, *Scottish Capital on the American Credit Frontier* (Austin: Texas State Historical Association, 1976).

21. New York (State) Attorney General's Office, *Report of the Attorney General of the State of New York* (New York: GPO, 1890), 236–41.

22. "Loans of Eastern Money on Western Mortgages," *Friends' Intelligencer and Journal*, March 17, 1888, 171.

23. Samuel M. Jarvis, "Letter from the Jarvis-Conklin Company," *Friends' Intelligencer and Journal*, March 17, 1888, 171–72.

24. See *Atchison Daily Globe*, December 18, 1890; and *Frank Leslie's Illustrated Newspaper*, January 17, 1891, 455.

25. *Dickerman's United States Treasury Counterfeit Detector*, October 1892, 15.

26. "Comes in Shackles," *Chicago Daily Tribune*, December 8, 1892; "Embezzler Kerr Brought Back," *New York Times*, December 6, 1892; "Arrest of the Jarvis-Conklin Embezzler," *Chicago Daily Tribune*, October 20, 1892, 9; "Because He Exposed the Company," *Washington Post*, November 18, 1892, 7.

27. "Embezzlement in a Kansas City Bank," *Brooklyn Daily Eagle*, September 23, 1892; *Dickerman's United States Treasury Counterfeit Detector*, October 1892, 16; *Hudson Register*, September 23, 1892.

28. On the panic, see Charles Albert Collman, *Our Mysterious Panics, 1830–1930* (New York: William Morrow, 1931), 153–79; Douglas Steeples and David O. Whitten, *Democracy in Desperation: The Depression of 1893* (Westport, CT: Greenwood Press, 1998), 27–41; Elmus Wicker, *Banking Panics of the Gilded Age* (Cambridge: Cambridge University Press, 2000), 52–81.

29. "Two Receivers Appointed," *New York Times*, September 29, 1893.

30. "Wants the Receivers Removed," *New York Times*, August 29, 1894; "Gross Mortgage Frauds Alleged," *Chicago Daily Tribune*, August 23, 1894; "A Big Mortgage," *Los Angeles Times*, January 3, 1894; "In and about Wall Street," *New York Times*, May 19, 1894; "Jarvis-Conklin Assets," *Wall Street Journal*, July 19, 1894; "Jarvis-Conklin Paper to Be Sold," *Chicago Daily Tribune*, August 18, 1894.

31. "Jarvis-Conklin Mortgage Trust Bonds," *Investors' Review* 2 (1893): 485. Similarly, see "American Land Mortgage Companies," *The Statist*, January 13, 1894, 49.

32. "The Methods of Messrs. Jarvis and Conklin," *Investors' Review* 4 (1894): 343–46.

33. Ibid.

34. "North American Trust Company," in *Comparative Statements of Trust Companies in the State of New York, Compiled from Annual Reports of the Superintendent of Banks, 1894–1904* (New York: George W. Young, 1905), 27.

35. "Securities Sold at Big Discount," *New York Times*, December 6, 1895.

36. "The Country Prosperous," *New York Times*, November 9, 1897; Julius W. Pratt, "American Business and the Spanish American War," *Hispanic American Historical Review* 12.2 (May 1934): 163–201.

37. *New York Times*, October 6, 1897.

38. See Harold F. Peterson, *Diplomat of the Americas: A Biography of William I. Buchanan* (Albany: State University of New York Press, 1977); John G. Carlisle, "Our Future Policy," *Harper's*, October 1898; John G. Carlisle, *Financial Statesman* (New York: Dodd, Mead, 1931), 495.

39. *New York Times*, January 20, 1898.

40. "Place for Col. Trenholm," *New York Times*, January 20, 1898.

41. *Representative Men of New York*, vol. 3, ed. Jay Henry Mowbrary (New York: New York Press, 1898), 95–96.

42. *New York Times*, July 22, 1898; *New York Times*, July 12, 1898; *New York Times*, October 14, 1898; William Howe Tolman, "Some Volunteer War Relief Associations," *American Monthly Review of Reviews* 19 (February 1899): 192.

43. Franklin Matthews, *The New Born Cuba* (New York: Harper and Brothers, 1899), 200.

44. E. F. Ladd, "Report of Major E. F. Ladd, Treasurer of the Island of Cuba," in *Civil Report of Major General Leonard Wood, Military Governor of Cuba*, vol. 5, *Finance* (Washington, DC: GPO, 1900), 13.

45. United States Adjutant-General's Office, *Correspondence Relating to the War with Spain and Conditions Growing out of the Same: Including the Insurrection in the Philippine Islands and the China Relief Expedition, between the Adjutant-General of the Army and Military Commanders in the United States, Cuba, Porto Rico, China, and the Philippine Islands, from April 15, 1898, to July 30, 1902* (Washington, DC: GPO, 1902), 1: 168.

46. *New York Herald*, July 29, 1898; *Banking Law Journal* 15.15 (January–December 1898): 487; *Lawrence Daily Journal*, August 1, 1898; W. A. Sadd, "Banking in Cuba," *Cuba Review* 10.4 (March 1912): n.p.; Walter A. Donaldson to Major General Wil-

liam R. Shafter, Governor General Cuba, Santiago de Cuba, August 24, 1898, William Rufus Shafter Papers, M0072, Dept. of Special Collections, Stanford University Libraries.

47. "American Colonial Bank in Porto Rico," *Washington Post*, April 29, 1899, 4; "Financial Institutions of Porto Rico," *Bankers' Magazine* 68.1 (January 1904): 28. Humberto García Muñiz discusses the history and activities of both de Ford and Muller, Schalle in *Sugar and Power in the Caribbean: The South Port Rico Sugar Company in Puerto Rico and the Dominican Republic, 1900–1921* (Miami: Ian Randle, 2010), 58–68, 146–48.

48. "Cuban Chamber of Commerce," *New York Times*, November 11, 1898.

49. *Bankers' Magazine* 57.3 (September 1898): 556.

50. "Banking Institutions in Cuba," *Monthly Bulletin of the Bureau of the American Republics* 6 (July–December, 1898): 633; Franklin Matthews, *The New-Born Cuba* (New York: Harper and Brothers, 1899), 198–99.

51. Samuel Miller Jarvis to Abner McKinley, January 9, 1899, The Papers of William McKinley, Library of Congress.

52. "Three Years to Upbuild Cuba," *Chicago Daily Tribune*, March 5, 1899.

53. "Fear to Invest in Cuba," *The World*, March 20, 1899; *The Butte Weekly Miner*, May 11, 1899.

54. Samuel Miller Jarvis to General Wager Swayne, August 10, 1898, William Rufus Shafter Papers, M0072.

55. "North American Trust Company," *United States Investor*, August 13, 1898, 1149.

56. "Hated Tax Collector," *Washington Post*, January 21, 1899. On the history of the Banco Español, see Inés Roldán de Montaud, *La banca de emisión en Cuba, 1856–1898* (Madrid: Banco de España, 2004); and Susan J. Fernandez, *Encumbered Cuba: Capital Markets and Revolt, 1878–1895* (Gainesville: University Press of Florida, 2002), 85–115.

57. Samuel Miller Jarvis to Abner McKinley, January 9, 1899, The Papers of William McKinley, Library of Congress.

58. "Depository of Cuban Revenues," *Washington Post*, May 7, 1899; F. W. Black, "Banking in Cuba," *Bulletin of the American Institute of Bank Clerks*, February 15, 1902, 5–7.

59. *New York Times*, August 14, 1898.

60. Roldán, *La banca de emisión en Cuba*, 184–85.

61. "Denies Charge of Cuban Extortion," *New York Herald*, March 3, 1899.

62. "Payment of the Costs of Exchange to the Fiscal Agents of the Government," in *Decisions of the Comptroller* (Washington, DC: U.S. Comptroller of Treasury, 1899–1900), 431.

63. "Depository of Cuban Revenues," *Washington Post*, May 7, 1899; "Depository of Cuban Funds," *Washington Post*, May 11, 1899.

64. *Weekly Rocky Mountain News*, June 29, 1899.

65. Investigation of Official Conduct of E. G. Rathbone, 59th Congress, 1st Session, Senate, Document no. 510, June 26, 1906, 50, 52, 53. For a succinct account of the Cuban postal affairs, see Russell H. Fitzgibbon, *Cuba and the United States, 1900–1935* (New York: Russell & Russell, 1964), 62–63.

66. Letter from the Secretary of War, in response to Resolution of the Senate of May 22, 1900, Relative to the North American Trust Company, 56th Congress, 1st Session, Senate, Document no. 440.

67. "Three Years to Upbuild Cuba," *Chicago Daily Tribune*, March 5, 1899.

68. *Final Report of the Habana Finance Commission, April 1, 1900, Report of Brig. Gen. William Ludlow, U.S.A., Annual Report of the Secretary of War*, vol. 1, pt. 4 (Washington, DC: GPO, 1900), 38.

69. S. M. Jarvis, "Civil Government Required in Cuba," *Chicago Banker* 2 (1899): 330–32.
70. Ibid.
71. For a general discussion of the context of corporate consolidation during this period, see Naomi Lamoreaux, *The Great Merger Movement in American Business, 1895–1904* (Cambridge: Cambridge University Press, 1985).
72. "A Banking Company with a Capital of Fifty Million," *Chicago Banker* 7.3 (March 1901): 253–55.
73. Incorporating the North American Trust Company for Cuba, Substitute for House Joint Resolution No. 265. 274, *Special Laws of Connecticut*, January 1899, 244–48.
74. "Trust Company Consolidation," *United States Investor*, March 2, 1901, 275.
75. For a survey of the history of the Platt Amendment, see Louis A. Pérez, Jr., *Cuba under the Platt Amendment, 1902–1934* (Pittsburgh: University of Pittsburgh Press, 1986).
76. Rafael Calzadilla, *La cuestión monetaria cubana en sus aspectos económico y político* (New York: S. Figueroa, 1898); Gordon Ireland, "Observations upon the Status of Corporations in Cuba since 1898," *Pennsylvania Law Review* 76.43 (1927): 43–73.
77. República de Cuba, Comisión Temporal Liquidación Bancaria, *Compendio de los trabajos* (Havana: Julio Arroyo, 1928), 13.
78. "National Bank of Cuba's Officers," *New York Times*, July 3, 1901; República de Cuba, "Contrato para la depositaria del gobierno," *Diario de Sesiones del Congreso de la República de Cuba*, Primera Legislatura, vol. 1, no. 49 (December 4, 1902), 533.
79. "Trust Company Consolidation," *United States Investor*, March 2, 1901, 275; "Vaughan in Havana," *Kansas City Journal*, January 4, 1899; *American Lawyer* 8.2 (February 1900), 78.
80. Henry C. Niese, "Trials of Cuban Paying Tellers," *Cuba Bulletin* 6.9 (August 1908): n.p. Also see J. C. Martine, "Cuban Financial Methods," *No. 8*, 2.4 (January 1907): n.p.
81. *Diario de Sesiones del Congreso de la República de Cuba*, Sexta Legislatura, Camara de Representates, vol. 6, no. 31 (January 22, 1905), 2–3.
82. José A. Pulido Ledesma, *Apuntes sobre el antiguo Banco nacional de cuba y su emisión de billetes de 1905* (Havana: Banco Nacional de Cuba, 1980); Jose Antonio Perez Martinez, "¿Billetes emitidos en 1905 por el Banco Nacional de Cuba?," *Revista del Banco Central de Cuba* 3 (2006): 30–32.
83. A. Goicochea to Manuel Rionda, December 11, 1903, Banco Nacional de Cuba and Bank of Cuba in New York, Record Group II, Series 1, Incoming Correspondence, 1896–1917, Braga Brothers Collection, University of Florida, Gainesville.
84. United States, *Cuban Sugar Sales* (Washington, DC: GPO, 1902), 161.
85. *Cuba Review* 8.1 (December 1909): 9. See Roland R. Conklin v. United Construction Company, 151 *New York Supplement* 626.
86. United States Corps of Engineers, Department of Cuba, *Report of Major H. F. Hodges for the Six Months Ending December 31, 1901* (Washington, DC: GPO, 1901).
87. *Printers' Ink* 28.1 (July 5, 1899): 41.
88. Notes of a conference with Dwight W. Morrow, January 26, 1926, Leland Hamilton Jenks Collection on the Cuban Sugar Industry (C0712), 1925–1934, Special Collections, Princeton University.
89. *Engineering News*, December 3, 1896, 195.
90. "Edmund Gustave Vaughan, Kansas City," in *The History of the Bench and Bar of Missouri*, ed. A. J. D. Stewart (Kansas City, MO: Legal Pub., 1898), 639–40.
91. Joseph H. Durrell, "Family History," vol. 1, "1879–1923" (unpublished manuscript), n.p.
92. "Office Building in Havana," *New York Times*, April 5, 1900. On the new headquarters,

see *La Habana y sus grandes edificios modernos: Obra conmemorativa del IV centenario de su fundación* (Havana: Pernas y Figueroa, 1919), 79; and *Cuba y America* 24.10 (1907): 146; Llilian Llanes, *1898–1921: La transformación de la Habana a través de la arquitectura* (Havana: Letras Cubanas, 1993), 45–48.

93. Banco Nacional de Cuba, Comparative Statement of the Deposits of the Banco Nacional de Cuba as at the close of business, June 30, 1902–1916 (Havana: Banco Nacional de Cuba, 1916), Frank. A Vanderlip Papers, Manuscripts and Special Collections, Columbia University Libraries. This document is also available in Joseph H. Durrell, comp., "Personal Files," vol. 1, "1918–1923" (unpublished manuscript), n.p.
94. Conference with Charles M. Lewis, Leland Hamilton Jenks Collection.
95. Alejandro García Álvarez, "Metamorfosis de una institución financiera: El Banco Español de la Isla de Cuba," *Tiempos de América* 2 (1998): 117–35; Ines Roldán de Montaud, "De banco de gobierno a banco comercial: El Banco Español de la isla de Cuba de la colonia a la república," in *Regards croisés: Cuba / Espagne (XIXe-XXe)* (Saint-Denis: Université Paris 8-Vincennes Saint-Denis, 2005), 61–82.
96. Clay Herrick, "Trust Companies," *Bankers' Magazine* 75.6 (December 1907): 817.
97. Duncan McDowall, *Quick to the Frontier: Canada's Royal Bank* (Toronto: McClelland & Stewart, 1993), 176–77. On the longer history of the Royal Bank of Canada in Cuba and the wider Caribbean, see Peter James Hudson, "Imperial Designs: The Royal Bank of Canada in the Caribbean," *Race & Class* 52.1 (July 2010): 33–48.
98. Charles Morris, *Our Island Empire: A Hand-Book of Cuba, Porto Rico, Hawaii, and the Philippine Islands* (Philadelphia: J. B. Lippincott, 1899), 158–59; William J. Clark, *Commercial Cuba: A Book for Business Men* (New York: Charles Scribner's Sons, 1898), 143–44; Enrique Collazo Peréz, "The Royal Bank of Canada: Establecimiento y breve reseña de sus operaciones en Cuba," *Santiago* 64 (1987): 167–75; J. Castell Hopkins, "Historical Sketch of the Royal Bank of Canada, 1869–1911," in *Royal Bank of Canada: Annual Report for 1911* (Montreal: Royal Bank of Canada, 1911), 82–86.
99. Frederico Mejer, "A Havana Old-Timer Recalls the Pioneer Days," *The Royal Bank Magazine*, July/August 1950, 5.
100. See the Royal Bank of Canada advertisements in various issues of *El Economista y Revista Comercial* (Havana) between 1903 and 1907.
101. For an overview of the politics of the second occupation, see Teresita Yglesia Martinez, *Cuba: Primera república, segunda ocupación* (Havana: Editorial de ciencias Sociales, 1976); Allan Reed Millett, *The Politics of Intervention: The Military Occupation of Cuba, 1906–1909* (Columbus: Ohio State University Press, 1968).
102. Martinez, *Cuba*, 330–36.
103. "Nova Scotia Branch Bank in Havana," *Washington Post*, December 20, 1898; Neil C. Quigley, "The Bank of Nova Scotia in the Caribbean, 1889–1940," *Business History Review* 63 (Winter 1989): 809–10; Joseph Schull and J. Douglas Gibson, *The Scotiabank Story: A History of the Bank of Nova Scotia, 1832–1982* (Toronto: Macmillan, 1982), 90; Bank of Nova Scotia, *Bank of Nova Scotia: One Hundredth Anniversary, 1832–1932* (Toronto: Bank of Nova Scotia, 1932). A branch of the Bank of Nova Scotia was also opened in Port of Spain, but it closed within six months when the manager, sent from Edmonton, died of yellow fever. It also moved to Puerto Rico in 1910 and the Dominican Republic in 1920.
104. Francis J. Sherman to William Howard Taft, October 9, 12, and 13, 1906, Fondo Secretaría de la Presidencia, Caja 67, num. 39, Archivo Nacional de Cuba.
105. Herman Harjes to Vivian Smith, April 22, 1908; Herman Harjes to Vivian H. Smith, April 24, 1908; Walter Burns to Harjes, April 28, 1908; Smith to Harjes, July 1,

1910, Vincent P. Carosso Papers, Box 32, Morgan & Co., Cuba, Morgan Library and Museum.

106. Leland Hamilton Jenks, *Our Cuban Colony: A Study in Sugar* (New York: Vanguard Press, 1928), 212.

107. Durrell, "Family History," vol. 1, n.p.

108. Conference with Charles M. Lewis, Leland Hamilton Jenks Collection.

109. Edmund retired from business and returned to New York City; William A. M. Vaughan went first to Sumatra, where he managed rubber plantations, and then returned to the United States, where he settled in Akron and began working with the Sieberling and Goodyear tire groups. *Bankers' Magazine* 86 (1913): 393; *Commercial and Financial Chronicle* 96.2487 (February 22, 1913): 530; *Los Angeles Times*, January 4, 1920; "W. A. M. Vaughan," *Rubber World* 115–16 (1946): 558.

110. Jenks, *Our Cuban Colony*, 212.

111. Conklin v. United Construction & Supply Co. et al. (No. 6814), Supreme Court, Appellate Division, First Department, February 1915, 151 *New York Supplement* 626.

112. Oscar Zanetti and Alejandro Garcia, *Sugar & Railroads: A Cuban History, 1837–1959*, trans. Franklin W. Knight and Mary Todd (Chapel Hill: University of North Carolina Press, 1998), 263–69.

113. *New York Times*, November 7, 1912.

114. S. M. Jarvis to Sir William Van Horne, November 8, 1912; Van Horne to Jarvis, November 21, 1912; vol. 29, file 41, Sir William Van Horne Fonds, Library and Archives of Canada.

115. "Buying an Old Road," *Cuba Review and Bulletin* 10.12 (November 1912): 23; S. M. Jarvis to Sir William Van Horne, November 8, 1912; Van Horne to Jarvis, November 21, 1912, vol. 31 file 6, Sir William Van Horne Fonds, Library and Archives of Canada.

116. "Banking in Santo Domingo," *Dun's Review* 96 (1912): 77; Julio C. Estrella, *La moneda, la banca, y las finanzas en la República Dominicana*, vol. 1, *1492–1947* (Santiago: Universidad Católica Madre y Maestra, 1971), 97.

117. The comprehensive account of the Santo Domingo Improvement Company is Cyrus Veeser, *A World Safe for Capitalism: Dollar Diplomacy and America's Rise to Global Power* (New York: Columbia University Press, 2002). For a succinct characterization of the Dominican debt crisis from the nineteenth century, see Jacob H. Hollander, "The Financial Difficulties of San Domingo," *Annals of the American Academy of Political and Social Science* 30 (July 1907): 93–103.

118. Dominican Republic, Oficina del Controller Receptor General de las Aduanas, *Report, Dominican Customs Receivership under the American-Dominican Convention, 1907 (August 1, 1907 to July 31, 1908)* (Washington, DC: Bureau of Insular Affairs/War Department, 1908), 5–6.

119. "Testimony of Walker W. Vick," in James D. Phelan, *In the Matter of the Investigation of Charges against American Minister to Santo Domingo*, pt. 1 (Washington, DC: GPO, 1915), 98b.

120. Cesar A. Herrera, *Las finanzas de la República Domincana* (Ciudad Trujillo: Impresora Dominicana, 1955), 140–47.

121. Walter B. Palmer, "Frank J. R. Mitchell," *The Scroll of Phi Delta Theta* 36.1 (September 1911): 3–7; F. J. R. Mitchell, "The Legal Effect of the Acquisition of the Philippines Islands: The Right and Power of the United States to Acquire Territory," *American Law Register*, n.s., 39 (April 1900): 85.

122. "Banco Nacional de Santo Domingo: Apertura solemna," *Listín Diario*, February 1, 1912; "Mr. Jarvis en *El Listín*," *Listín Diario*, April 13, 1912.

123. "Banco Nacional de Santo Domingo," *Listín Diario*, February 5, 1912 (reprint and translation of an article from the *Wall Street Journal*, January 30, 1912).

124. "Testimony of Roger L. Farnham," in Phelan, *In the Matter of the Investigation of Charges*, pt. 1, 308–34.

125. The diplomatic correspondence regarding the loan agreement, from which this section is largely derived, is found in "Financial Affairs—Conclusion of a Loan Contract Between the Dominican Republic and the National City Bank of New York, with the Approval of the United States," September 1, 1913, in *Papers Relating to the Foreign Relations of the United States* (Washington, DC: GPO, 1913), 456–67.

126. See Frank J. R. Mitchell, ed., *Opiniones jurídicas sobre el empréstito de $1500000* (Santo Domingo: La Cuna de América, 1913); Frank J. R. Mitchell, *La verdad del empréstito* (Santo Domingo: La Cuna de América, 1913). For a summary of the conflict surrounding the 1913 loan, see Estrella, *La moneda, la banca y las finanzas*, 28–29.

127. "Bryan Defends Minister Sullivan," *New York Times*, December 12, 1913.

128. "Contract between the Dominican Government and Santiago Michelena," in Phelan, *In the Matter of the Investigation of Charges*, pt. 1, 325; Mu-Kien A. Sang, *Ulises Heureaux: Biografía de un dictador* (Santo Domingo: Editora Corripio, C. por A., 1987), 65; "The City Bank in Santo Domingo," *Monthly Economic Letter*, April 1917, 12.

129. Quoted in James D. Phelan, *Santo Domingo Investigation* (Washington: Press of Gibson Brothers, 1916), 9.

130. Phelan, *Santo Domingo Investigation*, 28.

131. "Testimony of F. J. R. Mitchell," in Phelan, *In the Matter of the Investigation of Charges*, pt. 2, 942.

132. Unless otherwised noted, the following paragraph is derived from "Testimony of Jean B. Hestre," in Phelan, *In the Matter of the Investigation of Charges*, pt. 1, 1–42.

133. "Testimony of John L. Mann," in Phelan, *In the Matter of the Investigation of Charges*, pt. 1, 208.

134. James M. Sullivan, quoted in "Testimony of Jean B. Hestre," 6.

135. "Testimony of Walker W. Vick," 176.

136. "Exhibit 9: Statement of Walker W. Vick," in Phelan, *In the Matter of the Investigation of Charges*, pt. 1, 98a–98f.

137. "Testimony of Jean B. Hestre," 12.

138. "Testimony of Walker W. Vick," 133.

139. "Exhibit 89: James A. Sullivan to John Gray, January 31, 1914," in Phelan, *In the Matter of the Investigation of Charges*, pt. 2, 781e.

140. "Exhibit 51: Affidavit of Virgilo Abreu and Arturo Pellarano, June 5, 1914," in Phelan, *In the Matter of the Investigation of Charges*, pt. 1, 546a–e.

141. "Testimony of William E. Pulliman," in Phelan, *In the Matter of the Investigation of Charges*, pt. 1, 277.

142. "Domingo Probe Hits W. J. Bryan," *New York Times*, January 1, 1915.

143. "Testimony of William E. Pulliman," 277.

144. Clyde William Phelps, *The Foreign Expansion of American Banks: American Branch Banking Abroad* (New York: The Ronald Press, 1927), 162.

145. Walter A. Donaldson to Major General William R. Shafter, August 24, 1898, William Rufus Shafter Papers, M0072.

146. "Modern Financial Institutions and Their Equipment," *Bankers' Magazine* 91.2 (Au-

gust 1915): 242; *The Bankers Directory and Collection Guide* (New York: Bradford Rhodes, 1911), n.p.

CHAPTER TWO

1. James Morris Morgan, *Recollections of a Rebel Reefer* (New York: Houghton Mifflin, 1917), 474. On the IBC's original headquarters, see *Citicorp in China: A Colorful, Very Personal History since 1902* (New York: Citicorp/Citibank, 1989), 12; Citigroup, *Citibank: A Century in Asia* (Singapore: Editions Didier Millet, 2002), 34.

2. James Morris Morgan to Howell Morgan, November 26, 1903, James Morris Morgan Papers, #524, Southern Historical Collection, The Wilson Library, University of North Carolina at Chapel Hill.

3. For a history of the revolution in Panama, see Ovidio Diaz Espino, *How Wall Street Created a Nation: J. P. Morgan, Teddy Roosevelt, and the Panama Canal* (New York: Basic Books, 2003).

4. Morgan, *Recollections*, 475.

5. Ibid., 476.

6. Ibid.

7. "Panama Is All Right: Col. James M. Morgan Hopeful of New Republic," *Washington Post*, December 30, 1903, 4.

8. "Holland Writes of . . . ," *Washington Post*, November 3, 1915, 10.

9. *New York Times*, January 2, 1902, 6.

10. *Washington Post*, January 1, 1902.

11. "International Banking Corporation," in *Libro azul de Santo Domingo* (Santo Domingo: Compañia biografica, 1920), Collection Santiago Michelena, Centro de Investigaciónes Históricas, Universidad de Puerto Rico, University de Puerto Rico.

12. On the wider historical context in which the conference occurred and a description of the politics surrounding it, see José Martí, "The Washington Pan-American Congress," in *Inside the Monster: Writings on the United States and American Imperialism*, trans. Elinor Randall et al., ed. Philip S. Foner (New York: Monthly Review Press, 1975), 339–67; Francis Anthony Boyle, *Foundations of World Order: The Legalist Approach to International Relations (1898–1922)* (Durham, NC: Duke University Press, 1999), 103–22; David M. Pletcher, *The Diplomacy of Trade and Investment: American Economic Expansion in the Hemisphere, 1866–1900* (Columbia: University of Missouri Press, 1998), 237–55; Joseph Smith, "The First Conference of American States (1889–1890) and the Early Pan-American Policy of the United States," in *Beyond the Ideal: Pan-Americanism in Inter-American Affairs*, ed. David Sheinin (Westport, CT: Greenwood Press, 2000), 19–32.

13. The following year, Japanese businessman Nee Soko traveled to New York and San Francisco to gain support for the organization of an international banking institution, capitalized at $6 million, with branches in Japan, China, and the United States for Asian-American trade. Nothing appears to have come of his efforts. See "Plans for an International Bank System," *Bankers' Magazine* 44.10 (April 1890): 801.

14. International American Conference, "International American Bank," *Report of the Majority of the Committee on Banking, Reports of Committees and Discussions Thereon, Volume II* (Washington, DC: GPO, 1890), 829–37.

15. On the history of both institutions, see Geoffrey Jones, *British Multinational Banking, 1830-1990* (Oxford: Clarendon Press, 1993), 404–5, 410.

16. "South American Trade and Banking," *The Bankers' Magazine and Statistical Register* 44.11 (May 1890): 817.

17. "An International Bank," *New York Times*, October 16, 1897, 16.

18. "The Pan-American Bank," *New York Times*, June 18, 1898, 5.

19. Gail Bederman, *Manliness & Civilization: A Cultural History of Gender and Race in the United States, 1880–1917* (Chicago: University of Chicago Press, 1995); Emily S. Rosenberg, *Financial Missionaries to the World: The Politics and Culture of Dollar Diplomacy, 1900–1930* (Durham, NC: Duke University Press, 2003).

20. "Goes to Senate," *Chicago Daily Tribune*, June 18, 1898, 9; "The International Bank Bill," *New York Times*, January 26, 1898, 6; "The American International Bank," *Chicago Daily Tribune*, June 19, 1898, 28; "International American Bank," *Washington Post*, March 17, 1898, 4; "The Pan American Bank," *New York Times*, June 17, 1898, 4.

21. "An International Bank," *The Bankers' Magazine and Statistical Register* 59.1 (July 1899): 864.

22. Rafael Reyes, *Second International American Conference, Mexico, 1901–1902: Organization of the Conference, Projects, Reports, Motions, Debates and Resolution* (Mexico City: Typographical Department of Government Printing Office, 1902), 83–102; Theodore Roosevelt and United States, Delegates to the International American Conference, *Second International Conference of American States: Message from the President of the United States, Transmitting a Communication from the Secretary of State Submitting the Report, with Accompanying Papers, of the Delegates of the United States to the Second International Conference of American States, Held at the City of Mexico from October 22, 1901, to January 22, 1902* (Washington, DC: GPO, 1902), 7, 21, 173.

23. "Plan for Mexican Bank," *New York Times*, June 6, 1903, 2. Also see William Schell, Jr., *Integral Outsiders: The American Colony in Mexico City, 1876–1911* (Wilmington, DE: SR Books, 2001), 132. A brief survey of Mexico's banking laws during this period is found in Noel Maurer and Stephen Haber, "Institutional Change and Economic Growth: Banks, Financial Markets, and Mexican Industrialization, 1878–1913," in *The Mexican Economy, 1870–1930: Essays on the Economic History of Institutions, Revolutions, and Growth*, ed. Jeffrey L. Bortz and Stephen Haber (Stanford, CA: Stanford University Press, 2002), 25–26.

24. "Depositors but No Assets," *Chicago Daily Tribune*, March 11, 1905, 6; "Head Aches, Bank Closes," *Chicago Daily Tribune*, March 10, 1905, 4.

25. "William Hill Hunt: President of the International Bank and Trust Company of America," *The Successful American* 6.6 (December 1902): 742–43.

26. On the permissive context of the Díaz regime in Mexico, especially concerning foreign banking and finance, see Schell, *Integral Outsiders*, 90–101.

27. "International Bank Planned," *New York Times*, July 24, 1902, 11; "International Banking Corporation," *The New York Financier*, September 8, 1902, 898–99.

28. "Latin-American Bank Is Formed," *Chicago Daily Tribune*, September 5, 1902, 5; "To Control Mexican Banks," *Washington Post*, September 5, 1902, 4.

29. "The International Bank," *New York Times*, November 1, 1903, F1.

30. "Banks Close Their Doors," *Washington Post*, October 20, 1903, 3; "Mexican Bank Failure," *Los Angeles Times*, October 20, 1903, 2; "Bank to Be Re-organized," *New York Times*, December 15, 1903, 11; "The Pan American Bank," *Wall Street Journal*, January 5, 1904, 7; "Plan to Rehabilitate a Bank," *New York Times*, January 5, 1904, 11.

31. "To Reorganize Bank," *Los Angeles Times*, May 15, 1904, C1.

32. "Creditors Charge Collusion," *Washington Post*, February 16, 1905, 2; "Pan-American Bank Head Sentenced," *New York Times*, September 21, 1905, 2; "Banker Hunt Is Refused Liberty," *Chicago Daily Tribune*, August 3, 1906; "W. H. Hunt Pleads Guilty,"

New York Times, April 13, 1905, 8; "Bail for Banker Hunt," *Washington Post,* January 29, 1905; "Securities on Their Way," *Washington Post,* January 30, 1905, 1.

33. *New York Sun,* August 16, 1913; June 14, 1915.

34. Henry S. Burrage, *Thomas Hamlin Hubbard* (Portland, ME: N.p., 1923); "Thomas Hamlin Hubbard," in *The Historical Register,* ed. Edwin C. Hill (New York: Edward C. Hill, 1919), 193. For a complete list of Hubbard's directorships, see "Hubbard, Thomas H.," in *Directory of Directors in the City of New York* (New York: Audit Co., 1904), 457.

35. R. Carlyle Buley, *The Equitable Life Assurance Society of the United States, 1859–1964* (New York: Appleton-Century-Crofts, 1967), 1: 580–82; New York (State) Legislature, Joint Committee on Investigation of Life Insurance, William W. Armstrong, *Testimony Taken before the Joint Committee of the Senate and Assembly of the State of New York to Investigate and Examine into the Business and Affairs of Life Insurance Companies Doing Business in the State of New York* (Albany: J. B. Lyon, 1906), 2099.

36. See William L. Moyer, "International Banking," *New York Times,* January 1, 1903; William L. Moyer, "How Foreign Commerce Benefits the American Banker," in *Practical Problems in Banking and Currency: Being a Number of Selected Addresses Delivered in Recent Years by Prominent Bankers, Financiers, and Economists,* ed. Walter Henry Hull (New York: Macmillan, 1907), 15–23.

37. "Banks for Newly Acquired Territories," *Chicago Daily Tribune,* August 5, 1898, 7.

38. US Department of the Treasury, Comptroller of the Currency, *Annual Report of the Comptroller of the Currency to the Third Session of the Fifty-Fifth Congress of the United States, December 5, 1898* (Washington, DC: GPO, 1898), 1: XLIV.

39. International Banking Corporation, *Charter and By-Laws* (New York: International Banking Corporation, 1902).

40. See *Evening Telegram,* January 17, 1902; "Hon. John Randolph Dos Passos," *The Lawyer & Banker and Southern Bench & Bar Review* 6.7 (December 1913): 367.

41. "International Banking Corporation," *United States Investor* 15.6 (February 6, 1904): 9; "Banking and Financial News," *Bankers' Magazine* 63 (1902): 483; *Bankers' Magazine* 91.1 (July 1915): 744.

42. William Jay Gilpin and Henry E. Wallace, *Clearing House of New York City: New York Clearing House Association, 1854–1905* (New York: M. King, 1904), 62; "International Bank" and "International Banking Corporation," in *The Trow: Copartnership and Corporation Directory of the Boroughs of Manhattan and the Bronx, City of New York* (New York: The Trow, 1909), 379.

43. Frank H. H. King, "The Boxer Indemnity—'Nothing but Bad,'" *Modern Asian Studies* 40.3 (July 2006): 663–89 (esp. 669).

44. Memorandum regarding the Application of the International Banking Corporation, December 27, 1901, Theodore Roosevelt Papers, Library of Congress; also http://www .theodorerooseveltcenter.org/Research/Digital-Library/Record.aspx?libID=o36360, Theodore Roosevelt Digital Library, Dickinson State University; "Fiscal Agent of US for Chinese Payments," *Brooklyn Eagle,* December 31, 1901; "Government Fiscal Agents," *Brooklyn Eagle,* June 1, 1902, 6.

45. International Banking Corporation, *Charter and By-Laws.* On the American Asiatic Association, see James J. Lorence, "Coordinating Business Interests and the Open Door Policy: The American Asiatic Association, 1898–1904," in *Building the Organizational Society: Essays on Associated Activities in Modern America,* ed. Jerry Israel (New York: The Free Press, 1972), 127–42.

46. Citigroup, *Citibank: A Century in Asia,* 30. A general overview of the IBC's activities in

China can be found in Zhaojin Ji, *A History of Modern Shanghai Banking: The Rise and Decline of China's Finance Capitalism* (Armonk, NY: M. E. Sharpe, 2003), 76–77.

47. "Banks in the Philippines," *Washington Post*, June 11, 1903, 5; "American Dependencies," *Current Literature* 34.5 (May 1903): 520; US Bureau of Insular Affairs, *Report of the Chief of the Bureau of Insular Affairs to the Secretary of War* (Washington, DC: GPO, 1904), 17; US War Department, "Report for 1901," in *Five Years of the War Department following the War with Spain, 1899–1903, as Shown in the Reports of the Secretary of War* (Washington, DC: GPO, 1904), 228; "Manila's First American Bank," *New York Times*, June 15, 1902, 3.

48. Maurice Collis, *Wayfoong: The Hongkong and Shanghai Banking Corporation* (London: Faber and Faber, 1965).

49. Henry C. Ide, "Banking, Currency, and Finance in the Philippine Islands," *Annals of the American Academy of Political and Social Science* 30 (July 1907): 27–37.

50. "American Bank for the Orient," *Chicago Daily Tribune*, December 16, 1901, 1.

51. During this period, the Mutual Company also bought stock in the United States Mortgage Trust Company and other institutions. See Shepard B. Clough, *A Century of American Life Insurance: A History of the Mutual Life Insurance Company of New York, 1843–1943* (New York: Columbia University Press, 1946), 192–94.

52. For a general history of the Guaranty Trust Company, see A. W. Ferrin, "The Great Banks of New York, VII: The Guaranty Trust Company of New York," *Moody's Magazine* 17.8 (August 1914): 401; Guaranty Trust Company, *One Hundred Years of Banking Service, 1839–1939* (New York: Guaranty Trust Company, 1939).

53. Memorandum regarding the Application of the International Banking Corporation, December 27, 1901, Theodore Roosevelt Papers, Library of Congress; also available at http://www.theodorerooseveltcenter.org/Research/Digital-Library/Record.aspx ?libID=o36360, Theodore Roosevelt Digital Library, Dickinson State University; Theodore Roosevelt to Leslie M. Shaw, May 15, 1902, Theodore Roosevelt Papers; also at http://www.theodorerooseveltcenter.org/Research/Digital-Library/Record.aspx ?libID=o182251; Theodore Roosevelt to Philander C. Knox, May 22, 1902, Theodore Roosevelt Papers; also at http://www.theodorerooseveltcenter.org/Research/Digital -Library/Record.aspx?libID=o182301.

54. Morton Keller, *The Life Insurance Enterprise, 1885–1910: A Study in the Limits of Corporate Power* (Cambridge, MA: Harvard University Press, 1963), 149; Clough, *A Century of American Life Insurance*, 192–94.

55. "American Dependencies," *Current Literature* 34.5 (May 1903): 520; Henry W. Lucy, "Far East Bank Move," *New York Times*, February 7, 1904, 4. "Sharp Scramble for Place of Fiscal Agent," *Brooklyn Eagle*, April 22, 1902, 5; "War Department Relieved," *Brooklyn Eagle*, June 10, 1902, 5.

56. "Manila's First American Bank," *New York Times*, June 15, 1902.

57. Robert Taylor Swaine, *The Cravath Firm and Its Predecessors, 1891–1947*, Volume I (New York: The Lawbook Exchange, 2006), 1: 735–36.

58. "Banking in Mexico," *Bankers' Magazine* 77.6 (1908): 521–59. The best analysis of the IBC in Mexico is contained in John Mason Hart, *Empire and Revolution: The Americans in Mexico since the Civil War* (Berkeley: University of California Press, 2002), 91–105. Hart offers one of the few secondary accounts of the IBC, but he overemphasizes both the importance of Mexico to the IBC's operations and the IBC's ties to the City Bank in the years before 1914.

59. "The Banks of Mexico City," *Bankers' Magazine* 77.4 (October 1908): 558–59.

60. *Bankers' Magazine* 52 (January–June 1921): 293–94; "Personality in Banking," *The*

Financier, January 1, 1919, 113; "The Chemical Gets a Strong Man from the Coast," *Banking Law Journal* 35 (January–December 1918): 906–7.

61. "Testimony of W. Bundy Cole," in US Senate, Committee on Foreign Relations, *Convention between the United States and Nicaragua* (Washington, DC: GPO, 1914), 493.

62. "Seven Years of Successful Banking," *Bankers' Magazine* 79 (1909): 608; "The Banks of Mexico City," *Bankers' Magazine* 77.4 (October 1908): 558–59.

63. The first US financial institution in Panama was Wells Fargo, which had set up an agency on the isthmus in 1853 for US prospectors transiting to California. Wells Fargo abandoned Panama in 1868. See Juan Antonio Susto Lara and Jorge Conte Porras, *Evolución histórica del Banco Nacional de Panamá* (Panama City: Banco Nacional de Panamá, 1973), 18.

64. Joseph Bucklin Bishop to Theodore Roosevelt, January 21, 1904, Theodore Roosevelt Papers, Library of Congress; also at http://www.theodorerooseveltcenter.org/Research/Digital-Library/Record.aspx?libID=o43800, Theodore Roosevelt Digital Library, Dickinson State University; Theodore Roosevelt to Joseph Bucklin Bishop, January 20, 1904, Theodore Roosevelt Collection, bMS Am 1514 (67), Harvard College Library; also at http://www.theodorerooseveltcenter.org/Research/Digital-Library/Record.aspx?libID=o281256.

65. Theodore Roosevelt to Joseph Bucklin Bishop, January 17, 1904, Theodore Roosevelt Collection, bMS Am 1514 (65), Harvard College Library; also at http://www.theodorerooseveltcenter.org/Research/Digital-Library/Record.aspx?libID=o281242.

66. As a means of stabilizing the value of Panamanian silver pesos against the American dollar, the War Department maintained a $250,000 deposit in the vaults of the Bankers Trust Company in New York. This was stipulated by the United States' 1905 monetary agreement with Panama; the deposit equaled 15 percent of the total Panamanian currency emitted and was used as a means of guaranteeing the parity of the Panamanian silver coins with gold. See William H. Taft, "Paridad de la moneda Panameña," *La Estrella de Panamá,* June 10, 1905, 1.

67. "Statement of Hon. William H. Taft, Secretary of War," in *Monetary Agreements with Panama, Hearings before the Finance Committee of the United States Senate on the Monetary Agreements between the Secretary of War and the Government of Panama* (Washington, DC: GPO, 1906), 10–11.

68. *Panama Star and Herald,* February 19, 1907.

69. Susto and Porras, *Evolución histórica del Banco Nacional de Panamá,* 17.

70. *Investigation of Panama Canal Matters, Hearings before the Committee on Interoceanic Canals of the United States Senate in the Matter of the Senate Resolution adopted January 9, 1906, Providing for an Investigation of Matters Relating to the Panama Canal* (Washington, DC: GPO, 1907), 1: 202.

71. "Oldest Zone Bank Plays Vital Part in Canal Operation Employees' Lives," *Panama Canal Review* 6.9 (April 6, 1956): 8–9.

72. Velma Newton, *The Silver Men: West Indian Labour Migration to Panama, 1850–1914* (Mona, Jamaica: Sir Arthur Lewis Institute of Social and Economic Studies, 1984), 122–23; Bonham C. Richardson, *Panama Money in Barbados, 1900–1920* (Knoxville: University of Tennessee Press, 1985), 155–56.

73. Newton, *The Silver Men,* 104–5.

74. Olive Senior, *Dying to Better Themselves: West Indians and the Building of the Panama Canal* (Kingston: University of the West Indies Press, 2014), 323–24.

75. Joseph H. Durrell to Charles E. Mitchell, March 12, 1928, Joseph H. Durrell, comp., "Personal Files," vol. 2, "1924–1935" (unpublished manuscript), n.p.

76. "The International Banking Corporation," *Asia: Journal of the American Asiatic Society* 2.1 (February 1903): 25.

77. Discussion of Fearon's letter is derived from J. S. Fearon to shareholders, December 19, 1907, Van Horne, Business Correspondence, 1902–1903, Sir William Van Horne Fonds, Library and Archives Canada. For a description of banking in China from the perspective of the IBC, see Orin de Motte Walker, "Banking and Investment Opportunities in the Far East," *The Magazine of Wall Street* 22.11 (August 31, 1918): 795–98.

78. Tait's assessment of the situation in China is found in J. Selwyn Tait, "American Possibilities in the Far East," *Asia: Journal of the American Asiatic Association* 10.1 (February 1910): 22–23.

79. Charles Vevier, *The United States and China, 1906–1913: A Study of Finance and Diplomacy* (New Brunswick, NJ: Rutgers University Press, 1955), 88–111.

80. James Morris Morgan to Howell Morgan, December 29, 1903, James Morris Morgan Papers, #524, Southern Historical Collection, The Wilson Library, University of North Carolina at Chapel Hill.

81. "Business in Panama," *Washington Post*, March 31, 1905, 11.

82. On the "limping standard," see Charles A. Conant, *The Future of the Limping Standard* (Boston: Ginn & Co., 1903). On US perceptions of the monetary system of Panama, see *Report on the Introduction of the Gold-Exchange Standard into China, the Philippine Islands, Panama, and Other Silver-Using Countries and on the Stability of Exchange* (Washington, DC: GPO, 1904), 22–26, 313–33.

83. On the history of this creole elite, see Omar Jaén Suárez, "Burguesía criolla y mercaderes extranjeros (1850–1910)," in *Población, economía y sociedad en Panamá: Contribución a la crítica de la historiografía panameña*, ed. José Eulogio Torres Ábrego (Panamá: Editorial Universitaria Carlos Manuel Gasteazoro, 2001), 244–50; Peter A. Szok, *"La última gaviota": Liberalism and Nostalgia in Early Twentieth-Century Panama* (Westport, CT: Greenwood Press, 2001); Aims McGuinness, "Sovereignty on the Isthmus: Federalism, U.S. Empire, and the Struggle for Panama during the California Gold Rush," in *The State of Sovereignty: Territories, Laws, Populations*, ed. Douglas Howland and Luise White (Bloomington: Indiana University Press, 2009), 19–34.

84. "Panama Banking Company," in *The Republic of Panama: Its Economic, Financial, Commercial, and National Resources, and General Information*, ed. Sabas A. Villegas (Panamá: Imprenta Nacional, 1917), 187.

85. Morgan, *Recollections*, 476.

86. George S. Moore, *The Banker's Life* (New York: Norton, 1987), 176.

87. "J. Selwyn Tait," *The Engineering Magazine: An Industrial Review*, March 1896, 5.

88. Citigroup, *Citibank*, 34–37.

89. *Citicorp in China*, 14–16; Citigroup, *Citibank*, 31–39.

90. George W. Cullum, *Biographical Register of the Officers and Graduates of the U.S. Military Academy at West Point, N.Y.* (New York: Houghton, Mifflin and Company, 1891), 489.

91. James Morris Morgan to Howell Morgan, November 26, 1903, James Morris Morgan Papers.

92. "A Rolling Stone," *Eugenical News* 2.7 (July 1917): 50.

93. Morgan, *Recollections*, 2–3.

94. Ibid., 92–112, 325 ("English bulldog"), 326–30.

95. John E. Gardin to Frank A. Vanderlip, January 22, 1909, Frank A. Vanderlip Papers, Manuscripts and Special Collections, Columbia University Libraries.

96. Vanderlip to Stillman, February 18, 1909, Vanderlip Papers.

97. "The Commercial Conditions of Mexico," *Bulletin of the National Association of Credit Men* 14.11 (November 16, 1914): 931.

98. Yoshiko Nagano, *State and Finance in the Philippines, 1898–1941: The Management of an American Colony* (Singapore: NUS Press, 2015).

99. Geoffrey Jones, *British Multinational Banking, 1830–1990* (Oxford: Clarendon Press, 1993), 396.

100. *Washington Post*, November 13, 1918; Clyde William Phelps, *The Foreign Expansion of American Banks: American Branch Banking Abroad* (New York: The Ronald Press, 1927), 149.

101. "Chase National Bank of the City of New York," *Panama Star and Herald*, July 3, 1925; "American Foreign Banking Corporation," *Panama Star and Herald*, January 13, 1925.

102. "The Chase Bank on the Isthmus of Panama," *The Chase* 12.2 (May 1929): 70–79.

103. *New York Times*, April 23, 1928.

104. "What Shall We Do with the International Banking Corporation?," May 23, 1916, Frank A. Vanderlip Papers.

CHAPTER THREE

1. Descriptions of the Banque Nationale are drawn from W. H. Williams, "The Banque Nationale de la République d'Haïti," *No. 8*, 8.2 (1913): 9–10; "Banque Nationale de la République d'Haiti," in *The Blue Book of Haiti* (New York: Klebold Press, 1920), 98–99; Banque Nationale de la République D'Haiti, *Rapport de M. le Docteur Jacques Bergeaud, Commissaire nommé par la premier assemblée général constitutive du 30 Janvier 1911* (Paris: Imprimerie Chaix, 1911), 5. The comprehensive history of the Banque Nationale is Joseph Châtelain, *La banque nationale: Son histoire—ses problèmes* (Lausanne, France: Imprimerie Held, 1954).

2. Williams, "The Banque Nationale," 9.

3. Hesketh Prichard, *Where Black Rules White: A Journey across Hayti* (New York: Charles Scribner's Sons, 1900) 306–8. My thinking on the spatial character of banking practice is influenced by Walter Rodney, *How Europe Underdeveloped Africa* (Washington, DC: Howard University Press, 1974), 162–63.

4. Perceval Thoby, *Nos crises économiques et financières: Nos contrats de banque, nos émissions de monnaies, nos emprunts et la réforme monétaire, 1880 à 1888* (Port-au-Prince: published by the author, 1955), 16.

5. On the City Bank's history of diversification, decentralization, and deregulation, I have drawn from Harold Van B. Cleveland and Thomas F. Huertas, *Citibank, 1812–1970* (Cambridge, MA: Harvard University Press, 1985), 54–112; Alfred Chandler, "Development, Diversification, and Decentralization," in *The Essential Alfred Chandler: Essays Toward a Historical Theory of Big Business*, ed. Thomas K. Mcraw (Boston: Harvard Business School Press, 1988), 74–116; Alfred D. Chandler, *Scale and Scope: The Dynamics of Industrial Capitalism* (Cambridge, MA: Harvard University Press, 1990), 188–93.

6. The Banque Nationale de la République d'Haiti is mentioned only in passing in the bank's corporate histories. See Cleveland and Huertas, *Citibank*, 125; Citigroup, Inc., *Celebrating the Past, Defining the Future* (New York: Citigroup, 2011), 67.

7. C. L. R. James, *The Black Jacobins: Toussaint L'Ouverture and the San Domingo Revolution* (New York: Vintage, 1989), 394.

8. This chapter builds on a rich historiography of the US occupation that has drawn out the question of race and racism in US imperialism, though without necessarily considering racial capitalism or focusing on the history of the City Bank and the BNRH.

See, for instance, Hans Schmidt, *The United States Occupation of Haiti, 1915–1934* (New Brunswick, NJ: Rutgers University Press, 1971); Kethly Millet, *Les paysans haïtiens et l'occupation américaine d'Haïti, 1915–1930* (La Salle, Québec: Collectif Paroles, 1978); J. Michael Dash, *Literature and Ideology in Haiti, 1915–61* (Totowa, NJ: Barnes & Nobles Books, 1981); Suzy Castor, *L'occupation américaine d'Haiti* (Port-au-Prince: Société haïtienne d'histoire, 1988); Brenda Gayle Plummer, *Haiti and the Great Powers* (Baton Rouge: Louisiana State University Press, 1988); François Blancpain, *Haïti et les États-Unis, 1915–1934: Histoire d'une occupation* (Paris, L'Harmattan, 1999); Mary A. Renda, *Taking Haiti: Military Occupation and the Culture of U.S. Imperialism, 1915–1940* (Chapel Hill: University of North Carolina Press, 2001).

9. On the early history of the City Bank, see Cleveland and Heurtas, *Citibank*, 16–31.

10. On Taylor, see Roland T. Ely, *Cuando reinaba su majestad el azúcar* (Buenos Aires: Editorial Sudamericana, 1963), 119–55; Daniel Hodas, *The Business Career of Moses Taylor: Merchant, Finance Capitalist, and Industrialist* (New York: New York University Press, 1976), 22–23; John Moody and George Kibbe Turner, "Masters of Capital in America," *McClure's Magazine* 37.1 (1911): 74.

11. On Stillman père and fils, see Chauncey Devereux Stillman, *Charles Stillman, 1810–1875* (New York: Chauncey Devereux Stillman, 1956), esp. 26–27; John K. Winkler, *The First Billion: The Stillmans and the City Bank* (New York: Vanguard Press, 1934), 14–56; Anna Robeson Burr, *The Portrait of a Banker: James Stillman, 1850–1918* (New York: Duffield and Company, 1937); John Mason Hart, *Revolutionary Mexico: The Coming and Process of the Mexican Revolution* (Berkeley: University of California Press, 1989), 109–14; John Mason Hart, *Empire and Revolution: The Americans in Mexico since the Civil War* (Berkeley: University of California Press, 2002), 22–26.

12. On the development of correspondent banking, see Fritz Redlich, *The Molding of American Banking: Men and Ideas* (New York: Johnson Reprint Company, 1968), 16, 53; Cleveland and Heurtas, *Citibank*, 44.

13. Cleveland and Heurtas, *Citibank*, 34.

14. Stillman's vision is described in "Holland Writes of Our Trade with South American Nations," *Washington Post*, July 23, 1912.

15. John K. Winkler, *The First Billion: The Stillmans and the National City Bank* (New York: Vanguard Press, 1934), 272.

16. "Retrospect: From Foreign Parts," *No. 8*, 3.4 (January 1908): n.p.; "The Bond Market," *Wall Street Journal*, June 14, 1909, 5. On Morgan's Latin American loans, see Vincent P. Carosso, *The Morgans: Private International Bankers, 1854–1913* (Cambridge, MA: Harvard University Press, 1987), 209–11, 413–20.

17. Frank A. Vanderlip with Boyden Sparkes, *From Farm Boy to Financier* (New York: D. Appleton-Century, 1935).

18. Vanderlip also wrote a popular article on the Philippines that was among the first introductions to the country. He did his research for the essay at the Library of Congress, but finding little material there, relied on his imagination. Frank A. Vanderlip, "Facts about the Philippines with a Discussion of Pending Problems," *Century Illustrated Magazine* 56.4 (August 1898): 555–63.

19. Cleveland and Heurtas, *Citibank*, 46.

20. Vanderlip to Stillman, August 5, 1904, Frank A. Vanderlip Papers, Manuscripts and Special Collections, Columbia University Libraries.

21. Vanderlip, *From Farm Boy to Financier*, 158.

22. See United States Panama 2% Bonds, 1918–38, December 4, 1908, J. P. Morgan and Co. Syndicate Book, vol. 5, 83–88, Morgan Library and Museum.

23. Vanderlip, *From Farm Boy to Financier*, 228–31.
24. "People Met in Hotel Lobbies," *Washington Post*, October 20, 1902; and "Unwritten History," *Los Angeles Times*, August 16, 1904; "Roger L. Farnham, Vice-President," *No. 8*, 12.8 (1917): 18.
25. International American Conference, *Excursion Appendix, Narrative of the Tour of the Delegates through the United States; Together with Descriptions of Places Visited, and Reports of Addresses Delivered, Report of Committees and Discussions Thereon*, Volume III (Washington, DC: GPO, 1890), 9; Charles A. O'Rourke, *Congreso internacional americano* (New York: New York City Press Association, 1890), 17.
26. *The Paterson Sunday*, July 31, 1892.
27. "Testimony of William Nelson Cromwell, February 27 1906," in *Investigation of Panama Canal Matters, Testimony of Engineers before the Committee on Interoceanic Canals of the United States Senate* (Washington, DC: GPO, 1906), 1085.
28. Raymond Miller, *Kilowatts at Work: The Story of the Detroit Edison Company* (Detroit: Wayne State University Press, 1957), 112.
29. See Sullivan & Cromwell, comp., *Compilation of Executive Documents and Diplomatic Correspondence Relative to a Trans-isthmian Canal in Central America* (New York: The Evening Post Job Printing House, 1905); for Farnham's account of his work on Panama for Cromwell, see "Unwritten History," *Los Angeles Times*, August 16, 1904.
30. Statement of Roger L. Farnham to S. M. Williams, March 1, 1910, in Branch Office of *The World*, No. 25 Broad Street, New York, E. H. Harding Papers, Box 1, Folder 33, Special Collections Division, Georgetown University Library.
31. *Statement of Hon. William H. Taft, Secretary of War before the Committee on Interoceanic Canals of the United States Senate* (Washington, DC: GPO, 1906), 27–29; "Report of R. L. Farnham Concerning Purchase of Ships for Panama Railroad Company, and Papers Relating Thereto," in *Investigation of Panama Canal Matters*, 347–66; and "New Panama Board Is Named," *Chicago Daily Tribune*, April 18, 1905.
32. Vanderlip to Stillman, February 24, 1912, Frank A. Vanderlip Papers.
33. Vanderlip to Stillman, July 1, 1904; Vanderlip to Stillman, March 27, 1906, Frank A. Vanderlip Papers; "Standard Oil Interest after Bank in Panama," *New York Times*, May 18, 1904.
34. Vanderlip to Milton Ailes, March 1, 1905, Frank A. Vanderlip Papers.
35. Vanderlip to Stillman, June 16, 1905, Frank A. Vanderlip Papers.
36. It is unclear what the business in the Dominican Republic was. However, Sir Alexander Baird, a Scottish capitalist who had developed the Samana Railroad, had apparently approached the bank with the possibilities of raising funds. But the bank, according to Roger Farnham, did not seriously consider the proposition, given the instability there. Farnham stated that he examined the Samana properties in 1911. "Testimony of Mr. Roger L. Farnham," in *Inquiry into Occupation and Administration of Haiti and Santo Domingo* (Washington, DC: United States Senate, 1922), 314.
37. Vanderlip to Stillman, February 22, 1909, Frank A. Vanderlip Papers.
38. On Jacobs, see *New York Times*, November 25, 1900; *New York Times*, February 22, 1909.
39. Vanderlip to Stillman, April 8, 1909, Frank A. Vanderlip Papers.
40. "Compagnie des Chemins de Fer de la Plaine du Cul-de-S," in *Annuaire de legislation haïtienne* (Port-au-Prince: Verrollot, 1905), 51–64.
41. Vanderlip to Stillman, April 8, 1909, Frank A. Vanderlip Papers.
42. Vanderlip to Stillman, February 22, 1909, Frank A. Vanderlip Papers.
43. Vanderlip to Stillman, April 8, 1909, Frank A. Vanderlip Papers.

44. Rayford W. Logan, *The Diplomatic Relations of the United States with Haiti, 1776–1891* (Chapel Hill: University of North Carolina Press, 1941), 112–236.

45. H. Pauléus Sannon, Sténio Vincent, and Perceval Thoby, "Memoir on the Political, Economic, and Financial Conditions Existing in the Republic of Haiti under the American Occupation by the Delegates to the United States of the Union Patriotique d'Haïti," in *Inquiry into Occupation and Administration of Haiti and Santo Domingo*, 21; J. N. Léger, *Haiti: Her History and Her Detractors* (1907; repr., Westport, CT: Negro Universities Press, 1970), 184.

46. Châtelain, *La banque nationale*, 26.

47. Léger, *Haiti*, 230–32; Perceval Thoby, *Nos crises économiques et financières*, 36–38. For one Haitian official's defense, see Emanuel Monsanto Caspar, *Ma défense devant le public impartial et la chambre des députés de la république d'Haïti* (Curaçao, 1879).

48. Banque Nationale d'Haiti, *Projet de statuts de la Banque nationale d'Haiti* (Paris: V. Ethiou-Perou, 1880); Banque Nationale d'Haiti, *Réglement pour le service de la trésorie* (Paris: V. Ethiou-Perou, 1882).

49. Frédéric Marcelin, *La banque nationale d'Haïti: Une page d'histoire* (1890; repr., Port-au-Prince: Les Editions Fardin, 1985); Charles A. Conant, *A History of Modern Banks of Issue with an Account of the Economic Crises of the Nineteenth Century and the Crisis of 1907* (New York: G. P. Putnam's Sons, 1909), 529–30.

50. Frédéric Marcelin, *Finances d'Haïti: Emprunt nouveau, même banque* (Paris: Impr. Kugelmann, 1911), 88.

51. Letters to the Editor, *The Times* (London), November 8, 1887, 7; "The Treatment of British Subjects in Hayti," *The Times* (London), September 17, 1887, 6; "The Grievous Wrong Suffered by Mr. Coles," *The Times* (London), November 4, 1887, 9.

52. Marie Jean Joseph de la Myre Mory, *L'affaire de la consolidation: Documents et pièces judiciaires* (Port-au-Prince: J. Verrollot, 1906); Haiti, *L'affaire de la consolidation: Pourvoi en cassation des accusés* (Port-au-Prince: F. Smith, 1904).

53. Banque Nationale d'Haiti, *Assemblée générale des actionnaires du 25 Mai 1908* (Paris: Imprimerie et Librairie Centrales des chemins de Fer, 1908), 1–6; Banque Nationale d'Haiti, *Assemblée générale des actionnaires du June 7, 1909* (Paris: Imprimerie et Librairie Centrales des chemins de Fer, 1909), 1–4.

54. Banque Nationale d'Haiti, *Assemblée générale des actionnaires du June 6, 1910* (Paris: Imprimerie et Librairie Centrales des chemins de Fer, 1910), 1–4.

55. Schmidt, *The United States Occupation of Haiti*, 38–39.

56. Haitian historian Leslie Manigat shows that as early as 1905 the US minister to Port-au-Prince had suggested the desirability of organizing a US bank to displace the European presence in Haiti. Leslie Manigat, "La substitution de la prépondérance américaine à la preponderance française en Haïti au début du XXème siècle," *Revue d'Histoire Moderne et Contemporaine* 14 (October–December 1967): 341.

57. Memorandum on Loan Contract between Haitian Government and Banque de l'Union Parisienne (translation), October 17, 1912, US Department of State, Records of the Department of State Referring to the Internal Affairs of Haiti, Record Group 59, National Archives and Records Administration (hereafter RG 59, NARA); *Banque Nationale de la République d'Haiti, Status* (Paris: Imprimerie et Libraire centrales des chemins de fer, 1911); Memorandum of Maurice Casenave, December 30, 1915, US Department of State, Records of the Department of State Referring to the Internal Affairs of Haiti, RG 59, NARA.

58. See *Assemblée générale extraordinaire des actionnaires du 6 Janvier, 1911* (Paris: Imprimrie Librairie Centrales des chemins de Fer, 1911), 1–6; Banque Nationale d'Haiti, *As-*

semblée générale des actionnaires de la Banque Nationale d'Haiti du 8 Mai 1911 (Paris: Imprimerie et Librairie Centrales des chemins de Fer, 1911), 1–10.

59. Schmidt, *The United States Occupation of Haiti*, 38–39, 40; "Testimony of Mr. Roger L. Farnham," 105–6. For details of the new contract, see *Lois et contrats relatifs a la résiliation du contrat de la Banque nationale d'Haïti a l'établissement de la Banque nationale de la République d'Haïti et a l'emprunt exterieur 5% or 1910* (Port-au-Prince: Imprimerie Nationale, 1910); Marcelin, *Finances d'Haïti*, 17–24.

60. Hubert Bonin, *La Banque de l'union parisienne (1874/1904–1974): Histoire de la deuxième grande banque d'affaires française* (Paris: Éd. Plage, 2001), 47.

61. Mira Wilkins, *The History of Foreign Investment in the United States to 1914* (Cambridge, MA: Harvard University Press, 1989), 868–69n216.

62. "Bankers' Trust Co.," *Bradstreets*, November 18, 1899, 736; *Commercial and Financial Chronicle* 89.1 (August 7, 1909): 326; *The Bankers Directory and Collection Guide* (New York: Bradford Rhodes, 1900), 262; "John H. Allen, 86, A Former Banker," *New York Times*, January 21, 1958; "Armour Man in City Bank," *New York Times*, September 29 1909, 16; *Banque Nationale de la République d'Haiti: Renseignements financiers, statistiques et économiques sur la République d'Haiti, 31 Decembre 1912* (Paris: E. Cassegrain, 1913).

63. Roger L. Farnham to William Jennings Bryan, January 22, 1914, US Department of State, Records of the Department of State Referring to the Internal Affairs of Haiti, RG 59, NARA.

64. *Banque Nationale de la Republique d'Haiti: Renseignements financiers,* 63–64.

65. Farnham to Bryan, January 22, 1914, RG 59, NARA.

66. In Ecuador, his company had imported 6,000 Jamaican laborers; tensions soon emerged between the Jamaicans and the American foreman. Laborers were shot and killed while the Jamaicans took up arms against the company. *New York Times*, December 25, 1900.

67. Paul H. Douglas, "The National Railway of Haiti: A Study in Tropical Finance," *The Nation*, January 19, 1927, 59–60; *Report Covering Haiti Prepared in the Division of Latin American Affairs*, January 1, 1930, Harvard University Library; *Trow New York Copartnership and Corporation Directory, Boroughs of Manhattan and Bronx* (New York: Trow, 1919), 194.

68. See Haiti Company, Frank A. Vanderlip Papers.

69. Farnham to Bryan, January 22, 1914, RG 59, NARA.

70. Memorandum on Loan Contract between Haitian Government and Banque de l'Union Parisienne (translation), October 17, 1912, RG 59, NARA.

71. Extract from *Le Moniteur*, October 12, 1912, RG 59, NARA.

72. H. Desrue to Secretary of State, October 14, 1912; Allen to Secretary of State, October 4, 1912, RG 59, NARA.

73. Lespinasse to Director of Banque, September 30, 1912, RG 59, NARA.

74. Furniss to Secretary of State, October 15, 1912; Hallgarten et al. to Secretary of State, November 25, 1912, RG 59, NARA.

75. Memorandum on Loan Contract between Haitian Government and Banque de l'Union Parisienne (translation), October 17, 1912, RG 59, NARA.

76. Furniss to Secretary of State, October 15, 1912, RG 59, NARA.

77. Ibid.

78. Memorandum, Office of the Solicitor, Department of State, December 17, 1912, RG 59, NARA.

79. Hallgarten et al. to Secretary of State, November 25, 1912, RG 59, NARA.

80. Furniss to Secretary of State, November 15, 1912, RG 59, NARA.

81. See extract from *Le Matin*, February 14, 1913, RG 59, NARA.
82. Furniss to Secretary of State, February 25, 1913, RG 59, NARA.
83. Ibid.
84. Samuel McRoberts to Milton Ailes, March 7, 1913, RG 59, NARA.
85. Furniss to Secretary of State, May 5, 1913, May 28, 1913; Farnham to Secretary of State, February 2, 1914; Allen to Farnham, February 5, 1914, RG 59, NARA.
86. C. C. Woolard to R. L. Farnham, January 20, 1914, enclosed in Farnham to Secreatry of State, January 20, 1914, RG 59, NARA.
87. Smith to Secretary of State, January 21, 1914; Livingston to Secretary of State, January 23, 1914; Bryan to Consul, Cap-Haïtien, Livingston, January 25, 1914; Smith to Secretary of State, January 23, 1914; Roger L. Farnham to Secretary of State, January 24, 1914; Smith to Secretary of State, January 24, 1914; Bostwick, *USS Nashville*, Cap-Haïtien, Haiti, to Secretary of Navy, January 25, 1914; Smith to Secretary of State, January 25, 1914; copy of radiograph Bostick, *USS Nashville*, January 14, 1914, RG 59, NARA.
88. Smith to Secretary of State, January 31, 1914, February 4, 1914, RG 59, NARA.
89. Smith to Secretary of State, February 2, 1914; Farnham to Secretary of State, February 2, 1914; Farnham to Secretary of State, February 2, 1914, RG 59, NARA.
90. Smith to Secretary of State, February 2, 1914, RG 59, NARA.
91. Smith to Secretary of State, February 20, 1914, RG 59, NARA.
92. Allen to Wehrhane, March 4, 1914, RG 59, NARA.
93. Farnham to Bryan, January 22, 1914, RG 59, NARA.
94. Ibid. See also Allen to Farnham, March 21, 1914, RG 59, NARA.
95. Farnham to Bryan, January 22, 1914, RG 59, NARA.
96. Stabler to Bryan, February 3, 1914, RG 59, NARA.
97. Vanderlip to G. E. Gregory, March 5, 1914, Frank A. Vanderlip Papers.
98. Farnham to Boas Long, April 8, 1914; Bryan to American Consul, Cap-Haïtien, July 19, 1914, RG 59, NARA.
99. July 10, 1914, RG 59, NARA.
100. The document included settlement of all matters outstanding between the government of Haiti and the National Railroad of Haiti, settlement of questions outstanding between the government of Haiti and the bank, an agreement by Haiti to give full protection to all foreign interests in Haiti, and an agreement by Haiti never to lease any Haitian territory at Môle-Saint-Nicolas or anywhere else in the country to any European government for use as a naval or coaling station.
101. Bryan to A. Bailly-Blanchard; Bryan to American Consul, Cap-Haïtien, July 22, 1914; July 10, 1914; Bryan to Secretary of Navy; July 19, 1914, RG 59, NARA.
102. Bryan to Secretary of Navy, July 24, 1914, RG 59, NARA.
103. "Funeral Today Set for Ex-Banker," *Times Record* (Troy, NY), November 18, 1971.
104. Bryan to Secretary of Navy, July 24, 1914, RG 59, NARA.
105. H. C. Newland to W. R. Grace & Company, September 14, 1914, Haiti Company, Organization, Frank A. Vanderlip Papers.
106. Farnham to Bryan, October 14, 1914, RG 59, NARA.
107. Henry H. Wehrhane to BNRH, RG 59, NARA.
108. "Testimony of Mr. Roger L. Farnham," 122.
109. Memorandum of Maurice Casenave, December 30, 1915; Wehrhane to Bryan, December 8, 1914, RG 59, NARA.
110. Text of conversation between R. L. Farnham and Bryan, December 12, 1914, RG 59, NARA.

111. Robert Lansing to Secretary of the Navy, December 15, 1914; Bryan to American Legation, Port-au-Prince via Navy Radio, December 15, 1914, RG 59, NARA.

112. Wehrhane to Bryan, December 11, 1914; Wehrhane to Bryan, December 11, 1914;
Bryan to American Legation, December 12, 1914; Wehrane to American Legation,
December 10, 1914, RG 59, NARA.

113. Blanchard to Secretary of State, December 14, 1914, RG 59, NARA.

114. Bank to Wehrhane inserted in Blanchard to Secretary of State, December 14, 1914;
Bank to Wehrhane in State Department to Farnham, December 16, 1914, RG
59, NARA.

115. R. Bobo, "A Little Memorandum" (translation), December 14, 1914, RG 59, NARA.

116. Blanchard to Secretary of State, December 14, 1914, quoted in Bryan to Farnham,
December 16, 1914.

117. Commanding Officers, USS Hancock to Navy Department, December 19, 1914, RG
59, NARA.

118. Text of Wehrhane to BNRH in Wehrhane to Bryan, December 15, 1914, RG 59, NARA.

119. Radiogram from the *USS Wheeling*, quoted in *USS Hancock* to Navy Department,
December 16, 1914, RG 59, NARA.

120. Franklin D. Roosevelt to William Jennings Bryan, December, 1914; Commanding
Officer, *USS Wheeling*, to Secretary of the Navy, January 9, 1915; Josephus Daniels to
Bryan, December 16, 1914; Blanchard to Bryan, RG 59, NARA.

121. Commanding Officer, *USS Wheeling*, to Secretary of the Navy, January 9, 1915; "The
Question of the Day: The Bank and the State" (translation), *Le Nouvelliste*, Friday,
December 18, 1914; "The Incident Yesterday at the Bank" (translation), *Le Matin*,
December 18, 1914, RG 59, NARA.

122. *USS Wheeling* to Secretary of the Navy, December 22, 1914; Desrue to Wehrhane in
Blanchard to Secretary of State, December 26, 1914; Bryan to Blanchard, December 26, 1914; Bryan to Blanchard, January 4, 1914, RG 59, NARA.

123. Selon Ménos to Bryan, December 22, 1914; Blanchard to Secretary of State, December 22, 1914, RG 59, NARA.

124. William Jennings Bryan to Selon Ménos, December 31, 1914, RG 59, NARA.

125. Ménos to Bryan, January 11, 1915; translation of Ménos to Bryan, December 29, 1914,
RG 59, NARA.

126. Blanchard to Secretary of State, February 11, 1915; Blanchard to Secretary of State,
February 12, 1915; Desrue to Wehrhane via Robert Lansing, RG 59, NARA.

127. Woodrow Wilson to William Jennings Bryan, April 5, 1915, Wilson-Bryan Correspondence, 1913–1915, Box 59, William Jennings Bryan Papers, Library of Congress.

128. Bryan to Wilson, April 3, 1915, Wilson-Bryan Correspondence, 1913–1915, Box 59,
Bryan Papers, Library of Congress.

129. Wilson to Bryan, April 5, 1915, Wilson-Bryan Correspondence, 1913–1915, Box 59,
Bryan Papers, Library of Congress.

130. "Testimony of Mr. Roger L. Farnham," 119.

131. Wehrhane to Bryan, June 4, 1915, RG 59, NARA.

132. George Marvin, "Assassination and Intervention in Haiti," *World's Work* 31 (February 16, 1916): 404–10; Harry A. Franck, *Roaming through the West Indies* (New York:
Blue Ribbon Books, 1920), 128. On Davis, see Renda, *Taking Haiti*, 127.

133. On the initial insurrection between July and November of 1915, see Hans Schmidt,
*Maverick Marine: General Smedley D. Butler and the Contradictions of American Military
History* (Lexington: University Press of Kentucky, 1987), 75–82.

134. "Testimony of Mr. Roger L. Farnham," 108.

135. Weatherly, "Haiti and Experiment in Pragmatism," *American Journal of Sociology*, 32.3 (November 1926), 359.
136. Sannon et. al., "Memoir on the Political, Economic, and Financial Conditions Existing in the Republic of Haiti," in *Inquiry into Occupation and Administration of Haiti and Santo Domingo*, 5–33.
137. Schmidt, *Maverick Marine*, 76; Schmidt, *The United States Occupation of Haiti*, 101.
138. US Navy Department, *Annual Report of the Secretary of the Navy* (Washington, DC: GPO, 1921), 304. For more on the Cacos rebellions, see Roger Gaillard, *Les blancs débarquent*, 8 vols. (Port-au-Prince: Le Natal, 1973–87); Kelthy Millett, *Les paysans haïtiens et l'occupation américain 1915–1930* (La Salle, Québec: Collectif Paroles, 1978).
139. Dantès Bellegarde, *Pour une Haiti heureuse II: Par l'éducation et le travail* (Port-au-Prince: Cherquit, 1929), 7.
140. *Treaty between the United States and Haiti: Finances, Economic Development, and Tranquillity of Haiti, Signed at Port-Au-Prince, September 16, 1915* (Washington, DC: GPO, 1919).
141. Eldridge to Vanderlip, October 18, 1915; Eldridge to Vanderlip, November 3, 1915, Frank A. Vanderlip Papers.
142. Memorandum by John A. McIlhenny to L. S. Rowe, Port-au-Prince, Haiti, July 21, 1920, US Department of State, Papers Relating to the Foreign Relations of the United States, 1920; "Testimony of Mr. Roger L. Farnham," 124; J. C. M. Ogelsby, *Gringos from the Far North: Essays in the History of Canadian-Latin American Relations, 1866–1968* (Toronto: Macmillan of Canada, 1976), 113.
143. "A New Treaty and a New Era for Haiti," *The Americas* 2.7 (April 1916): 16–17.
144. "The National Bank of the Republic of Haiti," *Commercial and Financial Chronicle* 103.2664 (July 15, 1916): 211–12; "Haiti on Eve of a Financial Revival," *Wall Street Journal*, July 10, 1916.
145. *New York Herald*, July 12, 1916.
146. "Testimony of Mr. Roger L. Farnham," 106.
147. James Weldon Johnson, "Self-Determining Haiti: The American Occupation," *The Nation*, August 28, 1920, 236–38; "What the United States Has Accomplished," *The Nation*, September 4, 1920, 265–67; "Self-Determining Haiti: Government of, by, and for the National City Bank of New York," *The Nation*, September 11, 1920, 295–97; "The Haitian People," *The Nation*, September 25, 1920, 345–47.
148. Johnson, "The American Occupation," 236.
149. Johnson, "Government of, by, and for the National City Bank," 296, 295.
150. US Navy Department, *Annual Report of the Secretary of the Navy*, 174–78.
151. "Testimony of Mr. Roger L. Farnham," 114–15, 119.
152. Ibid., 124.
153. John H. Allen, "American Co-operation Assures a Better Era for Haiti," *The Americas* 6.8 (1920): 8.
154. John H. Allen, "Prosperous Caribbean Countries Turn to American Markets," *The Americas* 6.2 (November 1919): 7, 10.
155. Ibid.
156. J. Allen Palmer, "The Turning Point of Haiti," *The Americas* 3.9 (June 1917): 19-22. Palmer briefly worked for the City Bank in Port-au-Prince. See "J. Allen Palmer," *Bankers' Magazine* 100.2 (February 1920): 521.
157. Allen, "American Co-operation," 11.
158. Carl Kelsey, "Haiti and Santo Domingo," *Monthly Letter*, May 1922, 8–11.

159. James Weldon Johnson, *Along This Way* (New York: Viking Press, 1933), 358–60.

160. Medill McCormick et. al., "American Marines in Haiti Exonerated: Report of the Senate Committee," *Current History* 16.5 (July 1922): 841; US Navy Department, *Annual Report of the Secretary of the Navy*, 317.

161. Georges Sylvain to James Weldon Johnson, November 17, 1920, in *Dix années de lute pour la liberté, 1915-1925*, vol. 1, ed. Geoges Sylvain. (Port-au-Prince: Editions Henri Deschamps, 1927), 76.

162. "$16,000,000 Republic of Haiti Bonds Offered by National City Company," *Commercial and Financial Chronicle* 115.2990 (October 14, 1922): 1681.

163. Banque Nationale de la République d'Haïti, *Loi de Sanction, Contrat de Transfert, Acte de Constitution: Status* (Port-au-Prince: Banque Nationale de la République d'Haïti, 1922).

164. "Bank of Haiti Is Ours," *No. 8*, 17.10 (October 1922): 5. Also see "Our Banking and Bonds Follow the Flag in Haiti," *No. 8*, 17.11 (November 1922): 12–13, 21.

165. Cleveland and Huertas, *Citibank*, 123.

CHAPTER FOUR

1. "Branch Report Good," *New York Times*, May 1, 1915.

2. "Modern Financial Institutions and Their Equipment," *Bankers' Magazine* 91.2 (August 1915): 278; Pedro Martínez Inclán, *La Habana actual* (Havana: P. Fernandez y ca., 1925), 38; *La Habana y sus grandes edificios modernos: Obra conmemorativa del IV centenario de su fundación* (Havana: Pernas y Figueroa, 1919).

3. "American Banks May Withdraw Branches from Cuba," *New York Times*, May 29, 1921.

4. "Branch Bank Notes," *No. 8*, 13.4 (April 1918): 58; "Sagua la Grande Branch Club Christens Itself with Banquet," *No. 8*, 15.6 (June 1920): 23; "Souvenir del almuerzo celebrado por el 'City Bank Club'," *No. 8*, 15.6 (June 1920): 23.

5. Alexandre Lilavois, "Rapport financier: Régime financier des Américains en Haïti" (unpublished manuscript), University of Florida, Gainesville, Florida.

6. "The Bank of Havana Will Open Next Month," *New York Times*, June 30, 1906, 7; Enrique Collazo Perez, *Banco de la Habana: Un caso de penetracion interimperialista en Cuba* (Havana: Banco Nacional de Cuba, Centro de Documentacion, 1981).

7. Collazo Perez, *Banco de la Habana*.

8. David Joslin, *A Century of Banking in Latin America* (Oxford: Oxford University Press, 1963), 213; Richard Roberts, *Schroders: Merchants & Bankers* (London: Macmillan/ J. Henry Schroder Wagg & Co., 1992), 54–56, 59–61, 135–37.

9. Vanderlip to Wilbur, October 24, 1906, Frank A. Vanderlip Papers, Manuscripts and Special Collections, Columbia University Libraries.

10. *The Times* (London), April 20, 1907.

11. "Banco de la Habana," *El Economista y Revista Comercial* 8.2 (January 12, 1907).

12. Vanderlip to Stillman, May 25, 1906, Frank A. Vanderlip Papers.

13. Vanderlip to Stillman, June 1, 1906, Frank A. Vanderlip Papers.

14. Vanderlip to Stillman, June 22, 1906, Frank A. Vanderlip Papers.

15. J. C. Martine, "Cuban Financial Methods," *No. 8*, 2.4 (January 1907): n.p.; J. C. Martine, "Banking in Cuba," *Bulletin of the American Institute of Bank Clerks* 7.5 (November 1906): 1082; J. C. Martine, "Cuban Commerce," *Bulletin of the American Institute of Bank Clerks* 7.68 (December 1906): 1234.

16. "Modern Financial Institutions and Their Equipment," *Bankers' Magazine* 91.2 (August 1915): 244–49; "John H. Durland," *Bankers' Magazine* 95.1 (July 1917): 235; "New Banking House for Havana," *New-York Daily Tribune*, June 19, 1906; "Five New

Officers Are Appointed at Annual Meeting," *No. 8*, 16.2 (February 1921): 3; "New Bank in Havana," *Cuba Review and Bulletin* 4.8 (July 1906): 17; "Bank of Havana," *Havana Daily Post: Tourist Edition* (1910–11), n.p.

17. Vanderlip to Jerome J. Wilbur, October 24, 1906, Frank A. Vanderlip Papers.

18. Havana Manager, Banco de la Habana to Charles E. Magoon, October 12, 1906, Fondo Secretaría de la Presidencia, Caja 19, num. 57, Archivo Nacional de Cuba.

19. Francis J. Sherman to William Howard Taft, October 9, 12, and 13, 1906, Fondo Secretaría de la Presidencia, Caja 67, num. 39, Archivo Nacional de Cuba.

20. Vanderlip to Wilbur, October 4, 1906; Vanderlip to Stillman, May 25, 1906; Vanderlip to Stillman, June 22, 1906, Frank A. Vanderlip Papers; "Colonial Banks and Bankers," in *The Bankers Directory and Collection Guide* (New York: Bradford Rhodes, 1911); "Havana Bank Liquidating," *New York Times*, January 25, 1909, 13.

21. *Urbana Daily Courier*, November 16, 1906; Circular dirigida a Charles E. Magoon relativa a la constitución del Banco de la Habana, October 12 and 15, 1906, Fondo Secretaría de la Presidencia, Caja 19, num. 57, Archivo Nacional de Cuba; "Cuban Banks to Act as Depositors," *Wall Street Journal*, October 29, 1906, 4.

22. *The Times* (London), April 20, 1907; "City Intelligence," *The Times* (London), April 9, 1908.

23. "Havana Bank Liquidating," *New York Times*, January 25, 1909, 13; "National Bank of Cuba Absorbs the Banco de la Habana," *Cuba Bulletin* 7.1 (December 1908): 19; "Banco de la Havana," *Cuba Bulletin* 7.2 (January 1909): n.p.; "Bank of Havana's Future," *Cuba Bulletin* 7.3 (February 1909).

24. Vanderlip to Stillman, February 18, 1909, Frank A. Vanderlip Papers.

25. Vanderlip to Stillman, May 1, 1909; Vanderlip to Stillman, May 7, 1909; Vanderlip to Stillman, June 11, 1909, Frank A. Vanderlip Papers.

26. Vanderlip to Stillman, February 22, 1909, Frank A. Vanderlip Papers.

27. Liberia 5% Refunding Loan 1912, Syndicate Participation, The National City Company, Frank A. Vanderlip Papers.

28. "Defaulted Loans in Latin America," *Bankers' Magazine* 80.4 (April 1910): 605.

29. "Pan-American Bank," *Wall Street Journal*, January 28, 1910, 8.

30. For a full account of these negotiations, see Juan E. Paredes, *The Morgan-Honduran Loan* (New Orleans: L. Graham, 1911); Honduras, *The Republic of Honduras and J. P. Morgan & Co., Kuhn, Loeb & Co., National City Bank of New York and First National Bank of New York, Agreement, Dated February 15, 1911*.

31. William Schell, Jr., *Integral Outsiders: The American Colony in Mexico City, 1876–1911* (Wilmington, DE: SR Books, 2001), 92; Emilio Zebadúa, *Banqueros y revolucionarios: La a soberanía financiera de México, 1914–1929* (Mexico City: Fideicomiso Historia de la Americas / El Colegio de México, 1994), 210–11.

32. See John E. Gardin, Memorandum for the President, September 9, 1912, Frank A. Vanderlip Papers; Claude A. Smith, "Our National Banks around the World: Foreign Branches: Why Not?," *No. 8*, 5.1 (January 1910): n.p.; Samuel McRoberts, "The Extension of American Banking in Foreign Countries," *Annals of the American Academy of Political and Social Science* 36.3 (November 1910). 24–32.

33. Joseph T. Talbert to Frank A. Vanderlip, April 2, 1910, Frank A. Vanderlip Papers. On the Bank of Nova Scotia's Caribbean expansion and operations, see James D. Frost, "The 'Nationalization' of the Bank of Nova Scotia, 1880–1910," *Acadiensis* 12.1 (1982): 3–38; and Neil C. Quigley, "The Bank of Nova Scotia in the Caribbean, 1889–1940," *Business History Review* 63 (1989): 797–838.

34. A. A. Berle, "Promoter's Stock in Subsidiary Corporations," *Columbia Law Review* 29.1

(January 1929): 35–42; Jacob H. Hollander, "The Security Holdings of National Banks," *American Economic Review* 3.4 (December 1913): 793–814; W. Nelson Peach, *The Security Affiliates of National Banks* (Baltimore: Johns Hopkins University Press, 1941), 18–19.

35. Sheridan A. Logan, *George F. Baker and His Bank, 1840–1955: A Double Biography* (St. Joseph, MO: Sheridan A. Logan, 1981), 149–50.

36. US Congress, 62nd Congress, 3rd Session, *Report of the Committee Appointed Pursuant to House Resolutions 429 and 504 to Investigate the Concentration of Control of Money and Credit* (Washington, DC: GPO, 1913), 66–68, 72; Harold Van B. Cleveland and Thomas F. Huertas, *Citibank, 1812–1970* (Cambridge, MA: Harvard University Press, 1985), 63.

37. Cleveland and Huertas, *Citibank*, 65.

38. Vanderlip to Stillman, August 26, 1910; July 14, 1911, Frank A. Vanderlip Papers. Ailes, like Vanderlip, was a former assistant secretary of the treasury. He was also a vice president of the City Bank–controlled Riggs National Bank while being employed by the City Bank as its "special Washington representative." Cleveland and Huertas, *Citibank*, 350n49; Frank A. Vanderlip with Boyden Sparkes, *From Farm Boy to Financier* (New York: D. Appleton-Century, 1935), 117.

39. Vanderlip to Stillman, July 28, 1911; Vanderlip to Stillman, August 26, 1910; Vanderlip to Stillman, July 14, 1911; Vanderlip to Stillman, September 22, 1911, Frank A. Vanderlip Papers.

40. John Sterling was Stillman's personal lawyer and closest confidant. His firm, Shearman and Sterling, had represented both Charles Stillmans and the City Bank and was among the most prominent of Wall Street's corporate law firms. See Walter K. Earle, *Mr. Shearman and Mr. Sterling and How They Grew: Being Annals of Their Law Firm, with Biographical and Historical Highlights* (New York: Shearman & Sterling, 1963). On John Sterling, see Vanderlip, *From Farm Boy to Financier*, 95, 110, 300.

41. Vanderlip to Stillman, September 22, 1911, Frank A. Vanderlip Papers.

42. "Extends U.S. Finance," *Washington Post*, April 2, 1912.

43. W. Morgan Shuster, *The Strangling of Persia* (New York: The Century Co., 1912); "Cann, Henry Vibert," *Who's Who and Why, 1919–20*, ed. B. M. Greene (Toronto: International Press, 1920), 566.

44. Vanderlip to Stillman, March 16, 1912; Vanderlip to Stillman, March 29, 1912, Frank A. Vanderlip Papers.

45. The following section is based on Memorandum for Mr. Vanderlip by R. L. Farnham, October 17, 1912, Frank A. Vanderlip Papers.

46. *Report of the Committee Appointed Pursuant to House Resolutions . . . to Investigate the Concentration of Control of Money and Credit.*

47. Henry F. Pringle, *The Life and Times of William Howard Taft: A Biography* (New York: Farar & Rinehart, 1939), 676–77. For the text of the report, see "Frederick W. Lehmann to Charles W. Wickersham, November 6, 1911," in US Senate, Committee on Banking and Currency, *Stock Exchange Practices*, pt. 6 (Washington, DC: GPO, 1932), 2030–42. For opposing views of the question of the legality of the NCC, see John K. Winkler, *The First Billion: The Stillmans and the City Bank* (New York: Vanguard Press, 1934), 200–208; and Cleveland and Huertas, *Citibank*, 66–68.

48. "Testimony of R. L. Farnham, January 15, 1915," in James D. Phelan, *In the Matter of the Investigation of Charges against American Minister to Santo Domingo*, pt. 1 (Washington, DC: GPO, 1915), 309; George M. Smith, "The Dominican Republic," *No. 8*, 8.5 (May 1913): 10; La República Dominicana, Secretaría de Estado y Comercio, *Contrato*

de empréstito entre la República Dominicana y the National City Bank of New York, de fecha 22 de Febrero de 1913 (Santo Domingo: El Tiempo, 1913).

49. Cuban 6% Treasury Notes, 1913, J. P. Morgan and Co. Syndicate Book, vol. 7, 129, J. P. Morgan Library and Museum.

50. Vanderlip to Stillman, November 8, 1912, Frank A. Vanderlip Papers.

51. "As Morgan Shuster Saw South America," *New York Times Annalist*, June 16, 1913, 681; W. Morgan Shuster, "Address of Mr. W. Morgan Shuster," *No. 8*, 7.5 (May 1912): 1–15; H. V. Cann, *Pages from a Banker's Journal* (1933).

52. Beverly D. Harris, *Branch Banks and Foreign Trade* (New York: The City Bank of New York, 1916), 8.

53. See, for instance, John T. Madden, Marcus Nadler, and Harry C. Sauvain, *America's Experience as a Creditor Nation* (New York: Prentice-Hall, 1937), 41–56.

54. Graham F. Towers, *Financing Foreign Trade* (Montreal: The Royal Bank of Canada, 1921) 6–7; Stuart H. Patterson, *A Bank Catechism* (New York: Guaranty Trust Company of New York, 1925), 36–37.

55. E. E. Agger, "The Federal Reserve System," *Political Science Quarterly* 29.2 (June 1914): 279.

56. "Branch Banks Abroad," *Washington Post*, March 3, 1915, 6; H. Parker Willis, "What the Federal Reserve System Has Done," *American Economic Review* 7.2 (June 1917): 269–88.

57. See Smith, "Our National Banks around the World," n.p.; McRoberts, "The Extension of American Banking in Foreign Countries," 24–32.

58. Vanderlip, *From Farm Boy to Financier*, 216.

59. "Creation of a New Vice Presidency," *No. 8*, 4.5 (January 1909): n.p.; "J. E. Gardin Gives Up Office," *New York Times*, December 30, 1917; "J. E. Gardin Led Exchange Market," *Wall Street Journal*, December 29, 1926; "John E. Gardin, 73, Noted Banker, Dies," *New York Times*, December 24, 1926.

60. "Herbert Rucker Eldridge," *The Americas* 2.2 (November 1915): 3–4; "Herbert Rucker Eldridge," *National City Monthly Letter*, December 1915, n.p.

61. Joseph T. Cosby to Sir William Van Horne, October 19, 1908, Sir William Van Horne Fonds, Van Horne Business Correspondence, C, part 2, 1907–1908, National Archives of Canada; "Merchants Bank of Halifax," *Wall Street Journal*, July 8, 1899; "Royal Bank of Canada," *Wall Street Journal*, September 1, 1910, 8; *Wall Street Journal*, June 2, 1915; "Our New Vice-President: Stephen H. Voorhees," *No. 8*, 10.5 and 6 (July 1915): n.p.; *Bankers Monthly*, 32, pt. 2, no. 7 (July 1915): 61.

62. This paragraph draws from Cleveland and Huertas, *Citibank*, 78–79.

63. "First American Bank Abroad," *Chicago Commerce* 10.28 (November 13, 1914): 21.

64. Herbert R. Eldridge and S. H. Voorhees to Vanderlip, July 6, 1915, Frank A. Vanderlip Papers.

65. Philip Ziegler, *The Sixth Great Power: Barings, 1762–1929* (London: Collins, 1988), 324–25.

66. "Exhibit K: Foreign Branches Authorized," in *Fourth Annual Report of the Federal Reserve Board, Covering Operations for the Year 1917* (Washington, DC: GPO, 1918), 187.

67. Vanderlip to Stillman, July 30, 1915, Frank A. Vanderlip Papers.

68. J. J. McNamee, "The National City Bank's Economic Bulletin," *No. 8*, 18.8 (August 1923): 3–5.

69. Carlos Ignacio Parraza y Fernández, sobre la protocolizacion de estatutos del "The National City Bank of New York" y otros documentos relacionados con el misma, 11 de Agosta de 1915, Fondo Banco Nacional de Cuba, Caja 9, num. 12, Archivo

Nacional de Cuba; "National City Bank's Operations in Cuba," *Wall Street Journal*, November 20, 1915, 2; "Bank's West Indian Branch," *Wall Street Journal*, August 23, 1915, 2.

70. Havana Branch, Foreign Trade Department Files, October 26, 1915, Frank A. Vanderlip Papers.

71. Robert Mayer, "The Origins of the American Banking Empire in Latin America: Frank A. Vanderlip and the City Bank," *Journal of Interamerican Studies and World Affairs* 15.1 (February 1973): 60–76; James Addison, "Our Foreign Branches and Their Development," in *135 Years of Banking* (New York: City Bank of New York, 1947); Cleveland and Heurtas, *Citibank*, 78–70. On the history of the bank in Argentina, see Marcelo Zlotogwiazda and Luis Balaguer, *Citibank vs. Argentina: Historia de un país en bancarrota* (Buenos Aires: Sudamericana, 2003).

72. "National City Co. Buys International," *The Financier*, October 30, 1915, 1241; "Purchase of Stock of International Banking Corporation," *Federal Reserve Bulletin*, October 1, 1918, 937.

73. Lawrence M. Jacobs, "What Shall We Do with the International Banking Corporation," May 23, 1916, Frank A. Vanderlip Papers.

74. See annotations to International Banking Corporation, *Twenty-Eighth Semi-Annual Statement of International Banking Corporation, June 20, 1916* (New York: International Banking Corporation, 1916), Frank A. Vanderlip Papers; "International Banking Corporation," *The Financier*, December 16, 1916, 1648.

75. "The City Bank in Santo Domingo," *Monthly Economic Letter*, April 1917, 10; "The National City Bank of New York in Santo Domingo," *Bankers' Magazine* 94.5 (May 1917): 575.

76. James H. Perkins, "An American Bank in Argentina and Brazil: What the National City Bank of New York Is Trying to Do," *The World's Work* 29.2 (December 1914): 190–92; A. H. Titus, "Establishment of Branches by National Banks in Foreign Countries," *Journal of the American Bankers Association* 7.8 (February 1915): 615–19; E. A. Groff, *American Banks in Foreign Trade* (New York: The National City Bank of New York, 1920); "Commercial Relations with South America," *National City Monthly Letter*, August 1914.

77. For examples of these dispatches, see John H. Allen, *The Trends of Business and Credits in Argentina* (New York: The City Bank of New York, 1915); *The Market for Coal in Argentina* (New York: The City Bank of New York, 1915); and *Cotton Textiles in Argentina* (New York: The City Bank of New York, 1915).

78. See Joseph T. Cosby, *Latin American Monetary Systems and Exchange Conditions* (New York: City Bank of New York, 1915); *Guía Comercial* (New York: City Bank of New York, 1920), *A Handbook of Finance and Trade with South America* (New York: The City Bank of New York, 1919).

79. "Untitled," *The Americas* 1.1 (1914): n.p.

80. Oscar P. Austin, *Trading with the New Countries of Central Europe* (New York: City Bank of New York, 1921); Ferdinand C. Schwedtman, *The Development of Scandinavian-American Trade* (New York: The City Bank of New York, 1921); Frank O. Malley, *Our South American Trade and Its Financing* (New York: The City Bank of New York, 1920); Oscar P. Austin, *Trading with Our Neighbors in the Caribbean* (New York: The City Bank of New York, 1920); Oscar P. Austin, *Trading with the Far East* (New York: The City Bank of New York, 1920); George E. Roberts, *The Function of Imports in Our Foreign Trade* (New York: The City Bank of New York, 1920); "Oscar Phelps Austin: Statistician, The City Bank of New York," *No. 8*, 12.2 (February 1917): n.p.

81. John H. Allen, "Prosperous Caribbean Countries Turn to American Markets," *The Americas* 6.2 (November 1919): 10 (italics added).
82. "How Nationality Counts in Foreign Trade," *The Americas* 1.7 (April 1915), 4.
83. The following descriptions are drawn from Irving M. Barnhard, "Five Years in Jungle Land," *No. 8*, 12.4 (April 1917): 12–27 (quotations at 17 and 16).
84. "N. W. Halsey & Co. Sold to City Bank," *New York Times*, August 20, 1916, 3.
85. On the AIC's role in shipbuilding, specifically, see New York Shipbuilding Corporation, *History and Development of New York Shipbuilding Corporation* (New York: New York Shipbuilding Corporation, 1920).
86. See various issues of the *Bulletin of American International Corporation* between February 1917 and May 1920. For a general history of the AIC see Harry N. Scheiber, "World War I as Entrepreneurial Opportunity: Willard Straight and the American International Corporation," *Political Science Quarterly* 84.3 (September 1969): 486–511.
87. Minutes of the Branch Bank Committee, May 4, 1916, Frank A. Vanderlip Papers.
88. Minutes of the Branch Bank Committee, May 21, 1917; December 5, 1916, Frank A. Vanderlip Papers.
89. Minutes of the Branch Bank Committee, November 8, 1916; October 17, 1917, Frank A. Vanderlip Papers.
90. Minutes of the Branch Bank Committee, June 19, 1916, Frank A. Vanderlip Papers.
91. Minutes of the Branch Bank Committee, July 3, 1916, Frank A. Vanderlip Papers.
92. Minutes of the Branch Bank Committee, June 19, 1916, Frank A. Vanderlip Papers.
93. Minutes of the Branch Bank Committee, Feburary 23, 1917, Frank A. Vanderlip Papers.
94. The management of the Cuban branches was not systematized in a written document until more than a decade later. See Leopoldo Casas, *Branch Management* (Havana: The National City Bank of New York, 1933).
95. "Economic and Financial Conditions in Cuba," *Federal Reserve Bulletin*, November 1920, 1162.
96. W. H. Morales, "Money Legislation in Cuba," *Bankers' Magazine* 90.6 (June 1915): 730, reprinted in *Cuban Investments: An Intimate Statement of Investment Facts Existing in the Republic, with Some Comparisons on Securities in the United States* (New Orleans: Bankers' Loan and Security Company, 1916); Manuel Moreno Fraginals and José A. Pulido Ledesma, *Cuba: A través de su moneda* (Havana: Banco Nacional de Cuba, 1987), 144–46.
97. Eduardo C. Lens y Díaz, *La unidad monetaria en Cuba* (Havana: Imp. De Lloredo y Ca., 1916); Henry Christopher Wallich, *Monetary Problems of an Export Economy: The Cuban Experience, 1914–1947* (Cambridge, MA: Harvard University Press, 1950), 40–49.
98. Wallich, *Monetary Problems of an Export Economy*, 32–37.
99. For an overview, see Alberto Arredondo, *Cuba: Tierra indefensa* (Havana: Editorial Lex, 1945).
100. "New Offices of the Bank of Cuba in New York," *Bankers' Magazine* 96.4 (April 1918): 377–79.
101. Arredondo, *Cuba*, 318.
102. Manuel Rionda to W. A. Simonson, February 27, 1917; Manuel Rionda to W. A. Simonson, November 12, 1917, National City Bank, Record Group II, Series 10a-c; Manuel Rionda y Polledo, Subject Files, 1911–1943, Box 8, Braga Brothers Collection, University of Florida, Gainesville; Minutes of Special Meeting of the Board of Directors of Czarnikow-Rionda Company, Record Group II, Series 10a-c, Manuel Rionda y Polledo, Subject Files, 1911–1943, Box 7, Braga Brothers Collection, University of Florida, Gainesville.

103. Cuban-American Sugar Company, National City Company, *New Note Issue, $6,000,000 the Cuban-American Sugar Co. First Lien 6% Serial Gold Notes* (New York: National City Company, 1917); Cuban American Sugar Company, 6% Serial Notes, December 28, 1917, J. P. Morgan and Co. Syndicate Book, vol. 9, Morgan Library and Museum.

104. Albert L. Hoffman, "Current Conditions in Cuba," *The Americas* 3.6 (March 1917): 37–38; "Acuerdos sobre actividades bancarias," in *La República neocolonial*, ed. Juan Pérez de la Riva et al. (Havana: Instituto Cubano del Libro, Editorial de Ciencias Sociales, 1975), 398.

105. "National City Bank to Rigoberto Fernández, March 1, 1917," in *La República neocolonial*, ed. Juan Pérez de la Riva et al. (Havana: Instituto Cubano del Libro, Editorial de Ciencias Sociales, 1975), 405; Minutes of the Branch Bank Committee, Feburary 23, 1917, Frank A. Vanderlip Papers.

106. John K. Winkler, *The First Billion: The Stillmans and the National City Bank* (New York: Vanguard Press, 1934), 254.

107. George E. Roberts to Joseph H. Durrell, January 3, 1919; Roger L. Farnham to Joseph H. Durrell, January 3, 1919, Joseph H. Durrell, comp., "Personal Files," vol. 1, "1918–1923" (unpublished manuscript), n.p.

108. John H. Allen, "Team Work between America and Cuba Has Paid Well for Both," *The Americas* 226.10 (July 1920): 22–27.

109. "Six More Branches of the National City Bank opened in the Caribbean Territory," *No. 8*, 7 (July 1919): 15–17.

110. This incident is explored in more detail in Sean Ng Wai, "Why Do Banks Disappear? A History of Bank Failures and Acquisitions in Trinidad, 1836–1992," *Journal of Business, Finance, and Economics in Emerging Economies* 5.1 (2010): 165–205.

111. "City Bank Has Six More Cuban Branches," *No. 8*, 14.8 (August 1919): 34–36.

112. "The Bank Opens New Branches in Brazil and Cuba: IBC Announces a New Branch in San Domingo," *No. 8*, 9 (September 1919): 22–24; "City Bank Service Now Has Seventy Foreign Branches," *The Americas* 6.12 (September, 1920): 13–16; "Foreign Branches of National Banks," in *Report of the Comptroller of the Currency* (Washington, DC: GPO, 1918), 57; "Three New Branches in Tropics; Resume of the Year 1919 at the National City Bank of New York," *No. 8*, 15.1 (January 1920): 8–10; E. A. Groff, *American Banks in Foreign Trade* (New York: The National City Bank of New York, 1920), 12.

113. Joshua Bernhardt, *Government Control of the Sugar Industry in the United States* (New York: Macmillan Company, 1920); John Edward Dalton, *Sugar: A Case Study of Government Control* (New York: Macmillan, 1937).

114. See the comments of Ramón Mendoza of the Banco Nacional de Cuba in "Banco Nacional de Cuba Suspends," *New York Times*, April 10, 1921.

115. Frank Steinhardt interviewed by Leland Hamilton Jenks, Havana, Cuba, February 10, 1926, Leland Hamilton Jenks Collection on the Cuban Sugar Industry, 1925–1934, Special Collections, Princeton University.

116. Joseph Hergesheimer, *Cythrea* (New York: Knopf, 1922), 328; Robert B. Hoernel, "Sugar and Social Change in Oriente, Cuba, 1898–1946," *Journal of Latin American Studies* 8.2 (November 1976): 215–49; Louis A. Pérez, *Intervention, Revolution, and Politics in Cuba, 1913–1921* (Pittsburgh: University of Pittsburgh Press, 1978), 72.

117. This moment of Cuba's history is evoked in Joseph Hergesheimer, *San Cristóbal de la Habana*, (New York: Alfred A. Knopf, 1920); and Basil Woon, *When It's Cocktail Time in Cuba* (New York: Horace Liveright, 1928).

118. "Present Conditions in Cuba," *The Compass* 1.9 (September 1920): 257–63; *The Times of Cuba*, September 1920, 3; "What the Branch Bank Folk Are Doing: Havana Branch News," *No. 8*, 15.10 (October 1920): 27; "Sugar Property Deals More Alarming Than Crop Credits," *The Annalist*, October 25, 1920, 519.

119. Philip A. Howard, *Black Labor, White Sugar: Caribbean Braceros and Their Struggle for Power in the Cuban Sugar Industry* (Baton Rouge: Louisiana State University Press, 2015), 95–100.

120. *Louisiana Planter and Sugar Manufacturer* 63.17 (1920): 263.

121. J. H. Durrell to John H. Allen, May 24, 1920, in Durrell, "Personal Files," vol. 1, n.p.

122. John H. Allen, "Team Work between America and Cuba Has Paid Well for Both," *The Americas* 5.5 (July 1919): 22–28.

123. *The Times of Cuba*, September 1920, 127–28.

124. "Banking Conditions in Cuba Unsettled," *Christian Science Monitor*, October 12, 1920, 10.

125. Republic of Cuba, Secretaría de Hacienda, Sección de Acuñación de Moneda, Número recibido de los Estados Unidos desde el dia 12 de Octubre por los bancos y compañias que se Expresan, Fondo Secretaría de la Presidencia, Caja 12, exp. 1, Archivo Nacional de Cuba.

126. Memorandum de banqueros a Menocal, November 20, 1929, Fondo Secretaría de la Presidencia, Caja 12, num. 2, Archivo Nacional de Cuba.

127. On Rathbone's visit, see Leland Hamilton Jenks, *Our Cuban Colony* (New York: Vanguard Press, 1928), 233–34.

128. *The Times of Cuba*, October 1920, 60; "Sugar Property Deals More Alarming Than Crop Credits," *The Annalist*, October 25, 1920, 519.

129. Telegram, Colby Department of State to American Legation, November 12, 1920, Box 15, Vincent P. Carosso Papers, J. P. Morgan Library and Museum.

130. Hawley to Menocal, November 22, 1920, Fondo Secretaría de la Presidencia, Caja 12, exp. 2, Archivo Nacional de Cuba.

131. Menocal to Hawley, November 23, 1920, Fondo Secretaría de la Presidencia, Caja 12, exp. 2, Archivo Nacional de Cuba.

132. John H. Allen, "A Short Resume of Cuba's Present Business Situation," *The Americas* 7.1 (October 1920): 10.

133. Allen to Vanderlip, October 27, 1920, Frank A. Vanderlip Papers.

134. "John H. Allen, Vice President in Charge of Bank's Foreign Org., Resigns," *No. 8*, 15.12 (December 1920): 26.

135. The City Bank opened the National City Bank of New York, South Africa, in Cape Town in 1920. See Richard W. Hull, *American Enterprise in South Africa: Historical Dimensions of Engagement and Disengagement* (New York: New York University Press, 1990), 131–34.

136. Copy of "Report on Cuban Branches" made by Vere Brown, Executive Manager, Following His Visit to Cuba in October 1920, November 8, 1920, in Durrell, "Personal Files," vol. 1, n.p.

137. Frank Plachy, Jr., "What the City Bank Means to Cuba," *No. 8*, 17.10 (October 1921): 2–3.

138. "American Banks May Withdraw Branches in Cuba," *New York Times*, May 29, 1921; "Banks to Defend Cuban Business," *New York Times*, May 30, 1921; J. H. Durrell to Lee E. Olwell, January 21, 1925, in Durrell, "Personal Files," vol. 2.

139. "The National City Bank of New York," *The Times of Cuba*, November 1920, 134.

140. República de Cuba, Comisión Temporal de Liquidación Bancaria, *Compendio de los*

trabajos realizados desde 17 de Febrero de 1921, hasta 4 de Agosto de 1924 (Havana: Editorial Hermes, 1924).

141. Cleveland and Huertas, *Citibank*, 105–7.

142. "National City Bank Closes Colombia Branches," *Wall Street Journal*, August 20, 1921, 1.

143. *Directory of Directors of the City of New York* (New York: Directory of Directors Company, 1919), 211.

144. United States Circuit Court, Southern District of New York, José M. de Acosta, against Compagnie Nationale des Chemins de Fer d'Haiti, The Farmers' Loan & Trust Company, as Trustee, etc., against Roger L. Farnham, as Receiver, et al., In equity, No. E 18–196, Stenographer's Minutes, July 3, 1924, National Archives and Records Administration, New York.

145. Paul H. Douglas, "The American Occupation of Haiti II," *Political Science Quarterly* 42.3 (1927): 383.

CHAPTER FIVE

1. Descriptions of the opening and the building come from "Nos inaguramos," *Bamericuba* 1.1 (September 1919): 4–5; "Banco Mercantil Americano de Cuba," *The Financier*, October 1, 1919, 614; *La Habana y sus grandes edificios modernos* (Havana: Pernas y Figueroa, 1919), 110–18; "La inauguracion," *Bamericuba* 1.2 (October 1919), 8; "New Offices of Banco Mercantil Americano de Cuba Opens," *Guaranty News* 8.8 (October 1919): 246–47.

2. "Banco Mercantil Americano de Cuba," *The Financier*, October 1, 1919, 614–15.

3. "Nos inaguramos," *Bamericuba* 1.1 (September 1919): 5.

4. *La Habana y sus grandes edificios modernos*, 110.

5. Both the phrase "capitalism and slavery" and the description of the historical transition from merchant to bank are from Eric Williams, *Capitalism & Slavery* (Chapel Hill: University of North Carolina Press, 1944), 98–104.

6. On the history of Brown Brothers, see Brown Brothers and Co., *Experiences of a Century, 1818–1918* (Philadelphia: Brown Brothers and Company, 1919); John Crosby Brown, *One Hundred Years of Merchant Banking* (New York: Brown Brothers and Co., 1909); Edwin J. Perkins, *Financing Anglo-American Trade: The House of Brown, 1800–1880* (Cambridge, MA: Harvard University Press, 1975).

7. Clyde William Phelps, "American Banks Abroad," *Bankers' Magazine* 119.12 (December 1929): 994.

8. Ross L. Muir and Carl J. White, *Over the Long Term . . . The Story of J. & W. Seligman & Co., 1864–1964* (New York: J. & W. Seligman & Co., 1964).

9. Vincent P. Carosso, *The Morgans: Private International Bankers, 1854–1913* (Cambridge, MA: Harvard University Press, 1987), 217.

10. The history recounted in the next paragraphs draws on Statement of Pedro Rafael Cuadra, June 25, 1914, US Senate, Committee on Foreign Relations, *Convention between the United States and Nicaragua*, pt. 4 (Washington, DC: GPO, 1914), 115–34; and "Testimony of Severo Mallet-Prevost, Monday, June 29, 1914," in US Senate, Committee on Foreign Relations, *Convention between the United States and Nicaragua*, pt. 6 (Washington, DC: GPO, 1914), 169–281.

11. Otto Schoenrich, *Severo Mallet-Prevost, 1860–1948* (New York: privately printed, 1951), 10–19.

12. "Testimony of Severo Mallet-Prevost," 169–281.

13. Roscoe R. Hill, *Fiscal Intervention in Nicaragua* (New York: Paul Maisel, 1933), 11.

14. For Conant's assessment, see "Our Mission in Nicaragua," *North American Review* 196.553 (July 1912): 63–72; Charles A. Conant and F. C. Harrison, *Monetary Reform for Nicaragua: Report Presenting a Plan of Monetary Reform for Nicaragua, Submitted to Messrs. Brown Brothers & Company and Messrs. J & W Seligman & Company, by Messrs. F. C. Harrison and Charles A. Conant, April 23, 1912* (New York: W. R. Ficke, 1912).

15. A summary of the history of the National Bank of Nicaragua and its activities can be found in W. W. Cumberland, *Nicaragua: An Economic and Financial Survey* (Washington, DC: GPO, 1928), 136–37; Carlos Quijano, *Nicaragua: Ensayo sober el imperialismo de los Estados Unidos* (Managua: Ediorial Vanguardia, 1987), 66–71; Armando Occon Herradora, *Banco Nacional de Nicaragua y su Entorno Histórico, 1912–1998* (Managua: Banco Nacional de Nicaragua, 1988), 211–33.

16. Muir and White, *Over the Long Term,* 111.

17. "Testimony of Walter Bundy Cole," in US Senate, Committee on Foreign Relations, *Convention between the United States and Nicaragua,* pt. 10 (Washington, DC: GPO, 1914), 493–94; "The Guatemala Northern Railway," *Engineering News* 36.1 (July 9, 1896):14.

18. "The Banks of Mexico City," *Bankers' Magazine* 77.4 (October 1908): 558–59; "Seven Years of Successful Banking," *Bankers' Magazine* 79 (1909): 608.

19. W. Bundy Cole, "General Banking Business," in US Senate, Committee on Foreign Relations, *Convention between the United States and Nicaragua,* pt. 10 (Washington, DC: GPO, 1914), 510–15.

20. "Testimony of Walter Bundy Cole," 510, 513.

21. Ibid., 507.

22. Ibid., 511.

23. "Testimony of Albert Strauss, J. & W. Seligman," in US Senate, Committee on Foreign Relations, *Convention between the United States and Nicaragua* (Washington, DC: GPO, 1914).

24. "The Conflict with the Bankers," *The American* (Bluefields, Nicaragua), February 2, 1913, reprinted in US Senate, Committee on Foreign Relations, *Convention between the United States and Nicaragua,* pt. 8 (Washington, DC: GPO, 1914), 344–55.

25. "The Minister of Nicaragua and the Minister of the Treasury of Nicaragua to the Secretary of State," in *Papers Relating to the Foreign Relations of the United States* (Washington, DC: GPO, 1913), September 1, 1913, 1050.

26. John Atlee Kouwenhoven, *Partners in Banking: An Historical Portrait of a Great Private Bank, Brown Brothers Harriman & Co., 1818–1968* (Garden City, NY: Doubleday, 1968), 189; "The Republic of Brown Brothers," *The Nation* 114 (June 7, 1922): 667.

27. "James Brown," *The Compass* 1.4 (April 1920): 99; Brown Brothers and Co., *Experiences of a Century,* 67–69; "Foreign Branches of American Banks," *Federal Reserve Bulletin,* August 1, 1918, 736.

28. Brown Brothers and Co., *Experiences of a Century,* 67–69.

29. *Proceedings of the First Pan American Financial Conference* (Washington, DC: GPO, 1915), 9.

30. Mercantile Bank of the Americas, *Statement of Condition* (New York: Mercantile Bank of the Americas, 1918), n.p.

31. The Morgan firm—and J. P. Morgan himself—probably has the most extensive historiography of any US financial institution. For overviews, see Vincent P. Carosso, *The Morgans: Private International Bankers, 1854–1913* (Cambridge, MA: Harvard University Press, 1987); Jean Strouse, *Morgan: American Financier* (New York: Random House, 1999); Ron Chernow, *The House of Morgan* (New York: Atlantic Monthly

Press, 1990); John K. Winkler, *Morgan the Magnificent* (New York: The Vanguard Press, 1930).

32. "The Bond Market," *Wall Street Journal*, June 14, 1909, 5. On Morgan's Latin American loans, see Carosso, *The Morgans*, 209–11, 413–20.

33. Strouse, *Morgan*, 603–5; "Guaranty Trust Control," *United States Investor*, December 4, 1909, 2143; Thomas W. Lamont, *Henry P. Davison: The Record of a Useful Life* (New York: Harper and Brothers, 1933), 2, 115–21; Carosso, *The Morgans*, 619–28.

34. "Morton Trust Company," in *Historical Directory of the Banks of the State of New York*, comp. William H. Dillistin (New York: New York State Bankers Association, 1946), 53.

35. Bruce J. Calder, *The Impact of Intervention: The Dominican Republic during the U.S. Occupation of 1916-1924* (Austin: University of Texas Press, 1984), 80.

36. For a full account of these negotiations, see Juan E. Paredes, *The Morgan-Honduran Loan* (New Orleans: L. Graham, 1911); Honduras, *The Republic of Honduras and J. P. Morgan & Co., Kuhn, Loeb & Co., National City Bank of New York and First National Bank of New York, Agreement, Dated February 15, 1911*.

37. New York (State), Banking Department, *Annual Report of the Superintendent of the Banking Department of the State of New York* (Albany: Banking Department, 1916), 100.

38. "Branch Banks Abroad," *Washington Post*, March 3, 1915, 6; H. Parker Willis, "What the Federal Reserve System Has Done," *American Economic Review* 7.2 (June 1917): 269–88.

39. "Foreign Branches of National Banks," in *Report of the Comptroller of the Currency* (Washington, DC: GPO, 1918), 57.

40. See Frank O'Malley, "Our Awakening to the Possibilities of South American Trade," *The Americas* 7.8 (May 1921): 12; Leopold Grahame, "American Banks Abroad," *The Equitable Envoy* 1.4 (October 1921): 20–22, 39. Also see the editorial "Reciprocity in International Banking," *Bankers' Magazine* 95.2 (August 1917): 163–67. On the Irving National Bank's approach to American international banking, see "Foreign Banking Development," *Federal Reserve Bulletin*, January 1, 1919, 23.

41. *Federal Reserve Bulletin*, December 1, 1916, 665.

42. "Mercantile Bank of the Americas," *Wall Street Journal*, May 18, 1917; "Mercantile Bank of the Americas," *Wall Street Journal*, August 14, 1917. On the history of the Continental and Commercial National Bank of Chicago, see Arthur D. Welton, *The Making of a Modern Bank* (Chicago: The Continental and Commercial Banks, 1923).

43. "Development of American Banking Facilities for Foreign Trade," *Banking L. J.* 36 (January–December 1919): 638.

44. Ibid.

45. Albert Breton, *Banking Institutions to Finance Our Future Abroad* (New York: Guaranty Trust Co., 1918).

46. "Development of American Banking Facilities"; "Mercantile Bank of the Americas: Something More Than a Bank," *Barron's* 1.17 (August 29, 1921): 11.

47. Minutes of a Special Meeting of the Directors of the Banco Mercantil Americano de Cuba, Financial, Mercantile Bank of the Americas, Record Group II, Series 10a-c, Manuel Rionda y Polledo, Subject Files, 1911–1943, Box 7, Braga Brothers Collection, University of Florida, Gainesville.

48. Quijano, *Nicaragua*, 130–33.

49. "New Bank in Honduras," *Bankers' Magazine* 86.4 (April 1913): 752; "Banco Atlántida cumple 100 años de fundación en Honduras," *EFE News Service*, February 10, 2013; Thomas O'Brien, *The Revolutionary Mission: American Enterprise in Latin America*,

1900–1945 (Cambridge: Cambridge University Press, 1996), 93; Banco Atlántida, *75 aniversario: Banco Atlántida, S.A. 1913–1988* (Tegucigalpa: Banco Atlántida, 1988); Darío Euraque, *El capitalismo de San Pedro Sula y la historia política hondureña (1870–1972)* (Tegucigalpa: Editorial Guyamuras, 2001).

50. C. R. Beattie, "British Honduras," *Royal Bank Magazine* 87 (April 1928): 3–5.

51. "Canada Bank in Honduras," *New York Times*, December 11, 1912, 16.

52. Osgood Hardy, MA, "We Who Are about to Leave Salute You," *The Compass* 1.1 (January 1920): 14; "Banking in Costa Rica," *Bankers' Magazine* 82.1 (July 1911): 362; Rufino Gil Pacheco, *Ciento cinco años de vida bancaria en Costa Rica* (San José: Editorial Costa Rica, 1975), 105–10.

53. See the Banco de Guatemala advertisement in *The Times* (London), January 23, 1920, 57; "Mercantile Bank Hit By Falling Commodity Markets," *Wall Street Journal*, August 24, 1921.

54. Donald L. Kemmerer and Bruce R. Dalgaard, "Inflation, Intrigue, and Monetary Reform in Guatemala, 1919–1926," *The Historian* 46.1 (November 1983): 29; D. H. Dinwoodie, "Dollar Diplomacy in the Light of the Guatemalan Loan Project, 1909–1913," *The Americas* 26.3 (January 1970): 240.

55. *Commerical and Financial Chronicle* 102 (June 3, 1916): 2048.

56. "How an American Bank Is Pushing Ahead in the Foreign Field," *Bankers Monthly* 100.1 (January 1920): 97; F. J. Oehmichen, "New Offices of Banco Mercantil Americano de Cuba Opens," *Guaranty News* 8.8 (October 1919): 246–47; Manuel Landaeta Rosales, *La gran casa de la esquina de Camejo, hoy "Banco mercantil Americano de Caracas"* (Caracas: Banco mercantil Americano de Caracas, 1918); "Banco Mercantil del Peru at Lima Moves into New Quarters," *The Compass* 1.7 (July 1920), 203.

57. See "The MBA Enters the Argentine," *The Compass* 1.4 (April, 1920): 102–3.

58. "The MBA Enters the Argentine"; E. J. Lubo, "Ciego de Avila," *The Compass* 1.4 (April 1920): 115–16; the Mercantile Bank of the Americas advertisements in *Bamericuba* 1.2 (October 1919): 19 and in various issues of *The Compass*.

59. "Foreign Branches of American Banks," *Federal Reserve Bulletin*, August 1, 1918, 736; "Mercantile Bank Hit by Falling Commodity Markets," *Wall Street Journal*, August 24, 1921, 1. The history of the Mercantile Overseas Corporation predates the organization of the MBA. Its initial ancestor was the trading firm of H. Fogg & Co., organized in the 1850s for US trade with Japan. By the end of the century H. Fogg was reorganized as the China & Japan Trading Co., Ltd., and had, by 1908, offices in Yokohama, Kobe, Osaka, Nagasaki, Shanghai, and London. See Cleona Lewis, *America's Stake in International Investments* (Washington, DC: The Brookings Institution, 1938), 176–77.

60. Minutes of a Special Meeting of the Directors of the Banco Mercantil Americano de Cuba, Braga Brothers Collection.

61. "Plan New Bank for Cuba," *New York Times*, November 22, 1918; "New Cuban-American Bank," *Washington Post*, November 21, 1918.

62. Statement re: Foreign Bond and Share Corporation, January 19, 1922, Financial, Mercantile Bank of the Americas, Record Group II, Series 10a-c, Manuel Rionda y Polledo, Subject Files, 1911–1943, Box 7, Braga Brothers Collection.

63. Curtis Mallett-Prevost & Colt to Manuel Rionda, December 2, 1918, Financial, Mercantile Bank of the Americas, Record Group II, Series 10a-c, Manuel Rionda y Polledo, Subject Files, 1911–1943, Box 7, Braga Brothers Collection.

64. "Gracias," *Bamericuba* 1.2 (October 1919): 8–9.

65. See *Bamericuba* 1.1 (September 1919): 3.

66. "Twenty-Four Companies in Sugar Consolidation," *Wall Street Journal*, December 22, 1915; "Cuban Sugar Merger," *New York Times*, December 19, 1915.

67. Manuel Rionda to J. & W. Seligman & Co., December 16, 1915, Cuba Cane Sugar Corporation Syndicate, Corporations, Frank A. Vanderlip Papers, Manuscripts and Special Collections, Columbia University Libraries.

68. James L. Hunt, *Relationship Banker: Eugene W. Stetson, Wall Street, and American Business, 1916–1959* (Macon, GA: Mercer University Press, 2009).

69. J. Seligman to Frank A. Vanderlip, December 28, 1915, Cuba Cane Sugar Corporation Files; J. & W. Seligman & Co. to Frank A. Vanderlip, December 31, 1915, Cuba Cane Sugar Corporation, Organization, Frank A. Vanderlip Papers; Muriel McAvoy, *Sugar Baron: Manuel Rionda and the Fortunes of Pre-Castro Cuba* (Gainesville: University Press of Florida, 2003), 80–103. Vanderlip was offered, and subscribed for, 200 shares of preferred stock and 1,400 of common stock for the amount of $200,000. See Frank A. Vanderlip to J. & W. Seligman & Co, Cuba Cane Sugar Corporation Syndicate, January 3, 1916, Frank A. Vanderlip Papers.

70. Cuba Cane Sugar Corporation Stock Syndicate, Syndicate Records, December 24, 1915 J. P. Morgan and Co. Syndicate Book, vol. 8, 159–60, Morgan Library and Museum.

71. Jesse Seligman to Frank A. Vanderlip, February 3, 1916, Cuba Cane Sugar Corporation Syndicate, Frank A. Vanderlip Papers.

72. Hunt, *Relationship Banker*, 125.

73. E. J. Lubo, "Ciego de Avila," *Bamericuba*, 115–16.

74. Leland Hamilton Jenks, *Our Cuban Colony: A Study in Sugar* (New York: Vanguard Press, 1928).

75. Manuel Rionda to Banco Mercantil Americano de Cuba, March 3, 1919, Financial, Mercantile Bank of the Americas, Record Group II, Series 10a-c, Manuel Rionda y Polledo, Subject Files, 1911–1943, Box 7, Braga Brothers Collection.

76. Supplement F. to Statement of Banco Mercantil Americano de Cuba in Havana, Dated May 31, 1919, Mercantile Bank of the Americas, Financial, Mercantile Bank of the Americas, Record Group II, Series 10a-c, Manuel Rionda y Polledo, Subject Files, 1911–1943, Box 7, Braga Brothers Collection.

77. Loans Made by the Banco Mercantil Americano de Cuba to Colonos of Cuba Cana Sugar Corporation; Banco Mercantil Americano de Cuba, Loans and Advances as of August 31, 1919, Financial, Mercantile Bank of the Americas, Record Group II, Series 10a-c, Manuel Rionda y Polledo, Subject Files, 1911–1943, Box 7, Braga Brothers Collection.

78. McAvoy, *Sugar Baron*, 396 n 6.

79. Supplement F. to Statement of Banco Mercantil Americano de Cuba in Havana Dated May 31, 1919, Mercantile Bank of the Americas, Braga Brothers Collection.

80. Cable Received from F. J. Oehmichen, Manager, Banco Mercantil Americano de Cuba, n.d., Financial, Mercantile Bank of the Americas, Record Group II, Series 10a-c, Manuel Rionda y Polledo, Subject Files, 1911–1943, Box 7, Braga Brothers Collection.

81. Manuel Rionda to Walter M. Van Deusen, September 22, 1919, Financial, Mercantile Bank of the Americas, Record Group II, Series 10a-c, Manuel Rionda y Polledo, Subject Files, 1911–1943, Box 7, Braga Brothers Collection.

82. Banco Nacional de Cuba, Junta Liquidadora, *Memoria presentada a la Comisión Temporal de Liquidación Bancaria en 30 de Septiembre de 1926* (Havana: Imprenta La Prueba, 1926), 67.

83. Theodore S. Brooks interviewed by Leland Hamilton Jenks, February 25, Leland

Hamilton Jenks Collection on the Cuban Sugar Industry (C0712) 1925–1934, Special Collections, Princeton University.

84. República de Cuba, Comisión Temporal Liquidación Bancaria, *Compendio de los trabajos* (Havana: Julio Arroyo, 1928), 27; Alberto Arredondo, *Cuba: Tierra indefensa* (Havana: Editorial Lex, 1945), 318.

85. See the various country reports in *The Compass* in 1921.

86. Minutes of a Special Meeting of Banco Mercantile Americano de Cuba at 44 Pine Street, July 22, 1920, Mercantile Bank of the Americas, Record Group II, Series 10a-c, Manuel Rionda y Polledo, Subject Files, 1911–1943, Box 7, Braga Brothers Collection.

87. Manuel Rionda to W. A. Merchant, September 20, 1920, Mercantile Bank of the Americas, Record Group II, Series 10a-c, Manuel Rionda y Polledo, Subject Files, 1911–1943, Box 7, Braga Brothers Collection.

88. "Present Conditions in Cuba," *The Compass* 1.9 (September 1920): 257–63.

89. "Present Conditions in Cuba," *The Compass* 1.10 (October 1920): 334.

90. Republic of Cuba, Secretaría de Hacienda, Sección de Acuñación de Moneda, Número recibido de los Estados Unidos desde el dia 12 de Octubre por los bancos y compañias que se Expresan, Fondo Secretaría de la Presidencia, Caja 12, exp. 1, Archivo Nacional de Cuba

91. American Foreign Banking Corporation et. al. to Menocal, December 27, 1920, Fondo Secretaría de la Presidencia, Caja 12 exp. 3, Archivo Nacional de Cuba.

92. $12,000,000 Cuban sugar commercial acceptance credit, J. P. Morgan and Co. Syndicate Book, vol. 10, 35–36, Morgan Library and Museum.

93. Consta de una pequeña papa a Menocal, November 3, 1920, Fondo Secretaría de la Presidencia, Caja 12 exp. 3, Archivo Nacional de Cuba.

94. Statement re: Foreign Bond and Share Corporation, January 19, 1922, Braga Brothers Collection.

95. Ibid.

96. John Douglas Forbes, *Stettinius, Sr.: Portrait of a Morgan Partner* (Charlottesville: University Press of Virginia, 1974), 138.

97. "Bank Needs Met, Says Morgan Firm," *New York Times*, August 13, 1921.

98. Forbes, *Stettinius, Sr.*, 138.

99. "Cubans See Hope for Loan," *New York Times*, October 4, 1921, 24; P. R. Rodriguez to Manuel Rionda, October 19, 1921, Financial, Mercantile Bank of the Americas, Record Group II, Series 10a-c, Manuel Rionda y Polledo, Subject Files, 1911–1943, Box 7, Braga Brothers Collection.

100. "Bank of Americas to Close Branches," *New York Times*, September 30, 1921, 29.

101. "Mercantile Reduces Overhead," *Wall Street Journal*, September 20, 1921, 9.

102. Foreign Bond and Share Corporation to Czarnikow-Rionda Company, January 19, 1922, Financial, Mercantile Bank of the Americas, Record Group II, Series 10a-c, Manuel Rionda y Polledo, Subject Files, 1911–1943, Box 7, Braga Brothers Collection.

103. "Bank of Central and South America Succeeds Mercantile," *Wall Street Journal*, August 10, 1922, 4.

104. *The Mechanics & Metals National Bank of the City of New York* (New York: The Mechanics & Metals National Bank of the City of New York, 1920) n.p.; "Bank to Specialize in Latin America," *New York Times*, September 15, 1922.

105. "Bank Needs Met, Says Morgan Firm," *New York Times*, August 13, 1921; "To Close Cuban Branch," *New York Times*, September 17, 1921, 21.

106. Armando Occon Herradora, *Banco Nacional de Nicaragua y su entorno histórico: 1912–1998* (Managua: Banco Nacional de Nicaragua, 1988), 203.

107. Carlos Quijano, *Nicaragua: Ensayo sobre el imperialismo de los Estados Unidos* (Montevideo: Sandino, 1969), 89–95; "Nicaragua Bank Shows Big Profit," *Watertown Daily Times*, March 3, 1927.

108. "New Officer Added to Chase Official Staff," *The Chase* 13 (February–March 1931): 867; Herradora, *Banco Nacional de Nicaragua y su entorno histórico*, 203.

109. "Liberals Loot National Bank of Nicaragua," *Rochester Democrat and Chronicle and Rochester Herald*, May 6, 1926; Herradora, *Banco Nacional de Nicaragua y su entorno histórico*, 260; "Revolt Forces Control Valley," *Miami News*, May 5, 1926.

110. "Nicaragua Loan after Election," *Daily Worker*, August 13, 1927.

111. On the 1928 loan negotiations and the emergence of Sandino, see Emily Rosenberg, *Financial Missionaries to the World: The Politics and Culture of Dollar Diplomacy* (Durham, NC: Duke University Press, 2003), 232–34; and Gregorio Selser, *Sandino* (New York: Monthly Review Press, 1981), 60.

112. Conference with Judge Otto Schoenrich, January 13, 1925, Leland Hamilton Jenks Collection on the Cuban Sugar Industry, 1925–1934, Special Collections, Princeton University.

113. "Prosperous Cuba for 1923," *New York Times*, March 8, 1923.

114. "Cuban Banking Development," *The Times* (London), May 17, 1922, 1.

115. J. C. M. Ogelsby, *Gringos from the Far North: Essays in the History of Canadian-Latin American Relations, 1866–1968* (Toronto: Macmillan of Canada, 1976), 107.

116. "Prosperous Cuba for 1923," *New York Times*, March 8, 1923, 16.

117. "Bank of Canada Adds to Holdings," *New York Times*, February 4, 1925, 33.

118. Clifford H. Ince, *The Royal Bank of Canada: A Chronology, 1864-1969* (Montreal: Royal Bank of Canada, 1969), 22.

CHAPTER SIX

1. Descriptions of the new National City Bank of New York branch in Havana are drawn from "National City Bank Building Is a Marvel of Construction," "New National City Building a Triumph in Bank Architecture," "Praises National City Bank of New York" (translation from *Correo Español* under headline "Banking Progress in Cuba"); "Inauguración del nuevo edificio del National City Bank," "National City Bank a Wonder," and "New National City Building a Triumph in Bank Architecture," clippings in Joseph H. Durrell, comp., "Personal Files," vol. 2, "1924–1935" (unpublished manuscript), n.p.; "Opening of Bank's New Building at Havana a Brilliant Event," *No. 8*, 20.6 (June 1925): 2–5; T. Philip Terry, *Terry's Guide to Cuba* (Cambridge MA: The Riverside Press, 1926, 1929), 194.

2. On the convent, see Irene Wright, *Cuba* (New York: Macmillan, 1910), 39; Luis Bay Sevilla, "El convento de Santa Catalina de Sena," *Revista de Arquitectura* 28.276 (November–December 1943): 440–45.

3. Durrell's account of the opening is found in Joseph H. Durrell, "Family History," vol. 2, "1924–1930" (unpublished manuscript), n.p.; Charles E. Mitchell, "Mr. Charles E. Mitchell (Before Machado Spoke)," and also Mitchell, "Mr. Charles E. Mitchell (After General Machado's Speech)," in Durrell, "Personal Files," vol. 2, n.p.

4. Gerardo Machado y Morales, "A Few Paragraphs Taken from General Machado's Speech," in Durrell, "Personal Files," vol. 2, n.p.

5. "Ya está instalado en su suntuoso palacio de O'Reilly y Compostela the National City Bank of New York," undated newspaper clipping in Durrell, "Personal Files," vol. 2, n.p.

6. "Translation of Speech Delivered by Mr. J. A. Acosta, Manager of the Caibarién Branch," in Durrell, "Personal Files," vol. 2, n.p.
7. "Manager Overseas Division Is J. H. Durrell's Added Title," *No. 8*, 25.12 (December 1930): 3–4.
8. Durrell, like Roger L. Farnham, is mentioned only twice in Citibank's official history: Harold van B. Cleveland and Thomas F. Huertas, *Citibank: 1812–1870* (Cambridge, MA: Harvard University Press, 1985). However, his importance to the bank is as much as a historian as a historical figure: Durrell wrote a monograph titled "A History of Foreign Branches of American Banks and Overseas Division, N.C.B." (unpublished memoir, 1940) that the authors cite in their discussion of the City Bank's foreign expansion. The monograph was, according to Durrell's granddaughter, "borrowed" from the family by the bank during its research and has never been returned. See Cleveland and Huertas. *Citibank*, 110, 208; Joseph H. Durrell, "Family History," vol. 1, "1879–1923" (unpublished manuscript), n.p.; Connie Sheehy, pers. comm. via e-mail, October 5, 2009.
9. A. St. John, "Men in Wall Street's Eye: Introducing Mr. Charles E. Mitchell," *Barron's* 3.10 (March 5, 1923): 11; "Virility, in sparks, leaped from him," writes John K. Winkler, *The First Billion: The Stillmans and the City Bank* (New York: Vanguard Press, 1934), 262, also 26.
10. W. F. Walmsly, "The Ruler of the Largest Bank," *New York Times*, September 29, 1929.
11. When Durrell does appear, it is often not in the most flattering light. For instance, in his autobiography, George S. Moore claims that Durrell basically ran down the foreign department during his career. George S. Moore, *The Banker's Life* (New York: Norton, 1987), 169.
12. My thinking here draws on David Scott, "Colonial Governmentality," *Social Text* 43 (1995): 191–220; Michel Foucault, "Governmentality," in *The Foucault Effect: Studies in Governmentality*, ed. Graham Burchell et al. (Chicago: University of Chicago Press, 1992), 87–104; and Peter Miller and Nikolas Rose, *Governing the Present: Administering Economic, Social, and Political Life* (Cambridge: Polity Press, 2008).
13. Mitchell, "Mr. Charles E. Mitchell (Before Machado Spoke)," in Durrell, "Personal Files," vol. 2, n.p.
14. *The Visit of the President-Elect of Cuba General Gerardo Machado to the United States in April, 1925* (Washington, DC: Capitol Press, 1925), 55–56.
15. Gerardo Machado y Morales, "A Few Paragraphs Taken from General Machado's Speech," in Durrell, "Personal Files," vol. 2, n.p.
16. Brief biographical sketches of Durrell can be found in "Around the Bank: Joseph H. Durrell Appointed Assistant Vice-President," *No. 8*, 16.2 (February 1921): 26; "Joseph H. Durrell, Banker and Big-Game Hunter, 87," *New York Times*, February 23, 1967; and Joseph H. Durrell, "Untitled Biographical Document," in Durrell, "Personal Files," vol. 2, n.p.
17. "Manager Overseas Division Is J. H. Durrell's Added Title," 3.
18. The First National Bank of Dayton was part of a chain of banks owned by the Cheneys, of which the Fort Dodge National Bank was the parent.
19. I. A. Wright, *The Gem of the Caribbean* (Isles of Pines: Isle of Pines Publicity Company, 1909); "Isle of Pines Bank," in *West Virginia, Corporation Report of Secretary of State, March 4, 1905, to March 1, 1907* (Charleston: The Crossman Printing Company, 1907), 43.
20. Durrell, "Family History," vol. 1, n.p.

21. Durrell, "Family History," vol. 1, n.p. The characterization of Merchant is drawn from Conference with Charles M. Lewis, February 10, 1926, Leland Hamilton Jenks Collection on the Cuban Sugar Industry (C0712), 1925–1934, Special Collections, Princeton University. (Durrell traveled with Lewis to Cuba.)

22. Durrell, "Family History," vol. 1, n.p.

23. "Foreign Banking Operations of First National Bank of Boston," *Federal Reserve Bulletin*, November 1, 1918, 1079–81. On the early history of the First National Bank of Boston in Argentina, see Ramón Gutiérrez and Jorge Tartarini, *El Banco de Boston: La Casa Central en la Argentina, 1917–1997* (Buenos Aires: Fundación Banco de Boston, 1996), 19–31.

24. Joseph H. Durrell to George E. Roberts, March 28, 1918; George E. Roberts to Joseph H. Durrell, April 11, 1918, in Durrell, "Personal Files," vol. 1, n.p.

25. Durrell to F. A. Goodhue, July 13, 1918; Joseph H. Durrell to Daniel G. Wing, June 21, 1918; Goodhue to Joseph H. Durrell, July 9, 1918; Durrell to Goodhue, July 10, 1918; F. A. Goodhue to Durrell, July 20, 1918, in Durrell, "Personal Files," vol. 1, n.p.; "Manager Overseas Division Is J. H. Durrell's Added Title," *No. 8*, 25.12 (December 1930): 3–4.

26. J. H. Durrell to W. A. Merchant, June 24, 1918, in Durrell, "Personal Files," vol. 1, n.p.

27. Roger L. Farnham, "Memorandum in Respect of the Opening in Cuba of Additional Branches, September 15, 1919," in Durrell, "Personal Files," vol. 1, n.p.

28. Ibid.

29. Durrell to Roberts, November 30, 1919, in Durrell, "Personal Files," vol. 1, n.p.

30. Durrell to Roberts, January 10, 1919, in Durrell, "Personal Files," vol. 1, n.p.

31. Farnham to Durrell, January 3, 1919, in Durrell, "Personal Files," vol. 1, n.p.

32. Roberts to Durrell, January 3, 1919, in Durrell, "Personal Files," vol. 1, n.p.

33. Durrell to Charles E. Mitchell, February 10, 1922, in Durrell, "Personal Files," vol. 1, n.p.

34. "Six More Branches of the NCB Opened in the Caribbean Territory," *No. 8*, 14.7 (July 1919): 15; "City Bank Has Six More Cuban Branches: IBC Opens Two in the Far East," *No. 8*, 14.8 (August 1919): 34–36; "The Bank Opens New Branches in Brazil and Cuba: IBC Announces a New Branch in San Domingo," *No. 8*, 14.9 (September 1919): 22–24.

35. "Three New Branches in Tropics," *No. 8*, 15.3–4 (March–April 1920): 26.

36. Durrell to C. V. Rich, November 11, 1919, in Durrell, "Personal Files," vol. 1, n.p.

37. Durrell to Charles E. Mitchell, February 10, 1922, in Durrell, "Personal Files," vol. 1, n.p.

38. "Juan B. Roqué," *No. 8*, 13.1 (January 1918): 6.

39. Durrell to John H. Allen, December 24, 1919; Durrell to Allen, November 11, 1919; Durrell to C. V. Rich, November 11, 1919; Durrell to James A. Stillman, November 21, 1919; C. V. Rich to Durrell, November 25, 1919; Durrell to Gilbert Rubens, November 21, 1919; Gilbert Rubens to Durrell, November 26, 1919, in Durrell, "Personal Files," vol. 1, n.p.

40. Allen to Durrell, December 24, 1919; November 25, 1919; Durrell to Allen, n.d.; Allen to Durrell, November 28, 1919; November 29, 1919; December 1, 1919; December 24, 1919, in Durrell, "Personal Files," vol. 1, n.p.

41. A more extensive discussion of Durrell's impressions of Mexico can be found in "Mexican Events Warrant Belief That Better Times Are at Hand," *The Americas* 6.8 (May 1920): 1–5.

42. Durrell, "Family History," vol. 1, n.p.

43. Durrell to C. V. Rich, November 11, 1919, in Durrell, "Personal Files," vol. 1, n.p. On Mexico, see also Durrell to J. G. Durrell, May 18, 1920, in Durrell, "Personal Files," vol. 1, n.p.
44. Durrell, "Family History," vol. 1, n.p.
45. Durrell to Charles E. Mitchell, February 10, 1922, in Durrell, "Personal Files," vol. 1, n.p. On Rivera, see "Rivera's Friends Pleased with Rise," *Havana Post*, June 4, 1924, clipping in in Durrell, "Personal Files," vol. 1, n.p.
46. J. H. Durrell to John H. Allen, May 24, 1920, in Durrell, "Personal Files," vol. 1, n.p.
47. J. H. Durrell to John H. Allen, May 22, 1920, in Durrell, "Personal Files," vol. 1, n.p.
48. Durrell, "Family History," vol. 1, n.p.
49. "New Manager for Havana Branch," *No. 8*, 15.7 (July 1920): 26.
50. J. H. Durrell to James Addison, August 10, 1920; J. H. Durrell, "Memo for the Comptroller," August 10, 1920, in Durrell, "Personal Files," vol. 1, n.p.
51. John Brooks, *Once in Golconda: A True Drama of Wall Street, 1920–1938* (New York: Harper & Row, 1969), 1–20.
52. "J. H. Durrell Saw Explosion," untitled and undated clipping, in Durrell, "Personal Files," vol. 1, n.p.; *The Times of Cuba*, October, 1920, 68.
53. "John H. Allen," *No. 8*, 15.12 (December 1920): 26.
54. On Brady, see "Five New Officers Are Appointed at Annual Meeting," *No. 8*, 16.2 (February 1921): 3; *Commercial and Financial Chronicle* 103.2763 (September 1916): 1007; Moore, *The Banker's Life*, 25–26; Philip L. Zweig, *Wriston: Walter Wriston, Citibank, and the Rise and Fall of American Financial Supremacy* (New York: Crown Publishers, 1995), 48. Brady served as chairman of the City Bank from 1948 to 1952.
55. Durrell, "Family History," vol. 1, n.p.
56. *Commercial and Financial Chronicle* 112.1 (March 5, 1921): 901; *Wall Street Journal*, March 3, 1921.
57. Joseph H. Durrell, "Untitled Biographical Document," in Durrell, "Personal Files," vol. 2, n.p.
58. Durrell, "Family History," vol. 1, n.p.
59. Cleveland and Huertas, *Citibank*, 105–7.
60. Frank Plachy, Jr. "What the City Bank Means to Cuba," *No. 8*, 17.10 (October 1921): 2–3.
61. William G. Brady, Brady Report, in Durrell, "Personal Files," vol. 2, n.p.
62. Durrell, "Family History," vol. 1, n.p.
63. "Charles E. Mitchell Now Is President Both of Bank and City Company," *No. 8*, 16.5 (May 1921): 3; C. E. Mitchell to Frank A. Vanderlip, May 7, 1921, Frank A. Vanderlip Papers, Manuscripts and Special Collections, Columbia University Libraries.
64. This is a point made by Cleveland and Huertas in *Citibank*, 107. On Swenson's economic interests, see "Eric P. Swenson, 90, Retired Bank Head," *New York Times*, August 14, 1945; "E. P. Swenson Forms Holding Company," *New York Times*, November 29, 1927; and August Anderson, *Hyphenated or, The Life Story of S. M. Swenson* (Austin: E. L. Steck, 1916).
65. This section is based on Charles E. Mitchell, "National City Company," *No. 8*, 14.5 (May 1919): 1–6; Charles E. Mitchell, "The National City Company's Plans for World Wide Investments Service," *The Americas* 5.11 (August 1919): 16-18; Charles E. Mitchell, "The Story of the National City Company," *No. 8*, 19.1 (January 1924): 1–5; "Financial Notes," *New York Times*, March 18, 1916, 15; St. John, "Men in Wall Street's Eye," 11; "Charles E. Mitchell," *Bankers' Magazine* 122.6 (June 1931): 836.
66. "N. W. Halsey & Co. Sold to City Bank," *New York Times*, August 20, 1916, 3.

67. St. John, "Men in Wall Street's Eye," 11.
68. W. Nelson Peach, *The Security Affiliates of National Banks* (Baltimore: Johns Hopkins University Press, 1941), 104–5.
69. St. John, "Men in Wall Street's Eye," 11; "Testimony of Charles E. Mitchell," in US Senate, Committee on Banking and Currency, *Stock Exchange Practices*, pt. 1 (Washington, DC: GPO, 1932), 1772.
70. "Mitchell Will Run National City Bank," *New York Times*, June 8, 1921, 32.
71. *Commercial and Financial Chronicle* 112.2920 (June 11, 1921): 2500–2501. Two executive managers, John H. Fulton and W. A. Simonson, were made senior vice presidents; Vere Brown was made a vice president but left the bank soon thereafter; Charles Rich resigned from the bank. "Charles V. Rich Resigns from National City Bank," *Bankers' Magazine* 103.1 (July 1921): 151; Charles McD. Puckette, "Wall Street Harkens to C. E. Mitchell," *New York Times*, February 13, 1927.
72. Durrell, "Family History," vol. 1, n.p.
73. Charles E. Mitchell, "Speech by Mr. Charles E. Mitchell at the Banquet in His Honor at the Midday Club, Havana, on the 26th January, 1922," *Economic Bulletin of Cuba* 1.2 (February 1922): 68; also "Mr. Charles E. Mitchell Expresses Views on Cuban Situation," *Economic Bulletin of Cuba* 1.2 (February 1922): 71–72.
74. Rentschler served as chairman of Citigroup in 1940–48; he died of a heart attack in Havana and was succeeded by William G. Brady.
75. "Bank Executives Reach Havana by Air Route," *No. 8*, clipping in in Durrell, "Personal Files," vol. 2, n.p.
76. "Closer contact with Cuba Established in Trip through Island," *No. 8*, 17.3 (March 1922): 1–2.
77. See the clippings from the Cuban press in Durrell, "Personal Files," vol. 2, n.p.; and in the *New York Times*: January 20, 1922; January 26, 1922; January 27, 1922.
78. J. H. Durrell to Charles E. Mitchell, February 10, 1922, in Durrell, "Personal Files," vol. 2, n.p.
79. Durrell, "Family History," vol. 1, n.p.
80. Ibid.
81. Charles E. Mitchell to J. H. Durrell, April 11, 1922; Charles E. Mitchell to Joseph H. Durrell; Joseph H. Durrell to Charles E. Mitchell, April 18, 1922, in Durrell, "Personal Files," vol. 2, n.p. On Durrell's promotion and Farnham's resignation, also see the following clippings in Durrell, "Personal Files," vol. 2, n.p.: "Changes in Official Staff," *The National City Bank of New York, The National City Company Sales Letter*, April 11, 1922; "Durrell Promoted," *New York Sun*, April 11, 1922; "Farnham Resigns from National City Bank," *New York Times*, April 15, 1922; *Commercial and Financial Chronicle* 114.2964 (April 15, 1922); on Durrell's appointment, see "Durrill [*sic*] Elected Vice President," *Havana Post*, April, 15, 1922.
82. Charles E. Mitchell to J. H. Durrell, January 29, 1922; J. H. Durrell to Charles E. Mitchell, February 10, 1922, in Durrell, "Personal Files," vol. 2, n.p.
83. Cleveland and Huertas, *Citibank*, 109; J. H. Durrell to Charles E. Mitchell, February 10, 1922, in Durrell, "Personal Files," vol. 2, n.p.; Isaac Frederick Marcosson, *Colonel Deeds, Industrial Builder* (New York: Dodd, Mead, 1947), 306–11. The GSC was managed by George A. Houston but with Colonel Deeds and Gordon Rentschler as its principals; Rentschler's company manufactured steam engines and other machinery that was sold to Cuban planters.
84. "Camagüey Sugar Company," *Economic Bulletin of Cuba* 2.4 (December 1922): 156; Vertientes Sugar Co 1st Mortgage Sinking Fund 71/2 Bonds, 1942, J. P. Morgan and

Co. Syndicate Book, vol. 8, p. 97, Morgan Library and Museum; Camagüey Sugar Company (Compañia Azucarera de Camagüey, S.A.), National City Bank and National City Company; re: Cuban Dominican Sugar Company—Memoranda, Correspondence, and Prospectus, Box 145, Record Group 46, National Archives and Records Administration.

85. W. G. Brady, "Memorandum for Mr. C. E. Mitchell, President, January 11, 1923, in Durrell, "Personal Files," vol. 1, n.p.

86. Operating Profit or Loss, November 1, 1923, in Durrell, "Personal Files," vol. 1, n.p.

87. J. H. Durrell to Charles E. Mitchell, July 18, 1923, in Durrell, "Personal Files," vol. 1, n.p.; *Monthly Bulletin of the American Chamber of Commerce of Cuba* 3.3 (March 1924): 11. The price paid for the seven buildings was $336,030.49.

88. "Advancement from within the Promise of Our Chief: An Address Made by Mr. Mitchell before the Havana City Bank Club on February 14, 1923," clipping in Durrell, "Personal Files," vol. 1, n.p.; J. H. Durrell, Memorandum for Mr. Olwell, February 19, 1923, in Durrell, "Personal Files," vol. 1, n.p.

89. "J. H. Durrell Placed in Charge of District National City Bank," *Evening News*, July 6, 1923; J. H. Durrell to Charles E. Mitchell, July 18, 1923, in Durrell, "Personal Files," vol. 1, n.p.

90. See the following unidentified clippings in Durrell, "Personal Files," vol. 1: "Durrell Gets New Bank Job"; "Banquet for Durrell"; "National City Bank Employees Will Banquet J. H. Durrell Tonight"; "Los empleados del City Bank tributaron anoche un homenaje de simpatía a Mister Durrell por su ascenso en dicha entidad"; "Homenaje de los jefes y empleados del City Bank a Mr. J. H. Durrell," *Diario de la Marina*; "Homenaje al Vice President del City Bank"; "Bank Employees Dine Durrell on Eve of Leaving."

91. "Hard Cash the Only Means to Wind Up Crisis," *Havana Post*, September 19, 1922, clipping in Durrell, "Personal Files," vol. 1.

92. The Havana Clearing House was housed in the offices of the Trust Company of Cuba; its initial members were N. Gelats & Co., Pedro Gómez Mena e Hijo, Royal Bank of Canada, Trust Company of Cuba, Banco Mercantil Americano de Cuba, National City Bank, American Foreign Banking Corporation, Banco del Comercio, and Canadian Bank of Commerce. See Havana Clearing House, *Constitution and By-Laws* (Havana: La Moderna Poesía, 1921); *Cuba Review and Bulletin* 19.7 (June 1921): 11.

93. Also see "A Banking Law," *Economic Bulletin of Cuba* 1.4 (April 1922): 155; Luis Marino Perez, "The Proposed Cuban Bank Law," *Monthly Bulletin of the American Chamber of Commerce of Cuba* 2.5 (May 1923): 9.

94. A summary of the history of the Federal Reserve agencies in Cuba is found in Henry Christopher Wallich, *Monetary Problems of an Export Economy: The Cuban Experience, 1914–1947* (Cambridge, MA: Harvard University Press, 1950), 69–72.

95. *Federal Reserve Bulletin*, October 1923, 1089.

96. On the City Bank's complaints over the actions of the Federal Reserve, see the series of letters in 1923 between Durrell and Mitchell and the officials of the reserve bank in Correspondence with National Banks: Officers of the National City Bank of New York City, Papers of Benjamin Strong, Jr., Federal Reserve Bank of New York, https://fraser.stlouisfed.org/archival/1160.

97. J. H. Case to Charles E. Mitchell, July 17, 1923, Correspondence with National Banks: Officers of the National City Bank of New York City, Papers of Benjamin Strong, Jr., Federal Reserve Bank of New York.

98. "Office Building Adjoining Havana Branch Financed by City Company," *No. 8*, 21.4 (April 1926): 6.

99. "Opening of Bank's New Building at Havana a Brilliant Event," *No. 8*, 20.6 (June 1925):1–6.

100. General Receiver of Dominican Customs, *Report of the Nineteenth Fiscal Period, Dominican Customs Receivership, under the American-Dominican Convention of 1924, for the Calendar Year 1925* (Washington, DC: GPO, 1926), 6–7; Juan Daniel Balcácer, ed., *Citibank en la República Dominicana: En el país, con el país* (Santo Domingo: Citibank, 1987), in Colección Santiago Michelena Ariza, Instituto de Estudios del Caribe, Centro de Investigaciónes Históricas, Facultad de Humanidades, Universidad de Puerto Rico, Río Piedras.

101. International Banking Corporation, *Forty-Eighth Semi-Annual Statement, June 30, 1926* (New York: International Banking Corporation, 1926); "Bank Takes Over Panama IBC Branches, Colon and Panama City," *No. 8*, 21.3 (March 1926): 24. While the City Bank was taking over many of the IBC's branches, the IBC was making its own moves. In 1924, it had absorbed the Asia Banking Corporation, the Guaranty Trust Company's foreign banking corporation that had been in liquidation since the crash. The City Bank took over the seventeen Asia branches of the IBC to create the Far Eastern Division. See "IBC Absorbs Asia Banking Corporation," *No. 8*, 19.2 (February 1924): 7; "Asia Banking Corporation," J. P. Morgan and Co. Syndicate Book, vol. 10, 101, Morgan Library and Museum; "Bank Will Take Over 17 IBC Branches," *No. 8*, 21.12 (December 1926): 1.

102. St. John, "Men in Wall Street's Eye," 11; "Testimony of Charles E. Mitchell," 1772.

103. Mitchell, "The National City Company's Plans for World-Wide Investment Service," 16–18.

104. "Benjamin Franklin: Father of Thrift," *No. 8*, 18.1 (January 1923), 5. The efforts by bankers to encourage and teach savings were paralleled by similar educational work by the Federal Reserve System and the American Bankers Association. Meanwhile, journals such as *Bankers Monthly* offered articles on the "tendency to save" among different nationalities, women, and children. See issues in 1920, for instance.

105. *Bonds & Bankers* (New York: The National City Company, 1922), 4.

106. Mitchell, "National City Company," 1–5.

107. Peach, *The Securities Affiliates*, 10–12.

108. *Bonds & Bankers*, 29.

109. Frederick Lewis Allen, *Only Yesterday: An Informal History of the 1920s* (New York: Harper Brothers, 1931), 290–319.

110. Julian Sherrod, *Scapegoat* (New York: Brewer, Warren, and Putnam, 1931); Edmund Wilson, "Sunshine Charley," *New Republic*, June 28, 1933, 176–77.

111. "Automatic Savings at Work," *No. 8*, 18.1 (January 1923): 5.

112. "How a Home Budget Makes Good," *No. 8*, 17.10 (January 1923): 6.

113. "Benjamin Franklin: Father of Thrift," *No. 8*, 18.1 (January 1923), 5; "Following Franklin's Footsteps," *No. 8*, 18.1 (January 1923), 8. The bank created a ten-principle thrift program whose tenets were "Work; earn; make a budget; have a bank account; own your home; carry life insurance; make a will; invest in sound securities; pay bills promptly; share with others."

114. "Compound Interest Department Opens," *No. 8*, 17.1 (January 1922): 8; "The Beacon of Thrift at the Hub of New York," *No. 8*, 18.1 (January 1923): 12–13.

115. "The Beacon of Thrift at the Hub of New York," 12–13.

116. "THE CID Curtain Rises," *No. 8*, 93.4 (April 1923): 1–3.

117. "CID Contest Builds Thrift City of 45,226 New Depositors," *No. 8*, 18.6 (June 1923): 6; "Extend CID Services to Branches," *No. 8*, 18.11 (November 1923): 13; "How the CID Contest Came to Be," *No. 8*, 18.6 (June 1923): 7; "THE CID Curtain Rises," *No. 8*, 18.4 (April 1923): 1–3.
118. C. E. Mitchell, "From the Chief," *No. 8*, 21.1 (January 1926): 1.
119. "Cuba and Porto Rico Set a World Record in Savings Contest," *No. 8*, 21.1 (January 1926): 5.
120. "Cuba and Porto Rico Staffs in Stirring C.I.D. Contest," *No. 8*, 20.11 (November 1925): 6.
121. "All Colors Flying High as CID Contest Nears Close," *No. 8*, 18.5 (May 1923): 5.
122. "How Porto Rico Beat the World," *No. 8*, 23.8 (August 1928): 2–4.
123. "Cuba's Brilliant Record," *No. 8*, 23.8 (August 1928): 5–6.
124. I am borrowing the phrase "infrapolitics" to think about low-frequency resistance to American imperialism and banking from Robin D. G. Kelley, "'We are not what we seem': Rethinking Black Working-Class Opposition in the Jim Crow South," *Journal of American History* 80.1 (June 1993): 75.
125. "Nacionalismo económico," *El Mundo*, July 17, 1924, 16–18; "La compra del Banco Nacional por la Fedral Reserva sería un desastre para Cuba," *El Comercio*, August 5, 1925, 27–29; "La suerte del Banco Nacional y la suerte de Cuba," *El Mundo*, July 15, 1924, 30–31.
126. See the newspaper articles compiled in the publication *La reorganización del Banco Nacional de Cuba* (Havana: Imprenta "El Siglo XX", 1924).
127. "Rectificación oportuna," *El Mundo*, July 26, 1924, 33–35; "Palabras significativas," *El Mundo*, August 17, 1924; "El ambiente nacional y el problema bancario," *La Discusion*, July 31, 1924, 54–55; "La banca nacional," *El Heraldo*, August 2, 1924.
128. "La suerte del Banco Nacional y la suerte de Cuba," *El Mundo*, July 15, 1924, 30–31.
129. "El Banco Nacional: Sus enemigos en campaña," *El Triunfo*, August 13, 1924, 107–9; "La Banca Nacional," *El Heraldo*, July 29, 1924, 41–42.
130. "Necesidad de la Banca Nacional," *El Triunfo*, July 29, 1924; "Una moción oportuna," *El Mundo*, July 30, 1924, 46–47.
131. Translation of clipping from Havana newspaper *El Universal*, December 29, 1924, in Durrell, "Personal Files," vol. 2, n.p.
132. J. H. Durrell to Lee E. Olwell," January 21, 1925, in Durrell, "Personal Files," vol. 2, n.p.
133. Lee E. Olwell to J. H. Durrell, January 20, 1925, in Durrell, "Personal Files," vol. 2, n.p.
134. J. H. Durrell to Lee E. Olwell, January 21, 1925, in Durrell, "Personal Files," vol. 2, n.p.
135. Thomas F. O'Brien, "The Revolutionary Mission: American Enterprise in Cuba," *American Historical Review* 98.3 (June 1993): 765–85.
136. "Discurso pronunciado por Gerardo Machado en el 'Bankers Club' de Nueva York," April 24, 1925, in *Luchas obreras contra Machado*, ed. Mira Rosell (Havana: Editorial de Ciencias Sociales, Instituto Cubano del Libro, 1973), 53–55.
137. "A Few Paragraphs Taken from General Machado's Speech," in Durrell, "Personal Files," vol. 2, n.p.
138. Louis Perez, Jr., *Cuba under the Platt Amendment, 1902–1934* (Pittsburgh: University of Pittsburgh Press, 1986), 256–60.
139. *Economic Conditions, Governmental Finance, United States Securities* (May 1926), 87–88; for the statement from the Royal Bank of Canada, see *Wall Street Journal*, April 14, 1926.
140. *New York Times*, April 11, 1926; April 12, 1926; April 13, 1926.
141. "President Machado and the Banks," *Monthly Bulletin of the American Chamber of Com-*

merce of Cuba 5.4 (April 1926): 13; "Shrewd," Time, April 19, 1926, 15; "Cuban President Helps to Check Run on Banks," Washington Post, April 11, 1926; "$80,000,000 Cash Is Rushed to Cuba to Fortify Banks," Washington Post, April 12, 1926; "President Machado and the Banks," Monthly Bulletin of the American Chamber of Commerce of Cuba 5.4 (April 1926): 13.

142. New York Times, April 11, 1926.

143. Alberto Arredondo, Cuba: Tierra indefensa (Havana: Editorial Lex, 1945). The Banco del Comercio emerged out of the business interests of the Arguelles family, Spanish merchants who had been active in Cuba since the mid-nineteenth century. The bank survived the crisis of 1920–21 but had a rough time of it afterward, with repeated suspensions over the course of the next decade. Harold G. Hesler, "Cuba: Banking and Currency, 1942–1950" (unpublished manuscript, 1961), 120. On the City Bank loan to Céspedes, see "Convenio de préstamo otorgado por the National City Bank of New York a Carlos Miguel de Céspedes y José Manuel Cortina," in Luchas obreras contra Machado, ed. Mira Rosell (Havana: Editorial de Ciencias Sociales, Instituto Cubano del Libro, 1973), 215–21.

144. Wall Street Journal, April 14, 1926; "Our Own Dot and Dash Bridge to Havana," No. 8, 21.4 (April 1926): 5.

145. Richard H. Gamble, A History of the Federal Reserve Bank of Atlanta, 1914–1989 (Atlanta: Federal Reserve Bank of Atlanta, 1989), 40–45.

146. National City Monthly Letter, May, 1926, 87.

147. Ibid.

148. "President Machado and the Banks," Monthly Bulletin of the American Chamber of Commerce of Cuba 5.4 (April 1926): 13.

149. Joseph H. Durrell to Charles E. Mitchell, July 5, 1927, in Durrell, "Personal Files," vol. 2, n.p.

150. For details of Machado's April 1927 visit, see New York Times, April 24, 1927.

151. "A Visit from Cuba's President," No. 8, 22.4 (April 1927): 3.

152. New York Times, April 29, 1927.

153. Thomas W. Lamont, quoted in Alfred Betancourt to Reed Smoot, January 25, 1932, in US Senate, Committee on Finance, Sale of Foreign Bonds or Securities in the United States, pt. 4 (Washington, DC: GPO, 1932), 1932.

154. New York Times, May 26, 1927.

155. Durrell, "Family History," vol. 2, n.p.

156. Juan Santamaria Garcia, Sin azúcar no hay país: La industria azucarera y la economía cubana (1919–1939) (Sevilla: Consejo Superior de Investigaciónes Científicas, Escuela de Estudios Hispano-Americanos, 2001), 151; Moore, A Banker's Life, 72–73.

157. Minutes of Executive Committee of City Bank Farmers Trust Company, November 1928, National City Bank, and National City Company, Records of the Committee on Banking and Currency, 1913–1968, Record Group 46, National Archives and Records Administration. A succinct account of the General Sugar Company and the NCC is found in W. Nelson Peach, The Security Affiliates, 131–33. Also see Cleveland and Huertas, Citibank, 109–10.

158. Durrell to Mitchell, March 2, 1928, in Durrell, "Personal Files," vol. 2, n.p.

159. Ibid.

160. Joseph H. Durrell to Charles E. Mitchell, March 12, 1928, in Durrell, "Personal Files," vol. 2, n.p.

161. Durrell to Mitchell, March 12, 1928, in Durrell, "Personal Files," vol. 2, n.p.

162. Ibid.

163. "Our New Building in Panama," *No. 8*, 24.9–10 (September–October 1928): 5; "Expansion of Banking in Panama," *Pan-American Magazine* 41.4 (December 1928): 246–48.
164. Durrell to Mitchell, March 12, 1928, in Durrell, "Personal Files," vol. 2, n.p.
165. Ibid.
166. "Panama's Recent Financial Operations," *Pan-American Magazine* 41.3 (July–August, 1928): 180–82.
167. "In Honor of Haiti's President," *New York Amsterdam News*, June 16, 1926, 10.
168. Sidney de la Rue, *A Review of the Finances of the Republic of Haiti, 1924–1930* (Port-au-Prince: Bureau du conseiller financier-receveur général, 1930), 3; "World-Wide National City Service Is Increased in Many Fields," *No. 8*, 20.3 (March 1925): 1; Paul H. Douglas, "Economic and Financial Aspects," in *Occupied Haiti*, ed. Emily Balch Greene (New York: Writers Publishing Company, 1927), 37–56.
169. *Fourth Annual Report of the American High Commissioner at Port-au-Prince, Haiti to the Secretary of State, 1925* (Washington, DC: GPO, 1926), 10.
170. De la Rue, *A Review of the Finances of the Republic of Haiti*, 16.
171. W. W. Cumberland, quoted in George Séjourné, *Les États-Unis d'Amérique et la banque route d'Haïti* (Port-au-Prince: Imprimerie La Presse, 1932), n.p.
172. Arnold Roller, "Black Ivory and White Gold in Cuba," *The Nation*, January 9, 1929, 55-56.
173. "Bank of Central and South America Succeeds Mercantile," *Wall Street Journal*, August 10, 1922, 4.
174. Charles E. Mitchell, Memorandum for Mr. Durrell, July 23, 1929, in Durrell, "Personal Files," vol. 2, n.p.
175. Memorandum for Mr. Mitchell, Re: If I Were King, July, 1929, in Durrell, "Personal Files," vol. 2, n.p.
176. See correspondence between Durrell and A. M. Klender between November 8 and November 29, 1929, in Durrell, "Personal Files," vol. 2, n.p.

CHAPTER SEVEN

1. "The Chase Bank in Latin America," *The Chase* 7.10 (January 1925): 41, 415; "Havana Branch," *The Chase* 15.1 (April 1932): 3–5; Harold G. Hesler, "Cuba: Banking and Currency, 1942–1950" (unpublished manuscript, 1961), 121; Llilian Llanes, *1898–1921: La transformación de la Habana a través de la arquitectura* (Havana: Letras Cubanas, 1993), 295. The building was designed by Afro-Cuban architect Gustavo E. Urrutia. See Mercer Cook, "Urrutia," *Phylon* 4.3 (1943): 220–32.
2. *The Report of the Chairman of the Board of Directors at the Fifty-Third Annual Meeting of Shareholders.* (New York: The Chase National Bank of the City of New York, 1930), 3.
3. "Havana Correspondence," *Cuba Review* 16.5 (April 1918): 19.
4. The only accounts of the internationalism of the Chase Bank are Gino Cattani and Adrian E. Tschoegl, *An Evolutionary View of Internationalization: Chase Manhattan Bank, 1917 to 1996* (Philadelphia: Wharton Financial Institutions Center, 2002), and S. B. Prasad, "The Metamorphosis of City and Chase as Multinational Banks," *Business and Economic History* 28.2 (1999): 201–9. The authorized corporate biography of the Chase Bank, John Donald Wilson's *The Chase: The Chase Manhattan Bank, N.A., 1945–1985* (Cambridge. MA: Harvard Business School Press, 1986), provides but a quick overview of the bank's history before 1945 and says little about its international expansion.
5. *The Chase National Bank of the City of New York, 1877-1922* (New York: De Vinne Press, 1922), 9–14.

6. Wilson, *The Chase*, 9.
7. "Albert H. Wiggin, Financier, 83, Dies," *New York Times*, May 22, 1951.
8. *Boston: Its Commerce, Finance and Literature . . . 1892* (New York: A. F. Parsons, 1892), 137.
9. On the Eliot, see *Boston: Its Commerce, Finance and Literature*, 236. It was absorbed by the National Shawmut Bank in 1912. Asa S. Knowles, *Shawmut: 150 Years of Banking, 1836–1986* (Boston: Houghton Mifflin Company, 1986), 114.
10. Ernest Fletcher Clymer, *The Doorway: Being A Story of the Facilities within the Doorway of a Modern Commercial Bank* (New York: National Park Bank, 1920); Ernest Fletcher Clymer, *The Making of an Institution* (New York: National Park Bank, 1922); Ernest Fletcher Clymer, ed., *1856–1917: Some Mile-Stones in the History of the National Park Bank of New York* (New York: The National Park Bank, 1917).
11. D. C. Forbes, "Make Good First—and You Will Make Friends," *The American Magazine* 87.3 (March 1919): 16–17, 178.
12. On the formation of the Bankers Trust, see Thomas W. Lamont, *Henry P. Davison: The Record of a Useful Life* (New York: Harper, 1933), 51–65; Marjorie Wiggin Prescott, *New England Son* (New York: Dodd Mead, 1949), 82; *Twenty-Five Years of Bankers Trust Company: A Brief History of the Company with Graphs and Other Data Connected with Its Growth, 1903–1928* (New York: Bankers Trust Company, 1928); *The Five Decades of Bankers Trust Company, New York; 1903–1953* (New York: Bankers Trust Company, 1953).
13. Marjorie Wiggin Prescott, *New England Son* (New York: Dodd Mead & Company, 1949), 82.
14. "Foreign Credit Corporation Quits," *New York Times*, August 27, 1921.
15. Besides the Chase Bank, the organizers were the Merchants National Bank of Boston, the First National Bank of Cleveland, the Philadelphia National Bank of Philadelphia, the Canal Bank and Trust Company of New Orleans, the National Bank of Commerce in St. Louis, the Corn Exchange National Bank of Chicago, the First and Security National Bank of Minneapolis, the Fifth-Third National Bank of Cincinnati, the Anglo and London Paris National Bank of San Francisco, the First National Bank of Milwaukee, Hayden B. Harris (formerly of N. W. Harris and Co.) of New York City, Norman H. Davis of the Trust Company of Cuba, Havana, and Schmidt and Gallatin of New York City. *New York Times*, June 10, 1917; American Foreign Banking Corporation advertisement in *The Times of Cuba*, July 1920, 143.
16. Founded in Toronto in 1867 with a charter purchased by the dormant Bank of Canada, the Canadian Bank of Commerce (CBC) was a dominant financial presence on the Canadian prairies. Though it was (and remains) one of the largest Canadian banks, at the time of the organization of the AFBC, the CBC did not have the kind of extensive foreign or interimperial branch banking networks of its Dominion rivals, the Bank of Nova Scotia and the Royal Bank of Canada. It had one overseas branch, in Mexico City, that had been established in 1910, and used the AFBC as a stepping-stone for its own expansion into the Caribbean and Latin America. It would go on to organize branches in Cuba, Jamaica, Barbados, Trinidad, and Brazil in the 1920s. On the history of the CBC's foreign ventures, see Arnold Edinborough, *A History of the Canadian Imperial Bank of Commerce*, vol. 4, *1931–1973* (Toronto: CIBC, 1995), 53–79; Anne M. Logan, *From Tent to Tower: The Biography of Sydney H. Logan* (Don Mills, ON: n.p., 1974), passim. For the general history of the CBC, see Victor Ross, *A History of the Canadian Bank of Commerce, with an Account of the Other Banks Which Now Form Part of Its Organization* (Toronto: University of Toronto Press, 1922); and

various issues of *Caduceus: Staff Magazine of the Canadian Bank of Commerce*, 1920–1937.

17. "American Foreign Banking Corporation Leases Five-Story Building," *Banking Law Journal* 36 (January–December 1919): 518.

18. New York (State) Banking Department, *Annual Report of the Superintendent of the Banking Department of the State* (Albany: Banking Department, 1920), 93; *Annual Report of the Chamber of Commerce of the State of New York* (New York: Press of the Chamber of Commerce, 1920), 205.

19. Georges Corvington, *Port-au-Prince: Au cours des ans*, vol. 3 (Montreal: Les Éditions du CIDIHCA, 2007), 288.

20. According to the City Bank's Roger Farnham, the text of the agreement was negotiated by John H. Allen. Allen, at the time, worked for the BNRH; he would join the AFBC in November 1920. "Testimony of Roger Farnham," in *Inquiry into Occupation and Administration of Haiti and Santo Domingo* (Washington, DC: United States Senate, 1922), 124. See "The Royal Bank of Canada et. al. to Haitian Secretary of Finance, July 30, 1920," in *Inquiry into Occupation of Haiti and Santo Domingo*, 796.

21. *Washington Post*, November 13, 1918; Clyde William Phelps, *Foreign Expansion of American Banks* (New York: Ronald Press, 1927), 149; "The Chase Bank on the Isthmus of Panama," *The Chase* 12.2 (May, 1929): 70–79. An anecdotal account of the history of the Chase Manhattan Bank in Panama, and its predecessor, the Commercial National Bank, of Washington DC, is found in "Chase Manhattan Handles Varied Banking Business for Canal and Zone Residents," *Panama Canal Review*, June 1, 1956, 8–9; "Isthmus Commerce: Chase Manhattan," *Panama Canal Review*, November 1963, 6–7; *The Chase National Bank in the Caribbean Area* (New York: The Chase National Bank of the City of New York, 1944).

22. "Economic and Financial Affairs," *Bulletin of the Pan American Union* 51.2 (August 1920): 198; *Who's Who in California: A Biographical Directory, 1928–29*, ed. Justice B. Detwiler (San Francisco: Who's Who Publishing Company, 1929), 225.

23. "Foreign Branches," *Federal Reserve Bulletin*, December, 1920, 1298; Archibald Kains, "Foreign Trade and Foreign Banking," *The Chase* 1.3 (May 1918); 83–87; Melvin M. Knight, *The Americans in Santo Domingo* (1928; New York: Arnold Press, 1970), 136–37.

24. "American Foreign Banking Corporation," *Bankers' Magazine* 98.1 (January 1919): 76.

25. William B. Thompson to Manuel Rionda, re: Schmidlapp of the Chase, February 8, 1916, Record Group II, Series 10a-c, Manuel Rionda y Polledo, Subject Files, 1911–1943, Box 7, Braga Brothers Collection, University of Florida, Gainesville. On Upmann's accounts with the Chase, see "Comisión conferida al Dr. Clarence Marine en relación con los bancos norte-americanos," in Republic of Cuba, Comisión Temporal de Liquidación Bancaria, *Compendio de los trabajos realizados desde 17 de Febrero de 1921, hast 4 de Agosto de 1924* (Havana: Editorial "Hermes", 1924), 130.

26. "$100,000,000 Credit for Cuban Sugar," *New York Times*, February 20, 1918. On the 1921 crop, see *The Times of Cuba*, November 1920, 70–71, 81. The Chase, the AFBC, and the CSC participated in syndicates with J. P. Morgan, the Guaranty Trust Company, and the National City Company to purchase the 1921 Cuban sugar crop.

27. On Hayden, Stone, see the company-produced pamphlet *Hayden, Stone & Co., 1892–1958: 66 Years of Continuous Service to Investors* (Boston: Hayden, Stone, 1958).

28. H. O. Neville, "News of the Cuban Sugar Industry," *Facts about Sugar*, August 5, 1922, 110; Oscar Pino-Santos, *El asalto a Cuba por la oligarquía financiera yanqui* (Havana: Casa de las Américas, 1973), 153–54. On the history of Atkins and Punta Alegre, see Cesar J. Ayala, *American Sugar Kingdom: The Plantation Economy of the Spanish*

Caribbean, 1898–1934 (Chapel Hill: University of North Carolina Press, 1999), 89–94; Muriel McAvoy, *Sugar Baron: Manuel Rionda and the Fortunes of Pre-Castro Cuba* (Gainesville: University Press of Florida, 2003), 1, 80.

29. See *Agreement between Punta Alegre Sugar Company and Hayden, Stone & Company, Hornblower & Weeks, and the Merchants National Bank of Boston, Dated July 1st, 1916, Securing Collateral Trust Six Percent Convertible Gold Bonds to the Amount of $3,000,000* (Boston: Punta Alegre, 1916). On the history of the Atkins family in Cuba, see Edwin Farnsworth Atkins, *Sixty Years in Cuba: Reminiscences* (Cambridge, MA: Arno Press, 1926).

30. *The Chase National Bank of the City of New York, 1877–1922* (New York: Chase National Bank of the City of New York, 1922), 26–27, 30; Edwin F. Atkins, "Sugar Production in Cuba: The Influence of Political Changes on the Industry from 1870 to 1918," *The Chase* 1.6 (September 1918): 214.

31. "American Foreign Banking Corporation—Havana Branch," *Federal Reserve Bulletin*, November 1920, 1167; *International Banking Directory* (New York: Bankers Publishing Company, 1922), 718.

32. Joseph H. Durrell to Charles E. Mitchell, March 12, 1928, in Joseph H. Durrell, comp., "Personal Files," vol. 2, "1924–1935" (unpublished manuscript), n.p.

33. Exhibit C: Telegram, American Foreign Banking Corporation to National Bank of Commerce, St. Louis, Mo., September 27, 1920, American Foreign Banking Corporation, Record Group 2, Chase National Bank, Affiliates, JPMorganChase Archives.

34. The other participants in the syndicate were Corn Exchange National Bank, Chicago; Merchants Loan and & Trust Co., Chicago; Peoples State Bank, Detroit; First National Bank, Cleveland; Lincoln Trust Co., New York; Springfield National Bank, Springfield, MA; Merchants National Bank, Worcester, MA; Bank of Pittsburgh, N.A.; Fifth-Third National Bank, Cincinnati; Merchants National Bank, Los Angeles, CA; Philadelphia National Bank, Philadelphia, PA; First National Bank, Baltimore, MD; National Bank of Commerce, St. Louis; Merchants National Bank, St. Paul, MN; and National Bank of Commerce, Toledo, OH. Exhibit B: Participants in L. R. Munoz and Company acceptance credit, October 7, 1920, American Foreign Banking Corporation, Record Group 2, Chase National Bank, Affiliates, JPMorganChase Archives.

35. Exhibit D: M. M. Manasse to E. J. Mudd, October 14, 1920, American Foreign Banking Corporation, Record Group 2, Chase National Bank, Affiliates, JPMorganChase Archives. After he left the AFBC, Manasse joined the investment banking firm F. J. Lisman and Co., first as manager of its foreign department, later as partner. He investigated the possibility of Lisman loaning money to Colombia, El Salvador, and Peru. Swaine, *The Cravath Firm*, 442.

36. Exhibit E: J. Laughlin, Jr., to National Bank of Commerce, December 23, 1920, American Foreign Banking Corporation, Record Group 2, Chase National Bank, Affiliates, JPMorganChase Archives.

37. Ibid.

38. "Foreign Banking Election," *New York Times*, September 8, 1917.

39. John G. Lonsdale to Albert H. Wiggin, May 6, 1921; John G. Lonsdale to Albert H. Wiggin, May 11, 1921; see also John G. Londsdale to John H. Allen, May 7, 1921; Gerhard M. Dahl to John G. Lonsdale, May 9, 1921; John G. Lonsdale to Albert H. Wiggin, May 11, 1921, American Foreign Banking Corporation—Chase National Bank, Record Group 2, Chase National Bank, Affiliates, Subsidiaries, JPMorganChase Archives.

40. Report of E. J. Mudd and L. S. Mitchell in regards to the American Foreign Banking Corporation and Acceptance of L. R. Munoz and Company, May 16, 1921, American

Foreign Banking Corporation, Record Group 2, Chase National Bank, Affiliates, JPMorganChase Archives.

41. Ibid.

42. A detailed accounting of the collateral pledged is available in Exhibit F: Memorandum Concerning Status of Munoz & Company's Indebtedness and Collateral Securing the Same as of April 30th, 1921, American Foreign Banking Corporation—Chase National Bank, Record Group 2, Chase National Bank, Affiliates, Subsidiaries, JPMorganChase Archives.

43. For a list of participants and the amount of participation, see "Exhibit A, Proposed Participation in $9,200,000.000 Credit," in Report of E. J. Mudd and L. S. Mitchell.

44. This section is based on the Report of E. J. Mudd and L. S. Mitchell.

45. E. J. Mudd to Albert H. Wiggin, May 23, 1921; Albert H. Wiggin to E. J. Mudd, May 25, 1921, American Foreign Banking Corporation, Record Group 2, Chase National Bank, Affiliates, JPMorganChase Archives.

46. Conference with Judge Otto Schoenrich, January 13, 1925, Leland Hamilton Jenks Collection on the Cuban Sugar Industry, 1925–1934, Special Collections, Princeton University.

47. John H. Allen to Frank A. Vanderlip, New York, October 27, 1920, Frank A. Vanderlip Papers, Manuscripts and Special Collections, Columbia University Libraries; "American Foreign Banking Corporation," *Bankers' Magazine* 101 (1920): 863.

48. Report of E. J. Mudd and L. S. Mitchell.

49. It is unclear who was removed. However, Thayer left the AFBC.

50. Report of E. J. Mudd and L. S. Mitchell.

51. Ibid.

52. Banco Nacional de Cuba, Junta Liquidadora, *Memoria presentada a la Comisión Temporal de Liquidación Bancaria en 30 de Septiembre de 1926* (Havana: Imprenta La Prueba, 1926), 67.

53. Conference with Judge Otto Schoenrich, January 13, 1925, Interviews and Notes, 1925 to 1926, Leland Hamilton Jenks Collection on the Cuban Sugar Industry (C0712), 1925–1934, Special Collections, Princeton University; Interview with Theodore S. Brooks, February 25, 1926, Banco de Comercio Edificio, Leland Hamilton Jenks Collection on the Cuban Sugar Industry (C0712), 1925–1934, Special Collections, Princeton University.

54. See "Black, Frank W.," *Directory of Directors in the City of New York* (New York: Audit Co., 1916), 59; "Banking and Financial News," *Bankers' Magazine* 64 (1902): 113; F. W. Black, "Banking in Cuba: Cuban Banking Methods Described," *Bulletin of the American Institute of Bank Clerks* 1 (February 15, 1902): 5–7; "A Résumé of Mr. Black's Business Career," *The Equitable Envoy* 5.7 (January 1926): 3; Arthur Menzies Johnson, *Winthrop W. Aldrich: Lawyer, Banker, Diplomat* (Boston: Division of Research, Graduate School of Business Administration, Harvard University, 1968), 49; H. D. Nagel, "A Brief History of Our Foreign Department and Its Divisional Functions," *The Equitable Envoy* 2.8 (February 1923): 13.

55. Interview with Theodore S. Brooks, February 25, 1926, Banco de Comercio Edificio, Leland Hamilton Jenks Collection on the Cuban Sugar Industry (C0712), 1925–1934, Special Collections, Princeton University.

56. Interview with Frank Steinhart, February 19, 1926, Leland Hamilton Jenks Collection on the Cuban Sugar Industry (C0712), 1925–1934, Special Collections, Princeton University.

57. "New Charges in Lezama Case," *Facts about Sugar*, June 4, 1921, 447.

58. H. L. Darton, "American Foreign Banking Corporation," *Le Matin*, March 14, 1921.

59. "Foreign Banking Operations of First National Bank of Boston," *Federal Reserve Bulletin*, November 1, 1918, 1079–80.

60. "Banking Concern to Dissolve," *New York Times*, October 27, 1929; "The Chase Bank in Latin America," *The Chase* 7.10 (January 1925): 415; "Chase National Buys 3 Foreign Branches," *New York Times*, January 13, 1925, 26. For a detailed record of the transfer of the assets and liabilities of the American Foreign Banking Corporation to the Chase National Bank of New York, see *Schedules I, II, and III, Being Schedules Referred to in Agreement for Transfer and Pledge between American Foreign Banking Corporation and the Chase National Bank of the City of New York, et al., Dated December 19, 1924* (New York: Chase National Bank, 1924), American Foreign Banking Corporation, Record Group 2, Chase National Bank, Affiliates, JPMorganChase Archives.

61. "Dark Finance," *The Chase* 8.4 (July 1925): 151.

62. *The Chase National Bank in the Caribbean Area* (New York: The Chase National Bank of the City of New York, 1944), n.p.

63. *Schedule I, Being Schedules Referred to in Agreement for Transfer and Pledge between American Foreign Banking Corporation and The Chase National Bank of the City of New York, et al., Dated December 19, 1924* (New York: Chase National Bank of the City of New York, 1924) 1, American Foreign Banking Corporation, Record Group 2, Chase National Bank, Affiliates, JPMorganChase Archives.

64. "Amer. Foreign Banking Corp. Branches on Isthmus Taken Over by the Chase Bank," *Panama Star & Herald*, January 13, 1925; "American Foreign Banking Corporation," *Panama Star & Herald*, January 13, 1925; "Compra de una casa bancaria de Panamá," *La Estrella de Panamá*, January 13, 1925; "American Foreign Banking Corporation," *La Estrella de Panamá*, January 13, 1925.

65. Joseph H. Durrell to Charles E. Mitchell, March 12, 1928, Durrell, "Personal Files," vol. 2, n.p.

66. David Rockefeller, *Memoirs* (New York: Random House, 2002), 131.

67. On Machado's tour, see *The Visit of the President-Elect of Cuba General Gerardo Machado to the United States in April, 1925* (Washington, DC: Capitol Press, 1925); "Discurso pronunciado por Gerardo Machado en el 'Bankers Club' de Nueva York," in *Luchas obreros contra Machado*, ed. Mirta Rosell (Havana: Editorial de Ciencias Sociales, Instituto Cubano del Libro, 1973), 53–54.

68. Alberto Arredondo, *Cuba: Tierra indefensa* (Havana: Editorial Lex, 1945), 318.

69. Oscar Pino Santos, *El imperialismo norteamericano en la economía de Cuba* (Havana: Editorial de Ciencias Sociales 1973).

70. "Chase Securities Corporation," *The Chase* 6.2 (May 1923): 43–45. See "Testimony of Albert H. Wiggin, October 17, 1933," in US Senate, Committee on Banking and Currency, *Stock Exchange Practices*, pt. 5 (Washington: GPO, 1933), 2280.

71. "Testimony of Albert H. Wiggin," 2362.

72. The phrase "two-faced certificate" comes from a comment made by Senator Alva B. Adams during Albert H. Wiggin's congressional testimony. See "Testimony of Albert H. Wiggin," 2290.

73. "Chase Securities Corporation," *The Chase* 6.2 (May 1923): 43–45; "Testimony of Albert H. Wiggin," 2290.

74. Frank J. Williams, "Rise of New York's Great Investment Houses," *New York Evening Post*, October 15, 1926.

75. Robert T. Swaine, *The Cravath Firm and Its Predecessors, 1819–1947* (Clark, NJ: The Lawbook Exchange Limited, 2007), 199, 305, 433, 442n1.

76. "Testimony of Albert H. Wiggin," 2282; "The Chase-Metropolitan Merger," *The Chase* 4.9–10 (December 1921–January 1922): 283–86; *King's Handbook of New York City: An Outline History and Description* (Boston: Moses King, 1883), 677.

77. The relationship of the Metropolitan Life Insurance Company to these institutions is briefly discussed in Marquis James, *The Metropolitan Life: A Study in Business Growth* (New York: Viking Press, 1947), 154–55.

78. For details of the projects to be constructed, see Republic of Cuba, *Public Works Law under the Administration of Hon. President General Gerardo Machado, Carlos M. De Céspedes, Secretary of Public Works* (Havana: n.p., 1925), 1–18.

79. Karl A. Panthen to R. L. Clarkson, June 15, 1925, in Pinkerton Report re. Chase Securities Corporation, Republic of Cuba, October 7, 1933, Records of the Committee on Banking and Currency, 1913–1968, Record Group 46, National Archives and Records Administration (hereafter Pinkerton Report).

80. R. L. Clarkson to Karl A. Panthen, in US Senate, Committee on Banking and Currency, *Stock Exchange Practices*, pt. 5, 2654–55; "Testimony of Shepard Morgan," US Senate, Committee on Banking and Currency, *Stock Exchange Practices*, pt. 5, 2657–59. In the testimony, it is stated that Catlin refers to the Bank of Montreal. My sense is that he was referring to the Royal Bank of Canada, as the Bank of Montreal was, at that time, not present in Cuba, while the Royal Bank was based in Montreal.

81. "Guy W. Currier, Noted Lawyer, Dies," *New York Times*, June 22, 1930.

82. "Testimony of Shepard Morgan," 2657–59; Chase National Bank of the City of New York, *Cuban Public Works Financing: Reply to the Report of the Special Commission Created by Decree Law Number 140 of April 16, 1934* (New York: Chase National Bank of the City of New York, 1935), 421–23; for more details on this plan, see "Testimony of James C. Stewart," in US Senate, Committee on Banking and Currency, *Stock Exchange Practices*, pt. 5, 2719–32; Chase National Bank, *Cuban Public Works Financing*, 422.

83. "Brevities," *Monthly Bulletin of the American Chamber of Commerce of Cuba*, February 2, 1926, 29.

84. On Crowder's diplomacy in Cuba, see Leland Hamilton Jenks, *Our Cuban Colony: A Study in Sugar* (New York: Vanguard Press, 1928) 246–65; and David A. Lockmiller, *Enoch H. Crowder: Soldier, Lawyer, and Statesman* (Columbia: University of Missouri Studies, 1955), 217–46.

85. "Committee Exhibit No. 30: Cuba—Memorandum to Mr. Tinker, March 22, 1926," in US Senate, Committee on Banking and Currency, *Stock Exchange Practices*, pt. 5, 2607, 2608, 2610.

86. Chase National Bank, *Cuban Public Works Financing*, 367–69, 423.

87. Charles F. Batchelder to Edward Tinker, July 29, 1926, in US Senate, Committee on Banking and Currency, *Stock Exchange Practices*, pt. 5, 2568.

88. *Cuban Public Works Financing*, 401.

89. For the details of the contract, the following section draws on "Testimony of Carl J. Schmidlapp, C. P. Anderson, Jr., and A. M. Williams, January 27, 1932," US Senate, Committee on Finance, *Sale of Foreign Bonds or Securities in the United States*, pt. 4 (Washington, DC: GPO, 1932), 1978–86.

90. On Obregón, see Chase National Bank, *Cuban Public Works Financing*, 428.

91. "Honor Señor and Señora Obregón," *New York Times*, June 10, 1926; "4,000 at Eedding of Miss Machado," *New York Times*, June 1, 1926; "Machado's Son-in-Law with Bank," *New York Times*, April 14, 1927; León Primelles, *Crónica Cubana, 1919–1922: Menocal y la Liga Nacional, etc* (Havana: Editorial Lex, 1957), 239.

92. James Bruce to Joseph Rovensky, Feburary 23, 1931, quoted in "Testimony of Adam K.

Geiger," in US Senate, Committee on Banking and Currency, *Stock Exchange Practices*, pt. 5, 2631.

93. "Testimony of James C. Stewart," 2719–32.

94. "Testimony of Carl J. Schmidlapp," in US Senate, Committee on Banking and Currency, *Stock Exchange Practices*, pt. 4, (Washington, DC: GPO, 1932), 1949; Chase National Bank, *Cuban Public Works Financing*, 429.

95. Jose Obregón to Sherill Smith, January 6, 1928, in US Senate, Committee on Banking and Currency, *Stock Exchange Practices*, pt. 5, 2642.

96. Pinkerton Report.

97. One syndicate was composed of Warren Brothers Company and Compañía Cubana de Contratistas, in conjunction with the National City Bank of New York; and the other, in conjunction with Dillon, Read & Co., was composed of International Acceptance Bank, First National Bank of Boston, Bank of Italy, Blythe Witter & Company, and E. H. Rollins & Sons. Chase National Bank, *Cuban Public Works Financing*, 401.

98. Halstead G. Freeman to Albert H. Wiggin, April 30, 1928, in Pinkerton Report.

99. "Supplemental Agreement between Republic of Cuba and the Chase National Bank of the City of New York, June 22, 1928," in US Senate, Committee on Finance, *Sale of Foreign Bonds or Securities in the United States*, pt. 4, 1988–98.

100. Pinkerton Report.

101. "Supplemental Agreement between Republic of Cuba and the Chase National Bank of the City of New York, 1997–98.

102. Halstead A. Freeman to Albert Wiggin, April 30, 1928, in Pinkerton Report.

103. Kirwin Shaffer, "Contesting Internationalists: Transnational Anarchism, Anti-Imperialism, and US Expansion in the Caribbean, 1890s–1920s," *Estudios Interdisciplinarios de América Latina y el Caribe* 22.2 (2001): 30–31.

104. Louis S. Rosenthal to Ferdinand Pecora, October 2, 1933, Chase Securities Corp., Re: Republic of Cuba—Working Sheets, Senate Committee on Banking and Currency, Box 58, Record Group 46, National Archives and Records Administration.

105. Pinkerton Report.

106. James Bruce to Albert H. Wiggin, July 17, 1930, in US Senate, Committee on Banking and Currency, *Stock Exchange Practices*, pt. 6 (Washington, DC: GPO, 1932), 2765.

107. This paragraph draws on and quotes from Octavio Seigle, *Cuba's Finances* (New York: Octavio Seigle, 1930), in Chase Securities Corp., Re: Republic of Cuba—Remedies Re: Cuba, Chase Securities Corp.—Chase National Bank, Box 58, Investigation of Stock Exchange Practices, Records of the Committee on Banking and Currency, 1913–1968, Record Group 46, National Archives and Records Administration (hereafter Chase Securities Corp., Re: Republic of Cuba). On the background of *Cuba's Finances*, see Tiborio Cantaclaro to Ferdinand Pecora, October 16, 1933, Chase Securities Corporation, Re: Republic of Cuba. Seigle was murdered in 1936 by Fulgencio Batista. See Arthur Pincus, *Terror in Cuba* (New York: Workers Defense League, 1936), 19.

108. *El Mundo*, January 3, January 4, and January 8, 1931, reprinted in Pinkerton Report.

109. T. M. Findlay to Louis M. Rosenthal, November 9, 1932, in US Senate, Committee on Banking and Currency, *Stock Exchange Practices*, pt. 6, 2784.

110. Ibid.

111. Ibid.

112. C. S. Pinkerton to F. Pecora, October 7, 1933, in Pinkerton Report.

113. *The Chase Manhattan News*, Special Supplement: *The History of Chase Manhattan* (March 1982), 3-4, Kheel Center for Labor-Management Documentation and Archives, M. P. Catherwood Library, Cornell University; "Testimony of Albert H. Wiggin,

New York City, Retired, Tuesday, October 17, 1933," in US Senate, Committee on Finance, *Sale of Foreign Bonds or Securities in the United States*, pt. 4, 2280–2339.

114. Anon., *The Mirrors of Wall Street* (New York: G.P. Putnam's Sons, 1933), 116.

115. Forbes, "Make Good First," 178.

116. "Wiggin Is the Chase and the Chase Is Wiggin," *Business Week*, April 30, 1930, 22–24.

117. "Machado Adds to Guard against ABC in Montreal," *New York Times*, September 15, 1933; "Machado Is Barred from Bermuda Visit," *New York Times*, August 30, 1933; "Machado Happy and Contented in His Exile," *Sarasota Herald-Tribune*, August 14, 1933; August 30, 1933; Gerardo Machado y Morales to S. R. Noble, Royal Bank of Canada, Montreal, September 6, 1933, Series: I. Correspondence, 1923–1940; Subseries: A. From Machado, 1929–1936, Box No. 1, Folder No. 1, Folder Date: 1929–1934, Gerardo Machado y Morales Papers, Cuban Heritage Collection, University of Miami Libraries.

118. J. C. M. Ogelsby, *Gringos from the Far North: Essays in the History of Canadian-Latin American Relations, 1866–1968* (Toronto: Macmillan of Canada, 1976), 109.

119. Ramon Grau San Martin, quoted in *New York Times*, October 8, 1933, reprinted in Pinkerton Report; "President Grau San Martin Asks 'Fair Play' for Cuba," *Commercial and Financial Chronicle* 137.3654 (October 14, 1933): 2725.

120. Winthrop W. Aldrich, "Report of the Chairman of the Governing Board and President to Shareholders," in *The Report of the Chairman of the Governing Board and President at the Fifty-Seventh Annual Meeting of Shareholders, January 9, 1934* (New York: Chase National Bank, 1934), 14–18.

121. See Cuba, *Los empréstitos de obras públicas: Informe oficial rendido por La Comisión Especial de Investigación de las Obligaciones Contraídas con the Chase National Bank of the City of New York* (Havana: Talleres tipográficos de Carasa y ca, 1935).

122. "Letter of Winthrop W. Aldrich, June 29, 1934," in Chase National Bank, *Cuban Public Works Financing*, i–iv.

123. "Cuban High Court Upholds Machado Loans," *New York Times*, June 3, 1936, 1.

124. J. E. Higgs to F. Pecora, November 4, 1933, Chase Securities Corp., Re: Republic of Cuba.

125. Raymond Leslie Buell et al., *Problems of the New Cuba* (New York: Foreign Policy Association, 1935), 395–96.

126. Winthrop W. Aldrich, *Suggestions for Improving the Banking System* (New York: The Chase National Bank, 1933); Winthrop W. Aldrich, *Proposed Banking Act of 1935* (New York: The Chase National Bank of the City of New York, 1935).

CONCLUSION

1. "The New Home of the Chase National Bank," *The Chase* 10.4 (July 1927): 235–38; Alfred Shaw, "The Chase National Bank Building, New York," *Architectural Forum* 51.1 (July 1929): 1–5; "For Example: The Chase," *Fortune* 13 (January 1936): 55–60, 124–39; Sally A. Kitt Chappel, *Architecture and Planning of Graham, Anderson, Probst and White, 1912–1936: Transforming Tradition* (Chicago: University of Chicago Press, 1992), 191–96.

2. "World's Tallest Building for City Bank Farmers Trust Company," *No. 8*, 24.9–10 (September–October 1929): 4, 33; "New Building of City Bank Farmers Trust Company," *Bankers' Magazine* 122 (January–June 1931): 834–45; "New Bank Tower to Open Tuesday," *New York Evening Post*, February 19, 1931; "Around New York in an Airplane: No. 95—City Bank Farmers Trust Building," *New York Sun*, September 4, 1931; "The Design of a Bank's Skyscraper," *Architectural Forum* 55.1 (July 1931): 7–26;

"Structure and Equipment of the City Bank Farmers Trust Co.," *Architectural Forum* 55.1 (July 1931): 97–108

3. "Bull Market Architecture," *New Republic*, July 8, 1931, 192–93.
4. Julian Sherrod, *Scapegoat* (New York: Brewer, Warren, and Putnam, 1931); *The Mirrors of Wall Street* (New York: G. P. Putnam's Sons, 1933), 50.
5. On resistance to dollar diplomacy throughout the Caribbean and Latin America during this period, see Emily S. Rosenberg, *Financial Missionaries to the World: The Politics and Culture of Dollar Diplomacy* (Durham, NC: Duke University Press, 2003), 230–40.
6. Winthrop W. Aldrich, "Report of the Chairman of the Governing Board and President to Shareholders," in *The Report of the Chairman of the Governing Board and President at the Fifty-Seventh Annual Meeting of Shareholders, January 9, 1934* (New York: Chase National Bank, 1934), 1.
7. Joseph H. Durrell, "Family History," vol. 3, "1930–1936" (unpublished manuscript), n.p.
8. Harold van B. Cleveland and Thomas F. Huertas, *Citibank: 1812–1870* (Cambridge, MA: Harvard University Press, 1985), 159–72.
9. Susan Estabrook Kennedy, *The Banking Crisis of 1933* (Lexington: University Press of Kentucky, 1973), 109.
10. Ferdinand Pecora, *Wall Street under Oath* (New York: A. M. Kelley, 1968); Michael Perino, *The Hellhound of Wall Street* (New York: Penguin, 2010).
11. Durrell, "Family History," vol. 3, n.p.
12. "Testimony of Herbert D. Brown, January 27, 1932," in US Senate, Committee on Finance, *Sale of Foreign Bonds or Securities in the United States*, pt. 4 (Washington, DC: GPO, 1932), 1935.
13. George E. Roberts, *Investigación económica de la República de Panamá* (Managua, Nicaragua: Colección Cultural de Centro America, 2006).
14. George E. Roberts to Reed Smoot, February 1, 1932, in US Senate, Committee on Finance, *Sale of Foreign Bonds or Securities in the United States*, pt. 4, 1943.
15. Minutes of the Board of Directors of the City Bank Farmers Trust Company, January 9 and February 15, 1927, National City Bank and National City Company, Record Group 46, National Archives and Records Administration.
16. Durrell, "Family History," vol. 3, n.p.
17. For the text of the report, see "Frederick W. Lehmann to Charles W. Wickersham, November 6, 1911," in US Senate, Committee on Banking and Currency, *Stock Exchange Practices*, pt. 6 (Washington, DC: GPO, 1932), 2030–42.
18. Ibid.
19. Durrell, "Family History," vol. 3, n.p.
20. "Testimony of Albert H. Wiggin, New York City, Retired, Tuesday, October 17, 1933," in US Senate, Committee on Finance, *Sale of Foreign Bonds or Securities in the United States*, pt. 4, 2280–2339.
21. Ibid., 2451–52.
22. Cleveland and Huertas, *Citibank*, 197–98.
23. Durrell, "Family History," vol. 3, n.p.
24. Albert F. Nufer, Memorandum for the Ambassador, October 13, 1930, in US Department of State, *Confidential U.S. Diplomatic Post Records: Central America & the Caribbean, 1930–1945; Cuba*, pt. 1, *1930–1939*, reel 3 (Frederick, MD: University Publications of America, 1983).
25. Durrell, "Family History," vol. 3, n.p.
26. Exhibit 61–32A-C: T. M. Findlay to L. S. Rosenthal, November 9, 1932, Chase Securi-

ties Corp., Re: Republic of Cuba—Working Sheets, Senate Committee on Banking and Currency, Box 58, Record Group 46, National Archives and Records Administration.

27. "Havana Bank Is Bombed," *New York Times*, September 2, 1931; *Winnipeg Tribune*, September 2, 1931.

28. Robert Bruce Hoernel, "A Comparison of Sugar and Social Change in Puerto Rico and Oriente, Cuba, 1898–1958" (PhD diss., Johns Hopkins University, 1977), 140; Pablo de la Torriente-Brau, *Realengo 18 y Mella, Rubén y Machado* (Havana: Nuevo Mundo, 1962); and Alejandro de la Fuente and María de los Ángeles Meriño, "Vigilar las tiers del Estado: El Realengo 18 y la cuestión agraria en la República," in *Cuba de colonia a república*, ed. Martín Rodrigo y Alharilla (Madrid: Biblioteca Nueva, 2006), 209–24.

29. Harold Boyer, "Canada and Cuba: A Study in International Relations" (PhD diss., Simon Fraser University, 1972), 40. A slightly different account of the Palmira incident occurs in Duncan MacDowall, *Quick to the Frontier: Canada's Royal Bank* (Toronto: M&S, 1949), 262.

30. "City Bank Branch in Port Rico," *Wall Street Journal*, April 3, 1918.

31. "San Juan Branch Moves to New Building," *No. 8*, 24.12 (December 1929): 7.

32. Such protests from a colonial bourgeoisie also occurred when Durrell opened a branch of the City Bank in Mexico City in 1929. See, for instance, Miguel A. Quintana, "Quiene a hacer 'The National City Bank of New York' a Mexico," *Revista Mexicana de Economía* 1 (1929): 335–49; Miguel A. Quintana, *El imperialismo de la mercancia Americana y el establecimiento en México de The National City Bank of New York* (Villahermosa, Mexico: Ediciones de "Redención", 1931). On the opening of the branch, see "Bank Opens Branch in Mexico and Two in New York Area," *No. 8*, 24.7 (July 1929): 8.

33. "Fear National City's Size," *New York Times*, April 15, 1930; "Takes Porto Rican Bank," *New York Times*, April 24, 1930; "Bank Deal Opposed by Port Ricans," *New York Times*, April 2, 1930; "Takes Porto Rican Bank," *New York Times*, April 24, 1930.

34. "In addition, the economies of our people, which are deposited in the banks, go to the disposal of a foreign power. They are held by the National City Bank, the Royal Bank of Canada, and the Bank of Nova Scotia, which finance, with interest, enemies of the country." "Declaraciones de la Junta Nacional del Partido Nacionalista de Puerto Rico ante el momento politico, May 18, 1931," in *La conciencia nacional puertorriqueña por Pedro Albizu Campos*, ed. Manuel Maldonado-Denis (Mexico City: Siglo vientiuno editors, 1977), 79.

35. "Run on Porto Rican Bank," *New York Times*, May 23, 1931.

36. "Funds Sent to San Juan," *New York Times*, October 21, 1931.

37. "Puerto Rican Bank Opened," *New York Times*, March 5, 1933; "Puerto Rico Gets Cash," *New York Times*, March 7, 1933.

38. "The financial panic results in ruin for the miserable people of North America, but it is one of the efficient methods that the Yankee banking oligarchy uses to remain in power indefinitely." Pedro Albizu-Campos, "En torno a la situacion bancaria de Puerto Rico se dirige el Partido Nacionalista al Presidente del Senado, San Juan de Puerto Rico, 7 de Marzo de 1933," in *Pedro Albizu Campos: Obras Escogidas, 1923–1936*, vol. 1, ed. J. Benjamín Torres (San Juan: Editorial Jelofe, 1975), 243. Also see Pedro Albizu Campos and Jose Lameiro, "La bandera de la raza," in *Albizu Campos: Escritos*, ed. Laura Albizu-Campos Meneses and Fr. Mario A. Rodríguez León (Hato Rey, Puerto Rico: Publicaciones Puertorriqueñas, 2007), 28–32.

39. Albizu-Campos, "En torno a la situacion bancaria de Puerto Rico," 243.

40. "To Cut Interest Rates," *New York Times*, June 27, 1933; "15,000 Persons Thrown Out

of Work If United Puerto Rican Sugar Company Not Preserved," *New York Times*, September 8, 1933.

41. "United Puerto Rico Sale Held Up," *Wall Street Journal*, February 1, 1934; "Judge's Decree Assailed," *New York Times*, January 31, 1934.

42. "Plans Puerto Rican Bank," *New York Times*, September 20, 1933.

43. "Hoy se discutira la moción de nuevo juicio de los nacionalistas," *El Mundo* (San Juan), August 4, 1936; "Denegado el nuevo juicio a los nacionalistas,'" *El Mundo* (San Juan), August 5, 1936. Also see Vito Marcantonio, "Uncle Sam in Puerto Rico," *Labor Defender*, April 1937, 12.

44. "Tres jurados mas solicitan licencia para portar armas," *El Mundo*, August 12, 1936, 1, 4.

45. *The Bankers' Almanac and Year Book, 1968–1969* (Haywards Heath: T. Skinner, 1968), 650.

46. Rulhière Savaille, *La grève de 29* (Port-au-Prince: Les Ateliers Fardin, 1979).

47. W. Cameron Forbes, *Report of the President's Commission for the Study and Review of Conditions in the Republic of Haiti, March 26, 1930* (Washington, DC: GPO, 1930), 4, 8.

48. Herbert Hoover, "Message to Congress, December 10, 1931, on Foreign Affairs," in *The State Papers and Other Public Writings of Herbert Hoover*, vol. 2, *October 1, 1931–March 4, 1933*, ed. William Starr Myers (New York: Doubleday, Doran & Company, 1934), 79.

49. Joseph Jolibois Fils, *L'accord du 7 Août 1933* (Port-au-Prince: Le Courrier Haitien, 1933), 23; Beaucharnais Jean-Francois, *Le loup et l'agneau ou, le contrôle financier américan en Haïti* (Port-au-Prince: Impremerie nouvelle, 1933), 30; Alexandre Lilavois, "Rapport financier: Régime financier des Américains en Haïti" (unpublished manuscript, University of Florida, Gainesville).

50. "Testimony of Georges N. Léger, February 10, 1932," in US Senate, Committee on Finance, *Sale of Foreign Bonds or Securities in the United States*, pt. 4, 2127–61 (quotation at 2161).

51. Henry L. Stimson to Reed Smoot, February 15, 1932, in US Senate, Committee on Finance, *Sale of Foreign Bonds or Securities in the United States*, 2171–79.

52. For an overview, see Brenda Gayle Plummer, "The Afro-American Response to the Occupation of Haiti, 1915-1934," *Phylon* 43.2 (1982): 125–43.

53. Walter White to Reed Smoot, February 9, 1932, in US Senate, Committee on Finance, *Sale of Foreign Bonds or Securities in the United States*, pt. 4, 2161. See National Association for the Advancement of Colored People, "Memorandum to the Committee on Finance of the United States Senate," in US Senate, Committee on Finance, *Sale of Foreign Bonds or Securities in the United States*, pt. 4, 2162–66.

54. Langston Hughes, "White Shadows in a Black Land," *Crisis* 39 (May 1932): 157.

55. Robert Melvin Spector, *W. Cameron Forbes and the Hoover Commissions to Haiti (1930)* (New York: University Press of America, 1985), 197–98.

56. Hans Schmidt, *The United States Occupation of Haiti, 1915–1934* (New Brunswick, NJ: Rutgers University Press, 1971), 224–25; Ernest Gruening, *Many Battles: The Autobiography of Ernest Gruening* (New York: Liveright, 1973), 169–70.

57. US Department of State, "Sale of the Banque Nationale de la République d'Haiti by the National City Bank of New York to the Republic of Haiti," *Foreign Relations* 4 (1935): 703–28; Banque de la Republique d'Haiti, *Législation des banques et des institutions financières* (Port-au-Prince: Banque de la Republique D'Haiti, 1985), 5–12.

58. Haiti, *Annual Report of the Fiscal Representative for the Fiscal Year October 1934–September 1935* (Port-au-Prince: Bureau du représentant fiscal, 1935), 86–87.

59. Dispute between the Royal Bank of Canada and the Authorities of Hayti, October 26, 1931, Dominions Office, 35/459/4, The National Archives, Kew.

60. Spector, *W. Cameron Forbes and the Hoover Commissions*, 198; US Department of State, "Agreement to Replace the Agreement of August 7, 1933, Signed at Port-au-Prince, September 13, 1941," in *The Evolution of Our Latin-American Policy: A Documentary Record*, ed. James W. Gantenbein (New York: Columbia University Press, 1950), 937–42.

61. Banque Nationale de la Republique d'Haiti, *Annual Report of the Fiscal Deparment for the Year October 1946–September 1947* (Port-au-Prince: Imprimerie de l'Etat, 1947), 2.

62. Memorandum of Conversation, by the Assistant Chief of the Division of the American Republics, July 25, 1939, in US Department of State, *Foreign Relations of the United States, Diplomatic Papers, 1939, The American Republics* (Washington, DC: GPO, 1939), 584, 581.

63. Roberto B. Saladin Selin, *Historia del Banco de Reservas de la República a Dominicana, 1941–1981* (Santo Domingo: Editora del Caribe, 1982), 1–99.

64. Durrell's resignation was accepted on December 31, 1943. His final years in the bank were marked by a combination of inactivity and bitterness. He had a desk at 55 Wall Street but little role in the City Bank's daily operations. He was also unhappy with the way he was treated during his twilight years, suspecting that Gordon Rentschler didn't trust him because Durrell was too free with criticism, that he was loyal to Mitchell, and that he might expose bank secrets concerning the losses from sugar in Cuba in the 1920s. See Joseph H. Durrell, "My Quarter Century with the Bank," in "Family History," vol. 4, "1937–1943" (unpublished manuscript), n.p.

65. Frantz Fanon, *The Wretched of the Earth*, trans. Constance Farrington, (New York: Grove Press, 1963), 39. Also see Jemima Pierre, *The Predicament of Blackness: Postcolonial Ghana and the Politics of Race* (Chicago: University of Chicago Press, 2013), 69–99.

66. John H. Allen, "American Co-operation Assures a Better Era for Haiti," *The Americas* 6.8 (1920): 8.

67. Durrell, "Family History," vol. 3, n.p.

68. *No. 8*, 8.2 (February 1913): 24.

69. "Minstrel Show," *No. 8*, 7.3 (March 1912): 6.

70. Carleton Beals, *The Crime of Cuba* (Philadelphia: J. B. Lippincott, 1934), 25.

71. J. Wilenkin, "Dollar Diplomacy in Haiti," *Negro Worker* 2.5 (December 1929): 4–8; "The Haitian Revolt," *Negro Worker* 2.1–2 (January–February 1930): 5; Charles Alexander, "Negro Workers Starving in Cuba," *Negro Worker* 1.10–11 (October–November 1931): 18–19. On the Red International Labor Union, see *A Report of Proceedings and Decisions of the First International Conference of Negro Workers at Hamburg, Germany, July 1930* (Hamburg: International Trade Union, Committee of Negro Workers, 1930); Hakim Adi, "Pan-Africanism and Communism: The Comintern, the 'Negro Question' and the First International Conference of Negro Workers," *African and Black Diaspora: An International Journal* 1.2 (2008): 237–54; Holger Weiss, "The Road to Moscow: On Archival Sources Concerning the International Trade Union Committee of Negro Workers in the Comintern Archive," *History in Africa* 39.1 (2012): 361–93.

72. George Padmore, *Life and Struggles of Negro Toilers* (London: R.I.L.U. Magazine, 1931), 64–67; Padmore, *Haiti, an American Slave Colony* (Moscow: Centrizdat, 1931).

73. Padmore, *Life and Struggles*, 62.

74. "Esta es la grotesca sede de *companies y trusts*." Nicolás Guillén, *West Indies, Ltd.*

(Havana: Uca García y Cía, 1934), 43. Also see Regino Pedroso, "Y lo nuestro es la tierra," in *Poesías* (Havana: Editorial Letras Cubanas, 1984), 17.

75. Hernán Robleto, *Los estrangulados: El imperialismo yanqui en Nicaragua* (Madrid: Editorial Cenit, s. a., 1933). For more on Robleto, see Michel Gobat, *Confronting the American Dream: Nicaragua under U.S. Imperial Rule* (Durham, NC: Duke University Press, 2005), 133-35.

76. "To the Little Fort of San Lazaro on the Ocean Front, Havana," *New Masses* 6.12 (May 1931): 11.

77. See, for instance, Edith Efron, "The 'New Movement' in Haiti," *Caribbean Quarterly* 4.1 (1955): 14-31; Magdaline W. Shannon, *Jean Price-Mars, the Haitian Elite, and the American Occupation, 1915-1935* (London: Macmillan Press, 1996); J. Michael Dash, *Literature and Ideology in Haiti: 1915-1961* (Totowa, NJ: Barnes and Noble Books, 1981).

78. See Rafael Antonio Cisneros, *La danza de los millones: Novela historia de Cuba*, 3rd ed. (Hamburg: Hermann's Erben, 1923); Jesús Masdeu, *La Raza Triste: Novela Cubana* (Havana: Imprenta y Papeleria de Rambla, Bouza y Ca, 1924).

79. "They were seas of gold. The banknotes / Covered the avarice of the blank checks. / They were seas of numbers, of Bills, of money . . . / (And no one remembered that the sea is treacherous)." Agustín Acosta, *La zafra: Poema de combate* (Havana: Editorial Minerva, 1926), 135. For a detailed reading of the literary responses to the political economy of Cuban sugar and American finance capital, see Antonio Benitez Rojo, *The Repeating Island: The Caribbean and the Postmodern Perspective*, trans. James Maraniss (Durham, NC: Duke University Press, 1997), 112-49. On the overlapping anti-Machado literature, see Lionel Soto, *La revolución del 33*, vol. 2 (Havana: Editorial Pueblo y Educación, 1977), 66-69.

80. Acosta, *La zafra*, 13. Also see Acosta's account of Machado reprinted in Carlos González Peraza, *Machado crímenes y horrores de un régimen* (Havana: Cultural, 1933).

81. Alejo Carpentier, *¡Écue-Yamba-Ó! Historia afro-cubana* (Madrid: Editorial España, 1933), 129.

82. See "Cuban Crisis Grave," *Washington Post*, May 22, 1912, 1; "Fighting in Cuba; US Marines Go," *New York Times*, May 24, 1912, 1. For an account of 1912, see Aline Helg, *Our Rightful Share: The Afro-Cuban Struggle for Equality, 1886-1912* (Chapel Hill and London: University of North Carolina Press, 1995), 193-248.

83. Juan Pérez de la Riva, "Cuba y la migración antillana, 1900-1931," in *La República neocolonial 2*, ed. Juan Pérez de la Riva et al. (Havana: Instituto Cubano del Libro, Editorial de Ciencias Sociales, 1979), 23-30.

84. Mats Lundahl, "A Note on Haitian Migration to Cuba, 1890-1934," *Cuban Studies* 12 (1982) 21-36; Barry Carr, "Identity, Class, and Nation: Black Immigrant Workers, Cuban Communism, and the Sugar Insurgency, 1925-34," *Hispanic American Historical Review* 78.1 (February 1998): 83-116.

85. Padmore, *Life and Struggles*, 67.

86. "¿Cuba necesita inmigración?" *Bamericuba* 1.1 (September 1919): 18.

87. Luis Araquistáin, *La agonía antillana: El imperialismo yanqui en el mar Caribe* (Madrid: Espasa Calpe, S.A., 1928), 160.

88. "No more importation of cane workers." Ramiro Guerra y Sánchez, *Azúcar y población en las Antillas* (Havana: Editorial de ciencas socialies, 1970), 155.

89. "From the ABC to the Workmen of Cuba," Cuban Sugar Situation, 1934, Box 62, Aldrich Manuscript, Baker Library Historical Collections, Harvard Business School.

90. Pérez de la Riva, "Cuba y la migración antillana," 70-73; Elizabeth McLean Petras,

Jamaican Labor Migration: White Capital and Black Labor, 1850–1930 (Boulder, CO: Westview Press, 1988), 240–41.

91. See the statements by J. E. Wheeler and T. J. O'Connell, in *President Trujillo, His Work and the Dominican Republic,* ed. Lawrence de Besault et al. (Washington, DC: Washington Pub., 1926), 390–93, 396–402.

92. Albert C. Hicks, *Blood in the Streets: The Life and Rule of Trujillo* (New York: Creative Age Press, 1946), 130.

93. See Cleveland and Huertas, *Citibank,* 2; George David Smith, "Why Companies Can't Afford to Ignore the Past," in *Corporate Archives and History: Making the Past Work,* ed. Arnita A. Jones and Philip L. Cantelon (Malabar, FL: Krieger Publishing Co., 1993), 187; Thomas F. Huertas, "Can Banking and Commerce Mix?," in *The Financial Services Revolution: Policy Directions for the Future,* ed. Catherine England and Thomas Huertas (Boston: Kluwer 1988), 289–307; Thomas F. Huertas and Joan L. Silverman, "Charles E. Mitchell: Scapegoat of the Crash?," *Business History Review* 60.1 (Spring 1986): 81–103.

94. Aimé Césaire, *Discourse on Colonialism,* trans. Joan Pinkham (New York: Monthly Review Press, 2001), 77.

INDEX

Page numbers in italics refer to figures and tables.

legality of, 223–24, 240, 251–52; to China, 72–73; City Bank loans to Cuba, 242; to Honduras, 123, 161; Liberty Loans, 206–7, 209; to Mexico, 85; to Panama, 260; to Peru, 259; by Speyer and Co., 86, 89; US Senate investigation of foreign loans, 267; Victory Loans, 206. See also debts

London and River Plate Bank, 60, 78

London & Southwest Bank, 75

London Bank of Mexico and South America, 60, 120

Lonsdale, John G., 231–32

Lopez Fernandez, José, 248, 263

Loree, Robert F., 173–75

L. R. Muñoz and Co., 229–34

Luis, Manuel, 178

lynchings, 257, 274. See also violence

MacDonald, James P., 94

Machado y Morales, Gerardo, 178; bank holiday, 262; Chase Bank loans, 223–24, 238–44, 260–61; legitimacy of, 223–24, 244, 247, 251; overthrow, 224, 250, 263; repressive dictator-ship in Cuba, 216–17, 223–24, 244, 246–47, 263–64; support for US banks, 183, 210, 213–14, 263; US tour, 235–36

Machias (ship), 103–5

Magoon, Charles, 42, 121, 185

Maiden Lane Bank, 237

Maine (ship), 30

Malecón, 142, 185, 223

Mallet-Prevost, Severo, 155, 158

Manasse, Maurice M., 230, 332n35

Manhattan Trust Company, 87

Manigat, Leslie, 301n56

Manila syndicate, 68–69

Manning, J. L., 134

Marietta (ship), 104

Maroons, 109

Martine, James C., 121, 131

Martinez, Bartolomé, 174

Marx, Karl, 271

masculinity, 180–83

Masdeu, Jesús, 273

Masters of the Dew (Roumain), 272

Matin, Le, 97, 105

Mayer, Julius M., 149

Mazaurieta, J. H., 190–91

McConnell, T. J., 275

McGarrah, Gates W., 172

McKim, Mead, and White, 1

McKinley, Abner, 33–34

McKinley, William, 30–31, 67

McRoberts, Samuel, 86, 93–94, 96, 98, 131, 133

Mechanics and Metals National Bank, 173

Mena, Luis, 157

Mendieta, Carlos, 216, 251

Mendoza, Don Claudio, 217

Menocal, D. A., 138

Menocal, Mario García, 140, 142–45

Ménos, Solon, 105–6

Mercantile Bank of the Americas (MBA), 8, 17, 52, 152–53; chartered in Connecti-cut, 159, 161; City Bank's acquisition of, 138; collapse of, 172–76; commercial banks, 164–65; in Cuba, 147, 164–73, 188, 222 (see also Banco Mercantil Americano de Cuba); expansion, 163–64; government banks, 163–64; legal organization and management, 160–63; origins, 153, 226; participants in, 162, *166*

Mercantile Marine, 235

Mercantile Overseas Corporation, 165, 317n59

Merchant, William A., 43, 170, 186–87, 195

merchant banks, 163; in Cuba, 32, 39–41, 139; in Panama, 73–74

Merchants National Bank of Boston, 229

Metropolitan Bank, 237

Metropolitan Life Insurance Company, 64, 237

Mexican Trust Company (MTC), 58, 62–63

Mexico: banking industry, 62–63; British banks in, 69; City Bank in, 203, 221; J. P. Morgan and Co. loan, 85; political climate, 191–92; revolution, 78

Meyer, Alfred, 159–60, 165, 171

Michelena, Santiago, 48–49, 51, 134

military intervention, 6, 21, 58, 79; in Haiti, 16, 82, 100–106, 112–13, 115, 266, 268; in Nicaragua, 157–58. See also colonialism

minstrel shows, 14–15, 135–36, 270

Miro, Elias, 121

Missouri Commission Company, 26

Missouri Valley, 21